ANECDOTES FOR REFLECTION

Volumes One to Five

Written by Sayyid ʿAlī Akbar Ṣadāqat
Translated by Shahnawaz Mahdavi

BRITISH LIBRARY CATALOGUING IN PUBLICATION DATA
A catalogue record for this book is available from the British Library

ISBN: 978-1-78991-072-8
First Edition

Published by
The World Federation of Khoja Shia Ithna-Asheri Muslim Communities
Registered Charity in the UK No. 282303

*The World Federation is an NGO in Special Consultative Status with the Economic
and Social Council (ECOSOC) of the United Nations*

Islamic Centre, Wood Lane, Stanmore, Middlesex, United Kingdom, HA7 4LQ
www.world-federation.org

Cover Design & Layout by the Islamic Publishing House (www.iph.ca)

Contents

In the Name of Allah, the Most Gracious, the Most Merciful

Introduction

There are numerous ways for man to achieve guidance and emerge from darkness and move towards light. Allah, for the prosperity of man and perfection of his morals, has created proofs, evidences, and vestiges,[1] so great in number that they are beyond reckoning and computation. For the guidance of mankind, He sent the prophets with clear proofs,[2] books, miracles, and signs so that, perhaps, the people might perceive the right path and attain prosperity and success.

During the entire period of his prophethood, the Holy Prophet, with regards to the refinement of souls and perfection of morals, was an exemplar in speech and deed, and had said: 'I have been sent [as a prophet] to perfect the morals.'[3]

Man's problem lies in his disregard for virtues, his acquisition of vices, and his inclination towards lust and obedience to Shayṭān. Some men stoop so low that they lead their lives akin to animals. For the purpose of refinement and treatment of human morals, abatement of rebelliousness, and controlling the natural disposition, the Holy Prophet spared no effort and mentioned all that was necessary in this regard.

Attainment of prosperity in this world and the Hereafter is only accomplished under the auspices of a teacher, and, at the same time, not every person can completely identify the two extremes of moral behaviour in order to demonstrate a moderate and balanced path. Allah, the Absolute Wise, introduced all the prophets, especially the Holy Prophet, as the

---

[1] See Qur'an, 14:5.

[2] Ibid., 57:25.

[3] *Safīnat al-Biḥār*, vol. 1, p. 411.

teacher and trainer of morals, so that the people, by following in his footsteps, distance themselves from vices, and acquire honour in the two worlds.

In the Qur'an, there exists a chapter by the name of al-Qaṣaṣ (The Stories), which itself is proof that man is in need of stories and narratives.

In many places in the Qur'an, stories of prophets, kings, and nations have been mentioned. In addition, Allah has presented issues pertaining to wars, peace, family, religion, society, and other similar topics in the form of stories and narratives. By reading these accounts, people can comprehend and distinguish the paths of progress and regress, and ascent and descent in every field, especially in the field of morals.

The entire Sūrah Yūsuf has been devoted to the story of Prophet Yūsuf , Prophet Yaʿqūb , Zulaykhā, and Prophet Yūsuf's brothers. In the beginning of the chapter, Allah says: We will recount to you the best of narratives in what We have revealed to you of this Qur'an, and indeed prior to it you were among those who are unaware [of it]. (12:3)

And, in the concluding verse of that very chapter, He says: There is certainly a moral in their accounts for those who possess intellect. (12:111)

Indeed, one of the distinguished feats of the Qur'an is this very story of Prophet Yūsuf , to which it refers as 'the best of narratives'.

In this regard, Imam ʿAlī in *Nahj al-Balāghah* says to his son, Imam al-Ḥasan : 'Even though I have not reached the age which those before me have, I have looked into their behaviour and reflected over the events of their lives. I walked amongst their ruins till I was as one of them. In fact, by virtue of those of their affairs that have become known to me, it is as though I have lived with them from the first to the last. I have therefore been able to discern the impure from the clean and the beneficial from the harmful. I have selected for you the choicest of those matters and collected for you their good points while keeping away from you the useless ones.'

Years ago, I had written a book on ethics, by the name of *Iḥyāʾ al-Qulūb*. Ever since then, I had been reflecting over the idea of compiling a book on moral stories. It so happened that, by the grace of Allah, an opportunity presented itself to me, and with it the motivation for undertaking this assignment. In spite of a lack of necessary books, I contented myself with those that were available and commenced the compilation of this book, recording four to five stories for every topic.

I have certainly not come across any book which has been compiled in this fashion. Books such as *Namūnah-i Ma'ārif-i Islām* and *Pand-i Tārīkh* have been present for around thirty years and I too have made use of them. However, in those books the verses of the Qur'an, traditions, poems, and analogies have all been accumulated together, whereas I have sought to mention only the stories, and have abstained from presenting considerations relating to Qur'anic verses, traditions, poems, and analogies, which would not only have increased the size of the book but would also have made it difficult to understand for many readers. My method of collection caters for the general public, young and old alike, who are acquainted with general levels of reading and writing. As far as possible, I have endeavoured to omit scientific issues and those aspects pertaining to traditions whose comprehension would be demanding and exacting for the general masses.

Although it is possible some of the stories may not possess any aspect of reality and actuality, what I have focused on is the aspect of admonition and lesson contained in them, which, hopefully, the honourable readers would perceive and comprehend.

As far as the issue of associating a story to a particular topic is concerned, I do not claim that the stories allude to just one topic or to the particular topic under which it has been placed; rather, there are stories which can be associated with several topics, in addition to the topic under which it has been mentioned.

When narrating a text or presenting a translation, I have not restricted myself to the literal meaning; for a better understanding, I have resorted to paraphrasing, allusion, and conceptual explanation.

To avoid interference of topics with one another and the prolongation of discussion, I have refrained from bringing forth topics which are related to those already presented. For example, 'altruism' has been presented as one of the topics, but 'spending in the path of Allah' has been excluded.

To prevent the reader from experiencing exhaustion and boredom, and for the sake of variety, I have desisted from presenting stories of a monotonous kind, like those of the philosophers and poets, but have strived to make the collection varied. In this way, the readers will, hopefully, derive a greater pleasure from the narratives.

In view of the fact that trustworthiness ought to be adhered to, I have referred every narrative presented here to the book from which it has been extracted, also mentioning the volume and page. It is only with the objective of achieving a greater fluency of work that I have endeavoured to correct, polish, or alter some of the words or sentences of the original text.

It is hoped that the readers, after going through the stories and narratives, reflect upon and take lessons from them so that they are able to create within themselves a new impetus towards perfection of morals; and, God-willing, those who are endowed with laudable morals should relate them to others, for the rectification and remedy of the weaker souls.

Sayyid ʿAlī Akbar Ṣadāqat
And our final prayer (is): All praise is due to Allah, the Lord of the worlds.

Mordād 1378 AHS [July 1999]

1. Morals

Allah, the Wise, has said:

$$\text{وَإِنَّكَ لَعَلَىٰ خُلُقٍ عَظِيمٍ}$$

And indeed you possess a great character. (68:4)

The Holy Prophet ﷺ said:

$$\text{إِنَّـمَا بُعِثْتُ لِأُتَمِّمَ مَكَارِمَ الْأَخْلَاقِ}$$

Verily, I have been sent [as a prophet] only to perfect morals.[1]

Short explanation

For man, good morals bring grace and elegance in this world, and relief and happiness in the Hereafter. They elevate a person's status in proximity to Allah and aid him in the perfection of his religion. All the prophets, Imams, and the chosen ones of Allah possessed exemplary morals, and every believer ought to adorn himself with such morals, in order that his scales of deeds become weightier on the Day of Judgement.

The Holy Prophet ﷺ has said: 'The Ḥātim of our time is one who possesses good morals. Bad morals cause a person to suffer the squeezing of the grave and [the punishment of] hell [in the Hereafter], and a lack of friends in this world. Man should not be measured according to his knowledge, wealth, or position, but rather according to his commendable attributes which make him acceptable in the eyes of Allah and distinguished and praised in the eyes of people.'[2]

1 – The Holy Prophet ﷺ and Nuʿaymān

Nuʿaymān ibn ʿAmr Anṣārī was one of the early companions of the Holy Prophet and had a jovial and jocose nature. It has been reported that a tribal Bedouin once arrived in Medina and, resting his camel behind the mosque, entered inside to be in the presence of the Holy Prophet.

Some of the Prophet's companions incited Nuʿaymān, saying: 'If you

---

[1] *Jāmiʿ al-Saʿādāt*, vol. 1, p. 23.

[2] *Tadhkirat al-Ḥaqāʾiq*, p. 57.

kill this camel we could distribute its meat amongst ourselves, and the Holy Prophet would have to pay its price to the owner.'

Following their advice, Nu'aymān killed the animal. When the owner came out of the mosque and discovered his dead camel, he was furious and decided to bring the matter to the attention of the Holy Prophet. Nu'aymān, in the meantime, had taken flight.

The Holy Prophet came out of the mosque, saw the dead camel, and enquired: 'Who is responsible for this act?'

Those around him accused Nu'aymān so the Holy Prophet despatched someone to bring Nu'aymān before him. The word spread that Nu'aymān was hiding in the house of Ḍubā'ah bint Zubayr,[1] which was near the mosque. He had climbed into a pit and covered himself with fresh grass. The Holy Prophet was told about Nu'aymān's hideout and he and his companions set out towards Ḍubā'ah's house. Once there, the envoy revealed Nu'aymān's hideaway to the Holy Prophet who ordered him to uncover the pit. When it was done, Nu'aymān emerged, his cheeks and forehead covered with fresh grass. On seeing him, the Holy Prophet asked: 'O Nu'aymān! What is this that you have done?'

He replied: 'O Prophet of Allah! By Allah! Those people who have led you to my hiding place were the same ones who persuaded me to kill the camel.'

The Holy Prophet smiled and brushed away the grass from Nu'aymān's cheeks and forehead with his holy hands. He then paid the price of the camel to the Bedouin on Nu'aymān's behalf.[2]

2 – Khuzaymah and the Roman Emperor

Khuzaymah Abrash, the Arabian king, never embarked upon any task without first conferring with the Roman Emperor who was one of his closest friends. Once, with the intention of seeking the emperor's opinion regarding his children's fortune, he sent a letter to him with his herald. In

---

[1] She was the cousin of the Holy Prophet and the wife of Miqdād ibn al-Aswad.

[2] *Laṭā'if al-Ṭawā'if,* p. 26.

the letter, he wrote: 'I feel I should set aside great riches for each of my sons and daughters in order that they do not fall into bad times after me. What is your opinion in this regard?'

The Roman Emperor replied: 'Wealth is a sweetener – unfaithful and impermanent! The best service for your children would be to embellish them with good morals and laudable attributes, which will lead to permanent leadership in the world and forgiveness in the Hereafter.'[1]

3 – The conduct of Imam al-Sajjād

Once, a relative of Imam al-Sajjād approached the Imam and began to revile and insult him. The Imam did not utter a word in reply, but after the man had left the gathering, he turned to the people around him and said: 'You heard what this man said. Now I want you to accompany me and hear what I have to say in response to his abuses and insults.'

The companions complied and said: 'We shall surely accompany you; in fact we had hoped that you would reply to him at that very moment.'

The Imam set off towards the person's house and was heard reciting the following Qur'anic verse: Those who spend in ease and adversity, and suppress their anger, and excuse [the faults of] the people, and Allah loves the virtuous. (3:134)

The narrator says: 'When we heard the recitation of this verse we realised that the Imam intended to exhibit goodness towards the person who had just insulted him.'

When he reached the person's house, the Imam called out to him and announced his arrival. On seeing the Imam, the person immediately assumed that he had come to respond to his abuses. However, as soon as the Imam saw the man, he said: 'O brother! You came to me and uttered things which were appalling and unpleasant. If what you have attributed to me is true, I seek forgiveness for myself from Allah, but if it is not so, then I pray that Allah forgives you.'

The man was shocked to hear these words and he repented. He kissed

---

[1] *Namūnah-i Maʿārif*, vol. 1, p. 64; *Jawāmiʿ al-Ḥikāyāt*, p. 270.

Imam al-Sajjād 🕮 between the eyes and apologised, saying: 'My insults and abuse were unfounded and cannot be attributed to your character. In fact, those insults befit me more than you.'[1]

4 – Imam ʿAlī 🕮 and the discourteous trader

Imam ʿAlī 🕮, during his caliphate, would often undertake trips to observe the markets and advise and guide the traders there. One day, while passing through the date market, he noticed that a small girl was weeping. Imam asked her the reason for her tears at which she explained: 'My master had given me a dirham to purchase some dates. I purchased them from this trader here, but when I returned home my master did not approve of them. Now I wish to return them but the trader refuses to take them back.'

Imam ʿAlī 🕮 turned to the trader and said to him: 'This child is a slave-girl and has no authority of her own. Take back the dates and return her money to her.' The trader stepped forward and, in full view of the other traders and onlookers, struck the Imam on the chest in an attempt to shove him away from the front of his shop.

The people who were witnessing the incident, rushed forward and said to the man: 'What do you think you are doing? This is ʿAlī ibn Abī Ṭālib 🕮!'

The trader's face went pale as he stood flabbergasted. He immediately took the dates from the girl and handed back the money to her. Then, turning to the Imam, he implored: 'O Commander of the Faithful! Be pleased with me and forgive me.'

The Imam replied: 'I shall only be pleased with you when you change your behaviour for the better and pay close attention to morals and courtesy.'[2]

5 – Mālik Ashtar

Once, Mālik Ashtar was passing through the market of Kufa looking

---

[1] *Muntahā al-Aʿmāl*, vol. 2, p. 4.

[2] *Dāstān-hā Wa Pand-hā*, vol. 1, p. 46; *Biḥār al-Anwār*, vol. 9, p. 519.

very indigent. He was dressed in coarse, canvas apparel, and had placed canvas on his head instead of a turban. One of the traders was sitting in his shop when his eyes fell upon Mālik. He looked at him with contempt and scornfully hurled a lump of earth towards him. Mālik disregarded him and proceeded on his way. However, a person who had recognised Mālik and had witnessed the incident, reprimanded the trader: 'Shame on you! Do you know whom you have just humiliated?'

'No,' replied the trader.

'He was Mālik Ashtar, the companion of ʿAlī ﷺ.'

A shiver ran through the body of the trader at the thought of the evil deed he had committed. He immediately set off after Mālik in order to offer his apologies. He noticed that Mālik had entered a mosque where he was engaged in prayers, and he decided to wait for him. As soon as Mālik had finished praying, the trader fell at his feet and began kissing them. Mālik raised him and asked him what he was doing. 'I am apologising for the sin I have committed,' answered the trader.

Mālik explained: 'There is no sin upon you. By Allah, I came to the mosque especially to seek forgiveness for you.'[1]

2. Beneficence

Allah, the Wise, has said:

$$\text{إِنَّ اللّٰهَ مَعَ الَّذِينَ اتَّقَوا وَالَّذِينَ هُمْ مُـحْسِنُونَ}$$

Indeed Allah is with those who are God-wary and those who are virtuous.

(16:128)

Imam ʿAlī ﷺ has stated:

$$\text{عَاتِبْ أَخَاكَ بِالْإِحْسَانِ إِلَيْهِ}$$

Admonish your brother [in faith] by exhibiting kindness towards him.[2]

---

[1] *Muntahā al-Aʿmāl*, vol. 1, p. 212; *Majmūʿah Warrām* of Ibn Abī Farrās.

[2] *Nahj al-Balāghah*, p. 1165.

Short explanation

Allah loves one who possesses the attribute of beneficence. Just as Allah has exhibited kindness towards us, it is essential for us to exhibit a great beneficence towards others.

Even if a person has wronged us, we should respond with kindness and not repay evil with evil, as this would only add fuel to the fire and cause an increase in malice and enmity.

The conduct of divine personalities was such that if they were greeted they would return the greeting in a better and more complete manner, and if goodness was done to them they would repay it, augmented and amplified.

Those who perform goodness and exhibit beneficence towards others attract the hearts of the people; and these same good deeds hurt Shayṭān.

It should be noted that those who do good should not devalue or spoil their kind deeds by placing any kind of obligation.

1 – The Jew and the fire-worshipper

A poor Jew happened to meet a wealthy fire-worshipper during the course of his journey. The fire-worshipper, who owned a camel and also sufficient provisions for the journey, asked him: 'What is your faith and ideology?'

The Jew replied: 'I believe that this world has a creator and I worship him and seek refuge in him. I exhibit kindness towards anyone who professes my faith, but I shed the blood of whoever differs from me. What is your ideology?'

The fire-worshipper responded: 'I love all creatures, I never harm anyone, and I exhibit beneficence and goodness towards friend and foe alike. If anyone wrongs me, I respond with kindness because I am aware that this world has a creator.'

Hearing this, the Jew said: 'Do not lie so much. I am a human, just like you, but while you travel on a camel and are armed with provisions for the journey I trudge along on foot without any supplies; you do not offer me your food nor do you allow me to sit on your camel.'

The fire-worshipper dismounted from his camel and, spreading the tablecloth on the ground, placed his food before his fellow traveller. The Jew ate some bread and then sat on the camel to recover from fatigue. They had travelled some distance together when the Jew suddenly struck the camel with the whip, goading it to flee. The fire-worshipper called out after him: 'O man! I exhibited kindness towards you but now you repay my beneficence by leaving me alone in this desert!' However, no matter what he said, his pleas were to no avail.

'I mentioned to you that I destroy anyone who differs from me in faith and ideology,' the Jew shouted out to him as he fled.

The fire-worshipper looked up to the sky and beseeched: 'O my Lord! I treated this man well, but he has repaid me with evil. Grant me justice.'

Having said this, he proceeded on his way. He had only travelled a short distance when his eyes suddenly fell upon his camel, which stood alone having flung the Jew to the ground. The Jew, who was severely injured, wailed out in pain. Overjoyed, the fire-worshipper took hold of the camel, mounted on its back, and was about to move away when the Jew moaned: 'O beneficent person! You have reaped the fruits of your kindness and I have witnessed the consequence of my evil; now, in adherence to your own beliefs, do not turn away from the path of kindness; be kind to me and do not abandon me in this desert.'

The fire-worshipper was overcome with compassion and sympathy and allowed him to sit on his camel and took him to the city.[1]

2 – Imam al-Ḥusayn's 🕮 kindness to the camel-driver

Imam al-Ṣādiq 🕮 said:

'A man was trailing a woman when she was busy performing *ṭawāf* of the Kaʿbah. The woman was raising her hands in prayer when the man placed his hand upon her arm; at that moment Allah glued his hand to the women's arm.

'People thronged to witness this strange happening in such great

---

[1] *Jawāmiʿ al-Ḥikāyāt*, p. 24; *Namūnah-i Maʿārif*, vol. 1, p. 29.

numbers that all movement was hindered. A person was sent to the emir of Mecca to inform him of the incident. He gathered all the scholars around him and together they tried to settle on a suitable resolution to the problem. Many ordinary people also assembled, interested to know the sentence that would be pronounced for this crime.

'As they all stood perplexed over the issue, the emir finally said: "Is there anyone from the family of the Holy Prophet ﷺ here?"

'Those around him said: "Yes! Ḥusayn ibn ʿAlī ؑ is here."

'That night, the emir ordered the Imam ؑ to be brought before him. He sought to know the ruling for this incident from the Imam ؑ.

'First, the Imam ؑ turned towards the Kaʿbah and raised his hands. He stood in this position for a while, after which he supplicated. Then, approaching the man, the Imam separated his glued hand from the arm of the woman by the power of his Imamate.

'The emir asked the Imam ؑ: "O Ḥusayn! Should I not punish him?"

'"No," replied the Imam ؑ.'

The author says: This was kindness that the Imam exhibited towards the camel-driver, but it was this same person who repaid this act of kindness by cutting off the Imam's hands in order to snatch his belt in the darkness of the night of 11 Muḥarram.[1]

3 – Abū Ayyūb Anṣārī

Abū Ayyūb Anṣārī was one of the distinguished companions of the Holy Prophet. When the Holy Prophet migrated from Mecca to Medina, all the tribes of Medina requested him to stay with them; he said: 'The place where I stay shall depend on where my camel sits down.'

When the procession reached a place near the houses of Banī Mālik ibn Najjār, which later came to house the door of the Mosque of the Prophet, the camel sat down to rest. But a short while later it stood up again and began to walk, only to return and rest at the place where it had previously rested. The people began approaching the Holy Prophet, inviting him to be

---

[1] *Rāhnumā-yi Saʿādat*, vol. 1, p. 36; *Shajarah-i Ṭūbā*, p. 422.

their guest. Seeing this, Abū Ayyūb immediately lifted the Holy Prophet's saddlebag from the camel's back and carried it into his own house.

When the Holy Prophet noticed that the saddlebag was missing, he enquired: 'What has happened to the saddlebag?' Those around him informed him that Abū Ayyūb had taken it into his own house. The Holy Prophet remarked: 'A person should always accompany his luggage.' He then proceeded into Abū Ayyūb's house and stayed there until the time when the houses around the mosque were constructed.

Initially, the Holy Prophet was accommodated in a room on the ground floor, whereas Abū Ayyūb occupied the top storey, but later he requested: 'O Messenger of Allah! It is unbecoming that you stay below while we occupy the top storey; it would be more appropriate if you were to move to the top.' The Holy Prophet agreed and asked for his things to be moved to the top.

Abū Ayyūb was in the ranks of the Holy Prophet and participated in battles such as that of Badr and Uḥud, fighting against the enemies of Islam and putting on a scintillating exhibition of valour and courage.

One night, on the way back home after victory in the Battle of Khaybar, Abū Ayyūb stayed awake the entire night, guarding the tent of the Holy Prophet. When morning dawned, the Holy Prophet enquired: 'Who is out there?'

'It is I, Abū Ayyūb,' came the reply.

The Holy Prophet then said twice: 'May Allah exhibit mercy upon you!'

Thus, Abū Ayyūb, through the kindness he showed to the Prophet both with his money and his self, became the beneficiary of this supplication of the Holy Prophet.[1]

4 – Recompense for the poems

One Nawrūz day, Manṣūr Dawānīqī, the Abbasid caliph who took over the caliphate after his brother Abū al-ʿAbbās Saffāḥ, ordered Imam Mūsā al-Kāẓim ﷺ to present himself in the gathering of the Eid of Nawrūz.

---

[1] *Payghambar Wa Yārān*, vol. 1, pp. 20-27; *Biḥār al-Anwār*, vol. 6, p. 554.

This was so that the people could come and greet him and offer their gifts to him, which he should accept. The Imam told Manṣūr: 'Nawrūz is the customary Eid of the Iranians.'

Manṣūr replied: 'This act is politically motivated and is intended to keep my soldiers happy. I place you under the oath of Allah Almighty that you accept my request and present yourself at that gathering.'

The Imam agreed and arrived at the assembly. The army generals, nobles, and the common masses arrived in his august presence, greeted him, and presented their gifts to him.

In the meantime, Manṣūr had ordered one of his slaves to position himself near the Imam and maintain a record of the money and gifts presented to him. The last person who had come to meet the Imam was an old man, who said to him: 'O son of the Messenger of Allah! I am an impoverished person and lack the money to present you with gifts, but my gift for you today are three verses of elegy which my grandfather had composed for your grandfather, Ḥusayn ibn ʿAlī ﷺ.' He then recited the verses.

The Imam responded appreciatively, saying: 'I have accepted your gift,' after which he prayed for the man. Then, turning to the slave [of Manṣūr] he instructed: 'Go to Manṣūr, inform him of these gifts and ask him what is to be done with them.'

The slave did as he was told and upon returning, said to the Imam: 'The caliph has said: "I have given them to you as gifts. Spend them as you desire.'

The Imam told the old man: 'Take these riches and gifts, for I am giving them all to you as gifts.'[1]

5 – Prophet Yūsuf ﷺ and his brothers

Years after the brothers of Prophet Yūsuf ﷺ had deceptively taken him out of the city, beaten him, and flung him into the well thereby forcing their father into perpetual weeping and anguish over his loss, the brothers heard

---

[1] *Muntahā al-Aʿmāl,* vol. 2, p. 187.

that Prophet Yūsuf 🕮 had become the king of Egypt. Along with their father, they went to meet him.

The very first sentence which Prophet Yūsuf 🕮 uttered upon seeing them, was: 'He was certainly gracious to me when He brought me out of the prison [12:100].' Apparently, it was out of courtesy that Prophet Yūsuf 🕮 desisted from mentioning the troubles he had experienced; firstly, being flung into the well, his subsequent slavery, and then unpleasant incidents which he had to endure due to the acts of his brothers. He did not wish to revive those bitter memories which would cause his brothers to experience mortification and embarrassment.

He then added: 'It was Shayṭān who incited my brothers to commit those inappropriate deeds towards me, hurling me into the well and separating me from my father; however, Allah exhibited kindness towards me in that he made those very acts a means for granting eminence and reverence to our family!'

Attributing the unjust acts of his brothers to Shayṭān and regarding him as the prime culprit for the crimes of his brothers, was another example of Prophet Yūsuf's 🕮 magnanimity. He thus shielded his brothers from embarrassment and left them with an opportunity to apologise for their deeds. He said: 'There shall be no reproach on you today [12:92].' In other words: you can rest assured with respect to me, for I have forgiven you and chosen to disregard all that has happened previously, and on behalf of Allah, I can give you this good news and seek from Him that: 'Allah will forgive you, and He is the most merciful of the merciful.' (12:92) And: 'Indeed if one is God-wary and patient Allah does not waste the reward of the virtuous.' (12:90)[1]

The author says: The lesson that Prophet Yūsuf 🕮 has taught everyone is that of exhibiting kindness and beneficence in response to evil behaviour. Hopefully, we too can conduct ourselves in the same manner with respect to our brethren in faith, God-willing.

------

[1] *Tārīkh-i Anbiyā'*, pp. 334-347.

3. Sincerity

Allah, the Wise, has said:

فَٱعْبُدِ اللّٰهَ مُـخْلِصًا لَهُ الدِّينَ

So worship Allah, putting exclusive faith in Him. (39:2)

Imam ʿAlī said:

أَخْلِصِ الْعَمَلَ يُجْزِكَ مِنْهُ الْقَلِيلُ

Perform your deeds with sincerity, you will be rewarded for [even] a small amount [of those deeds performed with sincerity]. [1]

Short explanation

Sincerity is the key to the acceptance of all deeds. A person whose deeds are accepted by Allah, however trivial they may be, is a sincere person; and one whose deeds, in spite of being plentiful, are rejected by Allah, is not of the sincere ones.

A sincere person strives to purify his soul from vices and exerts himself to perform [good] deeds and maintain [sincerity of] intention so that Allah accepts his deeds.

The level of intention, knowledge, and deeds is related to spiritual purification and refinement, and if a sincere person were to pay due attention to his inner self, he would come to perceive the true concept of the unity of Allah. The lowest degree of sincerity is when a person exerts himself to the best of his ability, neither anticipating rewards for his deeds nor attaching any importance to them. [2]

1 – Three persons in a cave

The Holy Prophet has related:

'Three persons from the tribe of Banī Isrāʾīl got together and started out on a journey. On the way, clouds gathered above them and it started to pour with rain and so they sought shelter in a nearby cave.

---

[1] *Jāmiʿ al-Saʿādāt*, vol. 2, p. 404.

[2] *Tadhkirat al-Ḥaqāʾiq*, p. 73.

Suddenly, a large boulder slipped and blocked the entrance to the cave, trapping the three inside and transforming the day into a dark night for them. They had no other alternative except to turn to Allah for help.

'"Let us use our sincere deeds as a means to obtain deliverance from this predicament," suggested one of them. All the others agreed with the suggestion.

'One of them said: "O Lord! You are aware that I have an extremely attractive cousin and that I was infatuated and obsessed with her. One day, finding her alone, I took hold of her and wanted to satisfy my carnal desires when she spoke out to me saying: 'O my cousin! Fear Allah and do not harm my chastity.' Hearing this, I crushed my lustful tendencies and decided against the evil act. O Lord! If that deed of mine had been out of absolute sincerity and only for the purpose of acquiring Your pleasure, deliver us from grief and perdition." Suddenly they witnessed that the huge boulder had moved away a little, faintly brightening up the interior of the cave.

'The second person spoke out: "O Lord! You know that I had a father and a mother, so old that their bodies had bent over due to their excessive age, and that I used to tend to them regularly. One night, having brought them their food, I observed that both of them were asleep. I passed the entire night near them, with food in hand, without waking them up for fear of disturbing them. O Lord! If this deed of mine had been only for the sake of Your pleasure and happiness, open up a way for us and grant us salvation." As he completed his speech, the group noticed that the boulder had moved aside a little more.

'The third person supplicated: "O Knower of every hidden and manifest! You know that I had a worker who used to work for me. When his term had reached its termination, I handed over to him his wages, but he was not pleased and desired more and, in a state of dissatisfaction and displeasure, he went away. I used his wage to purchase a sheep which I looked after separately, and very soon I had a herd in my possession. After a period of time, the worker again approached me for his wage and I pointed towards the flock of sheep. Initially, he thought I was ridiculing him, but later, realising my seriousness, he took the entire flock and left.[1] O Lord! If this act had been prompted by sincerity and had only been for Your pleasure, deliver us from this quandary."

'At this point the entire boulder moved aside from the mouth of the cave and all three emerged from it, joyous and ecstatic, and continued their journey.'[2]

2 – Imam ʿAlī on the chest of ʿAmr

ʿAmr ibn ʿAbd Wudd was a warrior who, in battle, was a match for a thousand soldiers. In the Battle of Aḥzāb he challenged the Muslim soldiers to fight him, but none possessed the courage to stand before him until Imam ʿAlī presented himself before the Holy Prophet and sought permission to fight him.

The Holy Prophet said to ʿAlī: 'Do realise that this is ʿAmr ibn ʿAbd Wudd.'

Imam ʿAlī humbly stated: '[And] I am ʿAlī ibn Abī Ṭālib.' He then proceeded towards the battle-field and stood before ʿAmr. After a fierce encounter, Imam ʿAlī eventually knocked him down and sat on his chest.[3] Witnessing this, the entire Muslim army importuned the Holy Prophet: 'O Messenger of Allah, order ʿAlī to kill ʿAmr immediately.'

'Leave him alone for he is more aware of his deeds than anyone else,' replied the Holy Prophet.

When ʿAlī had severed the head of ʿAmr, he brought it to the Holy

---

[1] In the book *Maḥāsin*, it has been mentioned that his wage was half a dirham but when he returned to collect it, he was given 18,000 times over!

[2] *Namūnah-i Maʿārif*, vol. 1, p. 53; *Farajun Baʿd al-Shiddah*, p. 23; *Maḥāsin-i Barqī*, vol. 2, p. 253.

[3] Mawlānā, in his Mathnawī, has composed a poem over the incident, which is as follows:

از علی آموز اخلاص عمل شیر حق را دان منزه از دغل

در غزا بر پهلوانی دست یافت زود شمشیر برآورد و شتافت

او خدو انداخت بر روی علی افتخار هر نبی و هر ولی

Prophet who questioned him: 'O 'Alī! What caused you to hesitate before killing 'Amr?'

He replied: 'O Messenger of Allah! When I had floored him he abused me, as a result of which I was overcome by rage. I feared that if I were to kill him in that state of anger it would be for consoling myself and pacifying my soul. So I stepped away from him till my fury subsided, and then I returned to sever his head from his body only for the happiness of Allah and in obedience to Him.'

It was because of this sincerity and invaluable combat on the part of Imam 'Alī ﷺ that the Holy Prophet said: 'The strike of the sword of 'Alī on the day of the Battle of Khandaq is superior to the worship of all men and jinn.'[1]

3 – Shayṭān and the pious worshipper

In the tribe of Banī Isrā'īl, there once lived a pious worshipper. One day, the people informed him that at a certain location there existed a tree that was being worshipped by a tribe. When he heard this the man flew into a rage, picked up his axe, and set out to cut down the tree.

Iblīs, appearing before him in the form of an old man, asked: 'Where are you headed?'

He replied: 'I intend to cut down the tree that is being worshipped so that the people worship Allah instead.'

'Wait till you hear what I have to say,' said Iblīs to him. The worshipper urged him to speak. Iblīs continued: 'Allah has His own prophets and if it had been essential to cut down the tree He would have sent them to perform the task.' However, the worshipper did not agree with Iblīs and continued on his way. 'There is no way I shall let you do it,' said Iblīs angrily, and he began to wrestle with the man. In the ensuing contest, the pious worshipper hurled Iblīs onto the ground.

'Wait! I have something else to say to you,' pleaded Iblīs. 'Listen! You are a poor man. If you could possess some wealth by means of which you

---

[1] *Pand-i Tārīkh*, vol. 5, p. 199; *Anwār al-Nuʿmāniyyah*; *ʿAyn al-Ḥayāh*.

could give alms to the other worshippers it would be much better than cutting the tree. If you refrain from cutting the tree, I shall place two dinars beneath your pillow every day.'

The pious person said thoughtfully: 'If you speak the truth, I shall give one dinar in charity while the other dinar I shall put to my use. This is better than cutting down the tree. In any case, I have neither been ordered to perform this task nor am I a prophet to burden myself with unnecessary grief and anxiety.'

Thus, he acceded to the request of Shayṭān who then left him alone.

For two days he received the two dinars and utilised them, but on the third day there was no sign of the money. Upset and distressed, he picked up his axe and set out to cut down the tree. On the way, he encountered Shayṭān who asked him: 'Where are you going?'

'I am going to cut down that tree.'

'There is no way you are going to do it!' said Shayṭān. Once again they began to contest, but this time Iblīs overcame him. Upon hurling him to the ground, he ordered: 'Turn back or I shall sever your head from your body.'

The pious man said: 'Leave me alone and I shall return, but tell me how was it that I had managed to overcome you on the previous occasion?'

Iblīs answered: 'On that occasion you had set out only for Allah and you were sincere in your intention, as a result of which Allah subjugated me to you, but this time you were angry for your own self and for your dinars and so I could overpower you.'[1]

4 – The secret of a sincere slave

Sa'īd ibn Musayyab narrates:

'One year, there was a severe famine and so the people gathered together to pray for the rains. I looked around and my eyes fell upon a black slave who had separated himself from the crowd and emerged on top of a small hill. I advanced in his direction and when I came near him I

---

[1] *Namūnah-i Ma'ārif*, vol. 1, p. 54; *Iḥyā' al-'Ulūm*, vol. 4, p. 380; *Riyāḍ al-Ḥikāyāt*, p. 140.

noticed that his lips were moving in prayer. He had hardly completed his prayers, when a cloud appeared in the sky.

'Seeing the cloud the black slave praised Allah and moved away. Very soon rains lashed us so heavily that we thought we might perish. I ran after the slave and observed that he entered the house of Imam al-Sajjād ﷺ. I arrived before the Imam ﷺ and said: "O my master! In your house there is a black slave; oblige me by selling him to me."

'He replied: "O Saʿīd! I will gift him to you instead." He ordered the head of his slaves to bring all the servants before me. When they had assembled I noticed that the black slave was not amongst them.

'I said: "The one I desire is not amongst them."

'The Imam said: "There remains no other slave except one."

'He then ordered him to be brought forth. When the slave was brought before me, I saw that he was the very person whom I had sought and I said: "He is the one I need."

'The Imam ﷺ instructed: "O slave, henceforth, Saʿīd is your master so go with him."

'The slave turned to me and asked: "What prompted you to separate me from my master?"

'I replied: "When I witnessed your prayers for the rains being accepted, I wished that I could own you."

'When he heard this, the slave stretched out his hands in supplication and, turning his face towards the skies, beseeched: "O my Lord! This was a secret between You and me. Now that You have divulged it, grant me death and take me towards Yourself."

'The Imam and all those present wept over the position of the slave, while I, shedding tears, came out of the house. No sooner had I reached my own house than the Imam's messenger arrived and said: "Come along if you wish to take part in the funeral procession of your companion."

'I returned to the Imam's ﷺ house along with the messenger only to find that the slave had passed away.'[1]

---

[1] *Muntahā al-Aʿmāl*, vol. 2, p. 38; *Ithbāt al-Waṣiyyah* of Masʿūdī.

5 – The request of Prophet Mūsā 🕮

Prophet Mūsā 🕮 once requested Allah: 'O Lord! It is my wish to see that creature of Yours who has purified himself for Your worship and who is unpolluted in his obedience towards You.'

He was addressed: 'O Mūsā! Go near the shores of such and such sea in order that I may show you what you desire to see.'

Prophet Mūsā 🕮 proceeded till he reached near the sea. Looking around, he observed that on a branch of a tree that drooped over the water sat a bird, engrossed in the remembrance of Allah. When Prophet Mūsā 🕮 questioned the bird about itself, the bird said: 'From the time Allah has created me I have been on this branch, engaged in His worship and remembrance. From every remembrance of mine, there branch out a thousand other remembrances, and the pleasure which I derive from the remembrance of Allah provides me with nourishment.'

'Do you crave anything from this world?' asked Prophet Mūsā 🕮.

'Yes; I yearn to taste one drop of water from this sea,' replied the bird.

Prophet Mūsā 🕮 exclaimed: 'But there is not a great distance between your beak and the water! Why don't you dip your beak into it and drink it?'

The bird answered: 'Out of fear lest the enjoyment derived from the water should make me heedless of the pleasure of the remembrance of my Lord.'

Hearing this, Prophet Mūsā 🕮 clasped his head in intense astonishment.[1]

4. Perseverance

Allah, the Wise, has said:

$$فَٱسْتَقِمْ كَمَا أُمِرْتَ وَمَنْ تَابَ مَعَكَ$$

So be steadfast, just as you have been commanded – [you] and whoever has turned [to Allah] with you. (11:112)

---

[1] *Khazīnat al-Jawāhir*, p. 318.

Imam al-Ṣādiq ﷺ said:

مَنِ ٱبْتُلِيَ مِنَ الْمُؤْمِنِينَ بِبَلَاءٍ فَصَبَرَ عَلَيْهِ كَانَ لَهُ مِثْلُ أَجْرِ أَلْفِ شَهِيدٍ

Every believer who happens to be afflicted with a misfortune and [then] exhibits patience in the face of it, shall be granted the reward equivalent to that of a thousand martyrs.[1]

Short explanation

Endurance and perseverance can reduce the severity of misfortunes and calamities.

A person who possesses faith does not exhibit impatience when faced with trials, lest his faith should suffer.

It has been said that a believer is more resolute than a mountain. This is because he is steadfast against the enemies and displays fortitude in the face of misfortune, to the extent that no grief ever finds a way into the heart of a perfect believer.

Life, with its many troubles, will not present a problem for those with a firm resolve. It is only those who lack sincerity in their perseverance who tend to break down at the slightest of calamities. After all, if the religion of Allah has reached us today, it is due to the perseverance of the Holy Prophet and the patience of Imam ʿAlī ﷺ.

1 – The family of Yāsir

In the initial period of Islam, a small and oppressed family of four embraced the religion. Each of them displayed an incredible degree of perseverance in facing up to the ruthless torture of the polytheists. These four persons were Yāsir, his wife Sumayyah, and their two children ʿAmmār and ʿAbd Allāh.

Yāsir stood steadfast in his religion, suffering the abuses of the enemies, till he eventually died. His wife Sumayyah, in spite of her advanced age, resolutely bore the torture of the enemies until eventually Abū Jahl inflicted her final injury. Sumayyah therefore attained martyrdom as a result of a

---

[1] *Jāmiʿ al-Saʿādāt*, vol. 3, p. 404.

blow to her abdomen.

Abū Jahl, in addition to physically torturing Sumayyah, also tortured her psychologically at a time when she was old and frail. He used to taunt her, saying: 'You have brought faith upon Muḥammad not because of Allah, but because you are enamoured with Muḥammad and captivated by his good looks.'

Yāsir's son, 'Abd Allāh, was also subjected to great tortures but he too remained steadfast. The other son, 'Ammār, would be taken to the scorching desert, stripped under the hot sun, and have an iron coat-of-mail placed over his half-burnt body. He would then be forced to lie on the heated sand, the particles of which were like tiny smouldering pieces of iron from the blacksmith's furnace. As a result, the chains of the coat-of-mail would penetrate into 'Ammār's body and he would be told: 'Reject Muḥammad ﷺ and worship Lāt and 'Uzzā.' But 'Ammār never succumbed.

The burning metal left such traces imprinted upon his body that when the Holy Prophet saw him, 'Ammār appeared to resemble someone who was afflicted with leprosy. The disease-like marks upon the face, arms, and body of 'Ammār gave him the appearance of a leper.

The Holy Prophet used to say to this family: 'O family of Yāsir! Be patient and remain steadfast, for undoubtedly paradise is your abode.'[1]

2 – You are not inferior to an ant

Amīr Taymūr Gurgān was someone who was so firm and unfaltering in every predicament that he did not cower from any misfortune. When the reason for this was sought from him, he said:

'Once, having fled from my enemies and seeking refuge in the ruins of a run-down and dilapidated building, I was reflecting over my future when my eyes suddenly fell upon a small and weak ant carrying a grain bigger than itself, endeavouring to climb to the top of a wall.

'Looking carefully and counting accurately, I found that the grain had dropped from its clutches sixty-seven times before the ant finally managed

---

[1] *Ḥikāyat-hā-yi Shanīdanī*, vol. 5, p. 25; *Tafsīr al-Manār*, vol. 2, p. 367.

to make it to the top of the wall with it. The spectacle of this effort on the part of the ant infused within me strength of such great magnitude that I am never able to forget it.

'I said to myself: "O Taymūr! You are by no means inferior to an ant. Arise and get back to work!" I got up and gathered my resolve till I eventually came to acquire the courage that I now possess.'[1]

3 – Prophet Nūḥ

Prophet Nūḥ lived a very long and difficult life as a result of spending a lot of time amongst stout idol worshippers, whilst attempting to rid them of their false beliefs. However, in spite of this, he persevered and exhibited steadfastness, withstanding torments and troubles.

At times, the people would beat him up to such an extent that blood would flow from his ears, and for three whole days he would be in a state of unconsciousness. They would pick him up and throw him in a house, but upon regaining consciousness he would pray: 'O Lord! Guide my people for they comprehend not!'

For approximately 950 years he invited people towards Allah, but the people only increased in their rebellion and obstinacy. They would bring their children towards Prophet Nūḥ, point him out to them, and say: 'O children! If you happen to remain alive after us beware that you do not follow this insane person!' Then, they would say to him: 'O Nūḥ! If you do not stop your speeches you shall be stoned to death. These people who follow you are base and ignoble ones, who have listened to your talks and accepted your invitation without the slightest of reflection and deliberation.'

When Prophet Nūḥ spoke to them they would insert their fingers into their ears and pull their clothes over their heads so that they would neither hear his words nor see his face. The situation reached such an unbearable point that Prophet Nūḥ saw no alternative but to seek Allah's help and so he supplicated: 'O Allah! I am overpowered; assist me

---

[1] *Namūnah-i Maʿārif,* vol. 1, p. 174; *Akhlāq-i Ijtimāʿī,* p. 41.

and grant me relief from them.'[1]

4 – Sakkākī

Sirāj al-Dīn Sakkākī was an Islamic scholar and a native of Khwarazm.

Sakkākī was a blacksmith by profession. Once, having constructed a tiny and delicate iron chest with great effort and trouble, he decided to present it to the king of the time. The king and his ministers appreciated the delicate piece of work but while Sakkākī stood by awaiting his reward, a scholar entered the courtroom whereupon everybody honoured him and sat before him in veneration and respect. Sakkākī was very impressed and asked who he was. He was informed that he was one of the scholars of that period.

Sakkākī lamented the nature of his own profession and decided to seek knowledge instead. He was thirty years of age when he approached a school and expressed his desire to gain knowledge. The teacher of the school said to him: 'At your age I doubt if you can make any progress. Go away and do not waste your time unnecessarily.' But after a great deal of insistence Sakkākī procured the permission to engage himself in seeking knowledge.

His memory was very weak. Once, his teacher asked him to memorise the following religious ruling: The skin of a dog becomes pure by means of tanning; but, the next day, when he had to recite it before his teacher, he said: 'The dog said: "The skin of the teacher becomes pure by means of tanning."' Hearing this, the students as well as the teacher burst out laughing and ridiculed him.

Ten years of effort did not yield any result for Sakkākī, who became sad and despondent. He turned towards the mountains, but as he wandered he reached a place where drops of water were falling from a height onto a large slab of stone. The persistent falling of water had carved a hole in the stone. Sakkākī studied the stone for some time and then said to himself: 'Surely your heart is not as hard as this rock. If you persevere, you shall

---

[1] *Tārīkh-i Anbiyā'*, pp. 48-52.

finally succeed.' Having resolved on this, he returned to his school and from the age of forty began his studies with even greater diligence, vigour, and patience.

Sakkākī finally reached a stage whereby, in the field of Arabic grammar and literature, the scholars of his period looked upon him with wonder and awe. He wrote the book *Miftāḥ al-ʿUlūm* which comprises twelve sciences of Arabic literature and is regarded as one of the greatest and most distinguished works on the subject.[1]

5. Reconciliation

Allah, the Wise, has said:

وَإِنْ طَائِفَتَانِ مِنَ الْمُؤْمِنِينَ اقْتَتَلُوا فَأَصْلِحُوا بَيْنَهُمَا

If two groups of the faithful fight one another, make peace between them.
(49:9)

Imam al-Ṣādiq said:

لَأَنْ أُصْلِحَ بَيْنَ اثْنَيْنِ أَحَبُّ إِلَيَّ مِنْ أَنْ أَتَصَدَّقَ بِدِينَارَيْنِ

Reconciling between two [disputing] persons is dearer to me than giving two dinars in charity.[2]

Short explanation

One of the mandatory acts required of us is the inspection and rectification of our souls. Until a person reforms himself he would be unable to bring about reformation within others. Attempting or achieving reconciliation between the brethren in faith, relatives, or neighbours, is an attribute which is immensely loved by Allah.

For the purpose of establishing unity and harmony instead of disunity and discord, it is essential to make every possible effort to bring about reconciliation. In fact, in certain circumstances, it becomes permissible to resort to white lies. At times it may even become obligatory, so that

---

[1] *Dastān-hā-yi Mā*, vol. 3, p. 45.

[2] *Al-Kāfī*, vol. 2, p. 167.

dissension dies down and discord subsides.

1 – The order to reconcile

Once, during the time of Imam al-Ṣādiq ﷺ, Abū Ḥanīfah, the administrator of Ḥajjāj, had a quarrel with his son-in-law over some inheritance. Mufaḍḍal ibn 'Umar Kūfī (one of the special companions of Imam al-Ṣādiq ﷺ) happened to pass by at the time. When he overheard the dispute he stopped and said to both the men: 'Come with me to my house.'

They did as requested. Upon reaching the house he entered inside only to come out shortly afterwards with a bag containing 400 dirhams which he gave to both men and made peace between them. He then explained: 'This is not my money but Imam al-Ṣādiq's. He had instructed me: whenever you happen to see two of our Shi'as disputing over money, give them this and make peace between them.'[1]

2 – Exercise caution in reconciliation

'Abd al-Malik says:

'There arose a dispute between Imam al-Bāqir ﷺ and some of the children of Imam al-Ḥasan ﷺ. I approached the Imam and sought to intervene in the matter in order to reconcile them, but the Imam ﷺ advised: "Do not say a word in this dispute for our problem is like that of the old man from Banī Isrāʼīl who had two daughters. One of them was married to a farmer, while the other to a pottery-maker. Once, he decided to pay them a visit. He first visited the daughter who was the wife of the farmer and reaching her house, he enquired about her health. The daughter said: 'Dear father, my husband has cultivated a large area of land and if it were to rain we would be the most prosperous of the entire Banī Isrāʼīl.' Then, proceeding towards the house of the other daughter whose husband was a potter, he enquired about her health. The daughter said: 'Dear father, my husband has moulded pots in great quantity and if Allah were to withhold the rains till his pots dry up we would be better off than the entire Banī

---

[1] *Muntahā al-A'māl,* vol. 2, p. 249.

Isrāʾīl.' As he departed from the house of his second daughter, he prayed: 'O Allah! Act as You deem fit, for in this situation I cannot pray for either of them.'"

'The Imam then said to me: "You too cannot intervene in this matter. Be wary, lest you show disrespect to either of us. Your responsibility towards us, because of our relationship with the Holy Prophet, is to treat all of us with deference and esteem."'[1]

3 – Reward of reconciliation

Fuḍayl ibn ʿAyyāḍ says:

'A distressed man once took some rope which his wife had woven to the market to sell, so as to save himself and his family from hunger. Having sold it for one dirham, he intended to purchase some bread when he came across two persons quarrelling and trading blows with one another over a dirham. The man stepped forward, gave them a dirham, and established peace between them. Empty-handed once again, he went home and narrated the entire incident to his wife. She expressed happiness over his conduct. On searching the house she found an old dress which she handed to her husband, so that he could sell it and procure some food.

'The man brought the dress to the market but there was no one willing to buy it from him. Looking around, he saw a person with a putrefied fish in his hand. He approached the man and said: "Let us exchange our goods. You give me your fish and I shall hand you my dress."

'The fish-seller agreed and the man returned home with the fish. His wife busied herself with cleaning the fish when, suddenly, something valuable popped out of its stomach. She handed the object to her husband to sell in the market. The man sold it for a very good sum and returned home, but he had hardly entered the house when a destitute person came to the door and called out: "Provide me from that which Allah has granted to you."

'As soon as the man heard the cry, he brought out all the money and

---

[1] *Dāstān-hā Wa Pand-hā*, vol. 1, p. 134; *Rawḍat al-Kāfī*, p. 85.

invited the poor man to take as much as he wanted. The beggar picked up some money and started to walk away. He had just gone a few paces, when he returned and said: "I am not a poor person. I have been sent by Allah and have to inform you that the amount of money which has reached you is your reward for reconciling those two quarrelling persons."[1]

4 – Mīrzā Jawād Āghā Malikī

Regarding the mystic Mīrzā Jawād Āghā Malikī (d. 1343 AH), it has been recorded that during the initial stages of his journey in quest of spiritual purification and after having studied under his teacher, the great mystic Mullā Ḥusaynqulī Hamadānī (d. 1311 AH) for two years, he complained to the teacher: 'In my quest for spiritual purification, I have not been able to achieve anything as yet!'

'What is your name?' asked the teacher.

He replied: 'Don't you recognise me? I am Jawād Malikī Tabrīzī.'

Ḥusaynqulī Hamadānī enquired: 'Are you related to such and such Malikī family?'

Mīrzā Jawād replied in the affirmative, and then went on to speak critically of them.

'Whenever the time comes for you to place their shoes before them to wear, I shall personally come to guide you,' advised Ḥusaynqulī Hamadānī.

The next day, when Mīrzā Jawād went for his classes, he seated himself behind all the other students, and from that day on, slowly and steadily, he began to become acquainted and friendly with the students of the Malikī family living in Najaf. This continued until a stage was reached when he would even place their shoes before them to wear. When the relatives living in Tabriz came to know of this, the dissension and discord that existed among the members of the family subsided and peace was established amongst them.

Later, Mīrzā Jawād approached his teacher who said to him: 'There are no new instructions for you. Continue to act upon this order of the shariah

---

[1] *Namūnah-i Maʿārif*, vol. 1, p. 218; *Farajun Baʿd al-Shiddah.*

and derive benefits from it.'

The author says: Incidentally, the book *Miftāḥ al-Falāḥ* of the late Shaykh Bahā'ī is an excellent book to act upon.[1]

Slowly, Mīrzā progressed in his quest. He came to the Ḥawzah of Qum where he embarked upon training and guiding students in the field of spiritual purification. A great number of people – the common public as well as the educated elite – benefited from him and his teachings.

5 – The advice of Ma'mūn's minister

Once, Ma'mūn, the Abbasid caliph, became furious with 'Alī ibn Jahm Sāmī, the court poet, and in a fit of anger ordered his servants: 'Put him to death and confiscate all his possessions.'

Ma'mūn's minister, Aḥmad ibn Abī Du'ād, in a reconciliatory move, approached him and asked: 'If you kill him, from whom shall we confiscate his wealth?'

'From his heirs,' replied Ma'mūn.

Aḥmad said: 'In such an event, the caliph would not have confiscated his wealth but that of his heirs, for after his death he shall cease to be the owner of his possessions. And seizing the wealth of one for punishing another is an act of injustice, which does not befit the rank of the caliphate!'

Ma'mūn said: 'Well, if this is the case, imprison him, confiscate his wealth, and then put him to death.'

Aḥmad departed, imprisoned 'Alī ibn Jahm, and held him alive till Ma'mūn's anger had subsided. Ma'mūn pardoned 'Alī ibn Jahm and commended the minister for his conduct and elevated him in rank and status.[2]

6. Hopes

Allah, the Wise, has said:

$$ذَرْهُمْ يَأْكُلُوا وَيَتَمَتَّعُوا وَيُلْهِهِمُ الْأَمَلُ$$

---

[1] *Tārīkh-i Ḥukamā' Wa 'Urafā'*, p. 133.

[2] *Laṭā'if al-Ṭawā'if*, p. 98.

Leave them to eat and enjoy and to be diverted by longings. (15:3)

Imam ʿAlī ﷺ said:

الْآمَالُ لَا تَنْتَهِي

Hopes never come to an end.[1]

Short explanation

People who are not content with what they possess of this world and crave for things which they do not possess will keep chasing high hopes and lofty aspirations. A person who imagines that he will always remain young becomes heedless of death and goes after huge ambitions.

The majority of the inmates of hell would have gone there as a result of their procrastination. Instead of contenting themselves with what they possessed, they kept deferring the rectification of their souls and the repayment of their debts for later, and kept postponing their acts of worship for their old age.

Indeed, a person must lower his hopes and aspirations, perform every act at its appropriate time and occasion, and refrain from trusting the 'tomorrow', something that is entirely unknown and uncertain.[2]

1 – Prophet ʿĪsā ﷺ and the farmer

It is reported that once, Prophet ʿĪsā ﷺ son of Mary had been sitting and intently observing a farmer who, with a spade in hand, was hard at work in his field. At that moment Prophet ʿĪsā ﷺ prayed to Allah: 'O Lord! Take away from him his hopes and aspirations.' Suddenly, the person flung his spade aside and sat down in a corner.

'O Lord! Return his hopes and aspirations back to him,' Prophet ʿĪsā ﷺ prayed once again. The man moved from his place, picked up the spade, and began working again.

Prophet ʿĪsā ﷺ approached him and asked: 'Why did you behave in such a way?'

---

[1] *Ghurar al-Ḥikam*, p. 629.

[2] *Iḥyāʾ al-Qulūb*, p. 167.

The farmer answered: 'I said to myself: "You are an old man whose life has almost come to an end; how much more do you wish to work and exert yourself?" So I flung the spade aside and sat down in the corner. But, after a while, I said to myself: "Why don't you work? You are still alive and in need of livelihood." So, picking up the spade, I returned to my work.'[1]

2 – Ḥajjāj and the milk-seller

Once, Ḥajjāj ibn Yūsuf Thaqafī, the brutal tyrant [and the minister of the Abbasid caliph, 'Abd al-Malik ibn Marwān], was sauntering in the market when he witnessed a milk-seller talking to himself. Whilst standing in a corner, Ḥajjāj overheard him say: 'If I sell this milk, I shall earn a good income. I shall save the profit from this and future sales until I have sufficient money to buy a goat. I shall then purchase a ewe and utilise its milk to increase my capital, and within a few years I shall become a wealthy person, possessing several goats, cows, and [other] assets. I shall then seek the hand of Ḥajjāj's daughter in marriage, after which I shall come to acquire great importance and significance. And if, on any occasion, Ḥajjāj's daughter were to exhibit disobedience, I should kick her so hard that her ribs would break.'

As he said this he kicked out with his leg which unfortunately struck his milk container, spilling its entire contents in the process. Ḥajjāj came forward and ordered two of his soldiers to force the milk-seller onto the ground and to strike him 100 lashes. The milk-seller wailed: 'But for what crime are you punishing me?'

Ḥajjāj replied: 'Did you not say that if you married my daughter you would kick her so hard that her ribs would break? Now, as a punishment for that kick you must taste 100 lashes.'[2]

3 – Desire for martyrdom

'Amr ibn Jamūḥ, an inhabitant of Medina and from the tribe of Khazraj, was

---

[1] *Namūnah-i Ma'ārif*, vol. 1, p. 298; *Majmū'ah Warrām*.

[2] *Pand-i Tārīkh*, vol. 3, p. 150.

a generous and magnanimous person. The first time the people of Khazraj arrived in the presence of the Holy Prophet, he sought to know who the leader of their tribe was. They informed him that he was a person by the name of Jadd ibn Qays, a miser by nature. The Prophet said: 'Your chief should be 'Amr ibn Jamūḥ, the white-complexioned, curly-haired person.'

'Amr was lame in one foot and as per Islamic law, exempted from jihad. He had four sons and when the time for the Battle of Uḥud came, all of them prepared themselves to fight. 'I must come too and attain martyrdom,' said 'Amr, eagerly.

However, his sons stopped him and said: 'Father, we are going for battle. You stay in the house for it is not obligatory for you to fight.' The old man refused to budge and insisted on participating in the battle. The sons gathered their relatives in an effort to get him to change his mind, but it was to no avail.

'Amr approached the Holy Prophet and complained to him: 'I yearn to attain martyrdom. Why do my children prevent me from going for jihad and becoming martyred in the way of Allah?'

The Holy Prophet said to the sons: 'This man seeks martyrdom and although it is not obligatory for him to fight, it is not forbidden for him to do so.'

Overjoyed, 'Amr armed himself and set off for battle. During the battle, his sons kept an eye on him as he valiantly thrust himself into the heart of the enemy ranks, fighting heroically, until he was eventually martyred.

Before leaving for the battlefield, he had prayed: 'O Allah! Grant me martyrdom and do not return me to my house.' The Holy Prophet stated that his prayer had been answered. 'Amr was finally laid to rest in the cemetery of the martyrs of the Battle of Uḥud.[1]

4 – Ju'dah's state of disgrace and humiliation

Imam al-Ḥasan was extremely good-looking, possessed great forbearance and generosity, and was very kind and affectionate towards the members

---

[1] *Dāstān-hā-yi Ustād*, vol. 1, p. 48.

of his family. After the martyrdom of Imam ʿAlī ﷺ, Muʿāwiyah, for a period of ten years, embarked upon a mission of hatred, deception, and enmity with respect to Imam al-Ḥasan ﷺ. He subjected the Imam to harm and injury on several occasions, but did not achieve anything. He therefore resolved to use the Imam's wife, Juʿdah, the daughter of Ashʿath ibn Qays, to poison him.

Muʿāwiyah lured her by promising her that if she poisoned Imam al-Ḥasan ﷺ he would give her 100,000 dirhams and, in addition, he would marry her to his son Yazīd. In the hope of acquiring wealth and with the aspiration of becoming the wife of Yazīd, she agreed to comply with his request. Muʿāwiyah handed her the poison that he had acquired from the Roman Emperor.

On a very hot day, Imam al-Ḥasan ﷺ had observed a fast. At the time of *iftār*, the Imam was extremely thirsty. Juʿdah brought him a drink of milk in which she had mixed the poison. As soon as Imam drank the milk, he experienced the effect of the poison. He realised what had happened and cried out aloud: '*Innā lillāhi wa innā ilayhi rājiʿūn.*' After praising Allah that he would now be moving from the ephemeral world towards the eternal world, he turned towards Juʿdah and said to her: 'O enemy of Allah! You have killed me, may Allah kill you! By Allah, you shall not come to acquire the slightest of that for which you hope and aspire. That person has deceived you. May Allah humiliate you and him by means of His chastisement!'

The forbearance of Imam al-Ḥasan ﷺ can be gauged from the fact that when Imam al-Ḥusayn ﷺ sought to know the identity of his murderer, Imam al-Ḥasan ﷺ refused to divulge Juʿdah's name.

According to one tradition, for two days the Imam suffered from the ill effects of the poison, until he bid farewell to this material world on 28 Ṣafar in the year 50 AH at the age of forty-eight.

As for Juʿdah, she carried her hopes and desires to her grave, for Muʿāwiyah reasoned that if she could not be faithful to al-Ḥasan ﷺ, she could not be expected to be faithful to Yazīd; hence, he refused to fulfil any of his promises. As such, she died in a state of disgrace and humiliation.[1]

5 – Mughīrah becomes governor of Kufa

Mughīrah ibn Shuʿbah, who was originally an inhabitant of Taif and had embraced Islam in the fifth century AH, was a deceitful, devilish, and power-loving person.

When he heard that Muʿāwiyah had arranged for Ziyād ibn Abīh to settle in Kufa so that he could later take the governorship of Kufa away from him, he quickly appointed a deputy in Kufa and set off towards Shām to meet Muʿāwiyah. He expressed his wish to be transferred from Kufa, explaining to Muʿāwiyah: 'As I have grown old now, I have to request you to place a few small villages of Qirqīsiyā under my control, so that I can rest myself.'

Muʿāwiyah realised that one of his opponents, by the name of Qays, lived in Qirqīsiyā, and if Mughīrah were to go there he might form an alliance with him against Muʿāwiyah. 'We are in need of you and you must remain in Kufa,' said Muʿāwiyah.

Mughīrah declined the offer, but Muʿāwiyah's insistence persuaded him to give in. It was midnight when Mughīrah returned to Kufa. He immediately ordered his associates to dispatch Ziyād ibn Abīh towards Shām.

After a period, Muʿāwiyah appointed Saʿīd ibn ʿĀṣ as the governor of Kufa in place of Mughīrah, who incited Yazīd [son of Muʿāwiyah] by telling him: 'Why is Muʿāwiyah not thinking about you? It is imperative that he nominates you as his successor and crown prince!' Yazīd found the idea so appealing that he presented it to his father, Muʿāwiyah. With Mughīrah's support, Yazīd was eventually proclaimed successor to Muʿāwiyah.

In the meantime, Muʿāwiyah appointed ʿAmr ʿĀṣ as the governor of Egypt, and he placed Kufa under his son, ʿAbd Allāh ibn ʿAmr ʿĀṣ. When Mughīrah came to know of this, he warned Muʿāwiyah: 'By this act, have you not placed yourself between the mouths of two lions?' Having grasped

---

[1] *Muntahā al-Aʿmāl*, vol. 1, p. 231.

the message of this statement, Mu'āwiyah deposed 'Abd Allāh from Kufa and once again placed Mughīrah at the helm of affairs in Kufa.

Thus, by means of two cunning plots, Mughīrah became the governor of Kufa. After ruling for seven years and a few months, he died of plague at the age of forty-nine.[1]

7. Trustworthiness

Allah, the Wise, has said:

إِنَّ اللهَ يَأْمُرُكُمْ أَنْ تُؤَدُّوا الْأَمَانَاتِ إِلَى أَهْلِهَا

Indeed Allah commands you to deliver the trusts to their [rightful] owners.

(4:58)

Imam al-Bāqir ﷺ said:

فَلَوْ أَنَّ قَاتِلَ عَلِيِّ بْنِ أَبِي طَالِبٍ ائْتَمَنَنِي عَلَى أَمَانَةٍ لَأَدَّيْتُهَا إِلَيْهِ

If the murderer of Imam 'Alī ﷺ places a trust in my possession, I would surely return it back to him.[2]

Short explanation

If anything is placed in trust with someone, safeguarding of that thing is obligatory, and unfaithfulness with respect to it is prohibited, irrespective of whether its owner is a believer or a disbeliever.

A trustworthy person, as a result of safeguarding people's belongings, becomes the beneficiary of Allah's grace and favour.

A person who is unfaithful towards people's trusts can be compared to a thief, and Allah cloaks such a person with poverty and indigence.

One of the signs of perfect faith is not being unfaithful towards trusts.

A trust can be in the form of money, things, or even secrets. Shaytān leads astray a trustworthy person by causing him to become unfaithful towards the trust placed with him.

---

[1] *Payghambar Wa Yārān*, vol. 5, pp. 272-275.

[2] *Al-Kāfī*, vol. 5, p. 133

1 – Trustworthiness of Umm Salamah

When Imam 'Alī ﷺ decided to move to Iraq and settle there, he handed his letters and testament to Umm Salamah, who, in turn, passed them over to Imam al-Ḥasan ﷺ on his return to Medina.

In a similar manner, when Imam al-Ḥusayn ﷺ set out for Iraq, he too placed his letters and testament in the custody of Umm Salamah with instructions that she should hand them over to his eldest son whenever he sought them from her. After the martyrdom of Imam al-Ḥusayn ﷺ, Imam al-Sajjād ﷺ returned to Medina and she handed the documents over to him.[1]

'Umar, the son of Umm Salamah, narrates: 'My mother said: "Once, the Holy Prophet ﷺ, accompanied by 'Alī ﷺ, came to my house and asked for a sheepskin. After I had handed it to him, he wrote something on the sheepskin and returned it to me with the instruction: 'Whoever seeks this trust from you after mentioning these signs, hand it over to him.'"'

As time passed, the Holy Prophet departed from this world. More time passed and Imam 'Alī ﷺ became caliph but still no one came to claim this trust.

'Umar continued: 'On the day the people pledged allegiance to 'Alī ﷺ, I was seated among them. As he stepped down from the pulpit, the Imam's eyes fell on me whereupon he said: "Seek permission from your mother for I wish to meet her."

'I hurried to my mother and as soon as I informed her of Imam's ﷺ request, she announced that she had been waiting for that day.

'The Imam ﷺ entered and asked Umm Salamah to hand him the trust which contained certain signs. My mother got up and took out a small chest from inside a larger one and handed it to him. Then she turned to me and advised: "Do not forsake 'Alī ﷺ, for none other than him is the rightful Imam after the Holy Prophet ﷺ."'[2]

---

[1] *Safīnat al-Biḥār*, under s-l-m.

[2] *Payghambar Wa Yārān*, vol. 1, p. 275; *Biḥār al-Anwār*, vol. 6, p. 942.

2 – The unfaithful grocer

During the rule of ʿAḍud al-Dawlah Daylamī, a stranger once came to Baghdad wishing to sell a necklace worth 1000 dinars, but could not find any purchaser for it. As he intended to travel to Mecca, he began to search for a trustworthy person who would safeguard his necklace.

The people pointed him to a grocer who was known for his piety. The stranger placed the necklace in the grocer's trust and proceeded towards Mecca.

When he returned from Mecca, he approached the grocer and presented him with some gifts that he had brought with him. To the stranger's great surprise, the grocer pretended as if he did not know him and denied having possession of anything belonging to him. A quarrel ensued, as a result of which people gathered and threw the person out of the 'pious' grocer's shop.

The person approached the grocer for his necklace several times, only to receive abuse and invectives.

Someone advised him to complain to ʿAḍud al-Dawlah Daylamī. Heeding the advice, the man wrote a letter to the king, who replied: 'For three days, wait by the door of the grocery. On the fourth day, I shall pass there and when I greet you, reply to my greetings. The following day, seek your necklace from the grocer and then inform me of the outcome.'

The person did as instructed. On the fourth day, the king, with great pomp and grandeur, passed by the grocery and as soon as his eyes fell upon the person from Baghdad, he greeted him. The person returned the greeting. The king, exhibiting great respect and esteem, began to complain: 'You have come from Baghdad but you did not deem it fit to honour me with a visit and to grant me an opportunity to provide you with accommodation and comfort.' The stranger apologised for not having informed the king of his arrival. All the while, the grocer and the people around him looked on in amazement, wondering who this person was who was revered so greatly by the king. The grocer began to fear for his life.

As soon as the king's procession had passed, the grocer turned towards the stranger and said: 'Brother, when exactly did you place that necklace with me? Did it have any marks? Let me have another look, perhaps I might just be able to locate it.' The person described his necklace and the grocer, after a short search, found it. He handed it over to the person and said: 'Allah is aware of the fact that it had simply slipped out of my mind.'

Arriving before the king, the person related the entire episode to him. The king ordered the grocer to be arrested, placed the necklace around his neck, and sent him to the gallows. He then ordered the following announcement to be made all over the city: 'Such is the punishment for anyone who takes possession of a trust and then denies it. O people! Take heed from this incident!'

The king then returned the necklace to the stranger from Baghdad and sent him to his own city.[1]

3 – Remaining faithful when someone trusts you

'Abd Allāh ibn Sinān says:

'I approached Imam al-Ṣādiq ﷺ in the mosque at a time when he had completed his *ʿaṣr* prayers and was sitting down facing the qibla. I asked him: "Some of the governors and rulers consider us to be trustworthy and thus place their wealth with us, but at the same time they do not pay their *khums*. Do we return their money to them or do we keep it for our use?"

'The Imam ﷺ replied three times: "By the Lord of the Kaʿbah! Even if Ibn Muljim, the murderer of my father ʿAlī ﷺ, were to place something in trust with me, I would return it to him whenever he wanted it back."'[2]

4 – The shepherd and the sheep of the Jews

In the year 7 AH, the Holy Prophet with an army of 1600 soldiers set out to conquer the fort of Khaybar, which was about ninety-six miles from Medina. The Muslim soldiers had stationed themselves in the desert around Khaybar for some time but the conquest of the fort remained elusive.

---

[1] *Pand-i Tārīkh*, vol. 1, p. 202; *Mustaṭraf*, vol. 1, p. 118.

[2] *Namūnah-i Maʿārif*, vol. 1, p. 354; *Biḥār al-Anwār*, vol. 15, p. 149.

During this period they found themselves in a very difficult situation as far as food was concerned. The lack of food and intense hunger forced them to eat animals like horses and mules, whose meat is disapproved by Islam.

In these circumstances, a black shepherd, who used to graze the sheep of the Jews, arrived in the presence of the Holy Prophet. He embraced Islam and then said to the Holy Prophet: 'These sheep belong to the Jews and I hereby hand them over to you.'

The Holy Prophet replied unequivocally: 'These sheep have been placed in your possession as a trust and in our religion it is forbidden to be unfaithful to one's trust. It is incumbent upon you to lead the sheep to the door of the fort and hand them over to their owners.'

The shepherd, in compliance with his orders, handed the sheep over to their respective owners and then returned to join the Muslim army.[1]

5 – Possessions entrusted to the Holy Prophet

When the Holy Prophet migrated from Mecca to Medina, he left the Commander of the Faithful in Mecca so that he could return the possessions that had been entrusted to the Prophet back to their respective owners.

Ḥanẓalah ibn Abī Sufyān instructed 'Umayr ibn Wā'il to go to 'Alī and tell him: 'I had placed 100 *mithqāls*[2] of gold with the Holy Prophet ﷺ. Since he has fled to Medina and you are his representative here, please hand my property back to me.' Ḥanẓalah added that if 'Alī asked for witnesses to support the claim, all the Quraysh would testify to the veracity of 'Umayr's claim. Initially, 'Umayr was hesitant but Ḥanẓalah enticed him by presenting him with some gold and a necklace belonging to Hind, the wife of Abū Sufyān.

'Umayr approached 'Alī ﷺ and made the claim, adding that Abū Jahl, 'Ikrimah, 'Uqbah, Abū Sufyān, and Ḥanẓalah would testify for him. The Imam retorted: 'May their deception rebound on themselves.' He then asked him to bring his witnesses near the Ka'bah. When all of them had

---

[1] *Dāstān-hā Wa Pand-hā*, vol. 8, p. 114; *Sīrah Ibn Hishām*, vol. 3, p. 344.

[2] A legal mithqāl is a measure of weight equal to approximately 3.51 grams.

arrived, he began questioning each one, individually and separately, about the items being held in trust. He questioned 'Umayr first: 'What time was it when you had placed your possession with Muḥammad ﷺ?'

'It was morning when I gave him the gold and he handed it over to his servant,' replied 'Umayr.

Imam 'Alī ؏ asked Abū Jahl the same question. He replied: 'I have no idea.'

When Abū Sufyān was questioned, he responded: 'It was at sunset and he had placed it in his sleeves.'

When Ḥanẓalah was questioned, he gave the answer: 'He took possession of the gold at the time of *ẓuhr* and placed it in front of him.'

When 'Uqbah was questioned, he replied: 'It was *'aṣr* when the Prophet took the possession in his own hands and carried it to his house.'

And finally, when the Imam questioned 'Ikrimah, he answered: 'It was bright and early in the morning when Muḥammad took possession of it and sent it to the house of Fāṭimah.'

The Imam then informed them of their conflicting statements and their deception thus became apparent. Then, turning to 'Umayr, he asked him: 'Why is it that while you lied you appeared uneasy and your face had gone pale?'

'Umayr replied: 'By the Lord of the Ka'bah! I had not placed anything in trust with Muḥammad ﷺ. It was a deception Ḥanẓalah had bribed me into. This necklace here, belonging to Hind, with her name inscribed on it, is one of the things presented to me as a bribe.'[1]

8. Examination

Allah, the Wise, has said:

$$\text{الَّذِي خَلَقَ الْمَوْتَ وَالْـحَيَاةَ لِيَبْلُوَكُمْ أَيُّكُمْ أَحْسَنُ عَمَلًا}$$

He, who created death and life that He may test you [to see] which of you

---

[1] *Rāhnumā-yi Sa'ādat*, vol. 2, p. 435; *Nāsikh al-Tawārīkh* – Amīr al-Mu'minīn, p. 676.

is best in conduct. (67:2)

Imam al-Sajjād ﷺ said:

إِنَّمَا خَلَقَ الدُّنْيَا وَأَهْلَهَا لِيَبْلُوَهُمْ فِيهَا

Indeed, [Allah] created the world and its inhabitants in order to examine them in it.[1]

Short explanation

Man faces different types of examination in the world. He is tested through fear, hunger, disease, death of his near and dear ones, financial constraints, false accusations, evil neighbours, and so on.

Since this world is a place of deeds and examinations, blessed and happy are those who do not fail at any stage of life.

On one occasion, a person is tested by means of wealth and on another occasion by indigence. He achieves success by resorting to thanksgiving during affluence and patience during poverty. Everyone, without exception, is subjected to trials and examinations which vary only in their 'quality' and 'quantity'. Do you not see how some people, who are accustomed to boasting, lose their patience and fail miserably in the face of examinations?

1 – Hārūn Makkī

Sahl Khurāsānī approached Imam al-Ṣādiq ﷺ and complained: 'Why is it that in spite of the truth being on your side you do not stage an uprising? At the present time there are 100,000 of your Shiʿas who, upon your orders, would immediately unsheathe their swords for battle.'

The Imam, with the intention of giving him a practical answer, ordered the furnace to be lit. He then instructed Sahl to jump into the flames. Sahl said: 'O my master! May Allah shower you with His grace and favours! Do not place me in the fire. I take back my words and request you to withdraw your instruction too.'

Meanwhile, one of the sincere companions of the Imam by the name of Hārūn Makkī, happened to arrive. Just as he entered, the Imam told him to

---

[1] *Al-Kāfī* (new edition), vol. 8, p. 75.

take off his shoes and walk into the hot furnace. As soon as Hārūn heard the Imam's order he entered the furnace and sat within the flames.

The Imam then turned to Sahl and started to brief him about the circumstances prevailing in Khorasan, as if he had been there to witness the events taking place. After a while, he said to Sahl: 'Get up and have a look inside the furnace.'

When Sahl peered into the furnace, he saw Hārūn sitting cross-legged and unharmed inside, surrounded by the fiery flames. 'How many individuals like this one exist in Khorasan?' the Imam questioned Sahl.

'By Allah! Not a single person like Hārūn Makkī exists in Khorasan,' replied Sahl.

The Imam then explained: 'I shall not stage an uprising when I do not have even five sincere companions. [And remember]: we are very well aware as to when we should stage an uprising.'[1]

2 – Buhlūl succeeds!

Hārūn al-Rashīd, the Abbasid caliph, wished to appoint a judge in Baghdad. After conferring with his courtiers, it was unanimously agreed that none except Buhlūl possessed the right qualities for the post.

Buhlūl was summoned and the post was offered to him. But Buhlūl declined to accept, saying that he was neither worthy of the post nor capable of undertaking the task.

Hārūn said: 'All the inhabitants of Baghdad are of the opinion that none except you is worthy of the post and you deny it!'

Buhlūl explained: 'I am more aware of myself than any of you. Whatever I have stated is either true or false. If the reason I have given is true, then it would be improper of me to assume the office of judge when I am not capable. On the other hand, if I have lied to you, then a liar does not deserve to take this post.'

But Hārūn insisted that Buhlūl take up the responsibility. Buhlūl requested that he be granted one night to reflect over the offer. The next

---

[1] *Ḥikāyat-hā-yi Shanīdanī*, vol. 4, p. 65; *Safīnat al-Biḥār*, vol. 2, p. 714.

morning, Buhlūl feigned insanity, and placing a staff between his legs ran through the streets and markets of Baghdad, screaming: 'Make room for my horse and keep away lest it kicks you.'

As soon as the people noticed his antics they commented that Buhlūl had gone insane. When Hārūn al-Rashīd was informed of this, he said: 'Buhlūl has not become insane; rather he has saved his religion and has escaped our clutches. He has enacted this in order to prevent himself from interfering in the affairs and the rights of the people.'[1]

The author says: Yes, each one is subjected to a specific examination. Not only was Buhlūl offered authority, but the caliph would send him food. Buhlūl, however, would not eat it, saying: 'Throw it to the dogs behind the baths. Even they, if they were to realise that it was the caliph's food, would refuse to eat it!'

3 – Abū Hurayrah failed!

Abū Hurayrah embraced Islam in the year 8 AH. He was therefore in the company of the Holy Prophet for only two years. He died in the year 59 AH at the age of seventy-eight.

Abū Hurayrah had come to be regarded as one of the companions of the Holy Prophet. However, he failed to benefit from the Prophet's holy company and failed to protect himself from blunders and errors. On the contrary, he misused his position and sold himself for the material gains of this world.

Abū Hurayrah used to forge traditions and ascribe them to the Holy Prophet in return for riches. On the first of the occasions when this occurred, the Second Caliph prohibited him from narrating traditions; on the second occasion, the caliph punished him by lashing him; and on the third occasion, he had him expelled from the city.

When Aʿlā, the governor of Bahrain, passed away in the year 21 AH, ʿUmar appointed Abū Hurayrah as governor in his place. But within a short

---

[1] *Pand-i Tārīkh*, vol. 1, p. 181; *Rawḍāt al-Jannāt*, p. 36; *Gharāʾib al-Akhbār* of Sayyid Niʿmat Allāh Jazāʾirī.

period, a large amount of money (400,000 dinars) had found its way into Abū Hurayrah's pockets. As a result, ʿUmar dismissed him from his post.

Muʿāwiyah used to compel some of the Companions and Followers to forge traditions against the Commander of the Faithful and one of the principal personalities in this act was Abū Hurayrah. Once, Aṣbagh ibn Nubātah said to Abū Hurayrah: 'Contrary to the teachings of the Holy Prophet ﷺ you befriend ʿAlī's ؏ enemies and harbour enmity towards his friends!'

Hearing this, Abū Hurayrah sighed deeply and simply said: '*Innā lillāhi wa innā ilayhi rājiʿūn.*'

Another of the evil deeds committed by Abū Hurayrah was that in order to acquire riches from Muʿāwiyah, he accompanied the latter to the Mosque of Kufa, and slapping his forehead several times in full view of the gathering, said: 'O people of Iraq! Do you think I shall ascribe a lie to the Holy Prophet ﷺ and thereby burn myself in the fire of hell? By Allah! I have heard the Holy Prophet ﷺ say: "For every prophet there is a holy sanctuary and mine is in Medina, between the mountains of ʿAyr and Thawr. Whoever establishes an innovation in my sanctuary, may the curse of Allah, the angels, and all the people be upon him." I take Allah as my witness that ʿAlī introduced an innovation within the sanctuary of the Holy Prophet ﷺ.'

Muʿāwiyah was so pleased with this statement that he rewarded Abū Hurayrah and made him the ruler of Medina.[1]

4 – Prophet Ibrāhīm ؏ and the sacrifice of Prophet Ismāʿīl ؏

Allah ordered Prophet Ibrāhīm ؏ to sacrifice his son, Prophet Ismāʿīl ؏. He ordered this to examine Prophet Ibrāhīm's ؏ patience and obedience to Allah. If Prophet Ibrāhīm ؏ passed this test, he would demonstrate his worthiness of Allah's grace and favour.

Having been bestowed with a child after years of loneliness without any children, he was being ordered by Allah to sacrifice with his own

---

[1] *Payghambar Wa Yārān*, vol. 1, pp. 154-166.

hands the apple of his eyes, who had grown up to become a young boy of thirteen. Prophet Ibrāhīm ﷺ said to Prophet Ismāʿīl ﷺ: 'O my beloved son! I have dreamt that I am sacrificing you; what do you think about this?'

'Dear father! Act as you have been ordered and, God-willing, you shall find me of the steadfast ones,' Prophet Ismāʿīl ﷺ replied. He strengthened his father's resolve by advising: 'Father, death is very painful and I am so fearful of it that its very thought leaves me disturbed and distressed, so bind my hands and legs firmly, lest I beat about with them while my throat is being slit and thereby reduce the rewards ordained for me. In addition, sharpen the knife so that I am put at peace quickly. Also, place me with my face towards the ground and not upon my cheeks for I fear that if your eyes fall upon my face compassion might overtake you and prevent you from complying with the divine commandment. Take off your garments so that my blood does not taint them and my mother does not see my blood. If you deem it fit, take my clothes to my mother; they might serve to console her and lessen her grief at my death.'

Hearing this speech, Prophet Ibrāhīm ﷺ responded: 'O son! You are indeed an excellent aide in executing Allah's commandment.'

Prophet Ibrāhīm ﷺ took his son to Mina, sharpened the knife, bound Prophet Ismāʿīl's ﷺ hands and legs, and laid him with his face towards the ground. Prophet Ibrāhīm ﷺ then raised his head towards the heavens and placed the knife on his son's throat. But, as he did so, he realised that the knife did not cut. Looking at it, he noticed that the sharp knife had turned blunt. This occurrence was repeated several times, when suddenly a heavenly voice was heard, saying: 'O Ibrāhīm! Indeed, you have acted as you had dreamt and have complied with the commandment given to you.'

As a substitute for the sacrifice of Prophet Ismāʿīl ﷺ, Jibrīl brought a goat which Prophet Ibrāhīm ﷺ subsequently sacrificed. From here, it became a custom that those performing the hajj every year should offer a sacrifice at Mina.[1]

---

[1] *Tārīkh-i Anbiyāʾ*, vol. 1, pp. 164-169.

5 – Sa'd and the Holy Prophet

One of the companions of the Holy Prophet by the name of Sa'd was very poor and was regarded as one of the People of the Ledge.[1] He used to offer all his prayers behind the Holy Prophet who was greatly distressed by Sa'd's poverty. One day, the Holy Prophet promised him that if he got some money he would give it to Sa'd. Time passed but no money came to the Holy Prophet who became even more distressed at Sa'd's situation. It was at this time that Jibrīl descended from the skies, bringing with him two dirhams. He said to the Holy Prophet: 'Allah has said: "We are aware of your distress in connection with Sa'd's poverty. If you want him to emerge from this state give him these two dirhams and ask him to engage himself in trade."'

The Holy Prophet took the two dirhams and set out of the house for the *ẓuhr* prayers when he found Sa'd waiting for him near one of the rooms of the mosque. Turning to him, the Holy Prophet asked: 'Can you engage yourself in business?'

'By Allah! I have no capital with which I can do business,' replied Sa'd.

The Holy Prophet handed him the two dirhams and told him to start trading with this capital. Sa'd took the money and after offering the *ẓuhr* and *'aṣr* prayers set about to earn his livelihood.

Allah blessed him in such a way that whatever he purchased for a dirham he would sell it for double the amount. Consequently, his financial state gradually improved. This continued till he eventually purchased a shop near the mosque and began conducting his business from there.

As his business picked up, he began to become lax with respect to his acts of worship, even to the extent that when Bilāl recited the *adhān* he would not get ready for prayers. Previously, he was ready well before the *adhān* was recited!

When the Holy Prophet ﷺ noticed Sa'd's lateness for prayers, he said to him: 'Sa'd, this world has made you so busy that it has even weaned you

---

[1] These were people who did not possess a house of their own and so lived in the veranda or the rooms of the mosque.

away from your prayers.'

Sa'd replied: 'What can I do? If I leave my wealth unattended it will go to waste and I will end up in loss. From one person I have to collect the money for the goods sold, while from another I have to take possession of the goods purchased.'

The Holy Prophet was disturbed at Sa'd's involvement with his wealth and his negligence with respect to his acts of worship. At that moment, Jibrīl descended and said: 'Allah has said: "We possess knowledge of your distress. Which of the two states do you prefer for Sa'd?"'

The Holy Prophet indicated that the previous state was beneficial for Sa'd. Jibrīl agreed: 'Yes, love for the world causes man to become heedless of the Hereafter. Take back the two dirhams which you had previously given to him.'

The Holy Prophet approached Sa'd and asked him if he could return the two dirhams that he had given to him. 'If you desire, I shall even give you 200 dirhams,' said Sa'd.

'No, just give me the two dirhams which you had taken from me.'

Sa'd handed the money to the Holy Prophet and within a short time his financial situation turned a full circle, and before long he found himself in his previous state.[1]

9. Enjoining The Good And Forbidding The Evil

Allah, the Wise, has said:

$$ كُنْتُمْ خَيْرَ أُمَّةٍ أُخْرِجَتْ لِلنَّاسِ تَأْمُرُونَ بِالْمَعْرُوفِ وَتَنْهَوْنَ عَنِ الْمُنْكَرِ $$

You are the best nation [ever] brought forth for mankind: you bid what is right and forbid what is wrong. (3:110)

Imam 'Alī ﷺ said:

$$ مَنْ تَرَكَ إِنْكَارَ الْمُنْكَرِ بِقَلْبِهِ وَيَدِهِ وَلِسَانِهِ فَهُوَ مَيْتٌ بَيْنَ الْأَحْيَاءِ $$

One who refrains from prohibiting evil by means of his heart, hand, and

---

[1] *Dāstān-hā wa Pand-hā*, vol. 2, p. 78; *Ḥayāt al-Qulūb*, vol. 1, p. 578.

tongue, is [like] a dead amongst the living.[1]

Short explanation

Anyone who seeks to enjoin the good and forbid the evil must himself be aware of what is lawful and unlawful, and should not act contrary to what he preaches.

His aim should be to guide the people. He should talk nicely and be aware of the difference in the level of understanding of the people. If he is opposed, he should exhibit patience, and if he is supported and favoured, he should thank Allah.

1 – Bishr Ḥāfī

Once, Imam al-Kāẓim ﷺ was passing by the house of Bishr Ḥāfī, when he heard the sound of dance and music coming from inside. At that very moment a slave-girl came out of the house to throw some garbage. 'Is the owner of this house a free person or a slave?' the Imam asked her.

The slave-girl replied: 'He is a free man.'

Hearing this, the Imam remarked: 'You speak the truth, for had he been a slave he would have feared his master.'

When the slave-girl came back inside the house, Bishr, who had been consuming wine, asked her what took her so long. As soon as the slave-girl relayed what had happened, Bishr immediately got up and ran barefooted after the Imam. Once he had caught up with the Imam he expressed shame and repentance over his acts, sought forgiveness, and amended his wrongful ways.[2]

2 – Mullā Ḥasan Yazdī, the forbidder of evil

During the reign of Fatḥ ʿAlī Shāh, the Qājārī ruler, there lived in Yazd a scholar by the name of Mullā Ḥasan Yazdī,[3] who was held in high esteem by the people. The governor of the city of Yazd used to oppress the people

---

[1] *Jāmiʿ al-Saʿādāt*, vol. 2, p. 235.

[2] *Darsī Az Akhlāq*, p. 128; *Minhāj al-Karāmah* of ʿAllāmah Ḥillī.

[3] He was the author of *Muhīj al-Aḥzān*.

and treat them with great cruelty. Mullā Ḥasan advised him to stop his evil deeds. When he refused to mend his ways, Mullā complained to Fatḥ ʿAlī Shāh, but this also proved unproductive.

Since Mullā was particularly assiduous with respect to the issue of enjoining the good and forbidding the evil, he assembled the people of Yazd who, upon his orders, collectively threw the governor out of the city.

When Fatḥ ʿAlī Shāh was informed of this incident he was immensely upset and ordered Mullā Ḥasan Yazdī to be brought before him in Tehran. As soon as Mullā came, Fatḥ ʿAlī Shāh asked him about the incident in Yazd. Mullā replied: 'Your governor in Yazd was a tyrant and I wanted to relieve the people of his evils by throwing him out of Yazd.'

The answer so enraged the shah that he ordered Mullā's legs to be tied. Amīn al-Dawlah said to the shah: 'He is not at fault. It was without his permission that the people threw out the governor.'

In spite of his feet being fettered, Mullā Ḥasan spoke out: 'Why do we need to lie? I had the governor thrown out of Yazd because of his oppression.'

Eventually, due to the intervention of Amīn al-Dawlah, Mullā Ḥasan's legs were untied.

That night, the shah witnessed the Holy Prophet in his dream and observed that two of his toes were tied. 'Why are your toes tied?' he asked the Holy Prophet.

The Holy Prophet replied: 'It is you who has tied them.'

Fatḥ ʿAlī Shāh pointed out that he had never shown such disrespect.

The Holy Prophet explained: 'But was it not you who had ordered Mullā Ḥasan Yazdī's feet to be tied?'

Fatḥ ʿAlī Shāh woke up from his sleep, greatly alarmed. He ordered Mullā Ḥasan to be given resplendent clothes and to be returned to his city with great honour and respect. Mullā Ḥasan refused to accept the clothes and returned to Yazd. Later, he travelled to Karbala and remained there for the rest of his life.[1]

---

[1] *Ḥikāyat-hā-yi Shanīdanī*, vol. 3, p. 146; *Qaṣaṣ al-ʿUlamāʾ*, p. 101.

3 – Allah's command to destroy a city

Allah ordered two angels to destroy a city. On reaching there, the angels noticed one of the inhabitants beseeching and supplicating Allah. One of the angels said to the other: 'Don't you see this person supplicating?'

'Yes I do, but Allah's order has to be executed,' replied the other.

'Wait; let me ask Allah as to what should be done.'

Praying to Allah, the first angel enquired: 'In this city there is a person who entreats and beseeches you. Do we still impose the chastisement upon the city?'

The answer came from Allah: 'Execute the commandment which has been given to you, for that person has never been perturbed and distressed for My sake, nor did he show anger over the evil deeds committed by the other people.'[1]

4 – Yūnus ibn 'Abd al-Raḥmān

When Imam al-Kāẓim ﷺ departed from the world, his representatives had huge sums of wealth in their possession. As a result of their greed, some of them began to deny the Imam's death and thereby laid the foundation of a sect known as Wāqifiyyah. Ziyād Qandī possessed 70,000 gold coins while 'Alī ibn Abī Ḥamzah had 30,000.

Meanwhile, Yūnus ibn 'Abd al-Raḥmān invited the people towards the Imamate of Imam al-Riḍā ﷺ and regarded the Wāqifiyyah sect as false and erroneous. When Ziyād Qandī and 'Alī ibn Abī Ḥamzah realised what Yūnus was doing, they sent him a message, asking: 'Why do you invite the people towards Imam al-Riḍā ﷺ? If your objective is to acquire riches, we will make you rich.' They pledged to give him 10,000 gold coins if he kept quiet and refrained from inviting the people towards the Imam.

Yūnus ibn 'Abd al-Raḥmān[2] replied to them by quoting a narration from Imam al-Bāqir ﷺ and Imam al-Ṣādiq ﷺ, which says: 'When innovations

---

[1] *Jāmiʿ al-Saʿādāt*, vol. 2, p. 231.

[2] Imam al-Riḍā ﷺ had said: 'Yūnus ibn 'Abd al-Raḥmān in his time, is as Salmān Fārsī was in his.'

manifest themselves amongst the people, it is imperative for the elders and leaders to manifest what they know [so that people refrain from evil], and if they fail to do so, Allah shall take away from them the light of faith.' [Yūnus said:] 'Under no circumstances shall I abandon jihad in the path of religion and the affairs of Allah.'

After receiving this forthright and explicit reply from Yūnus, Ziyād Qandī and 'Alī ibn Abī Ḥamzah became his enemies.[1]

5 – The caliph on the rooftop!

One night, the Second Caliph was surveying the streets to ascertain the general state of affairs in the city. In the course of his inspection, he happened to pass by a house from which he heard suspicious noises. He climbed over the wall of the house and looked inside. A man and a woman were sitting together, with a jar of wine placed before them. Addressing them harshly, he said: 'You commit sins in solitude in the belief that Allah shall not make manifest your secret?'

The person turned to the caliph and said: 'Do not be so hasty, for if I have committed one sin, you have committed three. Firstly, Allah has said in the Qur'an: And do not spy [49:12]. You have been doing just that. Secondly, He has said in the Qur'an: And go into the houses by their doors [2:189]. You have entered from over the wall! Thirdly, He has said: So when you enter houses, greet your people with a salutation [24:61]. You have not done so.'

The caliph asked: 'If I were to pardon you, do you resolve to amend your ways?'

'By Allah! I shall never repeat this act again,' the man replied.

The caliph said: 'Now you can be at ease, for I have pardoned you.'[2]

---

[1] *Muntahā al-A'māl*, vol. 2, p. 253.

[2] *Pand-i Tārīkh*, vol. 5, p. 29; *al-Ghadīr*, vol. 6, p. 121.

10. Fairness

Allah, the Wise, has said:

كُونُوا قَوَّامِينَ لِلّٰهِ شُهَدَاءَ بِالْقِسْطِ

Be maintainers, as witnesses for the sake of Allah, of justice. (5:8)

Imam 'Alī ﷺ has said:

مَنْ يُنْصِفُ مِنْ نَفْسِهِ لَمْ يَزِدْهُ اللّٰهُ إِلَّا عِزًّا

One who exhibits fairness on his part, Allah shall increase him in glory.[1]

Short explanation

A person's faith does not become perfect until he observes fairness with respect to himself and others. In exchange, Allah shall increase his honour and glory.

Man, by nature, prefers his own self and loves everything that is associated with him. He also possesses a dislike for everything bad and evil. Thus, if he helps someone in need, he would be commended by one and all. Similarly, if he does not desire anything bad and evil for himself, he should also not desire it for the others.

This also holds true when mediating between two warring parties; never should he side unfairly with one against the other, even if the outcome results in his own detriment.

1 – An advice from the Holy Prophet

An Arab approached the Holy Prophet when he was about to embark upon a military expedition. Seizing the reins of the Prophet's camel, he said: 'O Prophet of Allah! Inform me of a deed that would earn me paradise.'

'Conduct yourself with people in the same manner as you would want them to behave towards you, and refrain from doing to them what you would not want them to do to you,' advised the Prophet. He then added: 'Let go of the reins [for I have to go for jihad].'[2]

---

[1] *Jāmiʿ al-Saʿādāt*, vol. 1, p. 368.

[2] *Al-Kāfī*, vol. 2, Chapter of Fairness, h. 10.

2 – The equity of ʿAlī 🕮

Shuʿbī narrates:

'Like the other youths, I entered the vast open ground of Kufa where I witnessed the Commander of the Faithful standing beside two containers which were filled with gold and silver coins. He had a small whip in his hand. A huge crowd had gathered around him and he kept them back by means of his whip, to prevent them from hampering the distribution of money.

'The Imam 🕮 began distributing the money amongst the people until nothing remained for himself and he returned home empty-handed. I returned home and said to my father: "I witnessed a very strange act today but I fail to comprehend if this person's action was good or bad because he never retained anything for himself!"

'My father enquired: "Who was the person?"

'"The Commander of the Faithful 🕮," I replied. I then narrated what had transpired earlier.

'Upon hearing ʿAlī's 🕮 fairness in distributing the money, my father began to weep and said to me: "My son, you have witnessed the most excellent person from amongst the people."'[1]

3 – ʿAdī ibn Ḥātim

ʿAdī, the son of the well-known Ḥātim Ṭāʾī, was one of the sincere and loyal companions of Imam ʿAlī 🕮. From the year 10 AH when he accepted Islam, ʿAdī had always remained in the service of the Imam and had fought alongside him in the Battles of Jamal, Ṣiffīn, and Nahrawān. In the Battle of Jamal he sustained an injury to one of his eyes as a result of which he lost his vision.

Once, he came to Muʿāwiyah for some purpose. Muʿāwiyah asked him why he had not brought his sons with him. 'They were killed fighting alongside the Commander of the Faithful 🕮,' he replied.

"ʿAlī has not been just to you, for he sent your sons to be killed while

____

[1] *Al-Ghārāt*, vol. 1, p. 55; *Dastān-hā Az Zindagī-yi ʿAlī*, p. 7.

he has kept his own sons alive!' said Mu'āwiyah.

'Adī retorted: '[On the contrary] I have not done justice to 'Alī for he has been killed, whereas I am still alive. O Mu'āwiyah! Our rage towards you still smoulders in our hearts. Do know that [the pain of] having our throats slit or the agony of death is easier for us to bear than hearing bad comments about 'Alī .'[1]

4 – The fairness of Abū Dharr

On the way towards the Battle of Tabūk,[2] Abū Dharr fell behind the army because he was mounted on a slow animal. When the others realised this they notified the Holy Prophet, who said: 'If he possesses goodness in him, Allah shall make him reach you.'

Meanwhile, Abū Dharr, disappointed with his animal, dismounted and proceeded on foot. The Holy Prophet found a convenient place and had decided to pitch the tents, when one of the Muslims shouted that there was someone in the distance approaching them. The Holy Prophet prayed: 'O Lord! May it be Abū Dharr!' The others informed him that it was indeed Abū Dharr. The Prophet supplicated: 'May Allah forgive Abū Dharr! He travels alone, shall die alone, and shall be resurrected alone.' He then asked the people to provide Abū Dharr with some water, as he appeared to be thirsty.

But when Abū Dharr arrived in his presence, the Prophet observed that he had a container of water in his possession, and so asked him: 'Abū Dharr! You had water with you and yet you remained thirsty?'

'Yes, O Prophet of Allah! May my parents be sacrificed for you! On the way, I was overcome by thirst. I reached a place where there was some water. Tasting it, I found it to be cold and delicious and so said to myself: "[It is not fair] if I drink this water before the Holy Prophet," replied Abū Dharr.

Hearing this, the Holy Prophet said: 'O Abū Dharr! May Allah forgive

---

[1] Ibid.

[2] Located 300 miles north of Medina.

your sins! You shall lead your life in solitude, die as a stranger, away from home, and enter paradise alone.'[1]

11. Altruism

Allah, the Wise, has said:

$$وَيُؤْثِرُونَ عَلَىٰ أَنْفُسِهِمْ وَلَوْ كَانَ بِهِمْ خَصَاصَةٌ$$

They (the Muhājirūn) prefer them over themselves though poverty may afflict them. (59:9)

The Holy Prophet said:

$$أَيُّمَا ٱمْرِئٍ ٱشْتَهَى شَهْوَةً فَرَدَّ شَهْوَتَهُ وَآثَرَ عَلَى نَفْسِهِ غُفِرَ لَهُ$$

One who covets something, [but] suppressing his desire gives others preference over himself, shall have his sins forgiven.[2]

Short explanation

The highest degree of generosity and munificence is altruism. An altruistic person, despite having his own acute needs and necessities, makes a sacrifice by giving others preference over himself.

Even the act of giving alms occupies a lower rank than altruism. Attaining the pleasure of Allah plays a pivotal role in it. If a person, in an effort to save the life of a drowning person, gets drowned himself, the commendation from the Lord for this self-sacrifice is a thousand times more than for the alms he pays.

1 – The altruistic slave

'Abd Allāh ibn Ja'far, the husband of Lady Zaynab ﷺ, was a person whose generosity was unparalleled. Once, as he happened to pass by a palm plantation, he noticed a slave working there. At that very moment the slave's food was brought and handed over to him. As he was about to start his meal, a hungry dog came before him, wagging its tail. The slave placed

---

[1] *Payghambar Wa Yārān*, vol. 1, p. 49; *al-Iṣābah*, vol. 4, p. 65

[2] *Jāmiʿ al-Saʿādāt*, vol. 2, p. 118.

a portion of his food before the dog and the animal immediately ate it up. The slave put some more food in front of the dog and before long it was eaten too. This continued till he had given his entire food to the dog.

'Abd Allāh, who had been witnessing the incident, asked the slave: 'What is your daily ration of food?'

'The amount you have just witnessed,' the slave answered.

'If that is the case, why then did you give the dog preference over yourself?' enquired 'Abd Allāh.

'This dog had come from afar and was hungry and I did not deem it appropriate to drive him away in that state of hunger.'

'With what then will you satiate yourself today?'

'I shall overcome my hunger by patience and steadfastness,' the slave explained.

'Abd Allāh, observing the slave's selflessness and altruism, thought to himself that the slave was more generous than himself. By way of commendation and compensation for his altruism, 'Abd Allāh purchased the slave and the plantation from the owner, freed the slave, and finally gifted the entire plantation to him.[1]

2 – The incident of the Mosque of Merv

Abū Muḥammad Azdī narrates:

'When the Mosque of Merv caught fire, the Muslims assumed that it was the work of the Christians and retaliated by setting their houses ablaze. When the king came to know of this act, he ordered those involved in the incident to be arrested and punished. He ordered that the culprits should face one of three types of punishment: death, severing of a hand, or whipping. Each punishment was to be written on a small piece of paper which was then placed in a box. Every guilty person was required to draw a piece from the box and would be subjected to the punishment written on it.

'When one of these people picked and read his paper, he broke down

---

[1] *Ḥikāyat-hā-yi Shanīdanī*, vol. 5, p. 114; *al-Maḥajjah al-Bayḍāʾ*, vol. 6, p. 80.

in tears because his sentence was the death penalty. A young boy, who appeared to be happy as he was to be punished with lashes, asked the distressed person: "Why are you agitated and weeping? These punishments should not be a problem in the path of serving the religion."

'The first person responded: "We have served our religion and therefore do not fear death, but the truth is that I have an old mother, and since I am her only son she is entirely dependent upon me. When she hears about my death she will not survive."

'Having heard this, the youth reflected for a while and then said: "Neither is my mother alive nor do I have an attachment with anyone. Let us exchange our punishments so that I get killed instead of you and you face the lashes, after which you can return home to care for your mother."

'The two exchanged their punishments; the youth was killed while the other person, after being lashed, returned home to his mother.'[1]

3 – The Battle of Yarmūk (or Tabūk)

In the Battle of Yarmūk, a group of Muslim soldiers would go out for battle every day. After a few hours of confrontation, the unhurt and those who had minor injuries would return, while the wounded or dead would be left on the battlefield.

Ḥudhayfah ʿUdwī recounts:

'One day, my cousin, together with some other soldiers, set out for the battlefield. Unfortunately, after the conclusion of the day's battle, he failed to return. Picking up a container of water, I set out for the battlefield hoping to provide him with a drink in case he happened to be alive.

'After searching for some time I found my cousin, who was barely alive. I stooped down beside him and asked him if he needed some water. He nodded. At that very moment, another soldier, who lay near him, heard me and then sighed loudly to indicate that he was very thirsty.

'My cousin signalled to me to provide water to the soldier first. As I went to attend to the injured soldier, I realised that he was Hishām ibn

---

[1] *Namūnah-i Maʿārif,* vol. 2, p. 435; *Mustaṭraf,* vol. 1, p. 157.

'Āṣ. I asked him whether he needed water. He signalled in the affirmative. Instantaneously, another injured soldier demanded water and Hishām also refused to drink the water before the other soldier had drank it. I moved towards the third soldier, but just as I reached him, he breathed his last. Returning to Hishām, I observed that in this ensuing period he too had died. I hastened towards my cousin, only to find him dead too!'[1]

4 – Imam 'Alī in place of the Holy Prophet

When the leaders of Quraysh realised that the inhabitants of Medina had pledged their loyalty to the Prophet, their hatred towards him intensified. Consequently, their leaders decided that on the eve of the first of Rabī' al-Awwal, one brave person from every tribe would gather together, besiege the Prophet's house, and kill him as he lay asleep in his bed.

Allah divulged their sinister plan to the Prophet, who said to the Commander of the Faithful: 'As the polytheists intend to murder me tonight, Allah has ordered me to migrate. Will you sleep in my place so that they do not find out I have gone?'

'O Prophet of Allah! Will you remain alive and well if I do this?' Imam 'Alī asked. The Holy Prophet confirmed that he would. Hearing this, the Commander of the Faithful's face lit up with delight and he fell down in prostration to give thanks [to Allah]. He then said: 'May my life be sacrificed for you! Go wherever Allah has ordered you to go; if you need me to do any work for you, just command me, and I shall unconditionally perform it, and from Allah I seek grace and success.'

The Holy Prophet took Imam 'Alī in his arms, wept profusely, and entrusted him to the protection of Allah. Then, Jibrīl took the Holy Prophet by the hand and led him out of the house and towards the cave of Thawr.

That night, the Commander of the Faithful slept in the Holy Prophet's bed and covered himself with his cloak. The infidels had initially intended to attack the house in the darkness of the night, but Abū Lahab, who was also with them, advised against it saying that it was night and the women

---

[1] *Dāstān-hā Wa Pand-hā*, vol. 1, p. 173; *Mustaṭraf*, vol. 1, p. 156.

and children were asleep. He told them to wait until morning. When morning dawned, they rushed into the house only to find Imam ʿAlī ⊕ in the Prophet's bed. They asked him where Muhammad was. 'Did you leave him with me [that you now ask me about him]? You wanted to get rid of him [and so] he has gone away himself,' he retorted. They left Imam ʿAlī ⊕ and set off in pursuit of the Holy Prophet.[1]

It was as a result of this act of self-sacrifice on the part of Imam ʿAlī ⊕ that the Holy Prophet remained alive and unharmed. Allah revealed the following verse on this occasion, pertaining to Imam ʿAlī ⊕: And among the people is he who sells his soul seeking the pleasure of Allah, and Allah is most kind to [His] servants. (2:207)

5 – The self-sacrifice of Ḥātim Ṭāʾī

Once, there was a severe famine in the place where Ḥātim Ṭāʾī was staying. The provisions had dwindled until there was nothing left and the people were suffering intense hunger and hardship.

Ḥātim's wife narrates:

'One night, there was not a morsel to be found in our house. Ḥātim, my two children ʿAdī and Safānah, and myself, found that we could not sleep due to our hunger. With great difficulty, Ḥātim put ʿAdī to sleep while I did the same with Safānah. Ḥātim then began to narrate a story with the intention of putting me to sleep, but the intensity of hunger kept me awake. All the same, I pretended to be so fast asleep that even when he called out to me several times I did not reply.

'Ḥātim had been gazing into the desert from a hole in the tent when he noticed a silhouette, advancing towards us. As it came nearer, Ḥātim realised that it was a lady and called out: "Who is it?"

'The lady bemoaned: "Ḥātim, my children are howling like wolves owing to their hunger."

---

[1] The Holy Prophet remained in the Cave of Thawr for three days, and on the fourth day proceeded towards Medina, entering it on 12 Rabīʿ al-Awwal in the thirteenth year after the proclamation of prophethood, and from this migration commenced the Islamic calendar.

'Ḥātim told the woman not to worry, as he would remove their hunger. Hearing this, I got up from my place and asked him how he would do it. He said: "I shall feed everyone." He then proceeded towards the only horse which we possessed and which we utilised to transport our belongings. He sacrificed it and gave a portion of it to the lady, saying: "Cook it and feed it to your children." Turning to me, he said: "Awaken the children so they can eat too." After a short while, he added: "It is a great shame to eat while others sleep beside you with an empty stomach."

'He proceeded to wake them up himself. Everyone ate the meat, except Ḥātim, who sat and derived pleasure out of watching them eat.'[1]

12. Harassment

Allah, the Wise, has said:

$$ إِنَّ الَّذِينَ يُؤْذُونَ اللهَ وَرَسُولَهُ لَعَنَهُمُ اللهُ فِي الدُّنْيَا وَالْآخِرَةِ $$

Indeed those who offend Allah and His Apostle are cursed by Allah in the world and the Hereafter. (33:57)

The Holy Prophet said:

$$ لَا يَحِلُّ لِلْمُسْلِمِ أَنْ يُشِيرَ إِلَى أَخِيهِ بِنَظْرَةٍ تُؤْذِيهِ $$

It is not permissible for a Muslim to look at a brother Muslim in a manner that hurts and inconveniences him.[2]

Short explanation

All creatures belong to the household of [the creation of] Allah and pre-eminent amongst them are the believers. Any person who is of benefit to the creation becomes the beloved of Allah, while one who harasses and inconveniences others, especially the believers, in any way, is as if he has declared war upon Allah.

On the Day of Judgement, Allah shall call out: 'Where are those who harassed and tormented My friends in the world?' A group of people whose

---

[1] *Rāhnumā-yi Saʿādat*, vol. 2, p. 350; *Safīnat al-Biḥār*, vol. 1, p. 208.

[2] *Jāmiʿ al-Saʿādāt*, vol. 2, p. 215.

bodies would be bare of flesh would step forward whereupon Allah shall order them to be hurled into hell.

Thus, it is essential to refrain from hurting and harassing others – parents, neighbours, friends, and so on. If one has committed this act, forgiveness ought to be sought from those concerned.

1 – Harassment of Imam al-Sajjād ﷺ

During the time of Imam al-Sajjād ﷺ, there lived a person in Medina who used to make people laugh to earn his livelihood.

Some people suggested that they should invite Imam al-Sajjād ﷺ and allow this person to make him laugh a little in an attempt to distract the Imam from his deep lamentation. They gathered together and were on their way to his house when they saw him coming towards them, accompanied by two of his slaves. When the Imam came near, the comedian took the cloak off Imam al-Sajjād's ﷺ shoulders and put it over his own. The people around burst out laughing when they saw this antic. The Imam enquired: 'Who is this person?'

The people around him answered: 'He is a person who makes people laugh and receives money from them for his antics.'

'Inform him that those who expend their lives in a futile way performing absurd acts shall be the losers on the Day of Judgement,' advised the Imam.

After hearing this, the comedian stopped his annoying behaviour and mended his ways.[1]

2 – Qārūn and Prophet Mūsā ﷺ

Prophet Mūsā ﷺ, in the course of propagating his religion, had to face severe adversity and hardship from the likes of Firʿawn, Balʿam Baʿūrā, and even his cousin Qārūn. Qārūn was immensely rich and possessed so much wealth that several strong youths were required to carry just the keys of his treasury. He was one of the high ranking and influential nobles, and he used to oppress his inferiors.

---

[1] *Darsī Az Akhlāq*, p. 120; *al-Amālī* of Shaykh Mufīd, p. 128.

Prophet Mūsā ﷺ, in compliance with Allah's orders, sought zakat from him but Qārūn used to say: 'I too possess knowledge of the Torah and am not inferior to Mūsā in any way; why should I pay zakat to him?'

Eventually, his arrogance forced him to resort to dirty tactics to try to demean Prophet Mūsā ﷺ. He approached a woman who was of bad character but was also extremely beautiful and attractive. He said to her: 'I shall pay you 100,000 dirhams provided that tomorrow, when Mūsā is delivering a sermon to the Banī Isrā'īl, you shout out in front of the people that Mūsā has committed adultery with you.'

The woman accepted the offer. The next day, the Banī Isrā'īl had gathered and Prophet Mūsā ﷺ, with the Torah in hand, was engaged in preaching to them. Qārūn, in all his finery, was also present in the crowd along with his attendants. Suddenly, the woman stood up, but as she looked at the saintly face of Prophet Mūsā ﷺ she experienced a change of heart and cried out aloud: 'O Mūsā! Do know that Qārūn has promised me 100,000 dirhams if I accuse you, in front of the Banī Isrā'īl, of having committing adultery with me; but [I declare that] you have never committed such an act and Allah has protected your holy personality from such uncleanness.'

When he heard this, Prophet Mūsā ﷺ was devastated and heartbroken and he cursed Qārūn by saying: 'O earth! Seize Qārūn and take him within you.'

Upon divine orders the ground underneath split apart and Qārūn and all his wealth fell in.

According to another report, Prophet Mūsā ﷺ had been preaching to the people about his shariah when, in the course of his lecture, he said: 'A person who does not have a spouse and indulges in adultery shall be punished with 100 lashes, and a person who possesses a spouse and commits adultery shall be stoned to death.'

At that moment Qārūn stood up and remarked: '[Would this be true] even if you were to commit such an offence?'

'Yes,' replied Prophet Mūsā ﷺ.

'The Banī Isrā'īl are under the impression that you have committed adultery with such and such woman.'

'Bring the lady here,' demanded Prophet Mūsā ﷺ. 'If she testifies to this claim, you are at liberty to act according to the law.'

The woman was brought before Prophet Mūsā ﷺ who, placing her under oath to speak the truth, asked her: 'Have I committed adultery with you?'

The woman suddenly began to experience a change in her thinking and gave an answer which was opposite to what she had intended.

'No! They lie!' she said. 'Qārūn paid me such and such amount in order that I level this accusation at you.'

Qārūn stood humiliated while Prophet Mūsā ﷺ began weeping, fell down in prostration, and supplicated: 'O Allah! Your enemy has hurt me and sought to disgrace me by means of calumny. If I am Your prophet, grant me ascendancy over him.'

Then he cursed Qārūn, whereupon divine punishment overtook him and the earth consumed him.[1]

3 – It is forbidden to hurt a believer

Ḥusayn ibn Abī al-Aʿlā narrates:

'I started out for Mecca in the company of twenty other persons. At every resting place I would slaughter a goat in order to provide the people with food. When I arrived in the presence of Imam al-Ṣādiq ﷺ, he said to me: "O Ḥusayn! Woe be to you that you hurt and cause inconvenience to the believers."

'"I seek refuge in Allah from such an act," I said.

'He explained: "I have been informed that at every resting place you used to slaughter a goat for your companions."

'"Yes, but by Allah it was only for His happiness that I acted in this manner."

'The Imam ﷺ continued: "Don't you realise that amongst the group there were some who desired to possess wealth so they too could perform good deeds like you, but not having the means they have become upset."

---

[1] *Ḥikāyat-hā-yi Shanīdanī*, vol. 5, p. 122; *Biḥār al-Anwār*, vol. 13, p. 253.

'"I repent over my actions and resolve never to act in that way again," I said.

'The Imam ﷺ advised: "A believer, in the eyes of Allah, is more honourable than the angels, the mountains, the seven skies, the seven earths, and everything that exists in them."'[1]

4 – Harassing Imam 'Alī ﷺ is akin to harassing the Holy Prophet

'Amr ibn Shās Aslamī, one of the companions present during the treaty of Ḥudaybiyyah, narrates:

'Once, 'Alī ﷺ and I had embarked upon a journey towards Yemen. During the journey, I happened to get upset with him and my heart was filled with malice towards him.

'As I returned from the trip, I proceeded to the mosque and complained to the people about his behaviour. Unfortunately, it so happened that my words eventually reached the ears of the Holy Prophet ﷺ.

'One morning, on entering the mosque, I noticed the Holy Prophet present there together with a few of his companions. As soon as his eyes fell upon me, he gazed at me in anger and continued to do so till I had seated myself. "O 'Amr! By Allah, you have surely harassed me!" he said crossly.

'I exclaimed: "I seek refuge in Allah from ever harassing or annoying you."

'He said: "Yes, you have troubled me; for whoever has troubled 'Alī has troubled me too."'[2]

5 – Mutawakkil

One of the worst Abbasid caliphs was Mutawakkil who left no stone unturned in his attempt to harass and torment Imam al-Hādī ﷺ, as well as the descendants of the Holy Prophet, the Shi'as, and the pilgrims of Imam

---

[1] *Namūnah-i Ma'ārif*, vol. 2, p. 453; *La'ālī al-Akhbār*, p. 135.

[2] *Dastān-hā Az Zindagī-yi 'Alī*, p. 112; *Mustadrak al-Ṣaḥīḥayn*, vol. 3, p. 122.

al-Ḥusayn ﷺ.

The governor of Medina, ʿAbd Allāh ibn Muḥammad, acting on Mutawakkil's instructions, troubled Imam al-Hādī ﷺ to such an extent that the Imam was compelled to write a letter of complaint to Mutawakkil.

Later on, Mutawakkil forced the Imam to move from Medina to Samarra. Here, he initiated a fresh wave of persecution and harassment, some instances of which are as follows:

One night, Mutawakkil called Saʿīd, his doorman, and instructed him to climb into Imam's house and snoop around with a view to finding wealth or weapons. If they were found, he should confiscate them. On another occasion, relying on a false accusation, he ordered a group of Turks to rush into the Imam's house, take possession of everything they could find, and bring him to the court. When the Imam was brought to the court, Mutawakkil was busy consuming wine and [out of mockery] offered it to the holy Imam and said: 'Recite poetry for me!'

On yet another occasion, he had the Imam brought before him and ordered four slaves to attack him with swords; but the Imam, utilising the power of Imamate, miraculously repulsed this attack.

In the year 237 AH, Mutawakkil ordered the grave of Imam al-Ḥusayn ﷺ and the houses in its vicinity to be destroyed; he wanted the area to be used for farming and cultivation.

He decreed that a hand or a leg of anyone who came for the pilgrimage of Imam al-Ḥusayn ﷺ should be amputated.

ʿUmar ibn Faraj, who was made the governor of Mecca and Medina by Mutawakkil, was ordered to prevent the people from helping or showing kindness to the descendants of the Holy Prophet. The people, out of fear, refrained from assisting these descendants whose condition became so miserable and adverse that they did not even have proper garments to wear. This harassment and torture reached a stage that Muntaṣir, Mutawakkil's son, out of love for Imam ʿAlī ﷺ was eventually prompted to murder his own father.[1]

---

[1] *Muntahā al-Aʿmāl,* vol. 2, pp. 378-384.

13. Faith

Allah, the Wise, has said:

$$\text{يَا أَيُّهَا الَّذِينَ آمَنُوا آمِنُوا بِاللهِ وَرَسُولِهِ وَالْكِتَابِ}$$

O you who have faith! Have faith in Allah and His Apostle and the Book.

(4:136)

The Holy Prophet said:

$$\text{الْإِيـمَانُ عَقْدٌ بِالْقَلْبِ وَنُطْقٌ بِاللِّسَانِ وَعَمَلٌ بِالْأَرْكَانِ}$$

Faith is [a combination of] conviction in the heart, speaking out by the tongue, and deeds by the limbs.[1]

Short explanation

The believers are ranked according to their level of faith. Faith has four pillars – trust in Allah, entrusting one's affairs to Allah, pleasure over the divine acts of Allah, and submission to Allah – and one who possesses these pillars acquires tranquillity and repose, and his faith attains stability and permanence. The faith of those who are weak in belief is neither stable nor permanent.

Did not Imam al-Ṣādiq ﷺ say: 'Allah grants the world to His friends and foes alike, but faith He bestows only to the chosen ones from amongst His creations'?

Hence, those possessing true and perfect faith have always been in the minority; forbearance being their 'minister' and wisdom the 'commander of their army'.

1 – Ḥārithah's martyrdom

One day, after offering the morning prayers in congregation, the Holy Prophet looked around the mosque and his eyes fell upon a youth, Ḥārithah ibn Mālik Anṣārī, who sat with his head lowered in a state of drowsiness. His face was pale, his body thin and weak, and his eyes appeared to have sunk into their sockets. The Holy Prophet approached Ḥārithah and

---

[1] *Biḥār al-Anwār*, vol. 69, p. 69.

enquired: 'What state are you in?'

'I find myself as a true believer,' replied the youth.

The Holy Prophet asked: 'Everything possesses a truth; what is the truth behind what you claim?'

'O Prophet of Allah! I have become disenchanted with the world,' he answered. 'I stay awake [in worship] in the night, and endure thirst [by observing fasts] in the day. It is as if I am witnessing the Throne of Allah and the scenario of reckoning, observing the inmates of paradise meeting each other and hearing the shrieks of the inmates of hell.'

The Holy Prophet remarked: 'This is a person whose heart Allah has illuminated.' Then, addressing Ḥārithah, he continued: 'You have acquired perception and insight, so remain steadfast.'

Ḥārithah beseeched: 'O Prophet of Allah! Request Allah to grant me martyrdom while fighting alongside you!'

The Prophet prayed to Allah to grant martyrdom to Ḥārithah. A few days later, he dispatched an army for battle and Ḥārithah was included in it. During the battle, Ḥārithah killed nine infidels before he himself was killed, being the tenth soldier from the Muslim force to taste the nectar of martyrdom.[1]

2 – Who is a youth?

Imam al-Ṣādiq once asked the students and companions who had gathered around him: 'Who is a 'youth'?'

A person answered: 'Someone who is young in age.'

The Imam said: 'Despite the old age of the People of the Cave, on account of the faith they possessed Allah has referred to them as 'youths'. In verse 10 of Sūrat al-Kahf, He says: When the youths sought refuge in the cave.' He then continued: 'Whoever believes in Allah and observes piety is a youth.'[2]

---

[1] *Al-Kāfī*, vol. 2, Chapter of Reality of Faith, h. 2 and 3.

[2] *Ḥikāyat-hā-yi Shanīdanī*, vol. 5, p. 58; *Tafsīr Nūr al-Thaqalayn*, vol. 3, p. 244.

3 – Levels of faith

Imam al-Ṣādiq ☙, addressing a saddler who used to serve him, said:

'Some Muslims possess one portion of faith, while there are others who possess two or three or even seven portions of it. It is inappropriate to burden a person possessing one portion of faith with acts suitable for a person possessing two portions of faith. Similarly, it is inappropriate to burden a person who has two portions of faith with acts suitable for a person with three portions of faith.'

The Imam continued: 'Let me present an example: once, there was a man whose neighbour was a Christian. The man invited him to Islam and the Christian agreed and converted to a Muslim. The next day at dawn the Muslim knocked on the door of the convert's house. When the convert answered the door, the man told him to perform *wuḍū'*, get dressed, and accompany him to the mosque for prayers. The neighbour duly obliged and both men proceeded to the mosque. They offered not only morning prayers but also many other prayers until it was sunrise.

'The new Muslim wished to return home, when the man asked him: "Where are you going? The days are short and very soon it will be time for the *ẓuhr* prayers. Let us wait until we have offered our *ẓuhr* prayers." So they waited till it was *ẓuhr*, when they offered their prayers. The convert prepared to leave but the man persuaded him to stay until *'aṣr* time. They offered *'aṣr* prayers after which the convert decided to go. The man told him that it was almost sunset and that they should not go before offering the *maghrib* prayers. He then persuaded his neighbour to stay for the *'ishā'* prayers also. Finally, they went back home.

'The next dawn, the man again knocked on the door of the convert and asked him to go to the mosque with him. The newly converted Muslim retorted: "For this religion of yours seek someone who has more time on his hands than me. I am a poor person and have a family to feed and look after!"'

The Imam concluded: 'The ignorant Muslim reverted him to his original faith of Christianity.'[1]

4 – The faith of Saʿīd ibn Jubayr

Saʿīd ibn Jubayr was one of the steadfast and loyal companions of Imam al-Sajjād ﷺ. Ḥajjāj was a bloodthirsty tyrant who had ruled over Kufa, Iraq, and Iran for almost twenty years after being appointed by the Banī Umayyah and Banī Marwān. He had killed nearly 120,000 people during his reign, and amongst the friends and descendants of Imam ʿAlī ﷺ murdered by him were individuals such as Kumayl ibn Ziyād, Qambar – the slave of Imam ʿAlī ﷺ, and Saʿīd ibn Jubayr.

Ḥajjāj ordered Saʿīd to be arrested when he became aware of Saʿīd's belief and inclination towards Imam ʿAlī ﷺ. Initially, Saʿīd fled to Isfahan, but when Ḥajjāj came to know of this he wrote to the governor of Isfahan seeking his arrest. The governor possessed a high regard for Saʿīd and therefore advised him to leave Isfahan for a safer resort.

Acting upon this advice, Saʿīd set out towards Qum and then proceeded to Azerbaijan and then to Iraq where he sought to enter the army of ʿAbd al-Raḥmān ibn Muḥammad, who had initiated a rebellion against Ḥajjāj.

ʿAbd al-Raḥmān was defeated and Saʿīd fled to Mecca where he lived in hiding. During that period, Mecca was under the rule of Khālid ibn ʿAbd Allāh Qaṣrī, a ruthless individual who had been placed there by the caliph, Walīd ibn ʿAbd al-Malik. Walīd wrote to him and gave him the order to arrest the well-known Iraqi personalities who were hiding in Mecca and to send them to Ḥajjāj. Thus, he arrested Saʿīd and had him dispatched to Kufa. At that time, Ḥajjāj was in Wāsiṭ, a city near Baghdad, and to where Saʿīd was eventually brought.

Ḥajjāj questioned him about himself, the Holy Prophet, Imam ʿAlī ﷺ, Abū Bakr, ʿUmar, ʿUthmān, and many others; he then asked him: 'How should I put you to death?'

'Whatever manner you may adopt to kill me, you are bound to be chastised accordingly on the Day of Judgement,' replied Saʿīd.

---

[1] *Namūnah-i Maʿārif*, vol. 2, p. 479; *al-Kāfī*, Chapter of Levels of Faith, h. 2.

'I would like to forgive you.'

'If the forgiveness is from Allah then I seek it, but if it is from you then I do not desire it,' responded Sa'īd.

Ḥajjāj ordered the executioner to sever Sa'īd's head before him. Despite his hands being tied behind his back, Sa'īd recited the following verse of the Holy Qur'an: 'Indeed I have turned my face toward Him who originated the heavens and the earth, as a *ḥanīf*, and I am not one of the polytheists [6:79].'

Hearing this, Ḥajjāj ordered his face to be turned away from the qibla, whereupon he recited the following verse: 'Whichever way you turn, there is the face of Allah [2:115]!'

When Ḥajjāj heard this he ordered his men to place Sa'īd's face down upon the ground. When this was done, Sa'īd recited the following verse: 'From it did We create you, into it shall We return you, and from it shall We bring you forth another time [20:55].'

Ḥajjāj shouted: 'Don't waste any more time! Kill him!'

Sa'īd testified to the unity of Allah and the prophethood of the Holy Prophet and prayed: 'O Allah! Do not grant Ḥajjāj respite after me so that he does not kill anyone else.' As he uttered these words, the executioner severed his head.

After the martyrdom of this epitome of perfect faith, Ḥajjāj suffered a derangement of his senses and did not live for more than fifteen nights. Before his death he would occasionally lose consciousness, but regaining it, he would repeatedly mutter: 'Why did I ever get involved with Sa'īd ibn Jubayr?'[1]

5 – Salmān Fārsī's rank

Faith has ten ranks and Salmān Fārsī was on its tenth rank. He possessed knowledge of the unseen, the ability to interpret dreams and misfortunes, he was well versed in genealogy, and had even been favoured with gifts of paradise in this world. The Holy Prophet said: 'Whenever Jibrīl would

---

[1] *Dāstān-hā-e-Mā*, vol. 2, pgs. 39-45.

descend he would, on behalf of Allah, say: "Convey my salutation to Salmān!"'

Here is an example of the high degree of Salmān's faith. Once, Abū Dharr paid Salmān a visit. Salmān had placed a utensil over the fire to heat its contents. The two men sat together for some time talking to each other, when suddenly the vessel toppled over, but to Abū Dharr's amazement its contents did not spill. Salmān, picking the utensil up, placed it back upon the fire. A little later the vessel fell over again, but once again its contents did not spill. Again Salmān picked it up and placed the vessel upright.

Amazed, Abū Dharr hurried out of Salmān's house and was lost in contemplation over what he had witnessed. He happened to come across the Commander of the Faithful on the way and narrated the incident to him.

Having heard Abū Dharr's narration, the Imam said: 'If Salmān were to inform you of all that he possesses knowledge of, you would surely say: "May Allah have mercy upon the murderer of Salmān." O Abū Dharr! Salmān is the 'door' of Allah upon the earth. One who recognises his status is a believer, while one who rejects him is an infidel. Salmān is [one] of us, Ahl al-Bayt.'[1]

14. Brotherhood

Allah, the Wise, has said:

$$\text{إِنَّمَا الْمُؤْمِنُونَ إِخْوَةٌ}$$

The faithful are indeed brothers. (49:10)

Imam al-Bāqir ﷺ said:

$$\text{عَلَيْكَ بِإِخْوَانِ الصِّدْقِ فَإِنَّهُمْ عُدَّةٌ عِنْدَ الرَّخَاءِ وَجُنَّةٌ عِنْدَ الْبَلَاءِ}$$

[It is incumbent] upon you to take true friends for yourself, for they are an asset in times of ease and a shield during adversities.[2]

---

[1] *Muntahā al-Aʿmāl,* vol. 1, p. 114.

[2] *Biḥār al-Anwār,* vol. 78, p. 251.

Short explanation

At any age, brotherhood and friendship are necessary for one who is worthy of them. Allah has not bestowed upon His servants a bounty more important than success in keeping and associating with religious friends.

But do you not observe that the primary grace which Allah granted to the prophets at the time of their prophethood was a friend, brother, and *walī*? It is apparent from this that after the bounty of cognisance of Allah and His prophets, there is no bounty more pure and pleasant than brotherhood and a righteous friend in the path of Allah.

One ought to refrain from entering into friendship and brotherhood with those who seek these alliances out of avarice or worldly motives. A few brothers [in religion] who possess great cognisance are better than numerous ones who lack this attribute.[1]

1 – A believer is the brother of a fellow believer

Imam al-Bāqir related:

'Once, a group of Muslims had set off on a journey, but in the course of their travel they lost their way. Their supplies were soon exhausted and they were overcome by intense thirst. [With no water in sight and imagining their end to be near,] they put on their shrouds and sat down, resting themselves against the trees. Suddenly, an old man in white apparels approached them and said: "Arise, for you have nothing to fear. Here is some water for you."

'They scrambled for the water and drank to their fill, after which, turning to the old man, they said: "May Allah have mercy upon you! Who are you?"

'"I belong to the jinn community who had pledged allegiance to the Holy Prophet. I had heard him say: 'A believer is the brother of a fellow believer. He is his eyes and his guide.' I could not allow you to die of thirst while I was here."'[2]

---

[1] *Tadhkirat al-Ḥaqāʾiq*, p. 52.

[2] *Al-Kāfī*, vol. 2, Chapter of Brotherhood of the Believers, h. 10.

2 – Bond of brotherhood

Muḥammad ibn ʿAjlān narrates:

'I was in the company of Imam al-Ṣādiq ﷺ when a man from a distant city arrived and greeted the gathering. "How were your brothers when you took leave of them?" the Imam ﷺ asked him.

'The man spoke well of them and praised them a great deal. The Imam ﷺ then asked: "Do the rich visit the indigent ones when they fall sick?" He said that they seldom did. The Imam ﷺ carried on: "Do the rich seek to know the condition of the impoverished ones?"

'"Rarely," answered the man.

'"Do the affluent ones help out the poor and the needy?"

'The man responded: "You speak of attributes which are rare amongst our people."

'The Imam ﷺ remarked: "How then do these people consider themselves to be [our] Shiʿas?!"'[1]

3 – At the door of a brother

Imam al-Bāqir ﷺ said:

'An angel was once passing by a house when he witnessed a man standing near its door. The angel questioned him: "Why do you stand here?"

'"This is the house of my brother and I wish to greet him," answered the man.

'The angel asked: "Is he of your kith and kin or is it that you are in need of his help that you have come to pay him a visit?"

'"The reality is not as you make it out to be. We are just brethren in faith and I only wish to meet him and greet him for the sake of Allah."

'"I am Allah's messenger towards you," the angel said. "He has sent you His greetings and has said: 'O My servant! You have paid Me a visit and desired My pleasure and so, as a reward for upholding the rights and sanctity of religious brotherhood, I have made paradise compulsory for

---

[1] *Al-Kāfī*, vol. 2, Chapter of the Right of a Believer upon his Brother, h. 10.

you and have distanced you from My fire and wrath.'"'[1]

4 – The benevolent governor

An inhabitant of the city of Rey narrates:

'One of the scribes of Yaḥyā ibn Khālid was appointed as governor of Rey. I had some taxes to pay and feared that the new governor would extract it from me, and if so then I would face very difficult times. Some of my friends informed me that he was a follower of the holy Imams ﷺ, but I was fearful that if it was not so he would not hesitate to put me behind bars.

'With the intention of performing hajj, I presented myself in the presence of Imam Mūsā al-Kāẓim ﷺ and informed him of my predicament. The Imam ﷺ wrote a letter to the governor, the contents of which were as follows: "In the name of Allah, the Most Beneficent, the Most Compassionate. Do know that beneath the Throne of Allah there exists a shade of mercy into which none shall enter except he who exhibits goodness and kindness towards his brother-in-faith, liberates him from his sorrow, and endeavours to make him happy. Behold! The bearer of this letter is one of your brethren. Peace."

'After returning from hajj, one night I proceeded to the governor's house and asked the sentry to tell the governor that a person had brought a message from Imam al-Kāẓim ﷺ. As soon as he was informed, the governor rushed out towards the door in sheer delight. He was barefooted and took me into his arms, repeatedly kissing my forehead and inquiring after the Imam's well-being.

'Having gone through the Imam's ﷺ letter, he gave me half of all the money and clothes he possessed, and as for the things which could not be divided he gave me the monetary equivalent of half its value, asking me after each distribution: "Have I made you happy?"

'I would reply: "By Allah! You have pleased me greatly."

'He took out his register, and erasing all the debts written across my

---

[1] *Namūnah-i Maʿārif*, vol. 1, p. 81; *Jāmiʿ al-Akhbār*, p. 118.

name handed me a letter which contained an order exempting me from all taxes.

'I took his leave and said to myself: "This person has been immensely kind to me and there is no way I can repay his munificence. Let me go for hajj again and pray for him there and also inform the Imam 🕮 of his generosity and kindness."

'That year I started out for Mecca, and presenting myself before the Imam 🕮 I informed him of what had transpired. As I narrated the events I observed that his face continually brightened up with delight and so I enquired: "Have his deeds pleased you?"

'He said: "By Allah! His deeds have truly pleased me and he has pleased Allah, the Holy Prophet 🕮, and the Commander of the Faithful 🕮.""[1]

5 – Imam ʿAlī 🕮, the brother of the Holy Prophet

One of the extremely significant steps undertaken by the Holy Prophet five or eight months after his migration to Medina was to establish the bond of brotherhood between the Muhājirūn and the Anṣār.

ʿAbd Allāh ibn ʿAbbās says:

'When the verse: The faithful are indeed brothers [49:10] was revealed, the Holy Prophet 🕮 proclaimed brotherhood to be a general law amongst the Muslims, and, taking into consideration their ranks and positions, established the bond between every two persons by making one the brother of the other; Abū Bakr with ʿUmar, ʿUthmān with ʿAbd al-Raḥmān, and so on.

'The Commander of the Faithful 🕮 had stretched himself on the ground; the Holy Prophet 🕮 approached him and said: "Arise, O Abū Turāb! By Allah! I have not made you the brother of anyone for I have kept you for myself.""[2]

---

[1] *Pand-i Tārīkh*, vol. 2, p. 47; *Biḥār al-Anwār*, vol. 11.

[2] *Namūnah-i Maʿārif*, vol. 1, p. 82; *Kashf al-Ghummah*; *Tafsīr al-Burhān*.

15. Independence

Allah, the Wise, has said:

$$\text{لَا تَمُدَّنَّ عَيْنَيْكَ إِلَى مَا مَتَّعْنَا بِهِ أَزْوَاجًا مِنْهُمْ}$$

Do not extend your glance toward what We have provided to certain groups of them. (15:88)

Imam al-Ṣādiq ﷺ said:

$$\text{شَرَفُ الْمُؤْمِنِ قِيَامُ اللَّيْلِ وَعِزُّهُ اسْتِغْنَاؤُهُ عَنِ النَّاسِ}$$

The honour of a believer lies in nocturnal worship, and his esteem lies in his being independent of people.[1]

Short explanation

Contrary to the reprehensible attribute of greed is the attribute of independence and self-reliance. In common usage, if it is said that a person has no need for anything, the immediate notion that comes to mind is that he is affluent. However, the actual meaning is to be self-sufficient, self-contained, and not avaricious with respect to that which others possess.

Persons who are independent with respect to Allah's creation are highly respected, and they possess trust in Allah which is, by far, the greatest asset.

The fact that begging and seeking from others is censured is because it erodes away the honour and status of a person, makes him a captive of others, and lessens his inclination towards Allah.

1 – A lesson from the Holy Prophet

One of the companions of the Holy Prophet once found himself in severe poverty. His wife advised him to go to the Holy Prophet and request his help. The man approached the Holy Prophet, but as soon as the Prophet's eyes fell upon the man, he said: 'If a person seeks something from me I shall certainly grant it to him, but if he were to exhibit himself as being self-sufficient and free from want, Allah shall make him affluent.'

---

[1] *Jāmiʿ al-Saʿādāt*, vol. 2, p. 108.

Hearing this, the man said to himself: 'The Holy Prophet ﷺ has intended me by this speech of his.'

Without uttering a word, he returned home and narrated the incident to his wife. His wife said: 'The Holy Prophet ﷺ is also human; explain your dilemma to him and see what he has to say.'

The man returned to the Holy Prophet for the second time but heard the same sentence from him and again came back home without saying a word. When this was repeated for the third time, the man borrowed a pickaxe from one of his friends and set off towards the mountains. Throughout the day he worked hard to gather firewood which he sold for some flour, and that night he and his wife had bread for dinner.

The next day, he worked harder and collected more firewood and this continued for several days until he was able to purchase a pickaxe for himself.

After some time, as a result of his hard work, he managed to purchase two camels and a slave, and slowly became one of the affluent ones.

One day, arriving before the Holy Prophet, he narrated to him the events of his life and the effect of his words, whereupon the Prophet responded: 'I had said [before]: one who seeks to be independent [of others], Allah shall make him independent.'[1]

2 – Alexander and Diogenes

When Alexander was selected the supreme commander of Greece, people from all walks of life approached him to congratulate him upon his selection. However, Diogenes, the well-known philosopher, did not go to meet him and so Alexander himself went to meet Diogenes. Diogenes was a person who followed the policy of contentment, self-sufficiency, and not depending on people.

As he was lying under the sun, he sensed that a large group of people was approaching him. He raised himself slightly, and when his eyes fell upon Alexander, who was advancing with great pomp and grandeur,

---

[1] *Pand-i Tārīkh*, vol. 3, p. 129; *al-Wāfī*, vol. 2, p. 139.

Diogenes behaved just as he would have behaved had any ordinary person visited him.

Alexander greeted him and said: 'If you need anything from me, just speak out!'

'I have only one request,' said Diogenes. 'I had been enjoying the warm sunshine and presently you are obstructing it. Could you move to one side?'

Those accompanying Alexander considered this speech to be very foolish and imprudent and spoke amongst themselves, saying: 'What a foolish man he is to have wasted such an opportunity!'

But Alexander, who felt dwarfed before the towering contentment and self-sufficiency of Diogenes, fell into deep reflection at these words.

On the way back he turned to his companions who had ridiculed Diogenes and remarked: 'Indeed, had I not been Alexander, I would have desired to be Diogenes.'[1]

3 – Not under the obligation of Avicenna

It has been narrated that once, Avicenna, in great ministerial splendour and fanfare, was passing by a sweeper who was reciting this poem loudly whilst performing his menial work: 'O soul! I have held you in high esteem so that you are a means of serenity for the heart.'

Hearing this, Avicenna smiled and said to him [derisively]: 'Indeed, you have truly held your soul in high esteem by engaging yourself in such [lowly] work.'

The sweeper stopped his work, turned to him and said: 'I make my living by means of this lowly work so that I am not compelled to be under the obligation of the lofty Avicenna.'[2]

4 – The recitation of Sūrat al-Wāqiʿah

ʿAbd Allāh ibn Masʿūd had been one of the close companions of the Holy

---

[1] *Riwāyat-hā Wa Hikāyat-hā*, p. 39; *Dāstān-hā-yi Parākandih*; vol. 2, p. 66.

[2] *Namūnah-i Maʿārif*, vol. 1, p. 162; *Nāmih-i Dānishwarān*.

Prophet and had developed into a distinguished and zealous personality of Islam. During the caliphate of ʿUthmān, he suffered a bout of illness which eventually resulted in his death.

ʿUthmān once came to pay him a visit and finding him distressed, asked: 'What distresses you so greatly?'

'My sins,' he answered.

'Tell me your wish so that I can fulfil it for you.'

'I desire Allah's mercy,' replied Ibn Masʿūd.

The caliph asked: 'If you permit I could call for the doctor.'

'It is the doctor who has made me sick.'

'If you want, I could present you with gifts from the public treasury.'

Ibn Masʿūd retorted: 'At the time when I was in need you did not give me a thing, and now that I am not in need you wish to shower me with presents!'

ʿUthmān insisted: 'Let these gifts be for your daughters then.'

'They are not in need of your presents,' Ibn Masʿūd replied tersely. 'I have instructed them to recite Sūrat al-Wāqiʿah every night, for surely I have heard the Holy Prophet ﷺ say: "One who recites Sūrat al-Wāqiʿah every night shall never be afflicted by poverty."'[1]

16. Stinginess

Allah, the Wise, has said:

$$ الَّذِينَ يَبْخَلُونَ وَيَأْمُرُونَ النَّاسَ بِالْبُخْلِ وَيَكْتُمُونَ مَا آتَاهُمُ اللهُ مِنْ فَضْلِهِ وَأَعْتَدْنَا لِلْكَافِرِينَ عَذَابًا مُهِينًا $$

Those who are stingy and bid [other] people to be stingy, and conceal whatever Allah has given them out of His grace; and We have prepared for (the faithless a humiliating punishment. (4:37

The Holy Prophet said:

$$ جَاهِلٌ سَخِيٌّ أَحَبُّ إِلَى اللهِ مِنْ عَابِدٍ بَخِيلٍ $$

---

[1] *Dāstān-hā Wa Pand-hā*, vol. 7, p. 112; *Majmaʿ al-Bayān*, vol. 9, p. 211.

An ignorant but generous person is more beloved to Allah than one who is devout but stingy.[1]

Short explanation

Stinginess, or refraining from giving things to others and collecting wealth and riches for oneself, is one of the signs of love for the world. It impedes one from adorning oneself with several praiseworthy virtues like charity, munificence, self-sacrifice, and helping others. It is for this reason that the Holy Prophet has said: 'No miser shall enter paradise.'

Stinginess is such a repugnant vice that if a person gets afflicted with it he keeps his family in poverty, detests guests coming to his house, abstains from visiting others in order that none visit him, withholds himself from associating with generous persons, and feels uneasy about other people's generosity. The Holy Prophet always sought refuge in Allah from this deadly vice.[2]

1 – The miser's sin

Once, the Holy Prophet was engaged in the *ṭawāf* of the Ka'bah when he witnessed a man holding the curtain of the Ka'bah and imploring: 'O Allah! By the sanctity of this house, forgive me!'

Approaching him, the Holy Prophet asked him about his sin. The man replied: 'My sin is too enormous for me to describe to you.'

'Woe be to you! Is your sin greater or the earth?' asked the Holy Prophet.

'My sin.'

'Is your sin greater or the mountains?'

'My sin.'

'Is your sin greater or the Throne of Allah?'

'My sin.'

The Holy Prophet then asked: 'Is your sin greater or Allah?'

To this the man replied: 'Allah is the Greatest, Loftiest, and the Most

---

[1] *Jāmiʿ al-Saʿādāt*, vol. 2, p. 110.

[2] *Iḥyāʾ al-Qulūb*, p. 96.

Glorious.'

The Holy Prophet exclaimed: 'Woe be to you! Inform me of you sin.'

The man explained: 'O Prophet of Allah! I am a wealthy person, but whenever a poor man approaches me for help I feel as if a bolt of fire has approached me.'

On hearing this, the Holy Prophet warned: 'Stay away from me and do not burn me in your fire! By He who has sent me with guidance and honour, if you were to offer prayers between al-Rukn and al-Maqām for 2000 years, and weep in such a measure that your tears flow as rivers and quench the trees, and after all this if you were to die while still possessing the vice of stinginess, Allah would hurl you into hell. Woe be to you! But do you not know that Allah has said: And whoever is niggardly is niggardly against his own soul [47:38]? And He has also said: And whoever is preserved from the niggardliness of his soul, is among the successful ones [59:9].'[1]

2 – Manṣūr Dawānīqī and his stinginess

Manṣūr Dawānīqī, the second Abbasid caliph, was well known for his stinginess and parsimony. For instance, as a result of his reluctance to part with his money, he would give the poets who came before him the following warning: if someone, other than you, also happens to know the poetry that you are about to recite or if it is established that it belongs to someone else, you should not expect any prize or reward. And if the poet happened to recite one which was his own, Manṣūr would give him money according to the weight of the scroll upon which the poetry was written! Furthermore, he possessed a sharp memory and also had a servant and a slave-girl who were extraordinarily quick at memorising things.

When a poet recited his poetry, Manṣūr would say to him: 'This which you have recited for me is not something new. Not only I, but even this slave of mine and the slave-girl behind the curtains know it.' Then, upon his orders, the slave would recite the poem, after which the slave-girl, having heard its recitation three times – once by the poet, once by Manṣūr,

---

[1] *Jāmiʿ al-Saʿādāt*, vol. 2, p. 110; *ʿIlm-i Akhlāq-i Islāmī*, vol. 2, p. 154.

and once by the slave – would also recite it. The astounded poet would then be sent off empty-handed and without any reward!

Aṣmaʿī, the renowned poet, became annoyed with the miserliness of Manṣūr and decided to compose a poem using difficult words and write it on a broken stone pillar. When this was done, he dressed himself up as a tribesman and covered his entire face except his eyes. He then presented himself before Manṣūr, and with a disguised accent informed him that he had composed some verses and sought his permission to recite them before him.

As usual, Manṣūr informed Aṣmaʿī of the conditions, which he accepted. Then Aṣmaʿī began reciting the poetry which comprised of difficult and uncommon words and intricate and complex sentences. Manṣūr, with all his acumen, and the slave and the slave-girl with all their sharpness of mind, were unable to memorise it, and for the first time appeared bewildered and taken aback. With no alternative left, Manṣūr said to him: 'O brother! It appears that the poetry is your own work. Bring me your scroll so that I can reward you according to its weight.'

Aṣmaʿī said: 'I could not find any paper and so I have written my poem on a stone pillar, which presently lies on my camel.' He brought the stone pillar and placed it before Manṣūr who was totally baffled. He realised that even if he were to place his entire treasury on one side of the scale it would not match up to the weight of the stone pillar. Turning to the poet, he enquired: 'O Arab! Are you not Aṣmaʿī?'

Aṣmaʿī took off the covering from his face and everyone observed that the poet was indeed Aṣmaʿī.[1]

3 – The Arab misers

It has been said that there were four Arab misers.

The first of them was Ḥaṭīʾah. It has been narrated that one day, Ḥaṭīʾah was standing at his doorstep with his staff in his hand when a person, passing by, said to him: 'O Ḥaṭīʾah! I am your guest today.'

---

[1] *Dastān-hā-yi Mā*, vol. 2, p. 102; *Iʿlām al-Nās*, p. 54.

Pointing to his staff, Ḥaṭī'ah tersely answered: 'I use this staff to welcome and entertain my guests!'

The second of the misers was Ḥamīd Arqaṭ. In connection with him, it has been reported that once, he invited a few people to be his guests and offered them dates to eat. The guests, while eating the dates, also consumed the seeds, whereupon Hameed created uproar by rebuking them for eating his seeds as well.

The third of the misers was a person by the name of Abū al-Aswad Du'alī. It has been related that one day, he gave one date to a pauper, who said: 'May Allah give you one date in paradise.'

Hearing this, Abū al-Aswad Du'alī commented: 'If we give our things to the miserable ones we shall become more miserable than them!'

The fourth of the misers was Khālid ibn Ṣafwān, about whom it has been reported that whenever a dirham would come into his hands, he would say to it: 'O money! How much you have wandered and travelled before coming into my hands. But [now that you have reached me,] I shall drop you into my safe and your captivity shall be a long and protracted one.' Saying this, he would drop the money into his chest and lock it.

The people said to him: 'Since you possess so much wealth and riches, why don't you give some of it as alms?'

He replied: 'I have a much longer life ahead of me.'[1]

4 – Zakat from Tha'labah Anṣārī is not accepted

Once, Tha'labah ibn Ḥāṭib Anṣārī approached the Holy Prophet and beseeched: 'O Prophet of Allah! Pray to Allah that He grants me wealth and riches.'

'Little wealth for which you are able to offer thanks is better than immense riches for which you are unable to offer thanks,' the Holy Prophet advised him.

Tha'labah went away but approached the Holy Prophet for the second time, repeating his request. The Holy Prophet said: 'You shall not obey me.

---

[1] *Namūnah-i Ma'ārif*, vol. 2, p. 493; *Mustaṭraf*, vol. 1, p. 171.

By Allah! If I wished that the mountains would turn into gold for me they would do so.'

For the second time Thaʿlabah went away, but returned a third time and again placed his request before the Holy Prophet and implored: 'Do pray for me. I avow that if Allah grants me wealth, whoever possesses a right in it I shall give it to him.'

The Holy Prophet prayed for him and Allah answered his prayers. Thaʿlabah initially purchased some sheep which slowly grew in number till they became plentiful. Earlier, he used to offer all his prayers behind the Holy Prophet, but after his wealth and riches began to increase he would only be present for the *zuhr* and *ʿaṣr* prayers, and spent the rest of his time looking after his sheep.

As time passed, his work increased to such an extent that he could only manage to come to Medina for the Friday prayers and eventually even this became a thing of the past. He would only come up to the road leading towards Medina and seek news of the city from the passers-by.

One day, the Holy Prophet enquired about him, whereupon he was informed that Thaʿlabah's sheep had increased manifold and that he had settled outside Medina. Hearing this, the Holy Prophet cried out three times: 'Woe be to Thaʿlabah!'

After a period of time, the verse pertaining to zakat was revealed. The Holy Prophet selected two people, one from Banī Sulaym and the other from Juhniyyah, and gave them written authority, empowering them to collect the zakat. Approaching Thaʿlabah, they read out the order for the collection of zakat. After some thought, Thaʿlabah said: 'This is *jizyah* (a tax) or something akin to it. Go and collect it from others and come back to me later.'

They proceeded to a person from the tribe of Banī Sulaym and read out the Holy Prophet's orders at which he handed over the best of his camels to them as his zakat. The collectors explained to him that they had not asked him to give the best of his camels, but he insisted by saying that he was giving the camels through his own choice.

The collectors collected the zakat from the others, and on the way back again approached Tha'labah and sought his zakat. He said: 'Let me have a look at that decree.' After reading it, he once again repeated: 'This appears to be *jizyah* or something similar to it. Go away and let me ponder over it.'

The collectors returned to the Holy Prophet, but before they could speak, he exclaimed: 'Woe unto Tha'labah!' He then prayed for the generous person from Banī Sulaym. The collectors explicitly narrated to him their encounter with Tha'labah whereupon the following verses were revealed:

Among them are those who made a pledge with Allah: 'If He gives us out of His grace, we will surely give the zakat and we will surely be among the righteous.' But when He gave them out of His grace, they begrudged it and turned away, being disregardful. So He caused hypocrisy to ensue in their hearts until the day they will encounter Him, because of their going back on what they had promised Allah and because of the lies they used to tell. (9:75-77)

One of Tha'labah's relatives who had been present during the revelation of these verses informed him of the incident. On hearing about it he hastened to the Holy Prophet and entreated him to accept his zakat, but he refused, saying: 'Allah has ordered me not to accept your zakat.' Tha'labah was devastated to hear this. 'This is a consequence of your own deeds. I had ordered you but you refused to comply with my orders,' the Holy Prophet said.

After the demise of the Holy Prophet, Tha'labah approached Abū Bakr who also refused to accept his zakat. During 'Umar's caliphate, Tha'labah approached him but he too refused, and 'Uthmān also followed suit, till death finally overtook Tha'labah.[1]

5 – Sa'īd ibn Hārūn, the miser

Sa'īd ibn Hārūn, the scribe from Baghdad and a contemporary of Ma'mūn, the Abbasid caliph, was notorious for his miserliness. Abū 'Alī Di'bil Khuzā'ī, the renowned poet (d. 245 AH), says:

---

[1] *Pand-i Tārīkh*, vol. 1, p. 73; *Asad al-Ghābbah*, vol. 1, p. 237.

'Accompanied by some other poets, I had gone to Sa'īd's house and we were with him from morning till afternoon. When the afternoon was approaching, we began to feel hungry and became restless and disturbed as a result. Sa'īd had an old slave, to whom he said: "If there is something to eat, bring it before us." The slave departed and returned a short while later bringing with him a dirty dinner-cloth. He spread this out before us and laid just one piece of dry bread on it. He then brought an old bowl, broken at the rim and filled with hot water, and which contained an old, raw, and headless rooster!

'As the slave placed the bowl on the dinner-cloth, Sa'īd's eyes fell upon it, and noticing the headless rooster he reflected for a moment and then said: "O slave! Where is the head of this rooster?!"

'The slave replied: "I have thrown it away."

'Hearing this, Sa'īd screamed: "I do not approve of one who throws away the legs of a rooster, never mind one who throws away its head! This act [of yours] augurs ill [for me], for the head of a rooster possesses many benefits: firstly, from its head emanates a sound which informs Allah's servants of the time for prayers; by means of it the sleeping ones awaken, and those who worship in the nights ready themselves for the night prayers. Secondly, the crown that lies on its head resembles the crown of the kings, and so it possesses a distinction in comparison to the other birds. Thirdly, it witnesses the angels by means of the two eyes which are located in its skull. In addition, poets liken coloured wine to its eyes because when they desire to describe red wine, they say: 'This wine is like the two eyes of the rooster.' Fourthly, the brain in its head is a cure for kidney problems. Besides, no bone is tastier than the bone of its head. If you have thrown it away under the impression that I would not eat it, you have erred greatly. And supposing that I do not eat it, my family would eat it, and if they do not eat it, these guests of mine, who have not eaten anything since morning, would eat it." He continued angrily: "Go and locate it, and should you fail to do so I shall punish you."

'The slave pleaded: "By Allah! I do not know where I have thrown it."

'Sa'īd retorted: "By Allah! I know where you have dropped it; you have dropped it in that ominous looking stomach of yours!"

"'By Allah! I have not eaten it," bemoaned the slave. "You are the one who is lying."

'Infuriated, Saʿīd stood up and seized the slave by the collar in an attempt to hurl him onto the floor, but in the process his foot struck the bowl, tipping it over and spilling its contents. A cat, which sat nearby, made the most of the opportunity, and picking up the headless rooster, darted away with it. We too came out of the house, leaving Saʿīd and his slave to themselves as they grappled with each other.'[1]

17. Evil

Allah, the Wise, says:

$$عَسَى أَنْ تُـحِبُّوا شَيْئًا وَهُوَ شَرٌّ لَكُمْ$$

It may be that you love something while it is bad for you. (2:216)

Imam al-Ṣādiq ﷺ has said:

$$وَإِنَّ الْعَمَلَ السَّيِّئَ أَسْرَعُ فِي صَاحِبِهِ مِنَ السِّكِّينِ فِي اللَّحْمِ$$

Indeed, the effect of an evil deed upon the doer is faster than that of a knife upon a piece of meat.[2]

Short explanation

The worst of people is one who sells his Hereafter in exchange for his worldly life, but worse still is one who sells his Hereafter for the worldly lives of others.

Evil manifests itself in numerous forms, all of which could be summarised as disobedience to Allah.

Since deeds are subordinate to intentions, evil thoughts generate evil deeds. When a person does not have Allah within his sights, he considers himself to be strong and powerful. He indulges in various acts of evil without his heart experiencing the slightest fear of hell.

---

[1] *Laṭāʾif al-Ṭawāʾif,* p. 341.

[2] *Jāmiʿ al-Saʿādāt,* vol. 3, p. 48.

For each limb and organ of the body there are evil actions which are associated with and specific to them: the ears to backbiting, the eyes to seeing prohibited things, the tongue to lying, and the hands to hurting orphans. It is therefore essential to preserve all of them from evil.

1 – Misfortune of Jālūdī

After the martyrdom of Imam al-Kāẓim ☝, the Abbasid caliph Hārūn al-Rashīd dispatched one of his commanders, a person by the name of Jālūdī, to Medina, and instructed him: 'Attack the houses of the progeny of Abū Ṭālib, loot the womenfolk, and leave behind nothing except one apparel for each of them!'

Once in Medina, Jālūdī started to execute Hārūn's orders. As he neared the house of Imam al-Riḍā ☝, the Imam gathered all the ladies of the house into one room and stood at the door, preventing Jālūdī from entering. Jālūdī insisted that he must enter the house and loot the ladies and take away their apparels. The Imam promised that he himself would collect their clothes and ornaments and hand them over to Jālūdī, on the condition that he should abstain from entering the room.

Jālūdī eventually acquiesced to the Imam's request, whereupon the Imam entered the room, gathered the ornaments and clothes of the ladies, and, together with the other things of the house, placed them at Jālūdī's disposal, which he promptly dispatched to Hārūn.

After Hārūn it was his son Ma'mūn who took over the reins of the caliphate. It so happened that one day he became angry with Jālūdī and sought to punish him with death. Imam al-Riḍā ☝ was present in that assembly and requested Ma'mūn to forgive him.

Jālūdī, recollecting his previous wickedness with respect to the Imam, thought that he would complain about it to Ma'mūn and so, turning to Ma'mūn, he said: 'I place you under the oath of Allah! Do not accept his words in connection with me.'

Ma'mūn said: 'By Allah! I shall not accept his words.' Saying this, he ordered Jālūdī to be beheaded.[1]

2 – Deceit by ʿAmr ibn ʿĀṣ

After the incident of arbitration – in which ʿAmr ibn ʿĀṣ tricked Abū Mūsā Ashaʿrī and deposed ʿAlī 🌸 from the caliphate – the Imam used to curse him, Muʿāwiyah, and Abū Mūsā after the *fajr* and *maghrib* prayers.

ʿAmr ibn ʿĀṣ was also part of the group that was involved in the incident of the night of ʿAqabah,[2] and he had subsequently been cursed by the Holy Prophet. [Regarding the issue of arbitration:]

When the dispute between Imam ʿAlī 🌸 and Muʿāwiyah intensified, it was decided that the issue should be resolved by means of arbitration. Unfortunately, the people of Iraq selected Abū Mūsā Ashaʿrī to represent the Imam (although the Imam himself was not happy at his selection), whereas Muʿāwiyah decided on ʿAmr ibn ʿĀṣ as his representative.

Abū Mūsā, who was in one of the villages of Shām, was asked to present himself in Ṣiffīn and 400 people, amongst them Shurayḥ ibn Hānī and Ibn ʿAbbās, accompanied him to Dūmat al-Jandal. ʿAmr ibn ʿĀṣ also arrived there with 400 of his companions.

All the counselling and recommendations provided to Abū Mūsā proved futile since ʿAmr ibn ʿĀṣ, with the evilness of intention and wickedness of character that he possessed, was far more powerful than him in shrewdness and deception.

One of ʿAmr ibn ʿĀṣ's techniques was to exhibit exaggerated deference towards Abū Mūsā. He sat him in the front of gatherings and insisted that he lead the prayers, while ʿAmr himself prayed behind him, and all the while addressing him as 'O companion of the Prophet of Allah'. He would

---

[1] *Rāhnumā-yi Saʿādat*, vol. 1, p. 177; *Aʿyān al-Shīʿah*, vol. 1, p. 60.

[2] After the Holy Prophet had proclaimed ʿAlī 🌸 his successor at Ghadīr Khumm, some individuals gathered together and conspired to conceal themselves near a mountain path and startle the camel of the Holy Prophet in order that he is hurled to the ground and killed, and in this manner sought to prevent the caliphate of ʿAlī 🌸 from being established in Medina; this is the night which is referred to as the 'night of ʿAqabah'.

to say to him: 'You have had a precedence over me with regards to the companionship of the Holy Prophet ﷺ and are elder to me, and thus it is unbecoming of me to speak on something before you have done so.'

He presented such an elaborate display of respect that the simple-minded Abū Mūsā Asha'rī was convinced of his uprightness and became certain that his only intention was to set aright the existing state of affairs. As part of his cunning plan, 'Amr ibn 'Āṣ initially took Abū Mūsā to a secluded place and spoke to him in solitude so as to prevent others from influencing Abū Mūsā in making a decision. 'Amr ibn 'Āṣ asked him: 'Abū Mūsā, what is your opinion regarding 'Alī and Mu'āwiyah?'

'Let us depose 'Alī and Mu'āwiyah from the caliphate, and allow the issue of caliphate to be managed by a council,' responded Abū Mūsā.

Hearing this, 'Amr ibn 'Āṣ said: 'By Allah! Your opinion is absolutely correct and we must put it into action.'

After agreeing this course of action, they came out in public. Abū Mūsā stood up first and began to speak when Ibn 'Abbās cried out: 'Be wary, for I fear 'Amr ibn 'Āṣ has tricked you. Allow him to speak before you.'

However, Abū Mūsā paid no heed and said: 'O people! 'Amr ibn 'Āṣ and I remove 'Alī and Mu'āwiyah from the caliphate and shall [only] approve of a caliph selected by means of a council. I hereby remove 'Alī from the caliphate.'

Then, the wicked 'Amr ibn 'Āṣ stood up and said: 'I too remove 'Alī from the caliphate but appoint Mu'āwiyah in his place; Mu'āwiyah seeks to avenge 'Uthmān's death and is therefore most deserving of this rank.'

'You are like a dog,' Abū Mūsā shrieked out, 'that attacks if one approaches it and does the same if one turns away from it.'

'Amr ibn 'Āṣ retaliated: 'And you are like a donkey which carries a hoard of books [but does not benefit from them in the least].'

In short, 'Amr ibn 'Āṣ, supported by his evil nature, emerged the victor in the issue of arbitration. Later, Ibn 'Abbās used to say: 'May Allah disgrace Abū Mūsā! I had warned him of the guile and the evil intentions of 'Amr ibn 'Āṣ and advised him rightly, but he turned a deaf ear and refused to take heed.'[1]

3 – Cruelty of Ḥajjāj ibn Yūsuf Thaqafī

It is not just evil deeds which merit chastisement but evil intentions also tend to have an impact. In fact, it is due to their evil intentions that the disbelievers and the enemies [of Islam] shall reside in hell eternally.

Ḥajjāj ibn Yūsuf Thaqafī used to exhibit great cruelty and evil by imprisoning and killing the descendants of the Holy Prophet. Once, while coming out of the mosque and hearing the wailing and crying of a great number of people, he asked: 'Who are these who wail?'

Those around him said: 'These are the wailings of the captives who are tormented due to the intense heat of the sun.'

He said: 'Tell them to scram away (*ikhsa'ū*),' which, in the Arabic language, is also employed for driving away a dog.[2]

His prison contained 120,000 males and 20,000 females; it was one large area, walled, but roofless. Each time the prisoners tried to shelter themselves from the scorching sun, either with their hands or some other means, the guards overlooking them would strike them with stones.

Their food was bread made of barley and mixed with sand, while their drink was bitter water. At times, the blood of the descendants of the Holy Prophet and the righteous ones would be utilised for preparing Ḥajjāj's bread, which he would eat with great relish!

This wicked person always regretted not having been in Karbala, and used to say: 'Oh how I wish I had been in Karbala so that I could have had a hand in killing Imam al-Ḥusayn and his companions!'[3]

4 – Justifying evil acts

Imam al-Ṣādiq ﷺ had heard that an old man had become famous for his

---

[1] *Payghambar Wa Yārān*, vol. 1, pp. 139-153; *Biḥār al-Anwār*, vol. 8, p. 544.

[2] Also used in the Holy Qur'an: 23:108. *Pand-i Tārīkh*, vol. 3, p. 163; *Rawḍāt al-Jannāt*, p. 133.

[3] *Pand-e-Tārīkh*, vol. 3, p. 163; *Rauḍāt al-Jannāt*, p. 133.

piety. One day, he saw him surrounded by a large crowd. A little later, the man came out of the crowd and, distancing himself from them, proceeded alone, whereupon the Imam began to follow him. After a short time, the Imam observed that he had stopped near a bakery from where he stealthily picked up two loaves of bread. After a short distance he stopped at a fruit store, picking up two pomegranates in the same manner and once again continued on his way.

As he walked further, the old man approached a sick person, handed over the loaves and fruits to him and was about to move on when Imam al-Ṣādiq ﷺ came up to him and said: 'I have witnessed something greatly astonishing from you,' and then proceeded to narrate the acts he had witnessed.

The old man said: 'I suppose you are Imam al-Ṣādiq.'

The Imam replied in the affirmative.

The man continued: 'It is really unfortunate that in spite of being of the progeny of the Holy Prophet ﷺ you do not seem to know anything.'

The Imam asked: 'What act of ignorance have you noticed from me?'

The man said: 'But do you not know that Allah has said in the Qur'an: Whoever brings virtue shall receive ten times its like; but whoever brings vice shall not be requited except with its like [6:160]? On this basis, since I have stolen two fruits and two loaves of bread, I have four sins in my account; but on the other hand, since I have given it in the way of Allah, I have earned forty good deeds. Reducing four from forty I still have thirty-six good deeds in my account; a pity that you possess no knowledge of such computations!'

The Imam explained to him: 'But have you not heard this verse of the Qur'an, which says: Allah accepts only from the God-wary [5:27]? You have earned four sins by stealing those four items and four more sins for giving them to someone else without the permission of the owners, so you have collected eight sins but not a single good deed.'

Later, the Imam said to his companions: 'With such interpretations and justifications, not only do they mislead themselves, but others as well.'[1]

5 – The consequence of evil deeds in *barzakh*

A distinguished scholar, renowned for his piety, narrates:

'One of my relatives had purchased a property during the last years of his life, utilising the abundant income derived from it for the fulfilment of his needs. After he died, I witnessed him in *barzakh* in a state of blindness. When I asked him the reason for it, he replied: "I had purchased a piece of land in the centre of which existed a well, the water of which was utilised by the inhabitants of a nearby village for themselves and their animals. But their passage through my land used to damage a portion of my crops, and so, in order to protect my income and to prevent them from coming in, I blocked the well by means of sand and stones, and covered it up. As a result, the hapless inhabitants were forced to travel a great distance to procure their water, and this blindness is an outcome of that act of mine."

'I asked him: "Is there any solution to this problem of yours?"

'He replied: "If my heirs were to exhibit mercy upon me and uncover the well so that others benefit from its water again, I shall come out of this predicament of mine."

'Approaching his heirs, I informed them of the incident. They agreed to do the necessary, and very soon the well was opened up and the people began to make use of it, as before.

'After a time I again witnessed the deceased, but this time noticed that his sight had been restored and he was thankful to me for helping him come out of his misery.'[2]

18. Misfortunes

Allah, the Wise, has said:

$$ \text{فَأَمَّا الْإِنْسَانُ إِذَا مَا ابْتَلَاهُ رَبُّهُ فَأَكْرَمَهُ وَنَعَّمَهُ فَيَقُولُ رَبِّي أَكْرَمَنِ} $$

---

[1] *Namunah-e-Ma'ārif*, vol. 4, p. 275; *Wasā'il al-Shī'a*, vol. 2, p. 57.

[2] *Dāstān-hā-yi Shigift*, p. 292.

As for man, whenever his Lord tests him and grants him honour and blesses him, he says: 'My Lord has honoured me.' (89:15)

The Holy Prophet said:

إِنَّ الْبَلَاءَ لِلظَّالِمِ أَدَبٌ وَلِلْمُؤْمِنِ آمْتِحَانٌ

Indeed, misfortune for an oppressor is a [corrective] chastisement, and for a believer a trial.[1]

Short explanation

For someone possessing intellect, misfortunes are a means of ornamentation and esteem. Exercising forbearance when faced with misfortune and being steadfast during trials strengthens one's faith.

One who bears hardship with patience shall acquire the grace of Allah and, as dictated by divine wisdom, shall attain salvation and comfort, either in this world or in the Hereafter.

From within the flames of misfortune and calamity emerge esoteric lights. A person who regards misfortune and calamity as a trial and combats it successfully will become that much wiser as a result of the extra knowledge and perception acquired. It is not good practice to constantly complain of worldly misfortunes like poverty, illness, family problems, and suchlike.

1 – In the company of angels

One of the patient Muslims, uncomplaining in the face of misfortunes, was a person by the name of 'Imrān. He had come to suffer from dropsy[2] and no amount of treatment proved productive.

For thirty years he lay upon his stomach, unable to rise, sit, or stand, and so a pit had been dug near his place of rest for his urine and excrement.

Once, his brother A'lā paid him a visit and, observing his pitiful state, burst into tears. 'Imrān asked: 'Why do you weep?'

---

[1] *Jāmiʿ al-Akhbār*, p. 113.

[2] A sickness in which a person suffers swelling of the stomach, consumes an inordinate quantity of water, and experiences extraordinary thirst.

His brother replied: 'It is because I see that for years you have been suffering in this pathetic condition.'

'Imrān said: 'Weep not and do not be disturbed because this state which Allah has ordained for me is dearer to me than anything else; I desire to remain in this condition which Allah desires for me for as long as I am alive. I shall now inform you of a secret which you must not divulge to anyone for as long as I am alive: I am in the company of the angels; they greet me and I reply to their greetings, and I enjoy a great bond with them.'[1]

2 – 'Alī 'Ābid in prison

'Alī 'Ābid ('Alī ibn al-Ḥasan al-Muthallath) was from the lineage of Imam al-Ḥasan 🖾 who had been imprisoned by Manṣūr Dawānīqī and had died in prison. 'Alī 'Ābid was unsurpassed in his patience, worship, and remembrance of Allah.

When Manṣūr arrested the descendants of the Holy Prophet and the children of Imam al-Ḥasan 🖾, he placed them in a prison that was so dark that day could not be differentiated from night except by means of the recitations and acts of worship of 'Alī 'Ābid. These acts were disciplined, orderly, and continuous, and therefore made the others aware of the time for prayers.

One day, due to the hardships of captivity and the weight of his fetters, 'Abd Allāh ibn al-Ḥasan al-Muthannā lost patience, and, in a state of great agitation, said to 'Alī 'Ābid: 'Do you not witness our misfortunes and adversities? Do you not pray to Allah to grant us relief from this suffering of ours?'

'Alī 'Ābid remained silent for a while after which he said: 'O uncle! There exists for us a [lofty] rank in paradise which we can never achieve except by exhibiting patience over these or even more severe adversities, and there exists for Manṣūr a dreadful place within hell which he shall never reach except by subjecting us to such persecution. If we are patient

---

[1] *Dāstān-hā Wa Pand-hā*, vol. 7, p. 148; *La'ālī al-Akhbār*, vol. 1, p. 346.

we shall soon find ourselves in ease and comfort, for death is not very far from us. But, if you desire, I shall pray for our deliverance; but in that case, Manṣūr shall not reach that stage of wretchedness which has been ordained for him within hell.'

Hearing this, 'Abd Allāh immediately said: 'We shall be patient.'

Hardly three days had passed when 'Alī 'Ābid passed away whilst in a state of prostration. 'Abd Allāh thought him to be asleep and said: 'Wake up my nephew.' As they attempted to move him they found that he would not wake up, and it was only then they realised that he had died.[1]

3 – An enemy ordained for a believer

Prophet Hūd ﷺ used to farm. Once, a group of people came to his house to meet him. His wife came to the door and asked: 'Who is it?'

They replied: 'We have come from such and such city, which has been afflicted with famine and we are on the verge of destruction. We have come to Prophet Hūd ﷺ to request him to pray for the rains.'

The wife of Hūd ﷺ remarked: 'If his prayers had been answered he would have prayed for himself; his own crops are withering away due to lack of water.'

They persisted: 'Where is he at present?'

She informed them of his whereabouts whereupon the group approached him and placed their request before him. Prophet Hūd ﷺ offered prayers and then supplicated, after which he turned to them and said: 'You may return for it has rained over your city.'

As they sought to take his leave, they asked him: 'When we approached your house we had come across a lady, who said: "If the prayers of Hūd were to have been answered, would he not have prayed for himself?"

Prophet Hūd ﷺ said: 'That woman is my wife and I pray to Allah to grant her a long life.'

'Why do you say that?' asked the people.

He replied: 'Allah has not created a believer except that He has also

---

[1] *Pand-i Tārīkh*, vol. 2, p. 172; *Maqtal-i Khwārazmī*, vol. 2, p. 108.

ordained an enemy for him to trouble him. This woman is my enemy; and an enemy of whom I am the master is better than an enemy who happens to be my master.'[1]

4 – Muḥammad ibn Abī ʿUmayr served three Imams

Muḥammad ibn Abī ʿUmayr had the opportunity of serving Imam al-Kāẓim ﷺ, Imam al-Riḍā ﷺ, and Imam al-Jawād ﷺ, and both the Sunnis and the Shiʿas have attested to his trustworthiness and uprightness.

He was a cloth-merchant by profession and financially very well off. He wrote ninety-four books on traditions and jurisprudence. Due to his stateliness and his knowledge of the names of the Shiʿas, he used to be greatly troubled during the period of Hārūn al-Rashīd and Maʾmūn; he would be abused, imprisoned, and his property would be seized. He was asked to become a judge, but he declined the offer; and since he was familiar with the Shiʿas of Iraq he was asked to reveal their names, but he refused to comply, and so they flung him into prison, and, on numerous occasions, he was whipped so severely that he was barely left alive.

Once, upon the orders of Hārūn al-Rashīd, Sindī ibn Shāhak subjected him to a 120 lashes and he had to purchase his freedom by paying 1000 dirhams. Financially, he suffered a loss of a 100,000 dirhams and his captivity extended for a period of four years.

His sister (by the name of Saʿīdah or Minnah) gathered all his books and concealed them, but it so happened that one day it rained and all his books were ruined. Later, the traditions that he used to narrate were either from the sharp memory he possessed or from copies which others had transcribed from his original books before their destruction.[2]

5 – A long life is associated with misfortunes

It has been reported that once, Jibrīl approached Prophet Sulaymān ﷺ, bringing with him a bowl containing the water of life, and said to him:

---

[1] *Namūnah-i Maʿārif,* vol. 2, p. 612.

[2] *Muntahā al-Aʿmāl,* vol. 2, p. 358.

'Your Lord has given you the choice that if you so choose you can drink this water and remain alive until the Day of Judgement.'

Prophet Sulaymān ﷺ, placing this issue before a group of men, jinn, and animals, consulted them and all of them recommended him to consume the water so that he could become eternal.

Prophet Sulaymān ﷺ, after some reflection, realised that he had not conferred with the porcupine, and so he sent a horse to call him but the porcupine did not arrive. He then sent a dog after him, whereupon he arrived immediately! Prophet Sulaymān ﷺ said to him: 'Before I confer with you about my issue, I would like to know: why, when I sent the horse – the most honourable of all animals after man – you did not arrive, but when I sent the dog – the most vile of all the animals – you presented yourself immediately?'

The porcupine replied: 'The horse, in spite of being an honourable animal, does not possess loyalty, whereas the dog, despite being the most despicable, possesses it; if it receives a loaf of bread from someone it would remain loyal to him all throughout its life.'

Prophet Sulaymān ﷺ then said: 'A bowl containing the water of life has been sent to me and I have been given the choice of either accepting it or refusing it. All the others have advised me to drink it in order that I become eternal.'

The porcupine said: 'Is this water of life only for you? Or are your children, family, and friends permitted to consume it as well?'

He said: 'No, it is solely for me.'

The porcupine then advised: 'It is advisable that you do not accept it, for when you acquire a long life, all your children, relatives, and friends shall depart before you, every passing day will bring you face to face with misfortune and sorrow, thereby making your life miserable for you.'

Prophet Sulaymān ﷺ approved of this advice and, heeding it, returned the water of life.[1]

---

[1] *Jawāmiʿ al-Ḥikāyāt*, p. 95.

19. Sickness

Allah, the Wise, says:

$$وَإِذَا مَرِضْتُ فَهُوَ يَشْفِينِ$$

And when I get sick, it is He who cures me. (26:80)

Imam ʿAlī said:

$$أَشَدُّ مِنَ الْفَاقَةِ مَرَضُ الْبَدَنِ$$

More calamitous than poverty is the sickness of the body.[1]

Short explanation

One of the treasures of paradise which reaches a believer in this world, is sickness. If a believer, occasionally and unintentionally, falters and commits sins, Allah does not like him to return to Him carrying the burden of his sins; He thus afflicts him with illness in order that his sins are forgiven.

A person who suffers from illness beseeches and supplicates to Allah to restore his good health and Allah likes this state of a sick person, for He desires His servant to converse and communicate with Him. At times, Allah afflicts a person with sickness in order to elevate him in spiritual rank and status.

The best amongst those who are ill is one who exercises patience in this suffering, conceals his pain, and desists from complaining about his disease to others until he regains his health and acquires the maximum reward ordained for him.

1 – The rank of a worshipper who suffers from illness

One day, the Holy Prophet raised his head towards the heavens and then laughed. One of his companions asked him the reason for his laughter to which the Prophet replied: 'My laughter was out of my astonishment. Two angels had descended from the heavens to record the deeds of a righteous believer. They always found him on his prayer mat, engaged in worship, but this time they noticed that he was not there. He was in his bed, having

---

[1] *Nahj al-Balāghah*, p. 1270.

been afflicted with sickness. They ascended towards the heavens and said to Allah: "O Lord! We did not find Your servant in his usual place of worship but instead found him lying on his bed in a state of sickness." Allah said to them: "Until he regains his health record for him all acts of worship and deeds of goodness that he used to perform when healthy. It is necessary for Us, for as long as he remains in the captivity *(of sickness)*,], to grant him rewards of all the good deeds that he used to perform when possessing soundness of health."'[1]

2 – My daughter has never fallen ill!

Once, the Holy Prophet sought a lady's hand in marriage. Her father began praising her, and while enumerating her virtues, he uttered: 'From the time she was born till today, she has never fallen sick.' As soon as the Holy Prophet heard this he immediately left the gathering.

Later, he said: 'There is no goodness in an entity which, like a zebra, never falls sick. Diseases and misfortunes are Allah's gifts to His servants that should they ever become negligent of Him, [those] diseases and misfortunes serve to make people mindful of Him.'[2]

3 – Patience in sickness

Abū Muḥammad Riqqī says:

'Once, I arrived in the presence of Imam al-Riḍā ﷺ and greeted him. He replied to my greetings, enquired after my health, and began to converse with me. In the course of the conversation, all of a sudden he said: "O Abū Muḥammad! Every believer whom Allah afflicts with a misfortune and who exhibits patience over it shall surely come to possess the rank and recompense of a martyr in the eyes of Allah."

'I wondered: "In what connection did the Imam ﷺ say this? We had not been talking about misfortunes and calamities for the Imam ﷺ to have suddenly come up with this kind of speech."

---

[1] *Dāstān-hā Wa Pand-hā*, vol. 6, p. 130; *Tafsīr Nūr al-Thaqalayn*, vol. 5, p. 68.

[2] *Pand-i Tārīkh*, vol. 2, p. 180.

'I bid farewell to the Imam ﷺ and proceeded towards my friends and fellow travellers, when suddenly I experienced a pain in my leg. I passed the night in great pain and when morning dawned I noticed that my legs had become inflamed. After a period, this inflammation became more severe. I remembered the speech of Imam al-Riḍā ﷺ in which he had recommended patience in the face of misfortune and how I had thought it to be out of place then.

'In this state I reached Medina, but there a large wound developed in my leg, oozing pus. The pain was so excruciating that I could not be at peace. I then realised that the Imam ﷺ had visualised such a phenomenon when he had spoken to me and advised me to keep calm by means of patience. For ten months I was bed-ridden as a result of this sickness.'

The narrator says: 'After a period, Abū Muḥammad regained his health only to fall ill once again, eventually passing away in that sickness.'[1]

4 – Imam al-Sajjād ﷺ helps the lepers

Once, Imam al-Sajjād ﷺ encountered some lepers sitting on the side of the road, eating their food. Greeting them, he passed by, when all of a sudden he stopped and said to himself: 'Allah does not like the haughty ones.' Having said this, he retraced his steps and approaching the lepers, said: 'Presently, I am in a state of fasting [and thus unable to sit down and share your food]. [However,] I invite you to come to my house and be my guests.'

They accepted the offer and went to his house, where the Imam fed them and helped them by giving them some money.[2]

5 – The sick person's debt is paid

Usāmah ibn Zayd was one of the companions of the Holy Prophet. Once, he fell ill and so Imam al-Ḥusayn ﷺ paid him a visit. Approaching him, the Imam observed him to be greatly disturbed, repeatedly moaning and

---

[1] *Ḥikāyat-hā-yi Shanīdanī*, vol. 1, p. 166; *Biḥār al-Anwār*, vol. 49, p. 51.

[2] *Bā Mardūm Īn Gūnih Barkhūrd Kunīm*, p. 38.

exhibiting great anguish. The Imam said to him: 'Brother, what causes you to be so disturbed and worried?'

'I am burdened by a debt of 60,000 dinars,' he replied.

The Imam consoled him by saying: 'I take the responsibility of clearing your debt.'

Usāmah persisted: 'I fear I may die before my debt is repaid.'

The Imam said: 'Do not worry! I shall clear your debt before your death.' Having said this, Imam al-Ḥusayn ﷺ ordered his debt to be paid off immediately.[1]

20. Parents

Allah, the Wise, has said:

$$\text{فَلَا تَقُلْ لَهُمَا أُفٍّ وَلَا تَنْهَرْهُمَا}$$

Do not say to them: 'Fie!' And do not chide them. (17:23)

The Holy Prophet said:

$$\text{بِرُّ الْوالِدَيْنِ أَفْضَلُ مِنَ الصَّلَاةِ وَالصَّوْمِ وَالْحَجِّ وَالْعُمْرَةِ والْجِهَادِ فِي سَبِيلِ اللهِ}$$

Kindness towards parents is better than prayers, fasting, ḥajj, 'umrah, and jihād in the path of Allah.[2]

Short explanation

In [several places in] the Qur'an, Allah has spoken about the very subtle issue of kindness towards parents, attaching such immense importance to it that He has even said: Do not say to them: 'Fie!' And do not chide them.

It is evident from this that it is not only forbidden to annoy parents in any way but it is obligatory to exhibit goodness and kindness towards them. People who hurt their parents, even occasionally, must seek their forgiveness and happiness before they suffer evil consequences. They should remember that their children, in turn, would ill-treat them too.

As for the repercussions in the Hereafter, the Holy Prophet has said

---

[1] *Payghambar Wa Yārān*, vol. 1, p. 193; *Biḥār al-Anwār*, vol. 10, p. 43.

[2] *Jāmiʿ al-Saʿādāt*, vol. 2, p. 264.

that if for every instance of hurting others one door of hell opens up for man, then two doors of hell will open up for he who causes inconvenience to his parents.[1]

1 – The mother's pleasure

The Holy Prophet approached a youth who was dying and said to him: 'O youth! Say *lā ilāha ill-allāh*,' but the youth's tongue would not move and he was unable to speak the sentence. The Holy Prophet asked the gathering crowd if the youth's mother was present. A lady, who stood near the head of the dying person, stepped forward and said she was his mother. The Holy Prophet asked her if she was pleased with her son to which she responded: 'No; I have not spoken to him for the past six years.'

He said: 'O lady! Forgive him and be pleased with him.'

The lady agreed and said: 'For your sake, I forgive him. May Allah be pleased with him!'

The Holy Prophet again turned to the youth and asked him to testify to the unity of Allah, and this time, having procured his mother's pleasure, the youth was able to do so. The Holy Prophet asked him: 'O youth! What do you witness at this moment?'

He said: 'I see an extremely ugly person who has a foul odour coming from him and who is waiting to strangle me.'

The Prophet then instructed the youth to recite the following supplication: O He who accepts trivial [good] deeds and disregards the immense sins! Accept from me my trivial [good] deeds and disregard my immense sins, for you are the All-forgiving and the All-merciful.

When the youth had recited this supplication, the Holy Prophet asked him once more what he was witnessing. He replied: 'I now see a man with a luminous and pleasing appearance. He is wearing beautiful clothes and possesses an enchanting fragrance. He is exhibiting kindness and courtesy towards me.' (Having said this, the youth passed away.)[2]

---

[1] *Iḥyā' al-Qulūb*, p. 129.

[2] *Dars-hā Az Zindagī-yi Payāmbar*, p. 116; *al-Amālī* of Shaykh Ṭūsī, vol. 1, p. 63.

2 – The companion of Prophet Mūsā 🕮 in paradise

Once, while conversing with Allah, Prophet Mūsā 🕮 requested: 'O Lord! I desire to meet the person who is to be my companion in paradise.'

Jibrīl descended and informed him that his companion was to be a butcher who lived in a certain place. Prophet Mūsā 🕮 set out in search of him and arrived at his shop, whereat he noticed a youth resembling a night watchman, busy selling meat.

When night fell, the youth took some meat and proceeded towards his house. Prophet Mūsā 🕮 followed him until they reached there. Prophet Mūsā 🕮 approached the youth and said: 'Would you not like to have a guest?' The youth willingly agreed and took him inside.

Prophet Mūsā 🕮 watched the youth preparing some food. When he had finished, he brought down a large basket from the upper storey. Bringing out an old and wizened woman from inside it, he washed her and then proceeded to feed her with his own hands. When the youth was about to carry the basket back to its original place, Prophet Mūsā 🕮 noticed the old lady's lips move as she mumbled something incomprehensible. The youth then brought food for him and both of them ate their dinner.

Prophet Mūsā 🕮 enquired: 'What is your relationship to this old lady?'

The youth replied: 'She is my mother and since my financial state does not allow me to purchase a slave-girl for her, I myself strive to serve and look after her.'

Prophet Mūsā 🕮 questioned further: 'What did your mother mumble before you took her upstairs?'

He responded: 'Whenever I wash her and feed her, she prays: "May Allah forgive you and place you in the company and in the rank of Prophet Mūsā 🕮 in paradise."'

Hearing this, Prophet Mūsā 🕮 said: 'O youth! I give you glad tidings; Allah has accepted your mother's prayers and Jibrīl has informed me that you shall be my companion in paradise!'[1]

---

[1] *Pand-i Tārīkh*, vol. 1, p. 68; *Tuḥfah-i Shāhī* of Fāḍil Kāshifī.

3 – The curse of a mother

In the tribe of Banī Isrāʾīl there lived a pious person by the name of Jurayḥ, who used to engage himself in Allah's worship in his monastery. One day, his mother approached him while he was busy in prayer and, as a result, he did not respond to her. She approached him for a second time, but again Jurayḥ did not answer. When this happened for the third time, she became angry and cursed him, saying: 'I pray to Allah that He does not help you!'

The next day a prostitute came to his monastery and, giving birth to a child there, declared: 'This is Jurayḥ's child to whom I have given birth.'

This created uproar among the people, who thought: 'The very person who used to rebuke us for fornication has committed it himself.' The king ordered him to be sent to the gallows.

When Jurayḥ's mother came to know of this, she began beating her face in distress whereupon he said to her: 'Keep quiet, for it is due to your curse that I find myself in this predicament.'

The people asked him: 'O Jurayḥ ! How can we know that you speak the truth?'

He told them to bring the child to him. When the child was brought, he prayed and then questioned the child: 'Who is your father?'

The child, with divine power and permission, said: 'My father is such and such a shepherd belonging to such and such a tribe.'

This incident saved Jurayḥ's life after which he vowed never to separate from his mother and to serve her throughout her life.[1]

4 – The truthful barber

The distinguished scholar, Shaykh Bāqir Kāẓimī, who lived near Najaf al-Ashraf, narrates that a truthful barber once related the following story:

'I had an old father whom I served diligently. I exercised such great care never to be neglectful towards him that I would even place water for him in the toilet and remain in wait outside till he emerged. All throughout [the week] I would be watchful of him except on the eve of Wednesday,

---

[1] *Namūnah-i Maʿārif*, vol. 2, p. 548; *Ḥayāt al-Qulūb*, vol. 1, p. 482.

when I would proceed to the Mosque of Sahlah, hoping to meet Imam al-Mahdī ﷼.

'One eve of Wednesday I was very busy and did not find a spare moment until it was almost sunset. Nevertheless, I set off towards the Mosque of Sahlah alone in the dark. It was a moonlit night and I still had one-third of the journey to cover when suddenly I observed an Arab, seated on a horse, coming towards me. I said to myself: "This Arab is surely going to loot me," but when he had come closer he spoke in the local dialect and sought to know where I was going.

'I told him that I intended to go to the Mosque of Sahlah, whereupon he enquired if I had anything with me to eat. When I replied that I did not, he spoke with some sternness, and said: "You have some food in your pocket."

'Putting my hand into my pocket I found some raisins which I had purchased for my son but had forgotten to give him. The Arab then said: "I recommend you to serve your father," and, repeating this three times, he suddenly disappeared.

'It was only later that I realised that it was Imam al-Mahdī ﷼ himself that I had seen and that he was not pleased that I stopped serving my father, even for the purpose of going to the Mosque of Sahlah on the eve of Wednesday.'[1]

5 – Striking the father

Abū Quhāfah, the father of Abū Bakr, was one of the enemies of the Holy Prophet. Once, he abused the Prophet and so his son Abū Bakr took hold of him and pounded him against the door.

When the news of this incident reached the ears of the Holy Prophet, he called for Abū Bakr and asked: 'Did you do such a thing to your father?'

Abū Bakr replied in the affirmative.

The Holy Prophet then said: 'Go, but from now on do not behave in

------

[1] *Muntahā al-Aʿmāl,* vol. 2, p. 476; *Najm al-Thāqib.*

this manner with your father.'[1]

21. God-wariness

Allah, the Wise, has said:

وَتَزَوَّدُوا فَإِنَّ خَيْرَ الزَّادِ التَّقْوَىٰ وَاتَّقُونِ يَا أُولِي الْأَلْبَابِ

And take provision, for indeed the best provision is God-wariness. So be
wary of Me, O you who possess intellects! (2:197)

Imam 'Alī said:

لَا يُقَلَّلُ عَمَلٌ مَعَ تَقْوَى

No deed, if accompanied by God-wariness, is trivial.[2]

Short explanation

Special God-wariness is acquired by refraining from prohibited and
dubious things, whereas general God-wariness is acquired out of fear of
punishment and the fire of hell.

God-wariness is similar to the water of a river that flows by the trees
growing along its banks, each tree benefiting from it in the measure of
its tenderness, covetousness, and essence. Although people benefit from
God-wariness according to their knowledge, perception, and level of faith,
their levels of God-wariness differ in deeds and sincerity. In reality, God-
wariness is absolute obedience without any transgression, and knowledge
without any ignorance. It becomes the cause for the acceptance of one's
deeds and makes one, who comes to possess it, distinguished and pre-
eminent.[3]

1 – Incorrect God-wariness

Once, during the time of the Holy Prophet, three ladies approached him to
complain about their husbands.

---

[1] *Dāstān-hā Wa Pand-hā*, vol. 10, p. 128; *Wasā'il al-Shī'ah*, vol. 1, p. 115.

[2] *Al-Kāfī*, vol. 2, p. 61.

[3] *Tadhkirat al-Ḥaqā'iq*, p. 79.

The first lady complained: 'My husband has stopped eating meat.'

The second one protested: 'My husband has abandoned the use of perfume.'

The third lady complained that her husband did not have intimate relations with her.

(By behaving in this manner, the husbands had desired to practice God-wariness and abstinence.)

This disturbed the Holy Prophet so much that as he came out of his house he did not even put on his cloak properly and thus it dragged along the ground behind him.

Climbing the pulpit before a gathering of the people, he praised Allah, and said: 'Why is it that some of my companions do not eat meat, they do not apply perfume, and they do not have intimate relations with their wives?! O Muslims! Do know that I too eat meat, make use of perfume, and am intimate with my wives. This is my tradition, and one who distances himself from my tradition is not from me.'

In this manner, the Holy Prophet destroyed the foundations of incorrect God-wariness and condemned its advocates.[1]

2 – Abū Dharr

Abū Dharr said: 'My provisions and savings during the time of the Noble Prophet had always been three kilogrammes of dates. As long as I live, I shall never seek to possess more than this quantity.'

'Aṭā' says: 'I noticed Abū Dharr offering prayers in an old garment. I asked him: "O Abū Dharr! Don't you have a better garment?"

'"If I had one, you would have seen me in it," he replied.

'"But for a period, I had seen you with two outfits," I said.

'"I gave the other one to my nephew, who was in greater need than me."

'"By Allah, you are needy yourself," I exclaimed.

'He raised his head towards the sky and implored: "Indeed, O Lord!

---

[1] *Ḥikāyat-hā-yi Shanīdanī*, vol. 2, p. 74; *al-Kāfī*, vol. 5, p. 496.

I am in need of Your forgiveness." He then turned to me and continued: "It appears that you have come to regard this world as something very important and significant. In addition to this garment that you presently see on me, I have one more garment which is exclusively for the mosque, some goats which provide me with milk, some food, a wooden case in which I carry my belongings, and a wife who relieves me from the troubles of cooking; what bounty could be greater than what I possess?"'

Some people suggested to Abū Dharr: 'Do you not desire to purchase properties for yourself as the others have done for themselves?'

'What need do I have to become an aristocrat or a nobleman?' he replied. 'A drink of milk and water and a [small] amount of wheat in a week are quite sufficient for me!'[1]

3 – A drunkard is not to be trusted

Ismā'īl, the eldest son of Imam al-Ṣādiq 🕮, had some money in his possession. When he learned that a person from the tribe of Quraysh who was living in Medina was about to set out for Yemen, he decided to hand him some money so that he could purchase for him some merchandise for trade.

When Ismā'īl consulted his father, Imam al-Ṣādiq 🕮, about the issue, the Imam enquired: 'Does the man consume intoxicants?'

Ismā'īl replied: 'People say so, but how do we know they speak the truth?'

The Imam advised him: 'It is not in your interest to give him the money.'

But Ismā'īl still gave his money to the person, who proceeded on his trip, and in the course of it, embezzled the funds.

During the season of hajj, both Imam al-Ṣādiq 🕮 and Ismā'īl went on pilgrimage. Ismā'īl was in the process of performing the *ṭawāf* of the Ka'bah when the Imam noticed that he was continually beseeching Allah

---

[1] *Payghambar Wa Yārān*, vol. 1, p. 47; *A'yān al-Shī'ah*, pp. 329-347.

to redeem his losses. Manoeuvring himself through the crowd, the Imam reached his son and placing his hand upon his shoulder, squeezed it lightly and said: 'My son! Do not seek anything from Allah needlessly, for you have no right upon Him. You should not have trusted the person in the first place. It is not upon others to rectify one's own wrongdoing.'

'The people used to say that he consumed intoxicants but I had not seen him consume it!' said Ismāʿīl.

The Imam advised him further: 'Consider the talks of the believers to be correct and do not trust a drunkard; be wary of giving money to those who are foolish and weak of understanding just as has been stated in the Qur'an.[1] Who could be more foolish than a drunkard? The suggestions and intermediation of a drunkard in issues related to marriage should not be accepted nor should one place trust in his possession for he is bound to misappropriate it. A person who relies on a drunkard has no right whatsoever upon Allah that he may seek from Him compensation for damages suffered by him.'[2]

4 – Shaykh Murtaḍā Anṣārī

The late Shaykh Murtaḍā Anṣārī, in the company of his brother, travelled from Kashan to Mashhad and then arrived in Tehran where he eventually settled down in a theological seminary, in which he shared a room with one of the students.

One day, the Shaykh gave the student some money so that he could buy some bread for both of them. When the student returned, Shaykh Anṣārī noticed that he had brought some sweetmeat too, which he had placed on top of the bread. Turning to the student, he said: 'From where did you get the money to purchase the sweetmeat?'

'I borrowed it,' replied the student.

The Shaykh took only that portion of the bread that had no sweetmeat on it, saying: 'I shall not eat the sweetmeat for I am not sure I may live long

---

[1] 5:5.

[2] *Bā Mardūm Īn Gūnih Barkhūrd Kunīm*, p. 35; *Biḥār al-Anwār*, vol. 4, p. 267.

enough to repay the debt!'

Years later, when that student came to Najaf, he went to the Shaykh and asked: 'Now that you are at the head of the Ḥawzah and the *marjaʿ* of the entire Shiʿa world, tell me, what did you do that Allah granted you this great success?'

'It is because I did not have the courage to eat even that portion of the bread which lay beneath the sweetmeat, but you had the audacity to eat the bread as well as the sweetmeat!' replied the Shaykh.[1]

5 – The objection of ʿAqīl

Once, after becoming the caliph, Imam ʿAlī ascended the pulpit, praised Allah, and said to the assembly: 'By Allah, as long as I have in my possession [even] one branch of a date-palm, I shall not extend my hand towards your wealth. I am depriving myself of this wealth and am giving it to you.'

At this point, ʿAqīl, the brother of Imam, stood up and said: 'By Allah! You have placed me on par with that black person from Medina.'

Imam ʿAlī cautioned him: 'Sit down! There is none except you who could have spoken out in this gathering. You do not possess any kind of superiority over that black person save for precedence in Islam, God-wariness, and reward, and these are issues which bring about superiority in the Hereafter.'[2]

22. Trust In Allah

Allah, the Wise, has said:

$$\text{فَإِذَا عَزَمْتَ فَتَوَكَّلْ عَلَى اللهِ إِنَّ اللهَ يُحِبُّ الْمُتَوَكِّلِينَ}$$

And once you are resolved, put your trust in Allah. Indeed Allah loves those who trust in Him. (3:159)

---

[1] *Dāstān-hā Wa Pand-hā*, vol. 4, p. 151; *Zindagī Wa Shakhṣiyyat-i Shaykh Anṣārī*, p. 70.

[2] *Namūnah-i Maʿārif*, vol. 3, p. 171; *al-Wāfī*, vol. 3, p. 60.

Imam ʿAlī said:

التَّوَكُّلُ عَلَى اللهِ نَجَاةٌ مِنْ كُلِّ سُوءٍ

Placing one's trust in Allah is the means of deliverance from every evil.[1]

Short explanation

Trust in Allah is a jar that has been sealed with Allah's seal, and only a person who does not rely on Allah and place his trust in Him shall break open the seal of the jar and consume its contents.

The lowest grade of trust in Allah is that a person does not strive to act upon his own statutes and principles before the right time, and does not endeavour to acquire more than what has been ordained for him.

The essence of trusting in Allah is entrusting one's affairs to Allah, and if a person is heedless towards the actual 'cause', i.e. Allah, he shall not achieve the reality of trust in Allah.

Trust in Allah can never be realised by mere words and claims; rather, it is an internal and esoteric issue which finds its roots in faith and belief, and it is by abandoning all hopes and aspirations that a person can arrive at the reality of trust in Allah.[2]

1 – The trader who placed his trust in Allah

During the time of the Holy Prophet there lived a trader who, in all his affairs, always placed his trust in Allah. He used to travel from Syria to Medina for trade, and during one of his trips he was confronted by a bandit who drew his sword and intended to kill him. 'If it is my wealth that you desire come and take it and leave me alone,' pleaded the trader.

'Killing you is a must, for if I let you go free you will identify me to the authorities,' said the bandit.

'In that case give me respite till I have offered a two-unit prayer,' requested the trader.

The bandit agreed and the trader engaged himself in prayers. Having

---

[1] *Biḥār al-Anwār*, vol. 78, p. 79.

[2] *Tadhkiraregt al-Ḥaqāʾiq*, p. 72.

completed the prayers, he raised his hands and beseeched: 'O Lord! I have heard from Your Prophet that whoever places his trust in You shall remain protected. I have no helper in this desert and Your grace is my only hope.'

Having placed all his trust in Allah he had hardly completed his supplication when a rider on a white horse loomed in the distance. When he came close, the rider confronted the bandit and killed him with one stroke of his sword. Then, turning to the trader, he said: 'O You who places your trust in Allah! I have killed the enemy of Allah and He has delivered you from him.'

'Who are you that you have come to my assistance in this desert?' the trader asked.

'I am your trust in Allah. Allah brought me out in the form of an angel and I was in the heavens when Jibrīl called out to me and said: "Hasten to the assistance of your master and exterminate his enemy." And here I have come and I have eliminated your enemy.' He then disappeared out of sight.

The trader fell down in prostration of thanksgiving to Allah and acquired a stronger conviction with respect to the instructions of the Holy Prophet regarding trusting in Allah. On arrival in Medina, he approached the Holy Prophet and narrated what had transpired. 'Indeed! Trust in Allah raises a person to the pinnacle of success and the rank of a person who possesses it is equivalent to the ranks of the prophets, the friends of Allah, the righteous ones, and the martyrs,' said the Prophet.[1]

2 – The Holy Prophet and trusting in Allah

When Abū Sufyān, the chief of the polytheists of Mecca, saw the 10,000 strong army of Islam [during the conquest of Mecca], he was filled with awe and astonishment. As he walked beside the battalions of the Holy Prophet, he murmured: 'I wish I knew why Muḥammad became victorious over me. How did he manage to gather for himself such a powerful army despite being alone and without support in Mecca?'

The Holy Prophet overheard him. 'We became victorious over you by

---

[1] *Khazīnat al-Jawāhir*, p. 679; *Majālis al-Muttaqīn* of Shahīd al-Thālith.

Allah's assistance!' he said, placing his hand upon Abū Sufyān's shoulder.

In the Battle of Ḥunayn, when the enemy suddenly and unsuspectingly attacked the forces of Islam, chaos reigned supreme within the Muslim ranks. When the Holy Prophet saw this state of the Muslim army, he sought Allah's help by placing his trust in Him, and supplicated: 'O Lord! All praise and thanks belong only to You. I place my complaint before You and it is only You from whom help and assistance ought to be sought.'

At that moment, Jibrīl descended from the heavens and said to him: 'O Prophet of Allah! You have recited a supplication which Mūsā 🕮 had recited and the sea had split for him and he was granted deliverance from the evils of Firʿawn.'[1]

3 – The illness of Prophet Mūsā 🕮

Once, Prophet Mūsā 🕮 became ill. The Banī Isrā'īl came to him, and realising what his illness was, advised him: 'If you consume such and such medicine you will recover from your sickness.'

'I shall not seek any cure, but will instead wait until Allah cures me without the help of any medicine,' said Prophet Mūsā 🕮 to them.

His illness became prolonged whereupon Allah revealed to him: 'By My majesty and glory! I shall never cure you till you have consumed the medicine which they had recommended to you.'

Prophet Mūsā 🕮 asked the Banī Isrā'īl to treat him with the medicine that they had previously suggested. They treated him and shortly afterwards Prophet Mūsā 🕮 regained his health. Allah revealed to him: 'You desired to annul My wisdom by means of your trust in Me! Is there one other than Me who has placed the medicinal and beneficial effects in plants and various things?'[2]

4 – Ḥammād ibn Ḥabīb

Ḥammād ibn Ḥabīb Kūfī narrates:

---

[1] *Dars-hā Az Zindagī-yi Payāmbar-i Islām*, p. 216; *Biḥār al-Anwār*, vol. 21, p. 150.

[2] *Jāmiʿ al-Saʿādāt*, vol. 3, p. 228; *ʿIlm-i Akhlāq-i Islāmī*, vol. 2, p. 290.

'One year, I had set out for hajj accompanied by some people. Just as we passed by a place called Zubālah, a dreadful wind with black dust began to blow. Its intensity was so great and severe that everyone in the group became scattered. I found myself alone and lost in a place with no water or trees. It was not long before night fell. Staring into the distance, my eyes perceived the silhouette of a single tree and I began trudging towards it. As I approached the tree, I witnessed that a youth, dressed in white apparel and scented with musk, also came up to the tree. "This person must be one of the close friends of Allah!" I thought.

'I concealed myself fearing that if I came forward he would move away to another place. The youth, as he was readying himself for his prayers, was reciting a supplication. He then started his prayers. I noticed that there was a spring of water nearby. I performed my ablution and stood behind the youth for my prayers. I observed that in the course of his prayers, when the youth reached the verses that narrated divine chastisement and punishment, he would repeat them with wailing, weeping, and lamentation. After the prayers, the youth began to walk away from his place, all the while supplicating.

'Fearing that I might lose him, I rushed toward him and pleaded: "I place you under the oath of He who has taken away exhaustion from you and instilled within you the ecstasy of this solitude! Have pity upon me for I have lost my way and I desire to be adorned with your traits and attributes."

'The youth replied: "If you had truly placed your trust in Allah you would never have lost your way. Now follow me."

'Saying this, he went to one side of the tree and, taking hold of my hand, brought me to a place by means of *ṭayy al-arḍ*.[1] It became apparent to me that morning had dawned. "Good news for you, for this place is Mecca," he said.

'I realised that I could hear the voices of the pilgrims who had come

---

[1] Literally: 'folding up of the earth'. Covering a great distance in a fraction of a moment, miraculously. (Tr.)

there to perform the hajj. I turned to the youth and asked: "I place you under the oath of He upon whom you have pinned your hopes for the Day of Judgement! Tell me, who are you?"

'"Since you have placed me under oath, I shall inform you of my identity. I am 'Alī ibn Ḥusayn (Zayn al-'Ābidīn)," the youth answered.'[1]

5 – Relying upon the butler

Jibrīl came to Prophet Yūsuf  while he was in prison and asked him: 'O Yūsuf! Who made you the most beautiful of all men?'

Prophet Yūsuf replied: 'Allah.'

Jibrīl questioned again: 'Who made you the most beloved of all children in the eyes of your father?'

'My Allah,' said Yūsuf.

'Who directed the caravan towards the well [into which you were thrown]?'

'My Lord,' replied Prophet Yūsuf.

'Who protected you from the stone which the people of the caravan had hurled into the well?'

'Allah.'

'Who delivered you from the well?'

'My Allah.'

'Who protected you from the deceit of the women?'

'My Lord.'

Jibrīl finally concluded: 'Allah says: "What made you seek your need from someone other than Me? For this act you shall stay in prison for seven years [for the offence of placing your trust in the king's butler and asking him to seek your freedom from the king]."'

❖ ❖ ❖

According to another tradition, Allah revealed to him: 'O Yūsuf! Who was it who showed you that dream?'

---

[1] *Pand-i Tārīkh*, vol. 5, p. 182; *Biḥār al-Anwār*, vol. 11, p. 24.

Prophet Yūsuf ﷺ replied: 'It was You, my Lord!'

'Who protected you from the guiles of the wife of the king of Egypt?' asked Allah.

'It was You, my Lord!'

Allah declared: '[Then] why did you seek help from someone else and not from Me? Had you placed your trust in Me I would have liberated you from your imprisonment, but now that you have placed your trust in someone else, you must stay in prison for seven years.'

Prophet Yūsuf ﷺ wept so much in prison that his inmates became frustrated with him and it was decided that he would only weep on alternate days.[1]

23. Submission

Allah, the Wise, has said:

$$وَأُمِرْنَا لِنُسْلِمَ لِرَبِّ الْعَالَمِينَ$$

And we have been commanded to submit to the Lord of all the worlds.

(6:71)

Imam al-Bāqir ﷺ said:

$$أَحَقُّ خَلْقِ اللهِ أَنْ يُسْلِمَ لِمَا قَضَى اللّٰهُ - مَنْ عَرِفَ اللّٰهَ، وَمَنْ رَضِيَ بِالْقَضَاءِ أَتَى عَلَيْهِ الْقَضَاءُ وَعَظَّمَ اللّٰهُ أَجْرَهُ$$

The most obliged of Allah's servants to submit to Allah's decree, is one who also has spiritual knowledge of Him. And [Based upon this knowledge that Allah only chooses the best for us] one who is satisfied with His decree, when it comes to pass, Allah increases his reward.[2]

Short explanation

The attribute of submitting to Allah holds a rank higher than those of pleasure in the divine decree of Allah and trust in Allah. This is because a person who possesses this attribute abandons his own quest for seeking

---

[1] *Namūnah-i Maʿārif*, vol. 3, p. 280; *Laʾālī al-Akhbār*, p. 92.

[2] *Jāmiʿ al-Saʿādāt*, vol. 3, p. 204.

solutions to the problems that plague him, and instead dissociates himself from his inner attachments to such an extent that he hands himself over to Allah completely.

In the attribute of pleasure in the divine decree of Allah, the actions are generally consistent with human inclination and temperament, whilst in trusting in Allah, people take Allah as their agent. But such is not the case in the attribute of submitting to Allah. The chosen ones of Allah are afflicted with various kinds of difficulties such as an ill-tempered spouse, poverty, disease, harassment by people, and so on; but having submitted themselves totally, they neither voice any protest nor do they experience any sort of unhappiness over these afflictions.

1 – The Imam's reply

It has been narrated that at times, Imam al-Ṣādiq ﷺ entertained his guests with sweetmeat and porridge, whereas at other times he presented them with olives and plain bread. A person once said to him: 'If you manage your affairs with prudence, you will always be consistent and will thus be able to entertain your guests in the same manner at all times.'

'The management of our affairs lies in Allah's hands [and we are in total submission to His will]. Whenever He grants us [an increased livelihood], we cater for our guests and ourselves liberally, but whenever He restrains our livelihood, we too adjust our lives accordingly,' replied the Imam.[1]

2 – Mu'ādh ibn Jabal

Mu'ādh embraced Islam at the age of eighteen and participated in the Battles of Badr, Uḥud, Khandaq, and some others. The Holy Prophet established the bond of brotherhood between him and 'Abd Allāh ibn Mas'ūd.

Mu'ādh was compassionate by nature and possessed a pleasant personality. The Holy Prophet sent him to Yemen as its governor and showered him with numerous advices, one of them being: 'Do not be too strict with the people; behave with them in such a manner that they are

---

[1] *Shanīdanī-hā-yi Tārīkh*, p. 32; *al-Maḥajjah al-Bayḍā'*, vol. 3, p. 43.

attracted to your speech and religion.'

During the caliphate of the Second Caliph, a battle ensued between the Muslims and the Romans, and Muʿādh took part in it. In the year 18 AH, in ʿAmwās, Syria, an epidemic of plague began to spread. Abū ʿUbaydah, the commander of the Muslim army, was afflicted with the disease and when he realised that his death was inevitable, he appointed Muʿādh as his successor. The soldiers requested Muʿādh to pray for an end to the calamity but he declined to do so, saying: 'This is not a calamity; instead, it is a prayer of your Prophet ﷺ: death of the pious and righteous ones, and martyrdom, which Allah grants to only a few from amongst you.' He then supplicated: 'O Lord! Grant the household of Muʿādh their complete share of this mercy [i.e. the plague].'

Shortly afterwards, members of his household were afflicted with the disease and succumbed to it. When he too sensed its effects in his finger, he placed the finger in his mouth, and biting it, said: 'O Lord! This is small and trivial; make it blessed [for me].'

He eventually died of this plague in the year 18 AH at the age of thirty-eight and was buried near Jordan.[1]

3 – Learn submission from the pigeons

During the time of one of the prophets, there lived a lady who had a son who was in his youth and whom she loved dearly. As divine decree would have it, the son died leaving the mother greatly aggrieved and immensely disturbed. She was in such a state that her relatives approached the prophet of the time and sought his help.

When he came to the mother, the prophet found her in a state of sorrow and agitation, and she was weeping. His eyes then fell upon a pigeon-nest nearby. He turned to the lady and asked: 'O lady! Is this a pigeon-nest?'

The lady replied that it was.

'Do the pigeons give birth to their young ones?' asked the prophet.

'Yes.'

---

[1] *Payghambar Wa Yārān*, pp. 264–259; *Ṭabaqāt Ibn Saʿd*, vol. 3, pp. 122-124.

'Do all the young ones grow up to be able to fly?'

'No, we kill some of them for their flesh,' said the lady.

The prophet continued: 'And despite this, these pigeons do not abandon their nest?'

'No, they do not move away to another place,' replied the lady.

The prophet then advised: 'O lady! Be apprehensive lest you be worse off than these pigeons in the eyes of your Lord. These pigeons, despite the fact that you kill and eat their young ones in front of their eyes, do not turn away from you. Whereas you, as a result of losing just one son, have directed your anger towards Allah, turned away from Him, exhibited all this agitation, and uttered things that are inappropriate.'

Hearing these words her tears ceased and she never displayed impatience and discontent again.[1]

4 – Ṣaʿṣaʿah

Aḥnaf ibn Qays narrates:

'Once, I complained to my paternal uncle Ṣaʿṣaʿah, of stomach ache. Instead of sympathising with me, he rebuked me severely, saying: "O nephew! Whenever you experience any discomfort and you complain about it to another being similar to yourself, there can exist only two possibilities on the issue: the person to whom you have narrated your problem is either your friend, in which case, quite obviously, he too would be concerned for you; or he is your enemy, in which case he would be delighted over your disturbed state. Do not manifest your problem to someone who is like you and does not possess the power to free you from it; instead seek shelter in, and present the problem to He who has afflicted you with it, for it is He who can rid you of it. O nephew! It has been forty years since one of my eyes lost its vision but I have not revealed this to anyone – not even my wife knows that I am blind in one eye!"[2]

---

[1] *Namūnah-i Maʿārif,* vol. 2, p. 761.

[2] *Pand-i Tārīkh,* vol. 5, p. 188; *al-Kunā Wa al-Alqāb,* vol. 2, p. 13.

5 – Submission before a ruling

The date plantation of Zubayr ibn ʿAwām (a cousin of the Holy Prophet) lay adjacent to that of one of the Anṣār. There arose a dispute between them in respect of the irrigation of their lands.

In order to resolve the dispute they approached the Holy Prophet and presented the problem to him. Taking into account the fact that the plantation of Zubayr lay near the upper part of the land – from where the water came – while that of the other person was near the lower section, the Holy Prophet ruled that it should be Zubayr who should water his plantation first, followed by the person from the Anṣār.

Despite the totally just nature of the ruling, the man from the Anṣār was displeased and protested to the Holy Prophet, saying: 'You have ruled in Zubayr's favour as he happens to be your cousin.'

The Holy Prophet was so greatly upset at this antagonistic statement that the colour of his face changed. At this juncture the following verse was revealed:

But no, by your Lord! They will not believe until they make you a judge in their disputes, then do not find within their hearts any dissent to your verdict and submit in full submission. (4:65)

This verse indicates that none can express dissatisfaction with the ruling of the leader of an Islamic government of the Holy Prophet and seek to follow his own inclinations, but should stand in total submission before it.[1]

24. Contemplation

Allah, the Wise, has said:

$$\text{أَوَلَمْ يَتَفَكَّرُوا فِي أَنْفُسِهِمْ مَا خَلَقَ اللهُ السَّمَاوَاتِ وَالْأَرْضَ وَمَا بَيْنَهُمَا إِلَّا بِالْحَقِّ}$$

$$\text{وَأَجَلٍ مُسَمًّى}$$

Have they not reflected in their own souls? Allah did not create the heavens

---

[1] *Dāstān-hā Wa Pand-hā*, vol. 9, p. 102; *Majmaʿ al-Bayān*, vol. 3, p. 69.

and the earth and whatever is between them except with reason and for a specified term. (30:8)

Imam 'Alī said:

التَّفَكُّرُ يَدْعُو إِلَى الْبِرِّ وَالْعَمَلِ بِهِ

Contemplation invites towards good and its performance.[1]

Short explanation

Reflecting over one's own state and that of other people leads to the manifestation of good, expiation of sins, and illumination of the heart. It draws a person's attention towards his Hereafter and brings about an increase in his or her deeds.

Contemplation is a quality and an act of worship, the like of which there is none – just as the Holy Prophet has said: 'An hour of contemplation is superior to an entire year's worship.' Only he, upon whose heart Allah has cast His glance and which Allah has illuminated with the light of His cognisance, can reach the station of contemplation, whereupon he then begins to perceive the world with a vision of comprehension and understanding, and never becomes heedless of Allah.[2]

1 – Rabī'ah

Rabī'ah ibn Ka'b reports:

'Once, the Holy Prophet said to me: "O Rabī'ah! You have been serving me for seven years; will you not ask for something from me in order that I grant it to you?"

'"O Prophet of Allah! Grant me some time in order that I may reflect over the matter," I requested.

'The next day, when I had arrived in his presence, the Prophet said: "O Rabī'ah! Speak your wish.'

'I said: "Pray to Allah that He makes me enter paradise along with you!"

---

[1] *Jāmi' al-Sa'ādāt*, vol. 1, p. 166.

[2] *Tadhkirat al-Ḥaqā'iq*, p. 29.

'Hearing this request, he enquired: "Who is it that has taught you to seek this from me?"

'"No one has taught it to me. I considered that if I sought great wealth it would eventually get exhausted; if I sought a long life and numerous children the ultimate eventuality would be death; hence, as a result of this contemplation, I eventually opted for this request," I replied.

'The Holy Prophet lowered his head for a few moments as he deliberated, after which, raising his head, he said: "I shall seek your wish from Allah, but you must help me too [in this matter] by prostrating excessively."'[1]

2 – Contemplation before action

One of the companions of the Holy Prophet said to him: 'I always tend to suffer losses in my business transactions. The guile and deception of the sellers or the purchasers act like magic and leave me cheated.'

The Holy Prophet advised: 'In every transaction in which you fear that you might be deceived, demand from the person with whom you are doing business the right to annul the transaction within a period of three days. This is for the reason that should you happen to suffer losses, you would be able to take back your money. In addition, be patient and forbearing in the course of the transaction.

'Do know that contemplation and patience are from Allah, while hastiness and impetuosity are from Shayṭān. You can learn this lesson from a dog, for when you throw a piece of bread to a dog it does not immediately begin to eat it but first smells it, and after finding it to be appropriate, begins eating it; similarly, you should smell every matter that comes up before you [i.e. reflect and ponder over the pros and cons of it and do not embark upon it without the required preliminariess]. You, with your intellect and wisdom, are no less than a dog; thus, contemplate and reflect before every action.'[2]

---

[1] *Khazīnat al-Jawāhir*, p. 345; *al-Daʿwāt* of Rāwandī.

[2] *Riwāyat-hā Wa Ḥikāyat-hā*, p. 195; *Dāstān-hā-yi Mathnawī*, vol. 2, p. 125.

3 – Types of contemplation

Miqdād, one of the loyal companions of Imam ʿAlī ☙, says: 'I went to Abū Hurayrah who said that he had heard the Noble Prophet ☙ say: "Contemplating for an hour is better than the worship of one year."

'I went to Ibn ʿAbbās and heard him say that the Noble Prophet ☙ said: "Contemplation for one hour is superior to seven years of worship."

'I went to another companion and heard him narrate that the Noble Prophet ☙ said: "An hour of contemplation is better than seventy years of worship."

'I was astonished to hear each of them narrating differently from the other and so I approached the Noble Prophet ☙ and informed him of the three different versions. He said: "All three of them speak the truth." Then, in order to prove his point, he summoned the three men. All of us gathered in the presence of the Noble Prophet ☙.

'The Noble Prophet ☙ asked Abū Hurayrah: "How do you contemplate?" He replied: "As stated by Allah in the Qurʾan: [Men of understanding] reflect on the creation of the heavens and the earth [3:191]. I too reflect upon the wonders of the heavens and the earth," he replied. The Noble Prophet ☙ remarked: "One hour of your contemplation is better than one year of worship."

'Then, turning to Ibn ʿAbbās, he asked: "How do you contemplate?" "I reflect upon death and the horrors of the Day of Judgement," replied Ibn ʿAbbās. The Noble Prophet ☙ said: "One hour of your contemplation is better than seven years of worship."

'Then, he asked the other companion: "In what manner do you contemplate?" The companion answered: "I reflect upon the fire of hell and its dreadfulness and severity." "One hour of your contemplation is better than seventy years of worship," the Noble Prophet ☙ stated.

'In this way the issue was solved and it became clear that the rewards for contemplation depended upon the intention that accompanied it.'[1]

---

[1] *Dāstān-hā Wa Pand-hā*, vol. 5, p. 87; *Tafsīr Rūḥ al-Bayān*, vol. 8, p. 440.

4 – Thoughts of leadership

Sa'dī narrates:

'One of my friends who was disturbed and distressed due to his meagre livelihood complained to me about his low income and large family. "In order to safeguard my reputation, I intend to shift to another city so that no one becomes aware of the abject state of my affairs. You are aware that I know accounting and can maintain accounts; I have approached you so that you use your rank and position to get me a job in the government so that I might lead my remaining life with peace of mind and will be grateful to you for your efforts!" he said.

'I said to him: "Handling the accounts of the king entails two aspects; on the one hand it carries hope while on the other hand it is also work which has to be feared. Do not place yourself in an ominous situation for the hope which the work possesses."

'"In view of my condition, your advice appears to be inappropriate; in addition, you have not responded correctly to my request," said the friend.

'"You surely possess piety, knowledge and trustworthiness but [realise that] envious and fault-finding individuals lie in wait for you. It is in your own interest that you lead your life with contentment and abandon the idea of a high rank and post," I explained.

'My friend was upset when he heard this and said: "What kind of reasoning and deliberation is this? It is in times of need that friends should step forward for help, for in good times even enemies pretend to be one's friend."

'Sensing his discomfort over my advice, I took him to the minister of the treasury, who was known to me. I narrated to him my friend's plight and the minister assigned him the responsibility of a petty task. As time passed, the officials found him to be vigilant and pleasant-mannered and they promoted him. After a long time, I embarked on a journey to Mecca with some of my friends. On the way back, not far from my city, I came across my friend who seemed to be in a state of distress. He came towards me looking depressed. "Why are you in such a state?" I asked him.

'"Just as you had predicted, a group of people became envious of me and accused me of treason," he responded. "The king, without any investigation, threw me into prison and subjected me to torture and punishment. I remained in prison until the news of the return of the pilgrims reached the city, whereupon I was set free. The king even went to the extent of confiscating the inheritance which I had received from my father."'

Sa'dī continues: 'I said to him: "I had advised you previously that working for kings is similar to a journey by sea – beneficial, but at the same time, dangerous – you might either strike treasure or end up in destruction, but you refused to take heed!"'[1]

5 – The kingdom of Rey or killing the Imam

Yazīd instructed his governor, 'Ubayd Allāh ibn Ziyād, that if Imam al-Ḥusayn ﷺ refused to pledge allegiance, he should fight the Imam.

Prior to the incident of Karbala, 'Ubayd Allāh ibn Ziyād had appointed 'Umar ibn Sa'd as governor of the province of Rey, but before he could go there, 'Ubayd Allāh ibn Ziyād sent him a letter which contained the following instructions: 'Ḥusayn has arrived in Iraq. First proceed to Iraq, fight with him, kill him, and then proceed towards Rey.'

'Umar ibn Sa'd approached 'Ubayd Allāh and requested: 'O Amir! Relieve me of this responsibility!'

'I shall relieve you of this responsibility but I shall also relieve you of the governorship of Rey,' 'Ubayd Allāh responded.

'Umar ibn Sa'd found himself hesitating between fighting the Imam and governing the great kingdom of Rey. He requested 'Ubayd Allāh to give him respite for a night so that he could reflect over the matter. 'Ubayd Allāh agreed and 'Umar ibn Sa'd passed the entire night pondering over the matter till he eventually opted for the kingdom of Rey, which lay before him at that moment, but chose to disregard hell and paradise, which were in the next life. He decided to fight the Imam.

The next morning he went to 'Ubayd Allāh and expressed his readiness

---

[1] *Ḥikāyat-hā-yi Gulistān*, p. 65.

to accept the responsibility of fighting the Imam. 'Ubayd Allāh placed a huge army at his disposal so that he could proceed to Karbala for this purpose.

Imam al-Ḥusayn ﷺ entered Karbala on 2 Muḥarram whilst 'Umar ibn Sa'd, in his capacity as the supreme commander of his army and with a 4000 strong cavalry, arrived there on 3 Muḥarram.

He appointed Shimr as the chief of his army and on the tenth of Muḥarram went to the extent of ordering the killing of Imam al-Ḥusayn ﷺ and seventy-two of his children and companions just for the purpose of acquiring the kingdom of Rey.[1]

25. Humiliation

Allah, the Wise, has said:

$$ يَا أَيُّهَا الَّذِينَ آمَنُوا لَا يَسْخَرْ قَوْمٌ مِنْ قَوْمٍ $$

O you who have faith! Let not any people ridicule another people. (49:11)

The Holy Prophet said:

$$ مَنْ حَقَّرَ مُؤْمِنًا مِسْكِينًا أَوْ غَيْرَ مِسْكِينٍ لَمْ يَزَلِ اللهُ عَزَّ وَجَلَّ حَاقِرًا لَهُ مَاقِتًا $$

If a person humiliates a believer, indigent or otherwise, Allah shall always abhor and humiliate him.[2]

Short explanation

Factors such as arrogance, malice, envy, and the like cause some individuals to view others who are either illiterate or lack strength, and whom they have compelled into performing base and lowly work, with contempt and humiliation.

Disparagement in every form is forbidden; moreover, if the humiliated person experiences a feeling of disgrace and injury this is bound to result in a metaphysical reaction that would reflect badly upon the esteem and personality of the offender. Thus, it is befitting to take regard of the

---

[1] *Muntahā al-A'māl*, vol. 1, p. 333.

[2] *Jāmi' al-Sa'ādāt*, vol. 2, p. 215.

weakest of Allah's creations so that we too are encompassed by His grace and compassion.

1 – Mufaḍḍal ibn ʿUmar

Once, a letter signed by some of the Shiʿa elders was brought to Imam al-Ṣādiq ☙ by a few of the signatories themselves. The letter complained of the friendship of Mufaḍḍal ibn ʿUmar, the Imam's representative in Kufa, with some pigeon-fanciers who were apparently not of good character.

After reading the letter, the Imam wrote and sent a letter to Mufaḍḍal through those very individuals who had brought the complaint to him.

Perchance, the Imam's letter reached Mufaḍḍal while some of the signatories of the letter of complaint were present in his house. Opening the letter in their presence, he read it and then handed it over to them. When the signatories read the letter, they found that it contained some instructions from Imam to Mufaḍḍal, requiring him to arrange a transaction involving a large amount of money. The letter did not make the slightest reference to Mufaḍḍal's association with the pigeon-fanciers.

Since the issue concerned the raising of money, Mufaḍḍal's guests lowered their heads and said that they needed time to think about it. They asked to be excused from making any monetary contribution. Mufaḍḍal, the intelligent person that he was, requested them to stay over for food and prevented them from leaving his house. In the meantime, he sent word to the pigeon-fanciers asking them to come to his house. When they had arrived, he read out the Imam's letter to them in full view of the previous group. Without wasting any time, the pigeon-fanciers left and while the previous group was still engaged in consuming the food they returned, handed over a large amount of money to Mufaḍḍal, and then took his leave.

At this point, Mufaḍḍal turned to the complainants and said: 'Despite the fact that these youths help the religion when the occasion demands and there exists a great possibility that they may turn to the right path, you desire that I should not entertain them and associate with them? Do you think Allah is in need of your prayers and fasts that you have become so haughty over them, but when it comes to money you seek excuses and refuse to answer the call of the Imam ?'

The elders, who had viewed Mufaḍḍal's friendship with those youths with contempt, were left mortified and speechless as they departed from his house.[1]

2 – The conduct of the Holy Prophet

The Holy Prophet and a few other individuals were having their meal when a person, suffering from smallpox, came to the gathering. His disease was so acute that the boils had become septic. Every person near whom this diseased person tried to sit would show his revulsion and loathing by rising up and moving away from him. The Holy Prophet made the person sit beside himself and exhibited great kindness towards him.

◈ ◈ ◈

On another occasion, the Holy Prophet, together with a few of his companions, was busy having his food when a leper arrived in the gathering. The people present expressed their abhorrence and detestation over his arrival but the Holy Prophet asked him to sit next to himself and invited him to eat the food.

A person from the Quraysh who had displayed his aversion was afflicted with the same disease before meeting his death.[2]

3 – The consequence of holding someone in contempt

There lived amongst the Banī Isrā'īl a person who was so sinful and immoral that they eventually had him expelled from their midst.

Once, while wandering around, he came across a pious worshipper, above whose head flew a pigeon casting its shadow over him [thus protecting him from the sun]. He said to himself: 'I am a person who has

---

[1] *Bā Mardūm Īn Gunih Barkhūrd Kunīm*, p. 78; *Manhaj al-Maqāl* of Astarābādī, p. 343.

[2] *ʿIlm-i Akhlāq-i Islāmī*, vol. 1, p. 435; *Jāmiʿ al-Saʿādāt*, vol. 1, p. 357.

been banished but this man is a pious individual; if I sit near him it is possible that due to his piety Allah may show mercy upon me too.'

With this in mind he approached the worshipper and sat down beside him. On seeing the exiled man sit next to him, the worshipper thought to himself: 'I am the pious worshipper of this tribe whilst he is a disreputable, banished, and despised sinner; how can he sit beside me?' Turning his head away from the man, the worshipper ordered him to go away from him.

Just as he had uttered these words, Allah revealed to the prophet of the time: 'Go to those two persons and ask them to start their deeds afresh, for I have forgiven all the sins of the immoral person and erased all the good deeds of the worshipper [for exhibiting self-conceit and holding the other person in contempt].'[1]

4 – The short and ugly son

Saʿdī narrates:

'A king had several sons, one of them being short, thin, and ugly, while the others were tall and good-looking. The king would look at the short son with scorn and contempt, thereby causing him humiliation. The son, being intelligent, realised why his father looked down upon him and so said to him: "O father! A short but wise person is better than a tall but ignorant one. He who is taller is not necessarily better and superior; a sheep is clean but an elephant, like a carcass, always possesses a foul smell." The son's words made the king laugh and the elders of the court approved of what he said, but his brothers were upset.

'Coincidentally, during those days it so happened that the enemy forces attacked the kingdom and the first person from the king's army to heroically attack the enemy was the king's short and ugly son. With a display of great courage, he felled a few of the enemy chiefs and then, returning to his father and paying his respects to him, said: "On the day of battle the lean horse comes of use." Despite the fact that a group of his soldiers had taken flight, the son returned to the battlefield. "O men!

---

[1] *Shanīdanī-hā-yi Tārīkh*, p. 373; *al-Maḥajjah al-Bayḍā'*, vol. 6, p. 239.

Endeavour hard or else put on the dress of womenfolk," he shouted with bitter sarcasm.

'This sarcasm breathed fresh life into the cavalry who fought with renewed vigour till they eventually overcame the enemy forces and became victorious. The king kissed his son all over the face and named him his successor. From then on, he looked at this son with great respect and esteem. These events caused his brothers to become so envious of him that they put poison into his food in order to get rid of him. Fortunately, his sister watched what was happening through a small door and sent a warning signal to her brother by shutting the door loudly. The intelligent brother became suspicious and abstained from eating the food. "It is impossible for skilled people to die while the unskilled ones continue to live on and take their place," he commented.

'When the king was informed of the incident he reprimanded the other brothers and sent each of them to the farthest part of his kingdom.'[1]

5 – Bring forth one worse than yourself!

Allah revealed to Prophet Mūsā ﷺ: 'The next time you come to converse with Me, bring along someone who is inferior to you.'

Prophet Mūsā ﷺ set out in quest of such a person but failed to find one, because he did not have the nerve to think himself superior to anyone he encountered.

Then, deciding to direct his search amongst the animals, his eyes fell upon a diseased dog. He decided to take it along with him. He tied a rope around the dog's neck and began pulling it, but after a short distance he regretted his action and set the dog free. He returned empty-handed to have his conversation with Allah.

'Why did you not bring someone along with you, in accordance with My order?' came the voice from Allah.

Prophet Mūsā ﷺ beseeched: 'O Lord! I failed to find anyone who could be inferior to me.'

---

[1] *Ḥikāyat-hā-yi Gulistān*, p. 43.

The reply came from Allah: 'By My might and glory! Had you brought someone regarding him to be inferior to yourself I would have surely erased your name from the list of prophets!'[1]

26. Pride

Allah, the Wise, has said:

$$\text{فَالَّذِينَ لَا يُؤْمِنُونَ بِالْآخِرَةِ قُلُوبُهُمْ مُنْكِرَةٌ وَهُمْ مُسْتَكْبِرُونَ}$$

Those who do not believe in the Hereafter, their hearts are amiss, and they are arrogant. (16:22)

The Holy Prophet said:

$$\text{لَا يَدْخُلُ الْجَنَّةَ مَنْ كَانَ فِي قَلْبِهِ مِثْقَالُ حَبَّةٍ مِنْ خَرْدَلٍ مِنْ كِبْرٍ}$$

One whose heart contains pride, [even] in the measure of a mustard-seed, shall not enter paradise.[2]

Short explanation

A proud and arrogant person regards himself better and superior to others, and by assuming vain and wishful thoughts in his mind adopts the conduct of Shayṭān, who said: 'I have been created of fire while Ādam has been created of earth, and fire possesses superiority over earth.' The first sin to have been committed in the world of creation was arrogance on the part of Shayṭān.

Thus, as for it being a vice, there can be no doubt or scepticism. Proud and arrogant individuals look down upon others and anticipate others to greet them and exhibit respect and deference towards them, always nurturing aspects of their superiority and greatness within their minds. The difference between self-admiration and pride is that someone who suffers from self-admiration is egocentric, whereas one who suffers from pride possesses an air of self-superiority with respect to others, and it is for this reason that his sickness is greater than one possessing self-admiration.

---

[1] *Namūnah-i Maʿārif*, vol. 2, p. 676; *Laʾālī al-Akhbār*, p. 197.

[2] *Jāmiʿ al-Saʿādāt*, vol. 1, p. 346.

1 – Abū Jahl

'Abd Allāh ibn Mas'ūd, a companion of the Holy Prophet, was the first person to openly recite the Qur'an in front of a gathering. He participated in all the battles of the Holy Prophet but was so short that even when he stood up among people who were sitting he would not rise above them! It was for this reason that in the Battle of Badr he requested the Holy Prophet: 'I do not possess the strength to fight in the battle; can you assign me some task by means of which I too can attain the same reward as those who fight?'

'Look amongst the dying infidels and if you happen to find anyone of them still alive, kill him,' the Prophet replied.

'Abd Allāh narrates: 'As I moved in the midst of people who seemed to be dead I came to Abū Jahl, the most unyielding enemy of the Noble Prophet. He still had some life left in him. "I thank Allah that He has humiliated you," I said as I sat on his chest.

'Abū Jahl opened his eyes and grunted: "Woe unto you! Who has been victorious?"

'"Victory is for Allah and His Prophet, and it is for this reason that I shall kill you," I replied, placing my foot on his neck.

'With great arrogance, he cried: "O tiny shepherd! You have placed your foot on a very exalted place. Do know that nothing is more painful for me than to be killed by a dwarf like you. Oh, why did one of the sons of 'Abd al-Muṭṭalib not kill me?"

'I severed his head from his body and appeared before the Noble Prophet ﷺ. "Glad tidings to you, O Prophet of Allah! This is the head of Abū Jahl."'[1]

Later, the Prophet remarked: 'Abū Jahl was more sinful and worse than Fir'awn of the time of Mūsā ؏. When Fir'awn was convinced that he would perish, he believed in Allah; whereas when Abū Jahl became certain of his impending doom, he called upon Lāt and 'Uzzā to save him.'[2]

---

[1] *Payghambar Wa Yārān*, vol. 4, p. 206; *Ṭabaqāt Ibn Sa'd*, vol. 3, p. 106.

[2] *Safīnat al-Biḥār*, vol. 1, p. 200.

2 – Walīd ibn Mughīrah

Three years after having been appointed a prophet and with only a handful of people having accepted Islam, it was revealed to the Holy Prophet: 'Openly proclaim your prophethood and disregard the ridicule and troubles from the polytheists, for We shall protect you from their evils.'

One of the opponents was Walīd ibn Mughīrah. Once, Jibrīl was with the Holy Prophet when Walīd happened to pass by. Seeing him, Jibrīl asked the Holy Prophet: 'This Walīd ibn Mughīrah, is he of those who ridicule you?' When the Holy Prophet replied in the affirmative, Jibrīl pointed towards Walīd's foot.

Walīd continued walking until he reached the place where a person from the tribe of Khuzā'ah was engaged in sharpening arrows. Walīd stepped on the sharp splinters and chippings on the ground, some of which penetrated into the heel of his foot. His heel was badly bruised and blood began to flow. Walīd's pride prevented him from bending down and plucking the splinters out of his heel. On reaching his home he heaved himself into a chair and dropped off to sleep while his daughter slept on the floor beside the chair.

Meanwhile, the blood gushed out so profusely from Walīd's wound that it reached the mattress of his daughter who woke up from her sleep. She asked her slave-girl why she had not shut the lid of the water-skin. Walīd explained: 'This is not the water from the water-skin. It is the blood of your father.'

He then dictated his will and left this world, departing for hell.[1]

3 – The rich near the poor

A rich person, dressed in clean and elegant clothes, arrived in the presence of the Holy Prophet and sat down before him. A short while later, a poor person wearing old and tattered clothes, came and sat down near the rich person, who immediately gathered his neat garments from near the poor person and drew them towards himself.

------

[1] *Muntahā al-A'māl*, vol. 1, p. 36.

Having observed this, the Holy Prophet remarked to the rich man: 'Did you fear that the poor person next to you might make your clothes dirty?'

'No,' replied the man.

'Then why did you behave so?' asked the Holy Prophet.

'I have a companion, [my soul], that makes good deeds appear evil to me, and vice versa. O Prophet of Allah! As a punishment for this reprehensible act of mine I gift half of my wealth to the poor man.'

Turning to the poor person, the Holy Prophet enquired: 'Do you accept the offer?'

'No, O Prophet of Allah,' said the man.

When the rich person wanted to know the reason, the poor man explained: 'I fear that I too might come to acquire the pride and self-conceit which has overwhelmed you.'[1]

4 – Sulaymān ibn ʿAbd al-Malik

One Friday, Sulaymān ibn ʿAbd al-Malik, (one of the caliphs of Banī Marwān) put on new clothes, applied perfume, and ordered that the chest containing the royal turbans be brought before him. With a mirror in one hand, he kept trying on one turban after another until he was eventually satisfied with one.

With pomp and glory, he set off for the mosque. As he entered the mosque, he ascended the pulpit, looking particularly pleased with his appearance, and kept adjusting his outfit. The sermon he delivered made him feel elated with himself, and several times during the sermon he appeared to be obsessed with his dress and thought to himself: 'I am a sultan, young, awe-inspiring, and immensely generous.'

At the end of his sermon he descended from the pulpit and headed towards his palace. Once inside, he asked a female who seemed to be one of his slave-girls: 'What is your opinion about me?'

'I find you to be honourable and joyous. Alas, had it not been for the

---

[1] *Rāhnumā-yi Saʿādat*, vol. 1, p. 161; *al-Kāfī*, vol. 2, Chapter on the Excellence of the Poor Muslims.

poem of a poet!' replied the slave-girl.

Sulaymān was taken aback by this comment. He insisted on hearing the poem, so she recited: 'You are a good commodity and investment, if only you remain forever, but alas! For man, there is no eternity.'

As soon as Sulaymān heard this he burst into tears and continued to weep for the entire day. In the evening, he summoned the slave-girl in order to find out what had prompted her to recite that poem but she swore that she had never before come before him nor had she recited any poem. All the other slave-girls vouched for her testimony. It then struck Sulaymān that the incident had a supernatural dimension attached to it and the thought filled him with great fear and apprehension.

Not long afterwards, he departed from the world with the self-conceit that had come to seize him.[1]

5 – Khusrow Parvez

Of the kings to whom the Holy Prophet had sent letters inviting them to Islam, one was Khusrow Parvez, the emperor of Iran. The letter was sent to him through someone called 'Abd Allāh.

On receiving the letter, Khusrow ordered it to be translated. When it was translated, he noticed that the Holy Prophet had written his own name before the emperor's and this proved too much for him to digest. He tore the letter in fury, totally ignored 'Abd Allāh, and refrained from responding to the letter.

When the Holy Prophet was informed of this act, he prayed: 'O Lord! You too tear apart his kingdom.'

Khusrow wrote to Bādhān, the king of Yemen: 'It has reached my ears that a person has claimed prophethood in Hijaz. Arrange to send two brave and courageous persons to him so that they may bring him to me as a captive.'

Bādhān sent two persons to Hijaz and they presented Bādhān's letter to the Holy Prophet. He said to them: 'You may rest now for I shall hand

---

[1] *Pand-i Tārīkh*, vol. 3, p. 37.

over my reply to you tomorrow.'

The next morning when they arrived before him, the Holy Prophet told them: 'Inform Bādhān that last night [10 Jamādī al-Awwal, 7 AH], when seven hours of the night had passed, my Lord killed Khusrow Parvez at the hands of his son Shīrwayh, and shortly we shall prevail over his empire. If you accept Islam you can continue to rule over your region.'[1]

27. Humbleness

Allah, the Wise, has said:

وَعِبَادُ الرَّحْمٰنِ الَّذِينَ يَمْشُونَ عَلَى الْأَرْضِ هَوْنًا وَإِذَا خَاطَبَهُمُ الْجَاهِلُونَ قَالُوا سَلَامًا

The servants of the All-beneficent are those who walk humbly on the earth, and when the ignorant address them, say: 'Peace!' (25:63)

The Holy Prophet has said:

مَا تَوَاضَعَ أَحَدٌ لِلّهِ إِلَّا رَفَعَهُ اللّهُ

There is none who exhibits humility for [the sake of] Allah, except that Allah grants him greatness and eminence.[2]

Short explanation

Humbleness is the root of all virtues. A humble person is always submissive before the majesty and greatness of Allah, and lays the foundation of his acts of worship on the platform of this significant virtue.

None can comprehend the reality of humility except the near ones from amongst the servants of Allah who have comprehended the unity of Allah. Submissiveness and fear [with respect to Allah] can only stem from humbleness, and it is for this reason that the humble ones possess an appearance which causes them to be recognised by the angels and divine gnostics.

Their appearance, demeanour, and social and domestic conduct clearly

---

[1] *Dāstān-hā Wa Pand-hā*, vol. 2, p. 126.

[2] *Jāmiʿ al-Saʿādāt*, vol. 1, p. 359.

reveal that they are far from every kind of pride and arrogance.[1]

1 – The humbleness of Salmān Fārsī

Salmān had been the governor of one of the cities of Syria for some time. His conduct during the period of his rule remained unchanged from that before his governorship; he would always wear ordinary clothing, travel on foot, and even place his household things as surety [for borrowing money].

Once, while moving through the bazaar, he saw a man who had purchased some alfalfa and was looking for someone to carry it to his house for him. Salmān approached the person, who failed to recognise him, and agreed to carry his load free of charge. The man placed the load of alfalfa on Salmān's back. As they were walking they came across a person who immediately recognised Salmān. 'O leader! Where are you carrying this burden?' he exclaimed.

Hearing these words, the owner of the load realised that the person carrying his load was Salmān. He fell down on his knees and implored: 'Forgive me, I had failed to recognise you.'

'Nevertheless I must carry this load to your house,' said Salmān.

When he had done so, he said to the man: 'I have fulfilled my promise; now it is for you to promise that henceforth you will never seek the services of anyone for anything. By you carrying things which you are able to, it will not reflect negatively upon your manliness.'[2]

2 – Bilāl the Abyssinian

Bilāl was one of those Muslims who had made great progress spiritually, to the extent that he became the muezzin of the Holy Prophet. The Holy Prophet would say to him: 'O Bilāl! Invigorate my soul [by means of your *adhān*].'

The Holy Prophet not only placed him in charge of the public treasury, but also treated him as if he were his blood brother. 'When I enter paradise,

---

[1] *Tadhkirat al-Ḥaqāʾiq*, p. 55.

[2] *Jawāmiʿ al-Ḥikāyāt*, p. 178.

I shall hear your footsteps ahead of me as you walk on its lush-green ground,' he had told Bilāl.

Consequently, the other Muslims would approach Bilāl and congratulate him for the lofty rank that he had come to acquire for himself, but he never allowed their compliments to make him arrogant, nor did he permit the people's praises to change him. With great humbleness he would respond to their praises by saying: 'I am an Abyssinian, and [until yesterday] I had been a slave.'[1]

3 – The humbleness of the Holy Prophet

Abū Dharr narrates:

'Once, I observed Salmān and Bilāl arriving in the presence of the Noble Prophet. Salmān, out of respect, fell down at the Prophet's feet and kissed them. The Noble Prophet endeavoured to prevent him from performing this act. "Do not perform acts that the non-Arabs perform for their emperors," advised the Noble Prophet. "I am a servant from amongst the servants of Allah – I eat what they eat and sit where they sit."'[2]

4 – Muḥammad ibn Muslim

Muḥammad ibn Muslim was a wealthy individual from the nobles of Kufa and a companion of Imam al-Bāqir 🕮 and Imam al-Ṣādiq 🕮. Once, Imam al-Bāqir 🕮 advised him: 'O Muḥammad! You must be humble and modest.'

On his return to Kufa from Medina, Muḥammad ibn Muslim picked up a pair of scales and a container of dates. He then sat down at the door of Kufa's main mosque and began calling out: 'Whoever needs dates should purchase them from me.' He acted thus so that not even the slightest arrogance should enter him.

His relatives objected to him by saying that he had disgraced them through this act of his. 'My Imam has instructed me to perform a task and I shall not disobey him; I shall not move from this place till I have sold all

---

¹ *Ḥikāyat-hā-yi Shanīdanī*, vol. 4, p. 173; *Ṭabaqāt Ibn Saʿd*, vol. 3, p. 238.

² *Dars-hā Az Zindagī-yi Payāmbar*, p. 162; *Biḥār al-Anwār*, vol. 76, p. 63.

the dates that are in this container,' said Muḥammad.

'If it is as you say then you might as well take up the work of a miller,' his relatives said to him sarcastically.

To their surprise, Muḥammad agreed. He purchased a handmill and busied himself with grinding wheat into flour, the intention being to emancipate himself from vanity and self-importance.[1]

5 – Prophet ʿĪsā 🕮 and the washing of his disciples' feet

Prophet ʿĪsā 🕮 son of Mary once told his disciples that he sought a favour from them. 'What do you want us to do?' they asked.

Prophet ʿĪsā 🕮 moved from his place and washed the feet of all the disciples. 'O Spirit of Allah! It is more befitting that we should wash your feet!' they exclaimed.

'The person who is the most deserving to serve is one who is a scholar. I have acted thus that I may have demonstrated humbleness. You too should develop the quality of humbleness and after I have gone you should behave with the people with humility and modesty just as I have behaved with you.' He continued: 'It is by means of humbleness and not arrogance that wisdom flourishes, just as it is on soft ground that plants grow, not on hard, mountainous terrain.'[2]

28. Repentance

Allah, the Wise, has said:

$$وَأَنِ ٱسْتَغْفِرُوا رَبَّكُمْ ثُمَّ تُوبُوا إِلَيْهِ$$

Plead with your Lord for forgiveness, then turn to Him penitently. (11:3)

Imam al-Ṣādiq 🕮 said:

$$إِذَا تَابَ الْعَبْدُ تَوْبَةً نَصُوحًا أَحَبَّهُ اللهُ فَسَتَرَ عَلَيْهِ$$

If a servant repents sincerely, Allah loves him, and therefore conceals his

---

[1] *Riwāyat-hā Wa Ḥikāyat-hā*, p. 103; *Dāstān-hā-yi Parākandih*, vol. 3, p. 18.

[2] *Namūnah-i Maʿārif*, vol. 3, p. 223; *al-Wāfī*, vol. 1, p. 4.

sins.[1]

Short explanation

Repentance is the cord of Allah which those repenting must necessarily grasp; they need to clean their interior of their sins and testify against themselves before their Lord.

They should be repentant from the depths of their hearts with regards to their past misdeeds and fearful with regards to the remaining period of their lives. The friends of Allah repent for the thoughts that may have passed through their minds, while the special ones repent for engaging themselves in anything other than Allah, even as the general masses repent for the sins they have committed.

It is vital, in order to make amends for past deeds and to refrain from committing sins in the future, that the person repenting should not look upon any sin as being trivial and insignificant, but should always experience regret over his past lapses, keep his soul away from various kinds of lusts, and guide it towards struggle and towards worship.[2]

1 – The inventor of a religion and repentance

Imam al-Ṣādiq ﷺ related:

'In ancient times there lived a man who sought to earn his livelihood and procure great wealth by lawful means, but was unsuccessful. He then strived to achieve his objectives by unlawful means, but once again failed. Shayṭān appeared before him and said to him: "You tried to acquire great wealth by lawful as well as unlawful means but were unsuccessful. Do you want me to show you a way by which you would not only become wealthy but you would also attract numerous followers?"

'The man expressed his willingness to know how he could get rich. "Concoct a religion and invite people to follow it," suggested Shayṭān.

'The man fabricated a religion, and soon he had a lot of followers through whom he became rich. One day, he realised that he had made a

---

[1] *Jāmiʿ al-Saʿādāt*, vol. 3, p. 65.

[2] *Tadhkirat al-Ḥaqāʾiq*, p. 75.

mistake by leading numerous people astray so he resolved to inform the people of the falsity of his religion and the error of his ways. But, however hard he stressed and emphasised this, the people simply refused to accept his word. "Your previous views were correct; have you become sceptical of your own religion now?" they asked.

'When he heard these words he got some shackles and chained himself. He pledged that he would not unchain himself until Allah accepted his repentance. Allah revealed to the prophet of the time to convey the following message to that person: "By My honour! Even if you weep and supplicate to the extent that every ligament of your body falls apart, I shall never accept your prayers until you inform those people who have died after having been led astray by you of the reality, and they turn back from your religion."'[1]

2 – The employee of Banī Umayyah

'Alī ibn Ḥamzah relates:

'I had a young friend who worked as a scribe within the Banī Umayyah administration. Once, he asked me to arrange an appointment for him to meet Imam al-Ṣādiq ☙. I sought permission from the Imam ☙ and he agreed to meet the man. At the appointed time, my friend and I arrived in the Imam's ☙ presence.

'My friend greeted the Imam ☙, sat down, and said: "May I be your ransom! I had occupied a position in the treasury of the Banī Umayyah and have managed to acquire great wealth, although I have committed some crimes too!"

'Imam al-Ṣādiq ☙ said: "If the Banī Umayyah did not have people like you to collect taxes for them and accompany them in their battles, they could not have usurped our rights."

'"Does there exist a way for my salvation?" pleaded the youth.

'The Imam ☙ asked: "If I tell you, would you act upon it?"

'The youth replied in the affirmative. "From the possessions that

---

[1] *Pand-i Tārīkh*, vol. 4, p. 251; *Biḥār al-Anwār*, vol. 2, p. 277.

remain with you, return those whose owners are known to you, and as for those things for which the owners are unknown, give them off in charity on behalf of their owners. In exchange for this act I shall guarantee you paradise!" said Imam ﷺ.

'Lowering his head, the youth responded after a long deliberation: "May I be your ransom! I shall do as you have instructed."'

'Alī ibn Ḥamzah says: 'We got up and proceeded towards Kufa. There, my friend divested himself of all his possessions – even his clothes – either returning them to their owners or giving them to charity. I collected some money from my friends to purchase some clothes for him and I used to send him money for his expenses.

'A few months after this incident he fell ill and we used to visit him regularly during his sickness. One day, when I paid him a visit, I found him on the verge of dying. Opening his eyes he said to me: "O 'Alī, the Imam ﷺ has fulfilled his promise." Then he departed from the world. We performed the washings, shrouded his body, and finally buried him.

'Some time later, I visited the Imam ﷺ. As soon as his eyes fell upon me, he said: "O 'Alī! I have fulfilled my promise to your friend."

'I said: "May I be your ransom! It is as you say. He too mentioned it to me before his death."'[1]

3 – Return before death

Mu'āwiyah ibn Wahab narrates:

'When we set out for Mecca, there was an old man with us who used to engage himself in acts of worship, but did not profess the Shi'a faith. He was accompanied by his nephew, who was of the Shi'as.

'During the journey, the old man fell sick. I said to his nephew: "Why don't you inform him of the true faith? It is possible that Allah may take him away from the world in the state of true faith and *wilāyah*."

'The other people advised him to leave the man alone and to let him die upon his own faith. However, his nephew did not heed their advice. He

---

[1] *Shanīdanī-hā-yi Tārīkh*, p. 55; *al-Maḥajjah al-Bayḍā'*, vol. 3, p. 254.

went to his uncle and said: "O uncle! After the death of the Noble Prophet ﷺ, the people, with the exception of a handful who had adhered to the Commander of the Faithful, became apostates despite the fact that the caliphate [of the Commander of the Faithful] had already been stipulated by the Noble Prophet ﷺ."

'Hearing these words, the old man heaved a sigh and said: "I accept this faith," and then breathed his last.'

Mu'āwiyah ibn Wahab relates further: 'We entered Medina and arrived before Imam al-Ṣādiq ؑ. 'Alī ibn Sarḥ, one of our companions, related the incident of the old man's repentance and his acceptance of Imamate just before his death to the Imam ؑ, who said: "He is of the inmates of paradise."

"'Alī ibn Sarḥ remarked in astonishment: "The old man did not know anything about our faith and was totally ignorant of its laws and rulings; it was only when his soul was about to separate from his body that he accepted this faith!"

'The Imam ؑ explained: "What (more) do you want of him? By Allah! He has entered paradise."'[1]

4 – Abū Lubābah

Abū Lubābah was one of the distinguished companions of the Holy Prophet and had participated in the Battle of Uḥud and the conquest of Mecca. One of the more prominent features of his life was the incident of his repentance.

When the tribe of Banī Qurayẓah violated their covenant with the Holy Prophet, the Holy Prophet initiated a military expedition against them and besieged their fort. Some persons from the tribe of Aws approached him and requested: 'Just as you had handed over the fate of the tribe of Banī Qaynuqā' to be decided by the tribe of Khazraj, leave it upon us to decide the fate of the tribe of Banī Qurayẓah.'

'Would you be satisfied if I were to appoint one person from your tribe

---

[1] *Khazīnat al-Jawāhir*, p. 312; *Rawḍat al-Anwār of Sabzawārī.*

to rule in this matter?' the Holy Prophet asked.

They agreed. The Holy Prophet suggested Saʿd ibn Muʿādh, but the Banī Qurayẓah refused to accept him. They told him to send Abū Lubābah to them so that they could confer with him. The Holy Prophet assigned Abū Lubābah – who had his house, property, and family in the fort of Banī Qurayẓah – the task of conducting consultations with them.

As soon as Abū Lubābah entered the fort, men and women, old and young, surrounded him and began lamenting and complaining to him with the intention of attracting his pity and compassion. Then they asked: 'Should we submit before the rule of the Noble Prophet?'

'You could do that,' he replied, making a gesture to indicate that submission was equivalent to death. He quickly realised that by performing this act he had been unfaithful and disloyal to the Holy Prophet. It was on this occasion that the following verses were revealed:

O you who have faith! Do not betray Allah and the Apostle, and do not betray your trusts knowingly. Know that your possessions and children are only a test, and that Allah – with Him is a great reward. (8:27-28)

Overcome with shame, he came out of the fort and proceeded straight towards the mosque of Medina and, tying himself to one of the pillars in the mosque, called out: 'None should untie me till Allah accepts my repentance.'

He remained in that state for ten to fifteen days, allowing himself to be untied only for prayers or to go to the washroom.

'If Abū Lubābah had come to me I would have sought forgiveness for him, but since he himself awaits Allah's forgiveness, leave him alone until Allah forgives him,' the Holy Prophet commented when he came to know what Abū Lubābah had done.

Umm Salamah states:

'One day at dawn, I saw the Noble Prophet ﷺ happy and smiling. "May Allah always keep you smiling! What is the reason for it?" I asked him.

'He said: "Jibrīl has informed me that Abū Lubābah's repentance has been accepted."

'I asked: "Do I have your permission to inform him of the good news?"

'"You may if you wish," he answered.

'From inside the room I called out: "Glad tidings, O Abū Lubābah! Allah has accepted your repentance."

'The people rushed forward to untie him but he ordered: "I place you under the oath of Allah that none except the Noble Prophet ﷺ should untie me."'

When the Holy Prophet arrived in the mosque for the morning prayers, he untied Abū Lubābah from the pillar that stands even today in the Mosque of the Prophet, and is popularly known as the Pillar of Repentance or the Pillar of Abū Lubābah.[1]

5 – Buhlūl[2] the gravedigger

Mu'ādh ibn Jabal was in tears when he arrived in the presence of the Holy Prophet and greeted him. The Holy Prophet replied to his greeting and asked: 'What makes you cry?'

'At the door of the mosque there is a good-looking youth who weeps as intensely as a mother whose young son has died, and he wishes to meet you,' replied Mu'ādh.

The Holy Prophet agreed to meet him. The youth entered and greeted the Holy Prophet who returned his greeting and enquired: 'Why do you weep?'

'Why should I not weep? I have committed sins which Allah will never forgive and He is bound to hurl me into hell,' said the youth.

The Prophet asked: 'Have you associated someone with Allah?'

'No.'

'Have you killed anybody?'

'No.'

'Even if your sins are of the magnitude of mountains, Allah shall forgive them,' said the Holy Prophet.

---

[1] *Payghambar Wa Yārān*, vol. 1, p. 129; *Majma' al-Bayān*, under the discussion regarding 9:102.

[2] Editor's note: Not to be confused with Buhlūl who lived during the time of Imam al-Riḍā ﷺ.

'My sins are greater than the mountains,' the youth explained.

'Are your sins in the magnitude of the seven earths, the seas, the sands, the trees, all that lies on the earth, in the skies, the stars, the Throne and the Chair?' asked the Holy Prophet.

'My sins are greater than all of these things.'

'Woe unto you! Are your sins greater than your Lord?'

The youth lowered his head and replied: 'Allah is devoid of all blemishes; it is my Lord who is greater.'

'Would you not relate one of your sins to me?' enquired the Holy Prophet.

'Why not?' responded the youth, whose name was Buhlūl. 'For seven years I used to dig up the graves of the dead, take out their shrouds, and sell them. One night, a maiden from amongst the Anṣār died and was buried in the cemetery. When I dug open her grave to remove the shroud from her body, Shayṭān tempted me and I committed a grave sin. As I was turning back, the body called out to me: "O youth! Don't you fear the Ruler of the Day of Judgement? Woe unto you of the fire of the Day of Judgement!"'

Having narrated this, the youth wanted to know what he should do. 'O sinner! Stay away from me for I fear that I might burn in your fire too!' cried out the Holy Prophet.

The youth left, heading straight towards the mountains. He tied his hands to his neck and became engrossed in worship, supplications, and seeking forgiveness. For forty days he wept day and night to the extent that even the wild beasts were affected by his weeping. After forty days he asked Allah to either punish him by means of fire or forgive him, so that he might not have to face humiliation on the Day of Judgement.

Allah revealed the following verse, which refers to the forgiveness of Buhlūl:

And those who, when they commit an indecent act or wrong themselves, remember Allah, and plead [Allah's] forgiveness for their sins – and who forgives sins except Allah? (3:135)

The Holy Prophet recited this verse with a smiling face and then asked: 'Who can take me to that youth?'

Muʿādh agreed to take him. Accompanied by Muʿādh, the Holy Prophet went to the place where the youth was. He saw him standing between two boulders, his hands tied to his neck, and engaged in supplication. His face had become dark due to the scorching sun and all his eyelashes had fallen off due to intense weeping. Wild beasts had gathered around him while the birds circled over his head, all of them weeping over his distressed and pitiable state.

The Holy Prophet advanced towards him, untied his hands, and cleared the soil from the top of his head. 'O Buhlūl! Glad tidings for you; you have been liberated by Allah from the fire [of hell],' he said.

Then, turning to his companions, he said: 'This is how you should make amends for your sins.'[1]

29. Ignorance

Allah, the Wise, has said:

$$\text{خُذِ الْعَفْوَ وَأْمُرْ بِالْعُرْفِ وَأَعْرِضْ عَنِ الْجَاهِلِينَ}$$

Adopt [a policy of] excusing [the faults of people], bid what is right, and turn away from the ignorant. (7:199)

Imam ʿAlī has said:

$$\text{الْجَهْلُ أَصْلُ كُلِّ شَرٍّ}$$

Ignorance is the root of all evils.[2]

Short explanation

Ignorance is a state that exists within humans and one who possesses it advances towards darkness, whereas one who keeps it away from himself reaches luminosity and acquires discernment and insight.

If a person chooses an incorrect path for himself and permits ignorance to guide him in his actions, he will be considered a sinner and of the inmates of hell. However, if he sets about on the correct path and acts on the basis

---

[1] *Risālah Liqāʾ Allāh*, p. 62; *Majālis al-Ṣadūq*.

[2] *Ghurar al-Ḥikam*, h. 819.

of knowledge and cognisance, he shall be of the delivered ones.

Being pleased and satisfied over one's actions is the key that opens the door of ignorance and the worst trait of an ignorant person is to claim to possess knowledge despite being ignorant.

An ignorant person, upon noticing his own faults, does not experience uneasiness and discomfort, and upon being advised does not pay heed to it. Despite having knowledge of his ignorance he still commits blunders.

1 – The ignorant commander

Ya'qūb Layth Ṣaffār (d. 265 AH) had a commander by the name of Ibrāhīm who, despite being brave and courageous, was extremely ignorant.

Once, during winter, Ya'qūb ordered that his personal winter clothes be given to Ibrāhīm. Ibrāhīm had a servant by the name of Aḥmad ibn 'Abd Allāh, who had hatred towards him. When Ibrāhīm returned home, Aḥmad asked him: 'Don't you know that whomsoever Ya'qūb Layth gives his personal clothes, he puts that person to death within that week?'

'Oh no! I was not aware of this. What is the way out?' asked Ibrāhīm.

Aḥmad suggested to him that he should flee from there. He even agreed to accompany Ibrāhīm and arranged to meet him the following day. Later, Aḥmad secretly went to Ya'qūb Layth and informed him that Ibrāhīm was intending to flee to Sistan from where he would initiate a rebellion against Ya'qūb Layth. Ya'qūb pondered for a while and was on the verge of ordering his army to prepare for battle with Ibrāhīm when Aḥmad made a request: 'Allow me to single-handedly bring Ibrāhīm's severed head before you,' he said to Ya'qūb.

Ya'qūb Layth agreed. As Ibrāhīm was about to leave the city with his soldiers, Aḥmad attacked him from behind, severed his head with his sword, and brought it before Ya'qūb Layth. Ya'qūb handed the position of Ibrāhīm, his ignorant commander, to Aḥmad who thus came to enjoy great esteem in his eyes.[1]

---

[1] *Namūnah-i Ma'ārif*, vol. 4, p. 93.

2 – The caliph's ignorant son

Mahdī, the third Abbasid caliph, had a son by the name of Ibrāhīm who was a misguided individual. He showed intense enmity and malice towards the Commander of the Faithful in particular.

Once, he approached Ma'mūn, the seventh Abbasid caliph, and said to him: 'I saw 'Alī in my dream. We were travelling together until we reached a bridge whereupon he granted me precedence in crossing it. I said to him: "You claim to be the Commander of the Faithful but we are more deserving of this status." 'Alī did not give me a proper answer.'

'How did he answer you?' Ma'mūn questioned.

'He simply greeted me several times by saying "Peace, peace",' replied Ibrāhīm.

'By Allah! He has answered you loud and clear,' explained Ma'mūn. Ibrāhīm was puzzled. Ma'mūn went on: 'He viewed you as an ignorant person, unworthy of responding to. This is because Allah, describing His special servants in the Qur'an, says: The servants of the All-beneficent are those who walk humbly on the earth, and when the ignorant address them, say: 'Peace' [25:63]. This is [an expression] indicative of their lack of regard [with respect to the ignorant ones] and also of their [own] greatness. 'Alī ﷺ looked upon you as an ignorant person and behaved with you as the Qur'an has recommended when dealing with ignorant persons.'[1]

3 – The handsome but ignorant person

A pleasant and dignified looking person entered the court of Abū Yūsuf Kūfī (d. 182 AH), the judge of Hārūn al-Rashīd, who regarded him with great respect. The person sat in the gathering with such silence and dignity that it prompted the judge to regard him as a person of great virtue. He asked the man if he wanted to say something. 'I seek an answer to a question,' said the person.

'Whatever I know, I shall answer you,' responded the judge, humbly.

The person enquired: 'When can a person break his fast?'

---

[1] *Ḥikāyat-hā-yi Shanīdanī*, vol. 2, p. 20; *Safīnat al-Biḥār*, vol. 1, p. 79.

'When the sun sets,' replied the judge.

'What if the sun does not set till midnight?'

Hearing this, the judge laughed out loud and said: 'How appropriately has the poet Jarīr ibn 'Aṭiyyah (a poet from the Umayyad period, who had died in the year 110 AH) said: "Silence is a beauty for a person who is weak and ignorant." Surely, the intelligence of a person is known by his speech, just as his lack of intelligence also becomes manifest as a result of his speech.'

Thus, the judge came to know of the ignorance of the good-looking person.[1]

4 – Qays ibn 'Āṣim

Qays ibn 'Āṣim was a tribal leader during the Age of Ignorance but he later accepted Islam. Once, during his old age, in order to seek ways to make amends for his past misdeeds, he arrived in the presence of the Holy Prophet and said: 'In the past, ignorance had instigated numerous fathers to bury their innocent daughters alive. I also had buried twelve of my daughters alive at short intervals. My wife gave birth to my thirteenth daughter in secret, and, making it appear to me as if it had been a stillborn child, she secretly sent the infant to her own relatives.

'Years passed till one day I returned home suddenly and unexpectedly from one of my trips, only to find a small girl in my house. Since she resembled my children, I found myself perplexed until I eventually came to know that she was my daughter.

'I immediately took hold of the girl who was weeping profusely, and took her to a remote location, refusing to permit myself to be affected by her wailing. She kept pleading: "I shall return to my maternal uncles and shall never come to your house again," but I paid no heed to her request and buried her alive.'

When he had narrated this, Qays noticed that tears flowed from the Holy Prophet's eyes and heard him murmuring: 'One who does not look

---

[1] *Laṭā'if al-Ṭawā'if,* p. 412.

upon others with mercy shall not be looked upon with mercy.' Then, turning to Qays, he said: 'You have difficult days ahead of you!'

'What should I do to lessen the burden of my misdeeds?' enquired Qays.

'For every daughter killed, set free a slave-girl,' replied the Holy Prophet.[1]

5 – A long beard

Jāḥiẓ Baṣrī, (d. 249 AH), who has a book to his name in every branch of science, states:

'Ma'mūn and a few other individuals had gathered together and were engaged in conversation. "A person who sports a long beard is stupid and foolish," one of them remarked.

'Some others objected by saying: "On the contrary, we have seen individuals with long beards and who were clever and intelligent."

'"Impossible!" exclaimed Ma'mūn. At that moment, a man with a long beard and riding a camel came towards them. Ma'mūn, in order to prove his point, summoned the person and asked him what his name was.

'"Abū Ḥamdawayh," replied the man.

'"What is your agnomen?" asked Ma'mūn.

'"'Alawiyyah."

'Ma'mūn said to those around him: "A person who is so ignorant so as to be unable to differentiate between a name and an agnomen, all his other acts would also be characterised with the same ignorance." Turning to the man once again, he asked: "What work do you do?"

'"I am a jurisprudent and an expert in various sciences. If the king desires, he can question me."

'"A person sold a sheep to another person, who took the animal in his possession. But he had not yet paid the price of the animal when it released its dung, which fell into the eyes of another person, blinding him. Under the circumstances, whose obligation is it to pay the compensation for the

---

[1] *Dāstān-hā Wa Pand-hā*, vol. 1, p. 15; *Jāhiliyyat Wa Islām*, p. 632.

injury caused?" asked Ma'mūn.

'The person with the long beard reflected for a while and then said: "The compensation should be paid by the seller and not the purchaser." Those around wanted to know why. "It is because the seller did not inform the purchaser that he had placed a catapult inside the rear of the sheep, which it used for hurling stones in order to protect itself," explained the person.

'Hearing this, Ma'mūn and those around him burst out in laughter. The man was given some money and he left.

'"The truth of my statement has become manifest before you that the elders have stated:[1] 'A long-bearded person is a dimwit,'" said Ma'mūn.'[2]

30. Greed

Allah, the Wise, has said:

$$إِنَّ الْإِنْسَانَ خُلِقَ هَلُوعًا$$

Indeed man has been created covetous. (70:19)

The Holy Prophet said:

$$يَشِيبُ ابْنُ آدَمَ وَتَشُبُّ فِيهِ خَصْلَتَانِ: الْحِرْصُ وَطُولُ الْأَمَلِ$$

[As] man becomes old, two attributes in him turn young: greed and lofty aspirations.[3]

Short explanation

If man is greedy in acquiring things, he shall not possess the proximity of Allah, since he has abandoned the attribute of trust in Allah, is not content with what Allah has appointed for him, and has adopted hastiness, which is an attribute of Shayṭān.

---

[1] There are traditions that censure the keeping of a long beard. One of the things that Imam 'Alī ﷺ mentioned in his criticism of the people of Basra was their long beards. The Holy Prophet regarded not sporting a long beard as being one of the felicities of man. (*Safīnat al-Biḥār*, vol.2, p. 509)

[2] *Jawāmi' al-Ḥikāyāt*, p. 300.

[3] *Jāmi' al-Sa'ādāt*, vol. 2, p. 100.

Allah has created the world similar to a shadow; following the shadow yields nothing except for exhaustion and fatigue. If one seeks the world in excess of what is necessary, not only does he not acquire it but he also suffers troubles and hardships.

The Holy Prophet has said: 'A greedy person remains excluded.' And an excluded person is hated and reproached.

A greedy person's thoughts are disturbed and his troubles are numerous; he is constantly involved in seeking and computing riches and is not at peace in this world nor inclined towards the Hereafter.[1]

1 – The mud from a grave is a greedy person's medicine

Saʿdī relates:

'I had heard that a trader who owned forty slaves and 150 camel-loads of goods used to travel from city to city for the purpose of trade. One night, on the island of Kish, he invited me into his room.

'I went to his room but throughout that night he was restless. He kept rambling on ceaselessly and would say: "Such and such storeroom of mine is in Turkistan, a certain cargo of mine is in India, this is the deed of sale of a particular land, another cargo is held up due to some merchandise, such and such person is the guarantor for a loan ... I am contemplating travelling to Alexandria but the Mediterranean Sea is stormy at the moment ... O Saʿdī! I have another journey before me which if I were to accomplish I would spend the rest of my life in solitude and never embark upon any more journeys, ever."

'"Which is that journey after which you will never undertake any other journey?" I asked him.

'He replied: "I wish to take Iranian sulphur to China, for I have heard that it sells at a very high price there; from China, I shall take porcelain bowls to Rome; in Rome I shall purchase the exquisite Roman silk for selling in India; in India, I shall take Indian iron to Halab [Syria] from where I shall purchase the Halabi mirror and glass, and proceed towards Yemen; there,

---

[1] *Tadhkirat al-Ḥaqāʾiq*, p. 33.

I shall purchase Yemeni clothes and bring them to Iran, after which I shall quit travelling and settle down to manage a shop." He continued to such an extent that he was eventually overcome with exhaustion and, unable to speak any more, he said to me: "O Sa'dī! Tell me what you think of what you have just heard."

'I said: "You surely know that at a very far place from the land of Ghour when a trader fell off his mount and died, a person commented: 'Only two things can satiate a greedy world-loving person: contentment or the earth of a grave.'"'[1]

2 – Greedy for pleasure

Yazīd ibn 'Abd al-Malik (the tenth Umayyad caliph) became caliph after 'Umar ibn 'Abd al-'Azīz. Contrary to his predecessor, he used to engage himself, day and night, in feasting, festive gatherings, drinking, and merry-making in the company of two of his slave-girls, Salīmah and Ḥabībah, who were beautiful singers.

Ḥabībah eventually brushed aside her rival Salīmah and took the reins of the caliph in her hands.

Maslamah ibn 'Abd al-Malik approached his brother Yazīd and said: "Umar ibn 'Abd al-'Azīz was extremely just, whereas you, in contrast, drink and engage yourself in various pleasures and have handed over the kingdom to a singer, Ḥabībah. Moreover, while the people are keen to catch a glimpse of you, you have dropped yourself into her arms. Leave her aside and pay attention to the affairs of the caliphate.'

Yazīd resolved to heed his brother's counsel and decided to lead the Friday prayers. Meanwhile, Ḥabībah had instructed her slave-girls to inform her the moment the caliph stepped out. As soon as the slave-girls informed her that the caliph had come out, she appeared before him and, with a lute in hand and in a melodious and enchanting voice, recited the following poem: 'If an enamoured one has lost his intelligence, do not censure him; the poor thing is exhibiting patience due to the intensity of

---

[1] *Ḥikāyat-hā-yi Gulistān*, p. 166.

his anguish.'

The caliph, seeing his beloved one in that engaging state and hearing her captivating voice, covered his face with his hands. 'Ḥabībah, enough! Stop it!' he cried and then recited the following poem: 'Life is nothing except living luxuriously and gratifying oneself; even if the people censure you.' And then he shrieked: 'O the beloved of the beloved ones! You have spoken the truth. May Allah destroy anyone who criticises me for being in love with you! O slave! Go and ask my brother Maslamah to go to the mosque and lead the prayers in my place.'

He then headed towards his pleasure-hall first, and later, for greater fun and enjoyment, proceeded towards Bayt al-Rass, which is situated near Damascus. Once there, he said to his slaves: 'People think that there is no pleasure without any bitterness and I wish to prove the falsity of this notion of theirs.' He remained there in order that no news or letters ever reached him. He remained completely engrossed in merry-making without the slightest of troubles.

However, as fate would have it, one day a seed of pomegranate got stuck in Ḥabībah's throat and, following a bout of severe coughing, she passed away. Day and night, the caliph held the lifeless body of Ḥabībah in his arms and shed tears over it, and it was only on the insistence of her relatives that her stinking body was eventually buried. The caliph too, after this incident, did not live for more than fifteen days and was laid to rest near the grave of Ḥabībah.[1]

3 – Prophet ʿĪsā 🕮 and the greedy person

Prophet ʿĪsā 🕮 had been travelling in the company of another person when, after having journeyed for a period, they were overcome by hunger. They reached a village where Prophet ʿĪsā 🕮 requested his companion to go and bring some bread while he engaged himself in prayers.

The man returned with three loaves of bread and waited for Prophet ʿĪsā 🕮 to join him, but since his prayers continued for a long time, the

---

[1] *Rāhnumā-yi Saʿādat*, vol. 3, p. 657; *Tārīkh-i Tamaddun-i Islām*, vol. 1, p. 86.

person quietly consumed one loaf of bread.

'Were there three loaves of bread?' Prophet 'Īsā ﷺ asked after completing his prayers.

'No, there were only two,' replied the man.

A short while after they had eaten their food they set off again, and on the way they encountered a herd of deer. Prophet 'Īsā ﷺ summoned one of the deer towards him, sacrificed it, and both the men sat down to eat it. When they had finished eating, Prophet 'Īsā ﷺ commanded: 'O deer! Move by the permission of Allah!' The deer immediately came to life and sprinted away.

Witnessing this, the man stood dumbfounded and uttered: '*Subḥān allāh* (glory be to Allah).'

Prophet 'Īsā ﷺ asked him: 'I put you under the oath of He who has manifested this sign of His power before you! Tell me what happened to the third loaf of bread?'

'There were only two loaves of bread!' the man insisted.

They continued on their journey and soon reached the outskirts of a large village where they happened to see three gold bricks lying before them. 'There appears to be great wealth here!' the man remarked.

'Yes; one brick is for you, the second for me, and I shall hand over the third to the person who ate the third loaf of bread,' said Prophet 'Īsā ﷺ.

The greedy man blurted out: 'I ate the third loaf of bread.'

Prophet 'Īsā ﷺ parted company with him, and handing him the bricks, said: 'All three bricks are your property now.'

The man sat down beside the gold bricks and was lost in thought as to how he would carry them and put them to good use, when three persons passed by. When their eyes fell upon the gold bricks they killed the man and took possession of the bricks. As they were hungry, they decided that one of them would go to the nearby village and arrange to get some bread. The person who had gone to get the bread, thought to himself: 'I shall poison the bread so that the other two are killed and then I shall have all the three bricks for myself.'

In the meantime, his other two friends had also conspired to kill him upon his return so that they could divide his share of the bricks between themselves. When he returned, they killed him as planned and with great satisfaction in their actions, began eating the bread. Before long they too died as a result of the poison contained in the bread.

On his return, Prophet 'Īsā ☙, observing four dead persons lying near the three gold bricks remarked: 'This is how the world conducts itself with those who covet it.'[1]

4 – Dhū al-Qarnayn[2]

Dhū al-Qarnayn, during the course of his journey, came across a palace in which he noticed a youth was standing, dressed in white, with his face raised towards the skies and his hands placed upon his lips. The youth, upon seeing him, asked him who he was. 'Dhū al-Qarnayn,' came the reply.

The youth (who was actually the angel Isrāfīl) said to him: 'When the Day of Judgment arrives I shall blow the Trumpet.' Then, picking up a stone and handing it to Dhū al-Qarnayn, he said: 'If this stone becomes satiated, you too shall become satiated, and if this stone happens to be hungry, you too shall be hungry!'

Dhū al-Qarnayn carried the stone to his friends and placed it on a scale in order to weigh it, but despite weighing against 1000 similar stones, it still weighed more than all of them put together.[3] At that moment, Prophet Khiḍr ☙ came to them. Placing a stone on the opposite scale, he put some earth over the stone, when suddenly all of them observed that the scales had balanced perfectly. Dhū al-Qarnayn wanted to know the reason for this, and Prophet Khiḍr ☙ explained: 'Allah wished to admonish you, that

---

[1] *Pand-i Tārīkh*, vol. 2, p. 124; *Anwār al-Nu'māniyyah*, p. 353.

[2] His name has been mentioned in Sūrat al-Kahf; he is the same Alexander, of the progeny of Prophet Nūḥ ☙, who had travelled to the east and the west of the world and constructed the city of Alexandria. Since he used to gather his hair in the form of two horns near his forehead, he came to be popularly known as Dhū al-Qarnayn (the possessor of two horns). He lived for nearly two centuries and had conquered around thirty-six countries all over the world.

[3] This was a supernatural act, performed to jolt Dhū al-Qarnayn into awareness and lead him towards subservience and obedience of Allah.

in spite of conquering so many nations you are still not satisfied; man can never become satiated except when a handful of earth is dropped over his face, and nothing can fill his stomach except earth.'

Dhū al-Qarnayn began to weep and turned back.

On another occasion, he came across a man sitting near a grave, fiddling with some decayed bones and decomposed skulls that lay before him. He asked the man what he was doing. The man replied: 'I want to separate the bones of the kings from those of the poor ones but find myself unable to do so.'

Dhū al-Qarnayn passed by and thought to himself: 'That act of his was intended for me.'

He then settled down in Dawmat al-Jandal,[1] abandoned his quest for global conquest, and engaged himself in Allah's worship.[2]

5 – Ashʿab ibn Jubayr Madanī (d. 154 AH)

Ashʿab ibn Jubayr Madanī was a person who was squint-eyed, bald on two sides of his head, and unable to pronounce the letters *rāʾ* and *lām*. He possessed such intense greed for material wealth and food that he never seemed to be fully satisfied in this regard. When questioned about this attribute of his, he replied: 'Each time I see smoke bellowing out of someone's house I feel as if they are preparing the food for me and I sit waiting for the food. But when, despite waiting for a very long time, there is no sign of any food, I dip dry bread in water and eat it!

'And whenever I hear the prayers being recited over a deceased, I feel that the deceased has set aside one-third of his wealth for me, and with this thought in mind I go to his house and assist in giving him the ablutions, covering him in his shroud, and finally participating in his burial. But when after his burial there is no sign of the wealth, I return home disappointed and dejected.

---

[1] Fakhr Rāzī states that Dhū al-Qarnayn returned to Iraq and fell sick in the city of Zur, where he eventually passed away. (*Safīnat al-Biḥār*, vol. 2, p. 426)

[2] *Namūnah-i Maʿārif*, vol. 4, p. 234; *Laʾālī al-Akhbār*, p. 46.

'And when I walk through the streets, I spread my cloak apart in the hope that perhaps a person, while throwing a thing from his roof or window to his neighbour, may slip-up and that thing may land in my cloak.'

It is said that once, while passing through a street, he came across some children engaged in playing games. He decided to tell them a lie. 'O children! Why do you stand here when at a crossroad further down there is a person distributing his load of red and white apples amongst the people for free?' he told them.

Hearing this, the children immediately rushed towards the crossroad. As they ran, Ashʿab was himself overcome with greed and he too started to run towards the crossroad. 'You have fabricated the story yourself, so why do you run?' the people asked him.

He replied: 'The children ran out of seriousness whereas I run out of greed. Maybe there is really someone out there distributing the apples; I do not wish to remain deprived of them.'[1]

31. Envy

Allah, the Wise, has said:

$$ أَمْ يَحْسُدُونَ النَّاسَ عَلَى مَا آتَاهُمُ اللهُ مِنْ فَضْلِهِ $$

Or do they envy the people for what Allah has given them out of His grace?

(4:54)

Imam al-Ṣādiq ﷺ has said:

$$ إِنَّ الْمُؤْمِنَ يَغْبِطُ وَلَا يَحْسُدُ $$

A true believer exults, but never envies.[2]

Short explanation

Envy stems from blindness of the heart and rejection of Allah's grace – the two wings of disbelief. An envious person's evil afflicts him before it can afflict the envied, just like Shayṭān, whose evil overtook his own self and

---

[1] *Laṭāʾif al-Ṭawāʾif*, p. 361.

[2] *Jāmiʿ al-Saʿādāt*, vol. 2, p. 195.

made him the eternally accursed one, whereas Ādam went on to attain the rank of prophethood.

The balance of deeds of a jealous person is light, thereby making hell his abode, whereas the balance of deeds of the envied person is heavy, thereby leading him to paradise. In view of this, Qābīl, who had murdered his brother Hābīl because of this vice, hurled himself in hell while sending his brother to paradise.

If this vice penetrates into the soul of a person he would never be able to repent but instead would always be on the lookout to cause harm and injury to those who are either superior to him or possess more than him.[1]

1 – The friend of Prophet ʿĪsā ﷺ

Imam al-Ṣādiq ﷺ said: 'Stay away from jealousy and do not harbour envy with respect to one another.' Having said this, the Imam continued: 'One of the practices which Prophet ʿĪsā ﷺ adopted for himself was to travel from city to city. During one of these journeys, he took along with him a companion who was of short build and who also happened to be one of his attendants.

'After a while, they reached the sea. ʿĪsā ﷺ recited the name of Allah, stepped onto the water, and began walking over it effortlessly. Repeating what ʿĪsā ﷺ had performed, the companion recited what the prophet had recited and began to follow him over the water. In the middle of the sea he thought to himself: "ʿĪsā ﷺ is a prophet and walks over water and I am walking over water too, so what superiority does he possess over me?"

'These thoughts hardly crossed his mind when he suddenly fell into the water and began to plead to ʿĪsā ﷺ for help. ʿĪsā ﷺ took hold of his hand and pulled him out of the water. "What did you say that caused you to fall into the water?" he asked.

'The companion confessed to the thoughts that had passed through his mind. "You placed yourself in a position other than what Allah had ordained for you, thus becoming the object of His wrath," remarked ʿĪsā

---

[1] *Tadhkirat al-Ḥaqāʾiq*, p. 49.

🖬. "Seek forgiveness so that you regain your previous rank once again."

'As soon as the companion sought forgiveness, he began to follow 'Īsā 🖬 over the water once again.'

After narrating this incident, Imam al-Ṣādiq 🖬 advised: 'Fear Allah and avoid jealousy.'[1]

2 – 'Abd Allāh ibn Ubayy

As the people of Medina were accepting the Holy Prophet in increasing numbers, 'Abd Allāh ibn Ubayy, one of the Jewish elders, became even more envious towards the Prophet and thus planned to kill him.

He invited the Holy Prophet, Imam 'Alī 🖬, and the other companions for his daughter's wedding feast. Meanwhile, he had a huge pit dug up in the courtyard of his house, filled its base with swords, arrows, and lances, and had it covered up with a carpet. In addition to this, he poisoned the food and also concealed some Jews, armed with poisoned swords, in the house. His idea was that when the Holy Prophet and his companions walked towards the pit, they would fall into it, whereupon the armed Jews would rush out and put them to death. He had poisoned the food so that should this plan fail, they would be killed by means of the poison.

Jibrīl, through the orders of Allah, revealed these two plans which stemmed from jealousy and envy to the Holy Prophet, and said to him: 'Your Lord says: "Go to 'Abd Allāh ibn Ubayy's house and sit wherever he requests you to sit and eat whatever he presents before you, for I shall suffice you and protect you from his evil designs."'

The Holy Prophet, the Commander of the Faithful, and the other companions entered 'Abd Allāh's house. 'Abd Allāh ushered them to the courtyard of his house, and as per his request all of them sat over the pit but nothing happened, much to 'Abd Allāh's astonishment.

He then ordered the poisoned food to be brought. When it was placed before them, the Holy Prophet told Imam 'Alī 🖬 to recite the following over the food: 'In the name of Allah, the Healer; in the name of Allah, the

---

[1] *Shanīdanī-hā-yi Tārīkh*, p. 316; *al-Maḥajjah al-Bayḍā'*, vol. 5, p. 328.

Sufficient; in the name of Allah, the Acquitter; in the name of Allah, with whose name no thing or sickness, in the earth or in the heaven, can cause harm, and He is the All-hearing, the All-knowing.' Then, all of them ate the food and came out of the gathering without being harmed in the slightest.

'Abd Allāh's bewilderment knew no bounds; he assumed that the food had not been poisoned and so ordered the armed Jews to eat it, as a result of which all of them died. Meanwhile, his daughter, who was the bride, decided to sit down on the carpet covering the pit. As soon as she did so, she plummeted into the pit. Her shrieks filled the air, only to subside with her death.

'Abd Allāh ordered his servants not to reveal the cause of all the deaths in the house. When the news of these incidents reached the Holy Prophet, he asked the jealous 'Abd Allāh what had happened. 'My daughter fell off the roof of the house; as for the others, they died due to diarrhoea,' he replied.[1]

3 – The strange act of the envious person

During the caliphate of Hādī the Abbasid,[2] there lived in Baghdad a wealthy person who was righteous and beneficent. In his vicinity there resided a person who was envious of his wealth, and no matter how much he tried to taint the wealthy person's prestige and bring him into disrepute, he could not succeed. Finally, he decided to purchase a slave, train him, and then use him to implement his evil intention.

One day, after a year had passed, he asked his slave: 'How obedient are you to your master?'

The slave replied: 'If you ask me to hurl myself into the fire I shall do so.' The man was overjoyed to hear this.

'My neighbour is rich and wealthy and I bear animosity towards him. I want you to carry out my instructions. Tonight, both of us shall climb onto

---

[1] *Khazīnat al-Jawāhir*, p. 344; *Biḥār al-Anwār*, vol. 6.

[2] He was the brother of Hārūn al-Rashīd and was the caliph for almost a year, after which the caliphate reached Hārūn.

the roof of his house where you will kill me so that he is accused of my murder and is put to death by the government as a punishment for killing me,' he said to the slave.

However much the slave insisted on not carrying out these instructions, it was to no avail and the man remained unyielding. At midnight, as per the orders of his envious master, the slave severed his master's head on top the roof of the rich neighbour and hurried back to his bed.

The next day, the death of the jealous person came to light and Hādī had the rich person arrested and subjected him to interrogation. He then summoned the slave and interrogated him as well.

The slave, observing that the rich person was totally innocent, divulged the incident of jealousy and the subsequent killing. Hearing the incident, the caliph lowered his head, reflected for a while, and then raised it again. 'Although you have killed a person, you exhibited courage and saved an innocent person from accusation; therefore, I shall set you free,' the caliph said to the slave.

In this manner, the harm of envy and jealousy rebounded upon the envious person himself.[1]

4 – The envy of the womenfolk

Ibn Abī Laylā was the judge during the caliphate of Manṣūr Dawānīqī. 'Many strange and interesting cases are brought before the judges and it is my desire that you relate one of them to me,' Manṣūr said to him.

Ibn Abī Laylā related: 'One day, an old and humble lady approached me and implored me to defend her right and punish her oppressor. I asked her about whom she wanted to complain. She replied: "My niece."

'I ordered the niece to be brought before me. When she arrived, I observed that she possessed charming looks and an appealing physique. I asked her the reason for her aunt's complaint whereupon she related the entire case as follows: "I am the daughter of this old woman's brother and she is my aunt. My father died while I was still a child and this aunt of mine

---

[1] *Dastān-hā-yi Mā*, vol. 2, p. 138; *Mustadrak al-Wasā'il*, vol. 3.

took care of me and was never negligent with respect to my upbringing. When I grew up, with my consent, she married me to a goldsmith.

'My comfortable life made my aunt envious of me. She ornamented her daughter and brought her before my husband who became captivated by her and sought her hand in marriage.

'This aunt of mine stipulated that she would marry her daughter to him only if the authority to retain or divorce me was placed in her hands. My husband agreed to this condition.

'After a period, my aunt had me divorced and I separated from my husband. Meanwhile, my aunt's husband, who had been away on a journey, returned home. After realising what had happened, he used to console me. I presented myself to him in such a manner that he found me attractive. Eventually, he fell for me and expressed his desire to marry me. I said to him: "I shall only agree upon the condition that the authority of divorcing my aunt be placed in my hands."

'He agreed, and after the marriage I had my aunt divorced and I continued to live with this husband, who died after a period of time. One day, my first husband approached me and expressed his inclination to marry me again. "I am willing to marry you again, but upon the condition that you should grant me the authority to either retain or divorce my aunt's daughter," I told him.

'He accepted and once again I got married to my first husband and, with the authority vested in me, I also had my aunt's daughter divorced.

'Now, you can judge that I have committed no offence; all that I have done is to recompense the baseless envy of this aunt of mine.'[1]

5 – The consequence of jealousy

Once, during the caliphate of Mu'taṣim the Abbasid, a learned person arrived in his court. Mu'taṣim was so impressed with his conversation and speeches that he ordered him to come to the court every few days. The man used to come regularly, and before long became one of the confidants

---

[1] *Pand-i Tārīkh*, vol. 2, p. 156; *I'lām al-Nās*, p. 44.

of the caliph. Another of the caliph's confidants became jealous of this person, and fearing that he would take over his ministry, considered ways of getting rid of him.

One day, at the time of *ẓuhr*, as he was leaving the caliph's gathering together with the learned person, he requested him to accompany him to his house so that they could talk and have lunch together. The learned man accepted his request.

When they sat for lunch, garlic was also served with the food and the man consumed a lot of it. At the time of *'aṣr*, the jealous person proceeded towards the caliph and said: 'As I am burdened by your favours and bounties, I cannot conceal this secret from you. This learned man who is your confidant has been secretly complaining to the people that the foul odour from the caliph's mouth is killing him, but the caliph repeatedly summons him to go to him.'

The caliph was horrified to hear this and ordered the learned man be brought before him. Since he had consumed a lot of garlic, he covered his mouth with a handkerchief and sat at a distance from the caliph. Observing this, the caliph became certain of the truthfulness of the minister's words. He wrote a letter to one of his assistants instructing him to kill the bearer of that letter and he asked the learned man to take it to the assistant.

The jealous confidant was waiting outside the room. As soon as the man came out of the caliph's court with the letter in his hand, the confidant thought that the letter contained the caliph's orders for a large sum of money to be given to him, and this added fuel to his already flaming envy. He offered 2000 dirhams to the man in return for the letter. The learned man accepted the money and also accepted the confidant's request not to go to the caliph for a few days. The jealous confidant took the letter to the caliph's assistant who immediately beheaded him.

Some days later, the caliph enquired: 'Where is the learned man? Has he gone on a journey?'

Those around him said: 'No, we have seen him just recently.'

The caliph ordered that he be brought before him. When he arrived, the caliph, with great astonishment, enquired: 'I had given you a letter to hand over to my assistant, did you not do as instructed?'

The man recounted the incident of the letter and the jealous minister.

The caliph said: 'I shall ask you a question; do not lie. Did you tell my confidant that the foul odour from the caliph's mouth troubled you?' The learned man replied in the negative. 'Why then did you sit away from me when you last came to see me and covered your mouth with a handkerchief?' asked the astounded caliph.

'Your confidant had taken me to his house and fed me garlic, and so when I arrived in your presence I feared lest the odour should inconvenience you,' replied the man.

Hearing this, the caliph uttered: '*Allāhu akbar!*' and then related the whole incident to those present around him. All of them were left astonished and amazed.[1]

32. Truth And Falsehood

Allah, the Wise, has said:

$$\text{وَقُلْ جَاءَ الْحَقُّ وَزَهَقَ الْبَاطِلُ إِنَّ الْبَاطِلَ كَانَ زَهُوقًا}$$

And say: 'The truth has come, and falsehood has vanished. Indeed falsehood is bound to vanish.' (17:81)

Imam 'Alī ؏ said:

$$\text{ظَلَمَ الْحَقَّ مَنْ نَصَرَ الْبَاطِلَ}$$

One who helps falsehood has oppressed the truth.[2]

Short explanation

There are several levels to comprehending truth and falsehood, and individuals differ vastly with respect to acceptance and rejection of them. The general rule with regards to the truth is that the heart should be inclined towards Allah and His commandments, whilst the rule with regards to falsehood is that the heart should be averse to things that are

---

[1] *Rangārang*, vol. 1, p. 358.

[2] *Ghurar al-Ḥikam*, h. 6041.

prohibited and related to other than Allah, and the interior should be kept away from dirty and impure carnal attachments.

A pious person comprehends that falsehood weans a person away from reality and it shall cease to exist, and that it is only truth that is deep-rooted and continues to exist. Thus, one must adhere to the people of truth and stay away from the people of falsehood.

1 – The right of a deceased Muslim

Zurārah relates:

'I was in the company of Imam al-Bāqir ﷺ in the funeral procession of a person from Quraysh. 'Aṭā', the jurist of Mecca, was amongst those present in the funeral procession. Suddenly, the air was filled with the wailing of a lady. 'Aṭā' instructed her to remain quiet as otherwise he would have to turn back, but the lady continued to wail and so 'Aṭā' left the procession.

'I informed the Imam ﷺ about 'Aṭā''s turning back. "Why?" enquired the Imam ﷺ.

'I replied: "Due to the lamentation of a lady. He asked her to keep quiet and when she did not, he left."

'Imam al-Bāqir ﷺ said: "Stay with me and we shall accompany the deceased. If we notice falsehood together with the truth and forsake the truth due to that falsehood, we would not have fulfilled the right of the Muslim. [i.e. escorting the funeral of the Muslim, which is his right, should not be forsaken for the sake of the wailing of that lady, which, according to the non-Shi'a sects is forbidden and prohibited]."

'When the prayers were offered for the dead person, his relative said to the Imam ﷺ: "May Allah have mercy upon you! You can turn back for you do not possess the strength to walk." Imam ﷺ continued to accompany the funeral procession.'

Zurārah continues: 'I said to Imam al-Bāqir ﷺ: "The relative of the deceased has permitted you to turn back."

'"If you have some work, you may go," said the Imam ﷺ. "I have neither come here with his permission nor do I need his permission to return. I have come here to seek rewards, since man shall be rewarded in the measure in which he accompanies a funeral procession.'"[1]

2 – Muʿāwiyah ibn Yazīd

After the three-year caliphate of Yazīd (which brought about the murder of Imam al-Ḥusayn), the lootings and crimes in Medina, and sacrilege with respect to the Kaʿbah, the caliphate reached his son, Muʿāwiyah. Whenever Muʿāwiyah slept at night, two slave-girls would remain awake, one near his head and the other near his feet, in order to protect him from inconveniences.

One night, thinking that the caliph was asleep, the slave-girls began conversing with each other. 'The caliph likes me more than you and if he does not set his eyes upon me three times a day, he gets restless and disturbed,' said the one that sat near the caliph's head.

'Hell is the abode for both of you,' commented the other slave-girl.

Not being able to sleep, Muʿāwiyah heard the conversation. Predictably, he felt the urge to get up and put the slave-girl to death, but he controlled himself and waited to hear more of their dialogue.

The first slave-girl wanted to know why the second one had made that remark. She got the following reply: 'Muʿāwiyah and Yazīd, the grandfather and father of this Muʿāwiyah, were the usurpers of the caliphate, since the rank was the right and privilege of the household of the Noble Prophet .' When Muʿāwiyah heard this he drifted into deep reflection and finally made up his mind to step down from the false caliphate and inform the people of the true leader.

The next morning he ordered all the people to be present in the mosque. When the mosque was full, he ascended the pulpit and after praising Allah, he said: 'O people! The caliphate is the right of Imam al-Sajjād whereas my grandfather, my father, and I were its usurpers.'

He descended from the pulpit, returned to his house, locked himself in,

---

[1] *Bā Mardūm Īn Gūnih Barkhūrd Kunīm*, p. 55; *al-Kāfī*, vol. 3, p. 171.

and refused to allow anyone to enter. When his mother was informed of the incident, she approached him, beating her head with her hands. 'Oh! How I wish that you had been the blood of my monthly cycle so that I might not have had to witness such an act from you!' she shouted.

Mu'āwiyah remarked: 'By Allah! I wish I had been just what you desired so that you had never given birth to me!'

For forty days he did not emerge from his house. In the meantime, Marwān ibn Ḥakam took over the reins of the caliphate. Marwān then married Mu'āwiyah's mother (Yazīd's wife) and a few days later he had Mu'āwiyah poisoned.[1]

3 – Accepting the truth

One night, Sa'īd ibn Musayyab entered the Mosque of the Prophet wherein he observed a person offering prayers. He was reciting them in a loud and beautiful voice. Sa'īd instructed his slave to go to the person and request him to recite his prayers softly. 'The mosque is not our property; this person has a right over it too,' the slave said.

Sa'īd decided to do it himself. He called out in a loud voice: 'O worshipper! If you are offering your prayers for Allah then lower your voice, but if you are offering it for the people, they shall not benefit you in the least.'

The person, appreciating the truth in this advice, lowered his voice and recited the remainder of the prayers in a low voice. As soon as he had completed his prayers, he picked up his shoes and left the mosque. After he had left, it transpired that the person was 'Umar ibn 'Abd al-'Azīz, the ruler of Medina.[2]

4 – The intoxicated turns grateful

Dhū al-Nūn Miṣrī relates:

'I had come out of Egypt for a walk and was strolling along the banks

---

[1] *Dāstān-hā Wa Pand-hā*, vol. 9, p. 154.

[2] *Shanīdanī-hā-yi Tārīkh*, p. 18; *al-Maḥajjah al-Bayḍā'*, vol. 2, p. 230.

of the River Nile gazing at its water, when I suddenly caught glimpse of a scorpion moving forward, hastily. I wondered where it was heading. As it reached the riverbank, a frog surfaced from within the water; the scorpion climbed onto its back and the frog began to swim through the water. "There is something mysterious about this event," I thought to myself. I jumped into the water and began to swim after them.

'I observed that when the frog had reached land, the scorpion got down from its back. I continued to follow the scorpion until I reached a tree. There, I found a youth lying in its shade. Beside him was a black snake that was about to bite him. Suddenly, the scorpion rushed forward and stung the snake in the back; the snake died instantly.

'After this, the scorpion proceeded towards the water, climbed onto the frog's back, and was ferried to the other side. I stood absolutely amazed. "This person is surely one of the close friends of Allah!" I whispered. I was about to kiss his feet when I realised that the man was intoxicated, and this only served to add to my amazement. I waited patiently for the youth to recover from his drunken state and when he regained consciousness, he saw me standing near him.

'"O one who is the leader of his time! You have come near this sinner and honoured him," he exclaimed in astonishment.

'I told him to leave aside the rhetoric but to look at the snake beside him. Seeing the snake near him, he slapped his forehead and enquired what had happened. I related to him the entire incident of the scorpion, frog, and the snake. On hearing about this and observing the grace of Allah upon him, he raised his head towards the heaven and cried: "O you! If Your grace upon the intoxicated ones is in such measure, how much would it be upon Your friends?"

'Then, after performing ablution in the Nile, he turned towards his house. From then on he engaged himself in self-rectification, until he reached such a stage and rank that every sick person for whom he prayed would become cured.'[1]

---

[1] *Jawāmiʿ al-Ḥikāyāt*, p. 46.

5 – The gratitude of Abū Dharr

When Abū Dharr received the news that a prophet had manifested himself in Mecca, he instructed his brother Anīs to go and acquire some information about him.

His brother went to Mecca, came back, and described the Holy Prophet to him. 'You have not been able to smother the flames that smoulder within my heart,' Abū Dharr complained.

He therefore made arrangements to undertake a journey to Mecca. On his arrival there, he took shelter until on the third day, under the guidance of Imam 'Alī ﷺ, he covertly approached the Holy Prophet and greeted him.

When the Holy Prophet asked him his name and enquired about him, Abū Dharr gave him the answers, following which he accepted Islam. The Holy Prophet advised him: 'Return to your city and do not stay in Mecca for I fear that you might be subjected to persecution.'

'By He in whose hand lies my soul! I shall shout out in front of the people and loudly proclaim my acceptance of Islam,' responded Abū Dharr.

He headed straight towards Masjid al-Ḥarām where, in a loud voice, he testified to the unity of Allah and the prophethood of the Holy Prophet. Hearing this, the people of Mecca rushed towards him to beat him up, until he fell unconscious. As 'Abbās, the paternal uncle of the Holy Prophet, witnessed the scene, he threw himself upon Abū Dharr and shouted out to the people: 'O people! Woe unto you! Do you not see that this person is from the tribe of Ghifār and was amidst you while on a journey towards Syria?' With these words he managed to save Abū Dharr's life.

The next day, his condition improved, but Abū Dharr again proclaimed his new faith and was again badly beaten up. For the second time in as many days, 'Abbās intervened and saved him from their beatings. After this, Abū Dharr left Mecca and returned to his city.[1]

---

[1] *Payghambar Wa Yārān*, vol. 1, p. 45; *A'yān al-Shī'ah*, p. 316.

33. Lawful And Unlawful

Allah, the Wise, has said:

$$\text{يَا أَيُّهَا النَّاسُ كُلُوا مِمَّا فِي الْأَرْضِ حَلَالًا طَيِّبًا}$$

O mankind! Eat of what is lawful and pure in the earth. (2:168)

Imam al-Kāẓim 🕊 said:

$$\text{إِنَّ الْحَرَامَ لَا يَنْمِي وَإِنْ نَـمَى لَمْ يُبَارَك فِيهِ}$$

Surely, the unlawful things do not grow, and if they ever do, they are not blessed.[1]

Short explanation

Consumption of lawful things results in soundness of health and a good Hereafter, whereas consumption of unlawful things causes hardening of the heart, which is the gravest of diseases for the heart. Its ill effects are also seen to manifest in one's progeny, and it even becomes the cause for a person to stand up in opposition to Allah! The prophets and the close friends of Allah never ate unlawful things and always counselled their nations to earn a lawful income and desist from unlawful things.

Why should one who shall eventually be in need of only a grave and a few metres of shroud strive to collect wealth by unlawful means only to leave it for the others, not to mention its burden and responsibility?

In regards to earning a lawful income, it has been reported from the Holy Prophet that worship consists of seventy parts, the most excellent of them being the earning of a lawful income. The act of earning a lawful income causes a person's heart to become illuminated, his acts of worship to be accepted, and the person finds himself in the continuous protection of Allah.[2]

1 – The Jews and the unlawful food

When the Holy Prophet was seven years of age, the Jews discussed amongst

---

[1] *Jāmiʿ al-Saʿādāt*, vol. 2, p. 167.

[2] *Safīnat al-Biḥār*, vol. 1, p. 297.

themselves: 'We have read in our scriptures that the Prophet will distance himself from unlawful and dubious food, so let us test him.'

Thus, they stole a fowl and gifted it to Abū Ṭālib so that the members of his family could eat it. All of them ate except for the Holy Prophet, who did not touch the food. When questioned, he replied: 'This fowl is unlawful and Allah has protected me from unlawful things.'

After this incident, the Jews got hold of a neighbour's fowl with the intention of paying him later and sent it to Abū Ṭālib, but once again the Holy Prophet refused to eat the food, saying: 'This food is dubious.'

When the Jews came to know of these incidents, they commented: 'This child shall come to possess a lofty rank and status.'[1]

2 – By unlawful means

During the period when Imam al-Bāqir ﷺ was in the captivity of Manṣūr Dawānīqī (the second Abbasid caliph), he used to eat very little food. Once, a righteous lady who was a follower of the Ahl al-Bayt prepared two loaves of bread by lawful means and sent it to the Imam so that he could eat them. The jail warden said to Imam: 'A certain pious lady, who happens to be your follower, has sent these loaves as a present for you and has sworn that it has been made out of lawful means and has requested you to eat them.'

The Imam refused to accept the loaves and asked for them to be returned to the lady. The Imam said: 'Tell her: we know that your food is lawful; however, since you have made it reach us by unlawful means, it does not befit us to eat it.'[2]

3 – Shayṭān's snare

One of the students of Ayatollah Shaykh Murtaḍā Anṣārī recounts:

'One night, while we were in Najaf engaged in studies under the tutelage of the Shaykh, I saw Shayṭān in my dreams. He was armed with

---

[1] *Dars-hā Az Zindagī-yi Payāmbar*, p. 31; *Biḥār al-Anwār*, vol. 15, p. 336.

[2] *Laṭā'if al-Ṭawā'if*, p. 44.

numerous ropes and cords in his hands. "What are these ropes for?" I asked him.

'He replied: "I put them around people's necks, draw them towards me, and ensnare them. Just last night I had put one of these strong cords around the Shaykh's neck and had managed to drag him from his room to the middle of the street in which his house is situated, but unfortunately he escaped from my clutches and returned home."

'The next morning when I went to the Shaykh, I related the previous night's dream to him. "Shayṭān has spoken the truth," the Shaykh explained. "That accursed had desired to beguile me, but by the grace of Allah I escaped from his grasp. Yesterday, I did not have any money to purchase something for the house. I said to myself: 'I have one rial from the money of Imam al-Zamān 🕌 and there is still some time before I can put it to use. I shall borrow it for now and repay it later.' I left the house with that money, but as I was about to purchase the item that I needed, I said to myself: 'How do I know I shall be able to repay this debt later?' I wavered, and then all of a sudden I decided against going ahead with the purchase. As soon as I returned home, I put the money back in its place."'[1]

4 – The caliph's food

Once, in a gathering of Hārūn al-Rashīd (the fifth Abbasid caliph), which included a number of aristocrats, the conversation drifted towards Buhlūl and his insanity.

When it was time for lunch, a king's luncheon was spread out and a delicacy especially prepared for Hārūn was placed before him. Hārūn handed this food to one of his slaves and ordered him to take the food to Buhlūl in the hope of drawing him towards himself with this benevolent act.

When the slave brought the food before Buhlūl, who was seated in the ruins of a house, he noticed that some dogs nearby were tearing apart and eating the carcass of a dead donkey. Buhlūl refused to accept the food.

---

[1] *Sīmā-yi Farzānigān*, p. 430; *Zindagī Wa Shakhṣiyyat-i Shaykh Anṣārī*, p. 88.

'Place the food before the dogs,' he said to the slave.

'This is the caliph's special food and he has sent it to you out of his respect for you. Do not insult the caliph!' ordered the slave.

Buhlūl responded: 'Lower your voice! For if the dogs come to know of this, even they would refuse to eat this food!'[1]

5 – 'Aqīl

Once, 'Aqīl, the brother of Imam 'Alī ☙, seeking some monetary help, asked the Imam to give him something because he was poor. The Imam said: 'Be patient until I distribute the money amongst the other Muslims, for then I shall also give you your share.'

But when 'Aqīl persisted with his request, the Imam said to a person: 'Take 'Aqīl by the hand towards the market and ask him to force open the lock of one of the shops and take everything from it!'

'Aqīl immediately asked: 'Do you want me to be arrested as a thief?'

'And by giving you money from the public treasury of the Muslims you want me to be looked upon as a thief?' the Imam retorted.

'I shall go to Mu'āwiyah,' replied 'Aqīl.

Imam 'Alī ☙ suggested to him to do as he pleased. 'Aqīl went to Mu'āwiyah to seek help from him, whereupon Mu'āwiyah gave him 100,000 dirhams and said: 'Ascend the pulpit and inform the people as to how 'Alī behaved with you and how I cooperated with you.'

'Aqīl climbed the pulpit and, after thanking and praising Allah, said: 'O people! When I sought from 'Alī his religion, he abandoned me, his own brother, and adhered to his religion. However, when I approached Mu'āwiyah, he gave me preference over his religion.'[2]

34. Forbearance

Allah, the Wise, has said:

---

[1] *Ḥikāyat-hā-yi Shanīdanī*, vol. 1, p. 120.

[2] *Pand-i Tārīkh*, vol. 1, p. 180; *al-Ṣawā'iq al-Muḥriqah*.

إِنَّ إِبْرَاهِيمَ لَحَلِيمٌ أَوَّاهٌ مُنِيبٌ

Ibrāhīm was indeed most forbearing, plaintive, [and] penitent. (11:75)

Imam al-Ṣādiq ﷺ said:

إِذَا لَـمْ تَكُنْ حَلِيمًا فَتَحَلَّمْ

If you are not forbearing then portray yourself as one possessing forbearance.[1]

Short explanation

Forbearance is Allah's lantern from which a person achieves the proximity of Allah. A forbearing person, in the face of ill treatment by his family, friends, and other people, exhibits patience for the sake of divine pleasure. The reality of forbearance is when a person, despite having the power and ability to extract revenge, pardons the person who has caused him harm and injury; we read in the supplications: 'O Lord! Your grace is expansive and Your forbearance is immense that You should punish me for my deeds and disgrace me for my sins.'

Since the significance of a true believer is more than anyone else, it is imperative for him to exhibit forbearance in the face of troubles and inconveniences of the foolish ones, for if he were to stand up in confrontation with them it would be tantamount to adding fuel to the fire and would only serve to aggravate the issue.[2]

1 – The nuisances of the pigeon-fancier

Shaykh Abū 'Alī Thaqafī had a neighbour who loved pigeons. His pigeons would perch on the roof of the Shaykh's house, and in order to make them fly away he would fling stones at them, an act that caused disturbance and inconvenience to the Shaykh.

One day, the Shaykh was sitting in his house reciting the Holy Qur'an when the neighbour hurled a stone at the pigeons. The stone struck the Shaykh on his forehead, injuring him and causing blood to flow down his

---

[1] *Jāmiʿ al-Saʿādāt*, vol. 1, p. 297.

[2] *Tadhkirat al-Ḥaqāʾiq*, p. 54.

forehead.

The Shaykh's companions were overjoyed and spoke amongst themselves: 'Tomorrow, the Shaykh is bound to complain to the governor of the city and we shall soon be relieved of the pigeon-fancier's nuisance.'

The Shaykh summoned his servant and instructed him to bring a long branch of a tree. When the slave had brought the branch, the Shaykh said to him: 'Now take this branch to the pigeon-fancier and ask him not to throw stones, but to use this instead to make the pigeons fly.'[1]

2 – Tolerance towards the commander's deeds

While Hishām ibn Ismāʿīl (the maternal uncle of ʿAbd al-Malik ibn Marwān) was the governor of Medina, having been appointed by Yazīd, he used to harass Imam al-Sajjād ﷺ immensely. When he was dismissed from the post Walīd took his place and ordered him to be arrested, and placed him in custody so that all those people who had grievances against him could come forward and seek compensation.

Hishām said: 'I do not fear anyone except ʿAlī ibn al-Ḥusayn.' This fear was because he had subjected the Imam to enormous troubles.

However, the Imam had instructed some of the individuals known to him (and who had a hand in Hishām's arrest) not to cause any harm to him, even by using a bad word. He even sent a message to Hishām stating: 'Listen, if you are unable to pay the money which they have imposed upon you as penalty and punishment, we can arrange to have it paid for you. Rest assured! You need not be worried, either with respect to us or with respect to our followers.'

When Hishām realised the Imam's civility and courteousness towards him in spite of his improper conduct, he recited aloud: 'Allah knows best where He places His message [6:124].'[2]

---

[1] *Namūnah-i Maʿārif,* vol. 4, p. 368.

[2] *Bā Mardūm Īn Gunih Barkhūrd Kunīm,* p. 22; *Tārīkh Ṭabarī,* vol. 8, p. 61.

3 – Qays Minqarī

A narrator says:

'I learnt to practice forbearance from Qays ibn ʿĀṣim Minqarī. Once, I watched him preaching and exhorting the people as he leaned on his sword in front of his house. In the course of his preaching, I observed that some people came to him with a dead body together with a person whose hands were tied. "This is your nephew and he has killed your son," they said to Qays.'

The narrator continues: 'By Allah! Qays neither discontinued his speech nor did he get up from his place. Instead, he continued until his speech finished, after which he turned to his nephew and said: "O nephew! You have committed an evil deed, disobeyed your Lord, severed your relationship, used your weapon to your own detriment, and dishonoured the people of your tribe!"

'Then, turning to his other son, he said: "Untie the hands of your cousin, bury your brother, and give your mother, from my property, 100 camels as blood money for the death of your brother, for she comes from a different family."'[1]

4 – Imam al-Ḥasan 🌸 and the Syrian

One day, Imam al-Ḥasan 🌸 was sitting in his place when he was confronted by a man who had come from Syria. As soon as the man set his eyes upon the Imam, he began to curse and revile him; but the Imam remained silent until he had completed his outburst.

When he had stopped, the Imam turned towards him, greeted him, smiled, and then said: 'Brother! You seem to be a stranger here and you have apparently made a mistake. If you want me to disregard your behaviour and forgive you, I shall do so; if you seek something from me, I shall grant it to you; if you want me to guide you, I shall do so; if you are hungry, I shall feed you; if you are in need of clothes, I shall provide them to you; if you are needy, I shall give you all that you need; if you have been

---

[1] *Payghambar Wa Yārān*, vol. 5, p. 180; *Asad al-Ghābbah*, vol. 4, p. 229.

expelled, I shall grant you shelter, and if you have a desire, I shall fulfil it for you. If you can be my guest for the duration of your stay here it would be to your benefit, since my house is large and contains all amenities.'

Hearing these words of Imam al-Ḥasan ﷺ the man burst into tears and said: 'I bear witness that you are Allah's caliph upon the earth and Allah knows best where He places His message and caliphate. Before this meeting of ours I regarded you and your father as my greatest enemies amongst the people, but now you are the most beloved of them all for me.'

The man stayed with Imam al-Ḥasan ﷺ as his guest for the entire duration of his stay in Medina, and eventually became one of the sincere followers of the Ahl al-Bayt.[1]

5 – Shaykh Jaʿfar Kāshif al-Ghiṭāʾ

Shaykh Kāshif al-Ghiṭāʾ was one of those illustrious scholars known to possess a high degree of forbearance.

One day, the Shaykh distributed some money amongst the impoverished people of the city of Isfahan after which he began to lead the congregational prayers. Between the two prayers, when the people were engaged in reciting their supplications, a poor sayyid entered the mosque, stood before the Shaykh, and shouted rudely: 'O Shaykh! Hand over the money of my grandfather [i.e. *khums*] to me.'

'You have arrived late; unfortunately, I have nothing left with me,' the Shaykh replied.

The sayyid, with great impertinence, spat on his beard!

Instead of reacting violently, the Shaykh spread out his cloak and began to walk amidst the rows of people, saying: 'Whoever loves and respects the Shaykh's beard, should help this sayyid.' The people, having witnessed what had transpired between the two, immediately obeyed, and very soon the Shaykh's cloak was filled with money. He handed all the money to the sayyid and proceeded to lead the congregation for the *ʿaṣr* prayers.[2]

---

[1] *Muntahā al-Aʿmāl*, vol. 1, p. 222.

[2] *Sīmā-yi Farzānigān*, p. 338; *Fawāʾid al-Raḍawiyyah*, p. 74.

35. Modesty

Allah, the Wise, has said:

$$إِنَّ ذَلِكُمْ كَانَ يُؤْذِي النَّبِيَّ فَيَسْتَحْيِي مِنْكُمْ وَاللهُ لَا يَسْتَحْيِي مِنَ الْحَقِّ$$

Indeed such conduct torments the Prophet, and he is ashamed of [asking] you [to leave]; but Allah is not ashamed of [expressing] the truth. (33:53)

The Holy Prophet said:

$$الْحَيَاءُ خَيْرٌ كُلُّهُ$$

Modesty is good in its entirety.[1]

Short explanation

Modesty is a luminosity, the essence of which is faith, and therefore modesty stems from faith and ought to be strengthened by means of it.

A person who possesses modesty enjoys every kind of goodness – restraining himself in the face of every repugnant and impure act – but one who lacks modesty and shame acquires every kind of evil, although he may appear to engage himself in acts of worship. A person who lacks this virtue shall be left deprived of God's mercy and will be afflicted with the punishment of the Hereafter. Modesty, in the initial stage, transforms into fear of Allah, while in the final stage, into perception of Allah.

A person in possession of this virtue is heedful of Allah, distant from sins and disobediences, and cloaked with honour and love.[2]

1 – Prophet Mūsā ﷺ and the daughters of Prophet Shuʿayb ﷺ

When Prophet Mūsā ﷺ killed the person from Qibt, the followers of Firʿawn schemed to have him murdered, and so he fled from Egypt. After travelling for between three and eight days and enduring great troubles, he reached the city of Madyan, where he stretched out to rest under a tree which was situated near a well.

He realised that there were two ladies standing near the well waiting

---

[1] *Jāmiʿ al-Saʿādāt*, vol. 2, p. 385.

[2] *Tadhkirat al-Ḥaqāʾiq*, p. 93.

for the shepherds to finish drawing water so they too could draw water from the well. He went to them and offered to help by drawing the water for them. As a result of his help, the women brought the water home sooner than usual and this prompted their father, Prophet Shuʿayb ﷺ, to enquire: 'How did you manage to bring the water sooner than usual today?' They narrated to him the entire episode, whereupon Prophet Shuʿayb ﷺ said: 'Go to the man and bring him to me that I may reward him for his act.'

The ladies approached Prophet Mūsā ﷺ. As soon as they conveyed their father's message to him, he immediately agreed, as he was hungry, tired, and a stranger in the place. The maidens led the way while Prophet Mūsā ﷺ followed them, but as they walked, the outlines of their bodies became visible and this appeared unsuitable to Prophet Mūsā's ﷺ modesty. Consequently, he said to them: 'I shall lead the way while you follow behind me; correct me if you find me heading in the wrong direction (or throw pebbles before me so that I know where to go) for we, the children of Yaʿqūb, do not look at the backs of women.'

When the ladies approached Prophet Shuʿayb ﷺ and related the incident to him, he gave his daughter in marriage to Prophet Mūsā ﷺ, owing to the latter's assistance, modesty, purity, trustworthiness, and physical strength.[1]

2 – The modesty of the eyes

It has been related in the commentary *Rūḥ al-Bayān* that there lived three brothers in a particular city. The eldest brother had been the muezzin of the mosque in the city and used to recite the *adhān* from the top of its minaret. After extending his services for ten years he died, and the second brother took over this task. A few years later this brother died too, and so the people approached the third brother and urged him to accept this responsibility and not to let the sound of *adhān* be terminated, but he flatly refused. 'We shall give you a large amount of money!' they said to him.

He replied: 'Even if you were to give me a hundred times more, I would

---

[1] *Tārīkh-i Anbiyāʾ*, vol. 2, pp. 65-71.

not accept this task.'

'Is the recitation of *adhān* an evil act?' they asked him.

'No, but I shall not recite it from the top of the minaret.' When they sought to know the reason for his refusal, he said: 'This minaret is a place that has caused my two wretched brothers to die without faith. I was near my eldest brother when he was breathing his last and I desired to recite Sūrah Yāsīn to ease the agony of his death, but he prohibited me from reciting it.

'The second brother too departed from the world in the same manner. In order to know the reason for this problem, Allah graced me and I saw my eldest brother in my dream, in a state of chastisement. I said to him: "I shall not leave you until you tell me what caused both of you to die without faith?" He said: "Whenever we ascended the minaret we would look at the womenfolk in the people's houses, without shame and modesty. This act of ours used to engage our hearts and occupy our thoughts leaving us neglectful and heedless of Allah, and this is what has caused us to become wretched and has earned for us an evil Hereafter."'[1]

3 – Zulaykhā

When Zulaykhā followed Prophet Yūsuf ﷺ to gratify herself and proposed to commit a sin with him, Prophet Yūsuf ﷺ suddenly observed that she had covered something with a piece of cloth. 'What did you do?' he asked her.

'I have covered the face of the idol so that it does not watch me while I commit this sin,' she replied.

Hearing this, Prophet Yūsuf ﷺ said: 'If you exhibit shyness and modesty before a stone that does not see, it is more befitting for me to exhibit shame and modesty before the one who sees and who is aware of what is manifest about me and what is concealed within me.'[2]

---

[1] *Riwāyat-hā Wa Ḥikāyat-hā*, p. 105; *Dāstān-hā-yi Parākandih*, vol. 1, p. 123.

[2] *Namūnah-i Ma'ārif*, vol. 4, p. 385; *Baḥr al-Maḥajjah* of Ghazzali, p. 94.

4 – The modesty of the Commander of the Faithful

The marriage formula between Imam ʿAlī 🕮 and Lady Zahrāʾ 🕮 had been recited in the year 2 AH, but the wedding ceremony took place only later (after one month or one year, as per varying reports).

During this period, Imam ʿAlī 🕮, out of shyness, would not utter the name of Lady Fāṭimah 🕮 and she behaved likewise. This continued until one day the wives of the Holy Prophet approached Imam ʿAlī 🕮 and asked: 'Why do you delay the wedding ceremony? If you experience a feeling of shyness and timidity, permit us to speak to the Noble Prophet 🕮 about it.' Imam ʿAlī 🕮 granted them permission.

En masse, they arrived in the presence of the Holy Prophet. 'O Prophet of Allah!' they said. 'Had Khadījah been alive, Fāṭimah's wedding ceremony would have left her overjoyed and Fāṭimah herself would be happy to set her eyes upon her husband. ʿAlī also awaits his wife and we look forward to this joyous occasion.'

Hearing Khadījah's name, tears welled up in the Holy Prophet's eyes. With a sigh, he said: 'Where is there the like of Khadījah ...?' And then added: 'But why did ʿAlī not approach me directly for this?'

The wives replied: 'His modesty restrained him from doing so.'

Hearing this, the Holy Prophet directed them to make preparations for the wedding ceremony.[1]

36. Fear

Allah, the Wise, has said:

$$\text{وَادْعُوهُ خَوْفًا وَطَمَعًا}$$

And supplicate Him with fear and hope. (7:56)

The Holy Prophet said:

$$\text{أَتَمُّكُمْ عَقْلًا أَشَدُّكُمْ خَوْفًا}$$

The most perfect and complete from amongst you in intellect is the one

---

[1] *Fāṭimah al-Zahrāʾ*, p. 283.

who is most fearful amongst you [of Allah].[1]

Short explanation

Fear of Allah is the sentinel of the heart; this is because a fearful person, by means of fear, remains mindful of divine pleasure and soars to lofty heights. He witnesses the divine threats and warnings and thus refrains from deeds that are dictated by his carnal and base desires.

A person who worships Allah out of His fear never gets deviated and eventually reaches his goal and objective. How can he afford not to be fearful especially since he does not possess knowledge of what his final outcome would be, and is unaware if his book of deeds would be light or heavy?

A fearful person finds himself torn between two fears – fear of the past and fear of the future. Fear serves to suppress one's soul and when a person's soul is suppressed with respect to carnal and capricious desires, his heart comes to life. This leads to steadfastness, which eventually prepares the ground for the heart to develop hope and become hopeful of divine mercy.[2]

1 – The fearful youth

Salmān Fārsī was passing through the blacksmiths' market of Kufa when he observed that a crowd had gathered around a youth who lay on the ground, senseless. When the people saw Salmān, they requested him to recite a supplication so that the youth could come out of his unconsciousness.

As soon as Salmān came closer, the youth got up and said: 'There is nothing wrong with me. It is just that I was passing through this market when I noticed the blacksmiths striking metal with their iron hammers and this made me recall what Allah has said in the Qur'an: And there will be clubs of iron for them [22:21]. As this verse crossed my mind, I was overcome by this state.'

Salmān became interested in the youth, grew fond of him, and made

---

[1] *Jāmiʿ al-Saʿādāt*, vol. 1, p. 225.

[2] *Tadhkirat al-Ḥaqāʾiq*, p. 83.

him his brother. They were always friends with each other until one day the youth fell ill and was on the verge of dying. Salmān sat down near his head and then, addressing 'Izrā'īl, said: 'O 'Izrā'īl! Be tolerant and lenient towards my young brother and be kind and gentle to him!'

'O servant of Allah! I am the friend of all the believers and kind to them all,' 'Izrā'īl replied.[1]

2 – The mute language of the stone

It has been reported that once, in the course of his journey, one of the prophets came across a small stone and observed that a large quantity of water flowed out from it. As the incident left him greatly astonished, Allah made speech come out from the stone, which said: 'Ever since I heard that men and stones would be the fuel of the fire of hell I have been in a state of weeping [out of fear that I should be one of those stones].'

The stone then requested the prophet to pray that it should remain protected from the fire [of hell] and the prophet, acceding to his request, prayed for it.

It so happened that after a period the prophet again passed by that place and, witnessing that the water still continued to flow from the stone as before, enquired: 'What is it that makes you weep now?'

The stone replied: 'Before I could be satisfied of my deliverance from the fire [of hell], my tears were out of fear, but now, I weep out of thanksgiving and joy and happiness.'[2]

3 – Punishment by fire

Once, the Commander of the Faithful was in the company of his companions when a person approached him and said: 'O Commander of the Faithful! Purify me for I have committed sodomy with a boy.'

'Go home for you appear to have been affected by bile or melancholia,' advised the Imam.

---

[1] *Dāstān-i Jawānān*, p. 94.

[2] *Shanīdanī-hā-yi Tārīkh*, p. 388; *al-Maḥajjah al-Bayḍā'*, vol. 7, p. 142.

The next day the person turned up again and confessed to his dirty act but the Imam repeated what he had previously stated. The third day he confessed once more and again Imam 'Alī ﷺ repeated his earlier advice. When the man arrived on the fourth day and confessed to his crime, the Imam said: 'Now that you have confessed four times, choose one of the three punishments which the Noble Prophet ﷺ has stipulated for this act: to be beheaded by means of a sword, to be hurled down from a height, or to be burned with your hands and feet tied.'

'Which of these three punishments would be the most severe for me?' the man asked.

'Burning by fire.'

'O 'Alī, I choose this punishment.'

The Imam told him to prepare for it. The man got up, offered a two-unit prayer and supplicated: 'O Lord! I have committed sin and You are aware of it. Fearing Your wrath, I have approached the successor and the cousin of the Noble Prophet ﷺ and have asked him to purify me of it. He asked me to choose one of the three punishments and I have chosen the most severe one. O Lord! I plead to You by Your mercy to make my burning in this world an expiation for my sin and not to burn me in the Hereafter!' Having said this, he got up, began to weep, and then hurled himself into the pit of roaring flames.

The Imam began to weep when he saw this and so did his companions; then he said in a loud voice: 'O man! Rise from within the fire for you have caused the angels to weep. Allah has accepted your repentance. Rise and henceforth do not conduct such an act!'

It is reported in another tradition that a person asked Imam 'Alī ﷺ: 'O Commander of the Faithful! Do you invalidate the punishment of Allah?'

Imam 'Alī ﷺ replied: 'Woe unto you! Whenever there exists an Imam appointed by Allah and a sinner repents for his sin, it is upon Allah to forgive him.'[1]

---

[1] *Dāstān-hā-yi Zindagī-yi 'Alī*, p. 51; *Qaḍāwat-hā-yi Muḥayyir al-ʿUqūl.*

4 – The fearful ones

'And indeed hell is the tryst of them all. It has seven gates, and to each gate belongs a separate portion of them.' (15:43-44)

When these verses were revealed to the Holy Prophet, he wept so intensely that it made his companions weep as well, but none knew what it was that Jibrīl had revealed which had made the Holy Prophet wail in such a fashion.

One of the companions went to Lady Fāṭimah 🏵 and informed her of the incident. Covering herself with her cloak, which was patched in twelve places by means of date palm leaves, she came out of the house. When Salmān Fārsī's eyes fell upon the cloak he looked at it in amazement and then, bursting into tears, said to himself: 'The emperors of Rome and Iran attire themselves in silken and gold-embroidered clothes but the daughter of the Noble Prophet 🏵 covers herself with such a cloak!'

When Lady Fāṭimah 🏵 came to the Holy Prophet, he said to Salmān: 'My daughter belongs to a group that has taken great precedence in subservience and obedience [to Allah].'

Lady Fāṭimah 🏵 then asked: 'Father! What was it that made you grieve?'

The Holy Prophet recited the verses that had been brought by Jibrīl. The mention of hell and the punishment of the fire left her so distraught that her knees failed to hold her weight and she collapsed onto the floor, saying: 'Woe unto he who enters the fire.'

'O I wish I had been a sheep that was eaten and my skin had been torn apart so that I would never have had to hear of the fire of hell,' uttered Salmān.

'O I wish my mother had never given birth to me so that I would never have heard of the hell-fire,' said Abū Dharr.

'I wish I was a bird in the desert so that I would not have had reckoning nor punishment, and would not have heard of the fire of hell,' muttered Miqdād.

The Commander of the Faithful said: 'I wish the wild animals had torn me into pieces and my mother had not given birth to me so that I would not have had to hear of the hell-fire.' Then, placing his hand upon his head, he began to cry and wailed: 'Oh, how distant is the journey of the Day of Judgement! Woe to those who did not make provision for the Day of Judgement. In this journey of the Day of Judgement they shall be led towards the fire; oh the sick ones who shall be in the binds of captivity and whose injuries shall never be treated! None shall step forward to untie them; fire shall be their food and water, and they shall be turned upside down in the various stations of hell.'[1]

5 – Prophet Yaḥyā

When Prophet Yaḥyā observed the clerics of Bayt al-Maqdas [in Jerusalem] wearing veils made of haircloth and headgears of cotton, he requested his mother to make a similar dress for him. Later, he began worshipping with them in Bayt al-Maqdas.

One day, Prophet Yaḥyā looked at his body, which had become considerably thin, and began to weep. Allah revealed to him: 'You cry over your body that has thinned down? By My glory and majesty! Had you possessed the slightest knowledge of the fire [of hell], you would have worn overcoats made of iron, not these woven clothes.' Hearing this, Prophet Yaḥyā wept to such an extent that the flesh of his cheeks became worn out.

Prophet Zakariyyā said to his son: 'I had sought you from Allah so that you could be the apple of my eyes. Why do you behave in such a manner?'

'Father, but was it not you who had said: "Surely, between paradise and hell there lies a pass and none except those who cry immensely due to fear of Allah shall be able to traverse it,"' Prophet Yaḥyā replied.

'Yes, I did!' admitted Prophet Zakariyyā.

Whenever Prophet Zakariyyā intended to preach and exhort the Banī Isrā'īl, he would first look around him, and if he noticed Prophet

---

[1] *Pand-i Tārīkh*, vol. 4, p. 221; *Biḥār al-Anwār*, vol. 10, p. 26.

Yaḥyā 🕮 amongst them, he would refrain from mentioning anything about paradise and hell. Once, Prophet Zakariyyā 🕮 was engaged in delivering a sermon to the people when Prophet Yaḥyā 🕮, his head covered with his cloak, arrived and sat down amongst the people. Prophet Zakariyyā 🕮, who had not noticed Prophet Yaḥyā 🕮, preached: 'Allah has said: "In hell there is a mountain by the name of Sakarān alongside which there lies a desert by the name of Ghadhabān, in which there is a well whose depth is equivalent to 100 years of travel. Within this well there exist caskets of fire, and within these caskets lie chests of fire, which in turn contain clothes and chains of fire."'

As soon as Prophet Yaḥyā 🕮 heard the name 'Sakarān', he raised his head, shrieked, and in a state of utter distress and disturbance, rushed out and headed towards the wilderness.

Prophet Zakariyyā 🕮 and Prophet Yaḥyā's 🕮 mother set off in search of him; some of the youths of Banī Isrā'īl, out of respect for Prophet Yaḥyā's 🕮 mother, joined them in their search. They came across a shepherd and asked him if he had seen a youth with Prophet Yaḥyā's 🕮 description. 'Are you looking for Yaḥyā ibn Zakariyyā?' enquired the shepherd.

'Yes,' they replied.

'He is presently in a particular place with his feet in the water and his eyes glued towards the heavens, praying and communicating with his Lord,' he explained.

The search party went to that place and located him. Calling Prophet Yaḥyā 🕮 towards herself, his mother placed him under the oath of Allah and requested him to return home. Soon, Prophet Yaḥyā 🕮 returned home with his mother.[1]

37. Treachery

Allah, the Wise, has said:

$$\text{إِنَّ اللَّهَ لَا يُحِبُّ مَنْ كَانَ خَوَّانًا أَثِيمًا}$$

---

[1] *Risālah Liqā' Allāh*, pp. 157-164; *al-Amālī* of Shaykh Ṣadūq.

Indeed Allah does not like someone who is treacherous and sinful. (4:107)

Imam al-Ṣādiq ﷺ said:

$$\text{لَيْسَ لَكَ أَنْ تَأْتَمِنَ الْخَائِنَ}$$

It is not for you to trust a treacherous person.[1]

Short explanation

If a thing such as money, a business, a car, or the like is placed as trust in one's possession, one should not be unfaithful to it, spoil or disfigure it, or deny having received it as a trust.

A person with this vice does not have credibility in the eyes of Allah nor in the eyes of the people. He drops down from the level of faith and the reaction of his deed rebounds – affecting him, his wealth, and his family in a detrimental way.

It has been strongly advised that one should not be deceived by a person's prayers and fasts – for it is possible that the person may have simply become fond of performing these acts – instead, one should test a person for truthfulness and faithfulness with respect to trusts.

One should never place a trust in the possession of an unfaithful person. Lending money or giving one's daughter in marriage to a treacherous person is disapproved, and if one does so and then happens to suffer loss or harm, it is only himself that he should censure and rebuke.

1 – The treacherous minister

During his reign, Gushtasp had a minister by the name of Rāst Rawshan.[2] As a result of this prestigious name, Gushtasp held him in high esteem and favoured him over the other ministers.

This minister exhorted Gushtasp into oppressing the subjects and confiscating their property in the belief that the orderliness of the kingdom's affairs was dependent upon the treasury, and that the subjects ought to be poor in order that they remained subservient and obedient. He

---

[1] *Biḥār al-Anwār*, vol. 78, p. 248.

[2] Literally, 'a truthful worker'.

himself had not only accumulated a lot of wealth but had come to harbour animosity towards Gushtasp.

One day, when Gushtasp came to the treasury, he realised that there was no money to pay his workers. Furthermore, his cities were falling into ruin and the people were in distress. This left Gushtasp in a state of bewilderment.

Out of sheer despair, he climbed onto his horse and set off into the wilderness. As he wandered, his eyes fell upon a flock of sheep in the distance. When he came nearer, he observed that the sheep were sleeping while a dog lay suspended from the gallows. In astonishment, he asked the shepherd the reason for killing the dog. The shepherd replied: 'This dog was a loyal animal; I nurtured him and trusted him to protect the sheep. After a period, he came in contact with a she-wolf and both became friends. When night fell, the she-wolf would take hold of a sheep, eat half of it, and leave the other half for the dog. One day, I noticed a decrease in the number of sheep, and after investigation I came to know of the dog's treachery. Therefore, I hung him on the gallows so that it is known that the consequence of treachery and evil is torture and punishment!'

Hearing this, Gushtasp thought to himself: 'My subjects are like these sheep and I am like the shepherd; I must investigate and study the condition of the people so that I know the cause for their deplorable state.'

He returned to his court and asked for the list of prisoners who were in his prisons. Studying the list, he concluded that his minister, Rāst Rawshan, had imprisoned all of them and that he was the cause of all the evils and troubles. He had the minister hanged and admitted to himself that he had been deceived by his name.

Gradually, he made the kingdom prosperous, rectified the past damages, paid attention to the state of the captives, and refrained from trusting anyone ever again.[1]

---

[1] *Jawāmiʿ al-Ḥikāyāt*, p. 313; *Siyāsatnāmih-i Khwājah Niẓām al-Mulk.*

2 – Treachery during *ziyārah*

Al-Ḥājj Ḥasan, the son of Ayatollah al-Ḥājj Ḥusayn Ṭabāṭabāʾī Qummī, relates:

'I had come to Tehran from Mashhad for the treatment of my eyes. During that time one of the traders of Tehran who was known to me had travelled to Khorasan for the *ziyārah* of Imam al-Riḍā 🖼.

'One night, I dreamt that I was in the sanctuary of Imam al-Riḍā 🖼 who was seated on the tomb. Suddenly, I observed that the trader shot an arrow at the Imam 🖼 which greatly troubled him. For the second time, from another direction of the tomb, he let fly another arrow towards the Imam 🖼 and again the Imam 🖼 was deeply troubled. The third time, the trader shot an arrow from behind, but on this occasion the Imam 🖼 collapsed on his back. Shocked and petrified, I woke up from my sleep.

'When my eye treatment was completed, I wished to go back to Khorasan but decided to stay on till the trader returned from Khorasan. When he returned, I spoke to him and asked him certain questions but could not get to the bottom of the matter. Eventually, I narrated my dream to him, whereupon, with tears flowing from his eyes, he explained: "One day, having entered the sanctuary of Imam al-Riḍā 🖼, I noticed that before me stood a lady with her hand placed on the tomb. I placed my hand on hers and so the lady went to the other side of the tomb. I followed her there and once again placed my hand on hers. This time, the lady went behind the tomb. When she had placed her hand upon it, I did exactly the same as before and asked her where she was from. She replied that she was from Tehran; we became friends and returned to Tehran together."'[1]

3 – The daughter's disloyalty towards the father

Satrun, whose title was Dhizan, was the king of Hadhar, a state located between the rivers Tigris and Euphrates. In Hadhar, there was a beautiful palace by the name of Jausaq.

Once, the king attacked a city that was under the control of Shapur;

---

[1] *Rāhnumā-yi Saʿādat*, vol. 1, p. 257; *Jāmiʿ al-Durar*, vol. 1, p. 448.

looting and plundering it, he massacred a great number of its people and eventually occupied it. In the process, he managed to take Shapur's sister as captive.

When Shapur came to know of this he gathered his army and set out towards the king. Dhizan had locked himself inside a strong fort to which Shapur laid siege. This siege continued for a period of four years during which Shapur was unable to penetrate the fort.

One day, Dhizan's daughter, Nadhirah, an extremely beautiful maiden, was strolling outside the fort when Shapur's eyes fell on her. He was instantly captivated by her beauty. He sent word to her that if she helped him conquer the fort he would marry her. During one of the nights, Nadhirah, who had also fallen for Shapur, got the guards of the fort intoxicated and opened its doors to Shapur's forces. In the battle that ensued, her father Dhizan was eventually killed.

In keeping with his promise, Shapur married Nadhirah. One night, he noticed that there was blood on her bed. As he set about to investigate the cause of it, he observed that a strand of thick hair lay on her bed and this had caused her delicate and subtle body to become scratched and injured. 'What did your father feed you with?' he asked her.

'Yolk of eggs, brain of lambs, butter, and honey,' she replied.

When he heard this, Shapur reflected for a while and then said: 'Despite these comforts provided by your father, you were not loyal to him; how can you ever be loyal and faithful to me?'

He ordered that she be tied to a horse's tail and the animal made to gallop through the desert so that the desert thorns become coloured by the blood of this treacherous and unfaithful daughter.[1]

4 – The Indian and the Sixth Imam

Imam al-Kāzim ﷺ narrates:

'One day, I was with my father in the house when a friend entered and told my father that some people were standing outside, waiting to see him.

---

[1] *Namūnah-i Maʿārif*, vol. 5, p. 142; *Mustaṭraf*, vol. 1, p. 210.

My father asked me to find out who they were. As I went outside, I saw numerous camels laden with chests and a man seated on a horse. "Who are you?" I asked the man.

'"I am from India and seek the honour of meeting the Imam ﷺ," he replied.

'I returned to my father and informed him about the man outside. "Don't let this impure and treacherous person enter the house," he instructed, and so I did as I was told.

'The people pitched their tents at that very place near the house and waited for a long time until Yazīd ibn Sulaymān and Muḥammad ibn Sulaymān intervened and procured permission for them to meet my father. When the Indian entered, he sat down before the Imam ﷺ with folded knees and said: "May you have good health! I am from India and the king has sent me with some presents which are to be handed over to you. For several days I have been seeking permission to enter but you have been refusing to meet me. Do the prophets' children conduct themselves in this manner?"

'My father ﷺ lowered his head and answered: "You will come to know the reason for it later." He then asked me to open the letter that the Indian had brought. In the letter, the king of India had extended his greetings. Then he had written: "It is because of you that I have been guided aright. I had been presented with an extremely beautiful slave-girl and I found none, save you, who could be worthy of possessing her; and so, in addition to some clothes, ornaments, and perfumes, I gift her to you. Out of 1000 persons I selected 100, and from them I selected ten, and from the ten I have shortlisted one person, Mīzān ibn Khabbāb, who is trustworthy. I send him to you together with the slave-girl and the presents."

'My father turned to the Indian and said: "O unfaithful person! Turn back, for I shall never accept a trust that has been subjected to unfaithfulness."

'The Indian swore that he had not been unfaithful, however my father told him: "If your clothes were to testify that you had been unfaithful with respect to the slave-girl, would you become a Muslim?"

'"Do forgive me!" implored Mīzān.

'"Then write your deeds to the king of India."

'"If you know something in connection with the issue, you write it down," said Mīzān.

'The man had a sheepskin over his shoulder; the Imam told him to place it on the ground. My father then offered a two-unit prayer after which he went into prostration and supplicated. Then, raising his head, he turned towards the sheepskin and said: "Speak out all that you know about this Indian."

'The sheepskin began to speak as if it were a sheep, and said: "O son of the Prophet of Allah! The king considered this person to be trustworthy and had laid great emphasis with regards to protecting the slave-girl and the gifts. When we had travelled some distance, we reached a desert where heavy rains lashed us. All our belongings had become soaked due to the rain. A short while later the clouds cleared away and the sun began to shine. At that point, this unfaithful person called out to the servant who had been accompanying the slave-girl, and dispatched him towards the city to purchase something. When the servant had gone, he said to the slave-girl: 'Enter into this tent which we have pitched beneath the sun so that your clothes and body may dry.' The slave-girl entered the tent and pulled up her clothes up to her calves. As soon as his eyes fell upon her legs he became mesmerised and persuaded the slave-girl into being unfaithful."

'The Indian, disturbed and distressed upon witnessing this, confessed to his misdemeanour and sought forgiveness. The sheepskin returned to its original state and the Imam ordered him to put it on. As soon as the Indian had placed it over his shoulder it encircled and tightened itself around his neck and the man was almost on the verge of being strangulated when the Imam said: "O sheepskin! Leave him so that he can return to the king who would be the most appropriate person to punish this man for his unfaithfulness."

'The sheepskin reverted back to its original state. The Indian, overcome with fright, implored the Imam to accept the gifts. "If you become a Muslim, I shall gift the slave-girl to you," said the Imam. He declined the offer. The Imam ﷺ then accepted the presents but refused to take the slave-girl, and the man returned to India.

'After a month, a letter arrived from the king of India in which, after extending his greetings, he wrote: "You accepted that which did not have any significant value and rejected that which was valuable. This left me greatly disturbed and I said to myself: 'The children of the prophets possess divine insight and wisdom and it is possible that the person who had escorted the slave-girl may have exhibited unfaithfulness.' And so, I wrote a letter in your name to myself and said to the man that your letter had reached me in which you had mentioned his unfaithfulness. I said to him: 'Nothing except the truth can save you,' whereupon he confessed and related to me the entire episode of his unfaithfulness with regards to the slave-girl and the incident of the sheepskin. The slave-girl also confessed and so I ordered both of them to be beheaded. I bear witness to the unity of Allah and the prophethood of the Noble Prophet ﷺ, and have to state that I shall personally arrive in your presence later."

'Before long, he arrived in Medina after having abdicated his kingship and transformed himself into a true Muslim.'[1]

38. The World

Allah, the Wise, has said:

$$وَمَا الْحَيَاةُ الدُّنْيَا إِلَّا لَعِبٌ وَلَهْوٌ$$

The life of the world is nothing but play and diversion. (6:32)

The Holy Prophet said:

$$مَنْ أَصْبَحَ وَالدُّنْيَا أَكْبَرُ هَمِّهِ فَلَيْسَ مِنَ اللهِ فِـي شَيْءٍ$$

He who rises in the morning whilst his greatest concern is the world, shall have nothing of [the guardianship] of Allah.[2]

---

[1] *Pand-i Tārīkh*, vol. 1, p. 217; *Biḥār al-Anwār*, vol. 11, p. 136.

[2] *Jāmiʿ al-Saʿādāt*, vol. 2, p. 24.

Short explanation

The world is like a figure whose head is pride; its eyes, greed; its ears, covetousness; its tongue, dissimulation; its hands, lust; its legs, vanity; and its heart, heedlessness. Whoever loves the world will be dragged by it towards arrogance and pride; whoever likes the world, will be made greedy by it towards itself; and whoever desires the world, will be hauled by it towards covetousness.

A person who has praised the world has cloaked himself with the garment of dissimulation, one whose goal and objective is this world his heart gets filled with vanity, and one who trusts this world is overcome by negligence and heedlessness [towards Allah] . Consequently, hell shall be the abode of the worldly people.[1]

1 – Esteem and humiliation

Hārūn al-Rashīd, the Abbasid caliph, was very fond of the Barmakī family. They were his close and special companions, generally occupying ministerial posts, and from amongst them he was particularly fond of Jaʿfar Barmakī. This mutual respect and esteem continued for over seventeen years. In 189 AH, due to certain events, the Barmakī family became the object of Hārūn's wrath, and consequently all of them went through very difficult times.

Muḥammad ibn ʿAbd al-Raḥmān Hāshimī narrates:

'On the day of Eid al-Aḍḥā I approached my mother who was having a conversation with a lady dressed in old clothes. "Do you recognise this lady?" my mother asked me. I said I did not. "This is ʿUbādah, the mother of Jaʿfar Barmakī," she said.

'I moved towards ʿUbādah and spoke to her for some time, all the while experiencing astonishment over the state she was in. "O my mother! What have you seen of the wonders of the world?" I asked her.

'ʿUbādah replied: "O son! I have experienced a day of Eid, similar to this day, when I had 400 slave-girls standing before me at my service and

---

[1] *Tadhkirat al-Ḥaqāʾiq*, p. 35.

[yet] I used to complain that my son Jaʿfar had not granted me my right for I should have had more slave-girls serving me. Today is another day of Eid but I am now faced with a situation in which the only things I require are two sheepskins: one for use as a mattress and the other for use as a blanket.'ʾ

Muḥammad Hāshimī continues: 'I gave her 500 dirhams which made her so happy that she almost died of delight. ʿUbādah kept coming to our house periodically, till she eventually passed away.'[1]

2 – Imam ʿAlī  and the public treasury

Shuʿbī narrates:

'Accompanying the other youths, I entered the vast open ground of Kufa where I saw the Commander of the Faithful ﷺ holding a small whip in his hand and standing near two containers filled with gold and silver coins. He used the whip to keep back the huge crowd that had gathered whilst he was distributing the money.

'The Imam ﷺ continued to distribute the money until there was nothing left for himself, and he returned home empty-handed at which point I went home too. I said to my father: "I have witnessed a very strange thing today and I fail to comprehend if this person's act was good or bad, in that he never retained anything for himself!"

'My father enquired as to what I was talking about. I narrated to him all that I had witnessed, whereupon my father, bursting out in tears, said to me: "Son, you have just watched the most excellent person from amongst all the people."'[2]

❖ ❖ ❖

Zadhān reports: 'Qambar and I set off to see the Commander of the Faithful ﷺ. When we reached him, Qambar said: "O Commander of the Faithful! Arise, for I have concealed a significant treasure for you."

---

¹ *Tatimmat al-Muntahā*, p. 181.

² *Al-Ghārāt*, vol. 1, p. 55; *Dastān-hā Az Zindagī-yi ʿAlī*, p. 114.

'"What is the treasure?" enquired the Imam ﷺ.

'"Arise and accompany me in order that I show it to you," insisted Qambar.

'The Imam ﷺ got up and followed him into the house. Qambar brought out a linen bag which was full of small sacs containing gold and silver coins. "O ʿAlī! I know that you distribute everything amongst the people and never retain anything for yourself, and so I have saved this especially for you!" said Qambar.

'Imam ﷺ remarked: "I would have preferred you to set this house on fire and burn down everything." As he said this, he struck the bag with his sword, causing the gold and silver coins to fall out. He then ordered us to distribute the coins among the people. After we had carried out his instructions, the Imam ﷺ said: "Bear witness that I have not taken anything for myself and have not been negligent with respect to the distribution of money amongst the Muslims. O gold and silver! Deceive someone other than ʿAlī."'[1]

3 – Prophet Sulaymān ﷺ

Prophet Sulaymān ibn Dāwūd ﷺ was one of those very few prophets to whom Allah had granted sovereignty over the east and the west of the world. For years he ruled over jinn, men, animals, birds, and wild beasts, and knew the language of all creatures – an authority so great and extensive that it was ineffable. He had prayed to Allah: 'Grant me a kingdom the like of which You shall never grant to anyone after me.'

After Allah had graced and honoured him with such a kingdom, Prophet Sulaymān ﷺ one day said to his servants: 'I have not passed one single day, from morning to night, in a state of happiness. Tomorrow I shall enter my palace, climb onto its roof, and view my subjects. Do not permit anyone to approach me lest my happiness should turn into sadness.'

The next morning, taking hold of his staff, he climbed to the uppermost

---

[1] *Dastān-hā Az Zindagī-yi ʿAlī*, p. 128; *Sharḥ Nahj al-Balāghah* of Ibn Abī al-Ḥadīd, vol. 8, p. 181.

portion of his palace and stood there, leaning upon his staff, observing his kingdom and subjects, and experiencing joy over what Allah had granted him. As he was looking around he suddenly noticed a good-looking youth, dressed in clean clothes, appearing from one corner of his palace.

'Who granted you permission to enter the palace?' he asked the youth.

'The Lord,' replied the youth.

'Who are you?' asked Prophet Sulaymān ﷺ.

''Izrā'īl.'

'Why have you come?'

'To seize your soul, Sulaymān.'

'I had wanted today to be my day of happiness but Allah desired otherwise; comply with the orders given to you,' said Prophet Sulaymān ﷺ.

'Izrā'īl seized his soul while he stood leaning on his staff, while the people, looking at him from afar, thought him to be alive.

When time passed, there arose a controversy amongst the people. Some said: 'It has been several days that he has not eaten or drunk anything and so he is our Allah!' Another group said: 'He is a sorcerer; he has made it appear to us that he stands, whereas, in reality, it is not so.' A third group said: 'He is a prophet of Allah.'

Allah sent an army of ants to eat through his staff; the staff broke and Prophet Sulaymān ﷺ collapsed. It was then that the people realised that he had passed away several days before.[1]

4 – Ṭalḥah and Zubayr's love for the world

Ṭalḥah and Zubayr had been of the foremost during the initial phase of Islam and had extended fitting contributions in the battles. After the death of the Holy Prophet, both of them, and Zubayr in particular, vehemently supported the Commander of the Faithful and never hesitated in offering their assistance to him.

Their support continued until 'Uthmān was murdered and the people

---

[1] *Ḥayāt al-Qulūb*, vol. 1, p. 370.

selected Imam ʿAlī 🖾 as their leader. When this happened, they approached Imam and formally requested him to appoint them as governors of some cities.

However, when they encountered a negative reply from Imam ʿAlī 🖾, they conveyed a harsh message to him through Muḥammad ibn Ṭalḥah, which said: 'We have had to make a lot of sacrifices for the sake of your caliphate, and now that you have the reins of power in your hand you act as a dictator, bringing to the fore the likes of Mālik Ashtar and pushing us into the background?!'

Imam ʿAlī 🖾 sent a message through Muḥammad ibn Ṭalḥah saying: 'What should I do in order that you may be pleased?'

'Appoint one of us as the governor of Basra and the other as the governor of Kufa,' they replied.

'By Allah! When I do not consider them to be trustworthy here in this place [Medina], how can I place them over the people of Basra and Kufa?' asked Imam ʿAlī 🖾. He then instructed Muḥammad ibn Ṭalḥah to go and tell them: 'O shaykhs! Fear Allah and His Prophet with respect to the *ummah* of the Noble Prophet 🖾 and do not oppress the Muslims; have you not heard Allah say: This is the abode of the Hereafter which We shall grant to those who do not desire to domineer in the earth nor to cause corruption, and the outcome will be in favour of the God-wary [28:83]?'

Having failed to realise their ambitions of power and riches, Ṭalḥah and Zubayr decided to go to Mecca. They approached Imam ʿAlī 🖾 to seek his permission to go to Mecca for performing ʿumrah. The Imam told them that they did not really intend to perform the ʿumrah, but they swore that they had no other motive and that they were firm and faithful in their pledge of allegiance.

Upon the Imam's orders they renewed their pledge with him and then set out for Mecca. There, they broke their pledge, raised an army, and in the company of ʿĀʾishah set out towards Basra for the Battle of Jamal. On the way, they met Yaʿlī ibn Munabbah who carried with him approximately 400,000 dinars for Imam ʿAlī 🖾 from Yemen. The two men forcefully took the money from him and utilised it for fighting the Imam.

In this battle (in the year 36 AH), 13,000 soldiers from the army of Ṭalḥah and Zubayr and 5000 soldiers from Imam ‘Alī's 🙶 army were killed. Ṭalḥah was eventually killed by an arrow shot by Marwān, who belonged to his own army. After killing him, Marwān declared: 'I have extracted revenge of ‘Uthmān's blood from Ṭalḥah.'

Zubayr withdrew from the battle and was murdered on the way by Ibn Jurmūz. The consequence of their penchant for power and proclivity towards worldly desires was nothing but an ignominious death.[1]

5 – What he desired and what eventually happened!

On 23 Muḥarram 169 AH, Mahdī the Abbasid died in Masabadhan and the caliphate passed on to his son, Mūsā, titled Hādī, who at that time had gone to Jorjān to fight the people of Tabaristan.[2]

Hārūn al-Rashīd, his brother, took the pledge of allegiance for him from the people of Masabadhan and Baghdad, and sent a message to inform him of the situation. Hādī quickly returned to the capital.

Harthamah ibn A‘yun recounts:

'One night, Hādī the Abbasid summoned me to a private meeting with him. "Do you know how disturbed I am because of this infidel dog, Yaḥyā ibn Khālid? He has turned the people against me and is coaxing them to support Hārūn. You must go to the prison immediately and behead him," he said. "Then proceed to the house of Hārūn and murder him. After this, survey the prison and kill every person from the progeny of Abū Ṭālib. When you have executed these instructions prepare the army and proceed towards Kufa; once there, drive out all the descendants of ‘Abbās from their houses and set their houses on fire."

'Hearing these instructions, a shiver ran through me. "I do not have the strength to carry out these great and difficult tasks," I pleaded.

'"If you exhibit negligence in obeying my orders, I shall kill you," he said, and ordered me to stand where I was whilst he went into the women's

---

[1] *Ḥikāyat-hā-yi Shanīdanī*, vol. 3, p. 20; *Tārīkh-i Ya‘qūbī*, vol. 2, p. 169.

[2] Modern day Mazandaran. (Tr.)

quarters.

'I thought that since I had exhibited aversion towards these acts he would assign them to someone else and then have me killed. I promised to myself that if I were delivered from this predicament I would set off for a place where no one would recognise me. Suddenly, a slave appeared and informed me that Hādī the Abbasid had summoned me. Anticipating death, I testified to the unity of Allah and the prophethood of the Noble Prophet ﷺ and advanced forward. Midway, I heard a lady speak out: "O Harthamah! I am Khayzurān, Hādī's mother. Come and see what calamity has befallen us."

'As I entered the room, Khayzurān, who was behind the curtains, said: "When Hādī entered the house I moved aside the covering from my head and begged pardon for Hārūn, but he refused. At that moment he was suddenly overcome by a fit of severe coughing. He drank some water but it did not help and he died there and then [on 18 Rabīʿ al-Awwal, 170 AH]. Now go and inform Yaḥyā ibn Khālid of his death so that he can take the pledge of allegiance for my son Hārūn."'

Harthamah continues: 'I informed Yaḥyā of Hādī's death and then proceeded towards Hārūn's house where I found him reciting the Holy Qurʾan. I informed him that he had become the caliph but he refused to believe it and so I narrated the entire incident to him. That very night, Hārūn was informed of the birth of his son, Maʾmūn.'[1]

39. Lies

Allah, the Wise, has said:

$$سَمَّاعُونَ لِلْكَذِبِ أَكَّالُونَ لِلسُّحْتِ$$

Eavesdroppers with the aim of [telling] lies, eaters of the unlawful. (5:42)

Imam al-ʿAskarī ﷺ said:

$$جُعِلَتِ الْخَبَائِثُ كُلُّهَا فِي بَيْتٍ وَجُعِلَ مِفْتَاحَهَا الْكَذِبُ$$

---

[1] *Rangārang*, vol. 1, p. 24.

All the evils have been placed in a house, and lies have been made its key.[1]

Short explanation

Speaking untruths – whether trivial or great, in jest or in seriousness – is not permitted, since it has been said: 'All the evils have been placed in a house, and lies have been made its key.' Hence, it becomes very important to abstain from this act.

Since lies refer to unrealities and one who utters lies neither does so for the purpose of exaggerating his point nor for effecting reconciliation between two warring factions, it causes the angels to distance themselves from him. It brings about destruction of his faith, reduction in his livelihood, and humiliation and disgrace in the eyes of the people, to the extent that if untruths are ascribed to Allah and the Holy Prophet in the month of Ramadan, it even results in the invalidation of fasts.[2]

1 – Walīd ibn ʿUqbah

Abū Muʿayṭ Walīd ibn ʿUqbah was a Muslim who initially appeared to be such a righteous individual that the Holy Prophet even assigned him the responsibility of collecting the zakat and alms from the tribe of Banī Muṣṭalaq. When the people of the tribe came to know of the arrival of a representative of the Holy Prophet, they came forward to welcome him.

During the Age of Ignorance there had existed enmity between Walīd and this tribe, and seeing the people come towards him in a large group, Walīd thought that they had prepared themselves to kill him. He quickly turned back and returned to Medina.

He went to the Holy Prophet and told him that the people of the tribe were not willing to pay their zakat, which was not true.

The Holy Prophet was upset to hear this and made up his mind to despatch an army towards the tribe, when Allah revealed the following verse: O you who have faith! If a profligate [person] should bring you some

---

[1] *Jāmiʿ al-Saʿādāt*, vol. 2, p. 323

[2] *Iḥyāʾ al-Qulūb*, p. 151.

news, verify it. (49:6)[1]

After the revelation of this verse, the liar Walīd came to be recognised as a corrupt person. 'He is of the inmates of hell,' the Holy Prophet said about him.

Walīd later teamed up with 'Amr ibn 'Āṣ and the two would consume intoxicants and harboured feelings of animosity towards the Holy Prophet and the Commander of the Faithful.

The Third Caliph, during his caliphate, appointed him the governor of Kufa, and one morning, in a state of intoxication, he led the morning congregational prayers by performing four-units instead of the stipulated two.[2]

2 – Hunger and lies

Asmā' bint 'Umays reported:

'On the night of 'Ā'ishah's marriage with the Noble Prophet ﷺ, a few ladies and I were with her, dressing her up. When we went to the house of the Noble Prophet ﷺ we did not find any food except a single bowl of milk. He drank a little milk from it and then handed it to 'Ā'ishah. Overcome by bashfulness, she did not take it.

'"Do not refuse the Prophet of Allah; take the bowl and drink the milk," I said to her. Shyly, she took the bowl and drank some milk from it.

'"Pass on the bowl to your companions in order that they may drink from it too," the Noble Prophet ﷺ instructed her.

'The ladies who were with us said: "We are not hungry."

'Hearing this, the Noble Prophet ﷺ remarked: "Do not gather hunger and lies together [i.e. why do you lie while at the same time you remain hungry?]."

'"O Prophet of Allah! If we were to possess an appetite for something but we deny having it, would we have uttered a lie?" I enquired.

'"A lie, even if trivial and insignificant, is recorded in the book of

---

[1] *Safīnat al-Biḥār*, vol. 2, p. 361.

[2] Ibid., p. 688.

deeds," stated the Noble Prophet 🌸.'[1]

3 – Zaynab the great liar

During the caliphate of Mutawakkil the Abbasid, a woman claimed that she was Zaynab, the daughter of Lady Fāṭimah al-Zahrā' 🌸. 'Years have passed since the time of Zaynab, but you appear to be young,' said Mutawakkil to her.

'The Noble Prophet 🌸 caressed my head and prayed that every forty years I should become young again!' said the woman.

Mutawakkil called for the elders from the progeny of Abū Ṭālib, 'Abbās, and the Quraysh, and placed the issue before them. All of them unanimously averred that the woman was lying because Zaynab had died in the year 62 AH.

Zaynab, the great liar, retorted: 'They are the ones who lie. I had concealed myself from the people and none knew of my whereabouts until today.'

'You must establish the falsity of her claims by means of proof,' insisted Mutawakkil to the elders.

'Ask Imam al-Hādī 🌸 to prove false her claims,' they advised. Mutawakkil called for the Imam and informed him of the issue.

'She lies, for Zaynab had died in such and such year,' said the Imam.

'Present your evidence to prove false her claim,' Mutawakkil demanded.

The Imam said: 'The flesh of the children of Fāṭimah 🌸 is forbidden upon the wild beasts; send her before the lions if she speaks the truth!'

Mutawakkil turned to the woman for an answer. 'In this way, he desires to kill me,' said the woman.

'A number of people from the progeny of Fāṭimah 🌸 are present here. You can send whoever you desire [before the wild beasts],' responded the Imam.

The narrator states: 'The faces of all the sayyids present in the gathering turned pale. Some said: "Why does he not go himself instead of referring

---

[1] *Shanīdanīhā-yi Tārīkh*, p. 294; *al-Maḥajjah al-Bayḍā'*, vol. 5, p. 249.

to others?"

'Mutawakkil asked the Imam ﷺ why he himself was not going before the lions. The Imam ﷺ instantly agreed to go. Mutawakkil ordered for a ladder, and the Imam ﷺ entered the enclosure where the lions were maintained. The wild beasts, in submission and humility, placed their heads on the ground before the Imam ﷺ and he in turn caressed their heads. A little later he ordered them to move aside and all of them obeyed!

'Mutawakkil's minister advised him: "Ask Imam al-Hādī ﷺ to come out immediately, for if the people witness this miracle all of them would flock to him."

'The ladder was placed and the Imam ﷺ climbed out.

'"Whoever is of the children of Fāṭimah ﷺ should come forward and sit amongst the wild beasts," proclaimed Imam al-Hādī ﷺ.

'The woman confessed: "O Imam! My claims are false. I am the daughter of a certain destitute, and poverty forced me to resort to this deception."

'Mutawakkil ordered his guards to throw the woman to the lions but his mother intervened and interceded for Zaynab who was then pardoned.'[1]

4 – The plain lie of Amīr Ḥusayn

Sultan Ḥusayn Bayqara who ruled over Khorasan and Zabolistan, and Yaʿqūb Mīrzā who ruled over Azerbaijan, were friends who frequently sent letters and gifts to each other.

Once, Sultan Ḥusayn handed over some exquisite and valuable items to a person named Amīr Ḥusayn Abyurdī and instructed him to pick the book *Kulliyāt Jāmī* from the library and present it to Sultan Yaʿqūb Mīrzā along with the other items.

Amīr Ḥusayn approached the librarian and asked for the book, but the librarian erroneously handed him Muhyiddin Arabi's book, *al-Futūḥāt al-Makkiyyah*, which greatly resembled the book *Kulliyāt Jāmī* in size and volume. Amīr Ḥusayn set out for Azerbaijan, and arriving in Yaʿqūb Mīrzā's presence handed him Sultan Ḥusayn's letter and presents.

---

[1] *Muntahā al-Aʿmāl*, vol. 2, p. 368.

After going through the contents of the letter, Yaʿqūb enquired after the health of Sultan Ḥusayn and the other ministers of the sultanate. He then asked about Amīr Ḥusayn's health and with reference to the long, two-month journey that Amīr Ḥusayn had undertaken to reach him, he said: 'You must surely have had a companion to make your journey pleasant.'

'Yes, I had in my possession the book *Kulliyāt Jāmī*, which has been transcribed recently. Throughout the journey I was engaged in reading it and thoroughly enjoyed it,' replied Amīr Ḥusayn.

As soon as Yaʿqūb Mīrzā heard the name of *Kulliyāt Jāmī*, he said: 'I had been desirous of this book and am extremely pleased that you have brought it.' Amīr Ḥusayn sent one of his servants to bring the book, and when it was brought he handed it to Yaʿqūb Mīrzā. When Yaʿqūb Mīrzā opened the book he observed that it was *al-Futūḥāt al-Makkiyyah*. He turned to Amīr Ḥusayn and asked: 'This is not *Kulliyāt Jāmī* – why did you lie?'

Amīr Ḥusayn, embarrassed and ashamed, did not even wait to take the reply of the letter, but immediately set out for Khorasan. 'When my lie had been exposed I wished that I had died,' said Amīr Ḥusayn later on.[1]

40. Theft

Allah, the Wise, has said:

$$\text{وَالسَّارِقُ وَالسَّارِقَةُ فَٱقْطَعُوا أَيْدِيَهُمَا}$$

As for the thief, man or woman, cut off their hands. (5:38)

Imam al-Ṣādiq ﷺ said:

$$\text{إِذَا سَرَقَ السَّارِقُ قُطِعَتْ يَدُهُ وَغُرِمَ مَا أَخَذَ}$$

When a thief commits a theft, his hands are cut and he must indemnify what he has taken.[2]

---

[1] *Khazīnat al-Jawāhir*, p. 640.

[2] *Tafsīr Muʿīn*, p. 114.

Short explanation

Denying the wife her dower, not repaying one's debts, not paying one's obligatory zakat, and so on, are examples of theft, but the meaning that immediately comes to mind upon hearing of theft is 'taking into possession the property and wealth of others, secretly and deceptively', and this is the meaning that is actually intended here.

If there was no security, people would be unable to sleep in peace for fear of thieves. It is for the purpose of establishing and maintaining security that Islam has ordered a thief's fingers to be severed; even if the act happens to be committed by a child, he has to be castigated in some manner so that he desists from committing this evil act in the future.

It is due to the non-implementation of this Qur'anic ruling that an increasing number of thieves are found even in Islamic societies these days.

1 – The Imam and the thief's confession

A person approached Imam 'Alī ☸ and confessed that he had committed a theft. 'Are you able to recite something from the Noble Qur'an?' Imam asked him.

'Yes, I know Sūrat al-Baqarah,' replied the man.

The Imam said: 'I forgive you because of Sūrat al-Baqarah.'

Ash'ath ibn Qays, who happened to witness this, asked the Imam whether he could repeal a punishment that had been stipulated by Allah. 'What do you know? If a person confesses to his crime an Imam has the authority to either punish him or pardon him, but if two persons testify to a person's crime it is not permissible to annul the punishment,' the Imam retorted.[1]

2 – The Bedouin's camel

Shaykh Ṭāwūs al-Ḥaramayn narrates:

'I had been standing near Masjid al-Ḥarām in Mecca when I witnessed a Bedouin advancing on his camel. When he reached the mosque he

---

[1] *Qaḍāwat-hā-yi Amīr al-Mu'minīn*, p. 119.

dismounted, made his camel sit down, tied its two knees, and then, raising his head towards the sky, implored: "O Lord! I entrust unto You this camel and the load that lies upon it." He then entered Masjid al- Ḥarām. When he had performed the *ṭawāf* of the Ka'bah and offered his prayers, he came out of the mosque and found his camel missing. He looked up towards the sky. "It has been said in the holy shariah that property should be sought from one unto whom it has been placed as trust. I had entrusted my camel to You, so return my camel to me," he said.

'Hardly had he uttered these words when I observed that someone emerged from behind the mountain of Abū Qubays with the rein of a camel in the left hand and the right hand severed and suspended from his neck. He came close to the Bedouin. "O youth! Take hold of your camel," he said.

'"Who are you and how did you come to be in this state?" asked the Bedouin.

'"I was impoverished and needy and hence stole your camel," said the stranger. "I went behind the mountain of Abū Qubays when I suddenly noticed a rider coming towards me. As he came closer to me, he shouted out: 'Bring your hand forward.' When I extended my hand, he severed it with a stroke of his sword and, hanging it on my neck, said to me: 'Return this camel to its owner immediately.'"'[1]

3 – Buhlūl and the thief

Whenever Buhlūl happened to have money in excess of his expenses, he would save it by concealing it in one corner of a ruined and broken-down house; this continued until the amount eventually reached a figure of 300 dirhams.

The next occasion when he had saved another ten dirhams and had gone to the place to add it to his concealed savings, a trader who lived in the neighbourhood found out about the hideout. As soon as Buhlūl had left the hiding place, the neighbour dug up the money that was concealed beneath the ground.

---

[1] *Rāhnumā-yi Sa'ādat*, vol. 2, p. 272.

The next time Buhlūl came to the place, he found his money missing and immediately realised that it was the work of the trader. He decided to approach him. 'I wish to trouble you by telling you about my secret,' Buhlūl said to the trader. 'I have placed my money in different places.' Then he began enumerating the places until the entire figure reached 3000 dirhams. 'The place where I have placed 310 dirhams is the safest of them all. I now wish to transfer all my money to this place in the ruined house.' Saying this, he bid the trader goodbye and left.

The trader decided to return the 310 dirhams to the place from where he had stolen the money with the intention that when Buhlūl placed all his money there, he would steal the increased amount. Some days later, Buhlūl returned to the ruins and found the 310 dirhams in its original location. Taking out the money, he defecated there and covered it with earth.

Immediately after Buhlūl had left the trader rushed towards the spot, and, removing the earth, sought to collect the entire money, only to find his hand dirtied by the excrement. He thus comprehended Buhlūl's deception. A few days later Buhlūl visited him. 'I want you to compute some figures associated with my money,' said Buhlūl. 'How much does eighty dirhams added to fifty dirhams added to 100 dirhams, added to the dirty odour that emanates from your hands, sum up to?' Saying this, he took to his heels. The trader rushed after him in hot pursuit but failed to catch him.[1]

4 – The Qur'an-reciting blind thief

'Allām ibn al-Thamān says:

'I was employed by a trader in Basra, when one day I had to undertake a journey to Ablah. I put 500 dirhams in a bag and set out for the journey. I reached the banks of the river Tigris where I hired a boat. As I was passing by the region named Mismār, I noticed a blind person sitting by the riverbank, reciting the Qur'an. In a very sad voice, he called out: "O seaman! Take me in the boat for I fear that the animals might kill me at night." Initially the boatman refused but when I rebuked him, he consented. The blind man sat

---

[1] *Dāstān-hā Wa Pand-hā*, vol. 2, p. 71; *Khazā'in Narāqī*.

in the boat and continually recited the Qur'an from memory till we came near Ablah, whereupon he stopped his recitation and began to disembark from the boat.

'All of a sudden, I realised that the trader's money, which had been given to me in trust, was missing. Both the boatman and the blind person removed their clothes to prove that they had not taken the money. I thought to myself: "The trader is bound to kill me." Thousands of thoughts whirled in my mind and I began to weep and pray.

'As I walked towards Ablah, a man came up to me and sought to know the reason for my lamentations. I informed him of the theft of the trader's money. "I shall show you a way," he said. "Purchase some good food, go to the prison, and plead to the prison warden to let you in. Inside the prison, go to Abū Bakr Naqqāsh and give him the food. He will enquire about your problem, and when he does so, narrate the entire story to him."

'I followed his instructions and when I had narrated my problem to Abū Bakr Naqqāsh, he said: "Now proceed towards the tribe of Banī Hilāl and go to a certain house. Open the door and enter the house. There you will notice some handkerchiefs hanging behind the door. Tie one of them to your waist and sit down in a corner. A group of people will enter and engage themselves in consuming intoxicants; you should pick up a bowl and after calling out, 'For the health of my uncle, Abū Bakr Naqqāsh' begin drinking from it. Upon hearing my name, they will enquire after my health. Pass this message to them: 'Yesterday, my nephew's money was stolen. Hand it back to him,' and they will hand over the money to you."

'I did as instructed and they too, without any protest, handed over the bag of money to me. I requested them to inform me as to how the theft had taken place. After great reluctance, one of them asked me if I recognised him. Looking closely at him, I realised he was the same blind man who had been reciting the Qur'an, while the other person was the boatman.

'"One of our associates swims underwater behind the boat," he explained. "When the Qur'an is recited, the traveller becomes so absorbed that he does not notice that we have thrown his money into the water. It is collected by the associate in the water and carried to the shore, to be distributed amongst ourselves when we gather together the next day. Today was the day for the distribution of the money, but since we have received orders from our chief, Abū Bakr Naqqāsh, we have returned the money to you."

'I took possession of the money and thanked Allah for having been delivered from this quandary.'[1]

41. Supplication

Allah, the Wise, has said:

اُدْعُونِي أَسْتَجِبْ لَكُمْ

Call Me, and I will answer you! (40:60)

Imam ʿAlī said:

اِدْفَعُوا أَمْوَاجَ الْبَلَاءِ عَنْكُمْ بِالدُّعَاءِ قَبْلَ وُرُودِ الْبَلَاءِ

Ward away, by means of supplication, the waves of misfortunes before the arrival of misfortunes.[2]

Short explanation

The etiquette and conditions of supplication ought to be taken into regard and adhered to; the supplicant should carefully consider whom he is invoking and for whom or what purpose he is supplicating.

The best of prayers is that man asks for obedience to Allah, drowning himself in His love, and entrusting all his affairs to Him.

If Allah had not ordered us to supplicate and pray to Him but we nevertheless had done so with sincerity, He, in His generosity, would have surely answered our prayers; accordingly, is it conceivable that the prayers of one who adheres to the etiquette and conditions for supplication which Allah has prescribed, would not be answered?

When one invokes Allah, He either grants him his desire immediately, sets aside for him something better than what he had desired, or wards

---

[1] *Jawāmiʿ al-Ḥikāyāt*, p. 357.

[2] *Biḥār al-Anwār*, vol. 10, p. 99.

away from him a great calamity.[1]

1 – The Supplication of Mashlūl

Imam al-Ḥusayn 🕮 narrates:

'One dark night, my father and I were engaged in the *ṭawāf* of the House of Allah when our attention was drawn towards the sound of weeping and lamentation. My father said to me: "O Ḥusayn! Do you hear the wailings of a sinner who has sought refuge in Allah? Locate him and bring him to me."

'In the darkness of the night I went in search of him; finding him between al-Rukn and al-Maqām, I brought him before my father. He was a young man possessing an elegant stature and dressed in expensive clothes. My father said to him: "Who are you?"

'He replied: "I am an Arab."

'My father enquired: "Why the wailing and lamentation?"

'He said: "Disobedience, sins, and my father's curse have shattered my life and affected my health."

'He asked: "What is your story?"

'The youth said: "I had a father who had become old and had been very loving and considerate towards me; however, I always used to indulge in inappropriate acts. Try as much as he would to guide me, I would not mend my ways and at times I even troubled and inconvenienced him. One day, I intended to take his money which he had kept in his trunk, but coming to know of my scheme he tried to stop me. In the ensuing melee I flung him to the ground; he attempted to rise but failed. I took the money and set about my way, but on the way out I heard him say: 'This year I shall go to the House of Allah and curse you.' For the next few days he engaged himself in prayers and fasts, and then started out for the Holy Ka'bah. I followed him and observed that taking hold of the Ka'bah's curtain, he cursed me. He had hardly finished cursing me when I suddenly found that one side of my body had become numb and paralysed." Having said this, the youth lifted his gown and pointed out his affliction. He then continued: "I repented and

---

[1] *Tadhkirat al-Ḥaqā'iq*, p. 20.

sought his forgiveness. Three years passed by and in the third year, during the season of hajj, he agreed to pray for me. Together, we set off for Mecca and it was night when we reached the valley of Arāk. In the darkness of the night a large bird suddenly took off in flight and startled my father's camel as a result of which my father was hurled to the ground and died. I buried him there but my affliction, due to my father's curse, still persists."

'The Imam ﷺ said: "The supplication recommended by the Noble Prophet ﷺ shall come to your aid. It contains the greatest name [of Allah] and every miserable, sick, or poor person who recites it shall have his desire fulfilled." Giving him the supplication, he ﷺ said: "Recite this supplication on the eve of the tenth of Dhū al-Ḥijjah – the eve of Eid al-Aḍḥā – and come to me the next morning."

'As instructed, the youth approached the Imam ﷺ having been completely cured of his affliction. The Imam ﷺ asked: "How were you cured?"

'He said: "I recited the supplication on the eve of the tenth of Dhū al-Ḥijjah all the while shedding tears of repentance. Having completed the recitation, I was about to recite it for the second time when I heard a voice say: 'O youth! Enough! You have invoked Allah by means of the greatest name.' I fell into a slumber and witnessed the Noble Prophet ﷺ in my dreams. He ﷺ placed his hand upon my body and said: 'You have been cured.' I woke up to find myself cured completely."'

The supplication which Imam 'Alī ﷺ had taught the youth was the Supplication of Mashlūl.

2 – Congregational supplication

Ḥafṣ ibn 'Umar Bajallī relates:

'I once complained to Imam al-Ṣādiq ﷺ about my abject financial condition and the dismal state of life whereupon he ﷺ advised: "When you return to Kufa, take ten dirhams and prepare some food, even if it means you have to sell the pillow upon which you sleep, and invite some of your brethren-in-faith for a meal and request them to pray for you."'

Ḥafṣ said: 'I returned to Kufa and despite all my efforts I was unable to make arrangements for the money. So, in accordance with the instructions of the Imam 🕮, I sold my pillow, prepared some food, invited some believers for a meal, and requested them to pray for the termination of my problems. After eating, they prayed for me. By Allah! Only a short period had passed since the incident when, one day, someone began to knock at my door. Opening the door I saw that the person knocking was one with whom I had previously engaged in trade and who owed me some money. He had come looking for me and handed me a large amount – around ten thousand – thus clearing off his debt to me. From that day on my work began to expand and my state began to improve until I was eventually drawn out of my poverty and relieved of my troubles.'[1]

3 – Repelling calamities

The late Ayatollah al-Ḥājj Shaykh ʿAbd al-Karīm Ḥāʾirī, the founder of the Ḥawzah of Qum, recounts:

'During the time when I was engaged in religious studies in the city of Samarra, an epidemic, in the form of a plague, spread amongst the inhabitants of the city, and several people would die of the disease every day.

'One day, some of the inhabitants of Samarra had gathered in the house of my teacher, the late Sayyid Muḥammad Fishārakī, when Ayatollah Mīrzā Muḥammad Taqī Shīrāzī (d. 1338 AH), who, in terms of knowledge, was at par with the late Sayyid Fishārakī, suddenly arrived. In the course of the conversation the talk drifted towards the issue of the plague that had threatened the lives of all the people. The late Mīrzā said: "If I were to issue an order (ḥukm), would it not be mandatory for it to be executed?" All those present said: "Yes." He said: "I rule that from today onwards, for a period of ten days, the entire Shiʿa community of Samarra should recite Ziyārah ʿĀshūrāʾ and gift the rewards of this recitation to Lady Narjis 🕮 – the mother of Imam al-Mahdī 🕮 – in order that this calamity is repelled

---

[1] *Bā Mardūm Īn Gūnih Barkhūrd Kunīm*, p. 107.

from them."

'Those present in the gathering informed the other Shi'as of this ruling and all of them engaged themselves in reciting Ziyārah 'Āshūrā'.

'The following days onward, it was observed that none of the Shi'as would die due to the disease, whereas the non-Shi'as continued to suffer deaths; and this became plainly manifest for all the inhabitants of the city, such that some of the non-Shi'as would question their Shi'as friends: "How is it that our people die due to the disease, whereas there are no deaths on your side?"

'The Shi'as would answer: "All of us recite Ziyārah 'Āshūrā' of Imam al-Ḥusayn 🕮 in order to remain protected from the epidemic and Allah wards away the calamity from us!"'[1]

4 – Supplicating for rain

Once, during the time of Prophet Dāwūd 🕮, a famine struck. The people selected three of their scholars who proceeded to go outside the city to pray for rain. The first of them pleaded: 'O Lord! You have ordered us to forgive one who has done injustice to us; we have done injustice to our own selves so forgive us.'

The second one implored: 'O Lord! You have instructed us to set free the slaves; we are Your slaves so set us free.'

The third of them supplicated: 'O Lord! In Your Torah you have commanded us not to drive away the poor and the unfortunate ones; we are the poor ones who now stand at Your door, so do not keep us deprived.'

The supplications of these sincere and practicing scholars had hardly finished when Allah sent down rain over the people.[2]

5 – Supplication for the dead

When Bāhiyah, a pious lady, was about to die, she raised her head towards the heaven and prayed: 'O the Lord who is my treasure! I place my trust

---

[1] *Dāstān-hā-yi Shigift*, p. 323.

[2] *Shanīdanī-hā-yi Tārīkh*, p. 22; *al-Maḥajjah al-Bayḍā'*, vol. 2, p. 299.

in You; do not abandon me at the time of death and deliver me from the terror of the grave.'

After she died her son used to visit her grave every Thursday night and Friday morning; he would recite Qur'an and supplications, and seek forgiveness for his mother and the other inmates of the cemetery.

One night, witnessing his mother in his dream, the youth greeted her and asked: 'How are you?'

She said: 'O my son! The intensity of death is indescribable, but praise be to Allah for I have been granted a beautiful place in *barzakh*.'

The youth asked: 'Mother, do you have any desire?'

She said: 'Yes, my son. Always continue to recite the Noble Qur'an, supplications, and *ziyārāt* for me. I am pleased when you visit me on Thursday nights and Friday mornings. When you come, the other deceased ones say to me: "Bāhiyah, your son has come." This good news makes me and the other inmates around my grave happy.'

The youth continued to recite the Holy Qur'an and supplications for his mother and the others, when one night he witnessed in his dreams that a large group had approached him. He asked them: 'Who are you?'

They replied: 'We are the inmates of the cemetery and have come to thank you for reciting the supplications and the Noble Qur'an for us. We request you not to abandon this practice of yours.'[1]

42. Religion

Allah, the Wise, has said:

$$ فَأَقِمْ وَجْهَكَ لِلدِّينِ حَنِيفًا $$

So set your heart on the religion as a people of pure faith. (30:30)

The Holy Prophet said:

$$ الْمُسْتَأْكِلُ بِدِيـنِهِ حَظُّهُ مِنْ دِيـنِهِ مَا يَأْكُلُهُ $$

One, who seeks to fill his stomach by means of religion, his share of

---

[1] *Muntakhab al-Tawārīkh*, p. 849; *Rawḍat al-Rayāḥīn*.

religion is what he fills in his stomach.[1]

Short explanation

Allah grants worldly provisions to His friends as well His enemies. However, He only bestows His religion to His friends, just as He has placed monotheism within the nature of every person, but grants His special religion to those whom He pleases.

One ought to sacrifice one's life and wealth for the religion of Allah and adorn oneself with the insignias of religion, such as truthfulness, steadfastness, faithfulness towards trusts, fulfilment of pledges and covenants, and goodness of behaviour.

1 – Religion has died

Imam ʿAlī ﷺ was passing by a place where a group of children were engaged in play. However, there was one boy who was not playing with them and stood aloof and sad. Imam approached him and asked: 'What is your name?'

He replied: 'Māt al-Dīn (which means 'religion has died').'

The Imam desired to know the reason for such a name and so enquired about the child's father. He was informed that his father had died, but his mother was alive. He called for his mother and enquired about the reason for such a strange name, whereupon the mother said: 'When this child was in my womb, his father had embarked upon a journey. After a period his companions approached me and said: "Your husband fell ill on the way and died, but before his death he requested us that if his child was born, he should be named Māt al-Dīn."'

Having heard this, the Imam comprehended the reason for such a name and ordered all the people to gather in the mosque. When the people had gathered, he said to them: 'Whenever I recite *allāhu akbar*, all of you should recite it in unison as well.'

He then called for the dead person's companions, who were four in number, and subjected them to individual and separate interrogation.

---

[1] *Biḥār al-Anwār*, vol. 78, p. 63.

Turning to the first person, he sought to know how he had killed the boy's father. The man, who was stunned to hear the question, blurted out: 'All I did was present the cord.' The Imam recited *allāhu akbar*, and the people in the mosque chorused.

The second one, in answer to the Imam's question, said: 'My only crime was to tie the cord around his neck.'

The third person said: 'I had brought the knife.'

The fourth person, recounting the incident explicitly, said: 'We collectively murdered him for the purpose of seizing and appropriating his wealth.' The Imam recited *allāhu akbar* and the people recited in unison.

Imam ʿAlī ◈ took possession of the wealth which they had stolen from the deceased and handed it to the boy's mother, and then subjected the killers to a severe punishment. Then, turning to the boy's mother, he said: 'Change his name to ʿĀsha al-Dīn (which means 'religion is alive').'[1]

2 – The religiousness of the learned one from Dezful

At the time of his death, Shaykh Murtaḍā Anṣārī, having become the highest-ranking religious authority with notable popularity and profundity in the methodology and science of Islamic jurisprudence, was not any different from a material point of life from the time when he had first set foot in Najaf as a poor student from Dezful. When people looked at his house they found that he led his life just as the most impoverished ones led theirs. A person once said to him: 'This is an immense work on your part that despite the large sum of money that comes to you, you refuse to use it for yourself.'

He said: 'What great work have I done?'

The man said: 'What work could be greater than what you are doing presently?'

The Shaykh said: 'At the very best my work is similar to the donkey-riders of Kashan who go to Isfahan and then return from there. The

---

[1] *Dāstān-hā Wa Pand-hā*, vol. 10, p. 168; in the book *Tārīkh al-Anbiyāʾ*, vol. 2, p. 215, this judgement has been attributed to Prophet Dāwūd ◈, and a similar one has been ascribed to the Commander of the Faithful.

donkey-riders are given money to travel to Isfahan, purchase goods from there, and bring them back to Kashan. Have you ever seen them exhibiting unfaithfulness and disloyalty with respect to the people's money? They are trustworthy individuals and do not possess any right [over the people's money]. This work of mine is not as important as it appears to you.'[1]

3 – Religion beside the royal throne

During the caliphate of the Second Caliph, Saʿd ibn Waqqās, in the company of a few others, started out for Iran. Yazdgard, the king of Persia who was in the city of Madain at that time, sent a herald to Saʿd inviting some of the people in his caravan to come to his court so that he could become aware of their destination.

They reached his court at a time when he had been busy consuming wine and so he ordered the drinks to be removed. When the group had entered the court, Mughīrah ibn ʿĀmir sat down alongside the king near the royal bed. Witnessing this, Yazdgard, in a state of protest, said: 'You Arabs initially came to our lands for trading and begging, and after you had consumed our tasty food and delicious water you went and informed your friends. Now you return and claim to have brought a new religion. Your example is similar to that of the fox that had entered a garden with the intention of eating the grapes. The owner of the garden allowed him to eat and did not hurt him. The next day the fox brought other foxes along with him and, entering the garden, began eating the grapes. When the owner of the garden arrived and witnessed the scene, he bolted all the exits and killed them all. If I wished I too could behave just like that but I know that you have drawn up your army because of your poverty and straitened livelihood. I shall give you abundant bounties and place over you a commander such that you would lead a life of ease and comfort.'

Mughīrah ibn ʿĀmir said: 'Your statement regarding a difficult livelihood is correct and we too agree that there was a time when we used to eat mice and lizards, could not differentiate the lawful from the unlawful,

---

[1] *Dāstān-hā-yi Ustād*, vol. 2, p. 68; *Sīrah-i Nabawī*, p. 29.

kill our cousins for the sake of one turnip, and even go on to brag about it. But then Allah, by means of His Prophet, sent for us a religion, stopped us from idolatry, guided us towards monotheism, and very soon we shall be targeting your country too. O Yazdgard! I give you the option to choose one out of three things: become a Muslim so that you can continue to rule, pay the *jizyah* tax, or prepare for war.'

Hearing this, Yazdgard was overcome with rage and said: 'Nothing save a sword can exist between you and me.' Having said this, he drove them out of his court. Later, a war ensued between the two forces in which the Muslims emerged victorious.[1]

4 – The religiousness of Abū Ja‘far Ḥusaynī

Abū Ja‘far Muḥammad Ḥusaynī[2] – whose lineage reached Imam al-Ḥusayn 🕮 through four generations – was a jurist and a pious and ascetic person, and had revolted against Mu‘taṣim – the Abbasid caliph – due to his oppression and injustices. Mu‘taṣam sought to crush his revolt and so he fled to Iran and into the cities of Khorasan, Sarakhs, Ṭāliqān, Nis, and Merv, and a great number of Iranians pledged allegiance to him.

In Merv, 40,000 Iranians pledged allegiance to him. One night, when his army had gathered, he heard the sound of weeping. Investigating, he came to know that one of his soldiers had forcefully taken felt from a weaver and it was this weaver who had been weeping. Abū Ja‘far called for the soldier and sought to know the reason for the evil act whereupon the soldier replied: 'We have pledged allegiance to you so that we can loot the people and do as we like.'

Abū Ja‘far returned the felt to its owner and then disbanded his army, saying: 'Assistance for the religion of Allah cannot be sought from such people.' Then, accompanied by his close companions, he left for Ṭāliqān.[3]

---

[1] *Namūnah-i Ma‘ārif,* vol. 5, p. 234; *Bazm-i Īrān,* p. 142.

[2] He was the son of Qāsim ibn ‘Umar ibn ‘Alī ibn Ḥusayn 🕮, while his mother, Ṣafiyyah, was the daughter of Musa ibn ‘Umar ibn ‘Alī ibn Ḥusayn 🕮.

[3] *Tatimmat al-Muntahā,* p. 221.

5 – Religion-selling by Samurah

Samurah ibn Jundab was of the inhabitants of Basra. After his father's death he accompanied his mother to Medina, where she married Ibn Shaybān – a companion of the Holy Prophet – and Samurah grew up under his care. Despite his young age he was an expert archer and the Holy Prophet permitted him to participate in the Battle of Uḥud; later, he participated in the other battles as well.

During the reign of Mu'āwiyah, Samurah, like some of the corrupt and lying companions of the Holy Prophet, began fabricating traditions in praise of Mu'āwiyah and in criticism of the Commander of the Faithful. Mu'āwiyah said to him: 'I shall give you 100,000 dirhams if you ascribe the following verse [which was revealed in criticism of the hypocrites] to 'Alī ibn Abī Ṭālib: Among the people is he whose talk about worldly life impresses you, and he holds Allah witness to what is in his heart, though he is the staunchest of enemies. And if he were to wield authority, he would try to cause corruption in the land, and to ruin the crop and the stock, and Allah does not like corruption [2:204-205]. And ascribe this verse [which was revealed in praise of Imam 'Alī 🕮 after he had slept on the bed of the Holy Prophet during the migration of the Holy Prophet to Medina] to Ibn Muljim: And among the people is he who sells his soul seeking the pleasure of Allah, and Allah is most kind to [His] servants [2:207].'

Initially, Samurah refused the offer and Mu'āwiyah raised the stakes, saying: 'I shall give you 200,000 dirhams.' Once again, Samurah refused. But when Mu'āwiyah offered him 400,000 dirhams, he agreed and then forged traditions ascribing the first verse, which was about the hypocrites, to the Commander of the Faithful, and attributing the second verse, which was for the Commander of the Faithful, to Ibn Muljim, and in this manner proved that he had indeed sold his religion.[1]

---

[1] *Payghambar Wa Yārān*, vol. 3, p. 258; *Sharḥ Nahj al-Balāghah* of Ibn Abī al-Ḥadīd, vol. 1, p. 471.

43. Remembrance Of Allah

Allah, the Wise, has said:

أَلَا بِذِكْرِ اللهِ تَطْمَئِنُّ الْقُلُوبُ

Look! The hearts find rest in Allah's remembrance! (13:28)

Allah said to Prophet Mūsā ﷺ:

لَا تَدَعْ ذِكْرِي عَلَى كُلِّ حَالٍ

Under no circumstance [should you] abandon My remembrance.[1]

Short explanation

Remembering Allah – with concentration and presence of heart – is the ultimate objective of all acts of worship. If one who is engaged in the remembrance of Allah is focussed towards Allah in heart and deeds, he shall come to possess a rank such that Shayṭān would be unable to overcome him and gain dominance over him.

If the tongue were to recite but the heart were to be heedless, the effects and the benefits would be reduced. At the same time if he were to regard his recitations as something very important and significant, he would be overcome by pride and vanity.

Accordingly, it is vital that in addition to remembering Allah a person should regard himself as trivial and insignificant; he should look upon himself as a non-entity before His bounties; he should beseech Him to never, ever make him heedless and negligent of His remembrance, but instead bestow an increase in it.

1 – Remembering Allah when confronting the enemy

The Holy Prophet had started out for a battle and on the way ordered his army to halt. In order to relieve himself he distanced himself from his forces and headed towards a secluded location. In the meantime, it began to rain and it rained so hard that water began to flood, as a result of which the Holy Prophet was cut off from his army.

---

[1] *Biḥār al-Anwār*, vol. 13, p. 342.

Having witnessed the change in weather, he sat beneath a tree when Ḥuwayrith ibn al-Ḥārith happened to see him. Speaking to his companions, he said: 'This man is Muḥammad and he has become isolated from his forces. May God kill me if I do not kill him!' He unsheathed his sword and rushed at him, saying: 'Who is it that can deliver you from me?'

The Holy Prophet said: 'Allah,' and then prayed softly: 'O Lord! Deliver me from the evils of Ḥuwayrith in any manner You please.' Just as Ḥuwayrith was about to inflict his blow, an angel struck him on his shoulder as a result of which he collapsed onto the ground and the sword fell from his grasp. The Holy Prophet picked it up and said to him: 'Who is it that can save you from me?'

Ḥuwayrith said: 'No one.'

The Holy Prophet advised: 'Accept Islam and I shall hand your sword back to you!'

Ḥuwayrith said: 'I shall not accept Islam but I shall pledge that neither shall I fight you and your followers, nor help anyone against you.'

The Holy Prophet returned his sword to him, whereupon Ḥuwayrith said: 'I swear that you are better than me.'[1]

2 – The enamoured one

Saʿdī states:

'Once, it so happened that I had been travelling throughout the night in the company of a group of people. Accompanying us on this journey was a person who was obsessed with Allah and drowned in His love. It was not yet dawn when we reached a jungle where we decided to rest, however, as soon as we arrived, the person uttered a cry, and rushing into the woods immediately engaged himself in supplicating and communicating with his Lord. When it was morning I asked him: "What was that state which overcame you last night?"

'He replied: "Looking into the jungle I witnessed the nightingales on the trees, the partridges on the mountains, the frogs in the water, and the

---

[1] *Dāstān-hā Wa Pand-hā*, vol. 2, p. 67; The Commentary of Abū al-Futūḥ.

various animals in the jungle weeping and lamenting [out of the fear of Allah], and so I thought to myself that it would be contrary to courtesy and civility that while all the other creations were engaged in His glorification, I slept heedless and unmindful of Him."'[1]

3 – The poor ones question the Holy Prophet

Some of the poor persons of Medina approached the Holy Prophet and said to him: 'The affluent ones perform acts of goodness like freeing slaves, giving charity, performing the hajj, etc., which are beyond our means [and therefore they shall be in possession of greater rewards than us].'

The Holy Prophet said: 'One who recites *allāhu akbar* 100 times shall be granted rewards which shall exceed the rewards of freeing 100 slaves; one who recites *Subḥān allāh* 100 times shall come to possess rewards better than the rewards associated with the performance of hajj; reciting *al-ḥamdu lillāh* 100 times is better than giving 100 fully laden horses as charity in the way of Allah; and who recites *lā ilāha ill-allāh* 100 times shall be of the best of the people on the Day of Judgement.'

When the affluent ones of Medina came to know of this they too began to act upon these recommendations, and so the poor ones again approached the Holy Prophet and complained: 'The affluent ones have also started to act upon your recommendations!'

Hearing their complaint, he remarked: 'This is Allah's grace and favour; He grants it to whomsoever He pleases.'[2]

4 – Remembering the beloved while in comfort

Allah had granted immense bounties to Prophet Ayyūb ﷺ such that it has been reported that he possessed 500 pairs of bulls for ploughing his fields and hundreds of slaves who used to cultivate his farms. His cargo-carrying camels were 3000 in number, while his sheep totalled 7000.

In addition to this, Allah had also granted him good health and

---

[1] *Ḥikāyat-hā-yi Gulistān*, p. 127.

[2] *Shanīdanī-hā-yi Tārīkh*, p. 18; *al-Maḥajjah al-Bayḍā'*, vol. 2, p. 274.

numerous children. On his part, Prophet Ayyūb ﷺ perpetually praised and thanked his Lord, and when faced with two acts of obedience he would always choose the more difficult of the two.

But then he became the object of divine trials – not for having committed any sin but rather for raising his rank and status – such that Allah took back all the bounties that He had given him and afflicted his body with an incurable disease.

However, despite the severity of the adversity, when Prophet Ayyūb ﷺ never abandoned thanking, praising, and remembering Allah, Shayṭān got into the act. He began whispering into his wife's mind as a result of which she started to complain of the hard times that had befallen them and would moan: 'Everyone has deserted us and we do not possess anything.'

Prophet Ayyūb ﷺ said: 'For eighty years we had been receiving the bounties of Allah and so we should not complain for seven years of hardships, but instead continue to remember Him in all circumstances!'

But his wife continued to complain and protest, and persistently placed before him irrational ideas, until eventually, enraged, he hollered: 'Go away from me such that I do not set my eyes upon you ever again.'

When his wife had left him, Prophet Ayyūb ﷺ found himself alone and without a caretaker; going into prostration, he began praying to his Lord and communicating with Him. On this occasion Allah answered the prayers of His servant who had continued to praise and thank Him, and once again granted him all the bounties.

Meanwhile, his wife thought to herself: 'Although he has driven me away, it is inappropriate for me to leave him alone. He has none to look after him and he may perish out of hunger.' With this in mind she returned to the place where she had left him but found him missing, while in his place sat a youth.

As she began to weep, the youth asked her: 'Why do you weep?'

She replied: 'I had left my old husband here but I do not see him anymore.'

The youth said: 'If you were to see him, would you recognise him?'

She said: 'Yes.'

Having answered him, she then looked at him hard and realised that he possessed a great resemblance to her husband. The youth then said to her: 'I am the same Ayyūb.'[1]

5 – Nafīsah

Sayyidah Nafīsah, the daughter of Ḥasan ibn Zayd ibn Ḥasan al-Mujtabā ﷺ, married Isḥāq Muʾtamin, the pious and virtuous son of Imam Jaʿfar al-Ṣādiq ﷺ. She was of the rare and distinguished ladies of her time and stood apart from the rest with regards to worship and remembrance of Allah.

Zaynab, her niece, states:

'I had been in the services of my aunt for forty years and throughout this period neither did I ever observe her sleep at night [for she would be engaged in worship] nor eat in the day [for she would be engaged in fasting]. I once said to her: "Would it not be better if you were to ease things upon yourself?"

'She replied: "How can I place myself in ease when I have before me the bottlenecks of *barzakh* and the Day of Judgement which none can cross save the delivered ones!"

'She possessed great wealth which she used to spend on the sick, the bed-ridden, and the impoverished ones for the pleasure of Allah. She had the honour of performing the hajj on thirty occasions – most of her journeys to the House of Allah were accomplished on foot. Once, in the company of her husband, she started out from Medina for Palestine in order to visit the grave of Prophet Ibrāhīm ﷺ, after which she proceeded towards Egypt.

'The inhabitants of Egypt requested her to settle there and she agreed. She dug a grave in her house and perpetually engaged herself in worship and remembrance of Allah, reportedly completing thousands of recitations of the Noble Qur'an in the grave.

'According to Ḥadīth al-Qudsī, when Allah observes that a servant of His continually engages himself in His remembrance, He manifests the person's worth amongst the people and makes him respected and revered.

---

[1] *Tārīkh-i Anbiyā'*, vol. 2, p. 20.

'In the neighbourhood of Nafīsah there lived a Jew who had a daughter who was blind. By means of the water of Nafīsah's *wuḍū'*, the Jew's daughter regained her sight and this prompted numerous Jews of Egypt to accept Islam.

'One day, whilst fasting, as she recited Sūrat al-Anʿām of the Noble Qur'an, upon reciting the verse: For them shall be the abode of peace near their Lord, her soul departed from her body. The people wanted her to be buried in Egypt, but her husband, desiring to take her to Medina, refused. At night the Holy Prophet appeared to him in his dream and said: "Do not oppose the people of Egypt in connection with Nafīsah's burial since Allah shall descend His mercy upon them as a result of her blessed presence there."'[1]

44. Sustenance

Allah, the Wise, has said:

$$\text{وَمَا مِنْ دَابَّةٍ فِي الْأَرْضِ إِلَّا عَلَى اللهِ رِزْقُهَا}$$

There is no animal on the earth, but that its sustenance lies with Allah.

(11:6)

The Holy Prophet said:

$$\text{الرِّزْقُ يَطْلُبُ الْعَبْدَ أَشَدَّ طَلَبًا مِنْ أَجَلِهِ}$$

Sustenance seeks a person more intensely than his death does.[2]

Short explanation

There exists no creature except that Allah has apportioned a livelihood for it, and no soul departs from the world before it has consumed the last morsel that had been ordained for it. One should strive to procure lawful sustenance and, in the event of delay and stoppages in this path, desist from attempting to obtain it by unlawful means; the best approach being

---

[1] *Shāgirdān-i Maktab-i Aʼimmah*, p. 168.

[2] *Jāmiʿ al-Akhbār*, p. 126.

that of patience and self-control.

Every person has his sustenance placed in a particular thing: one has his sustenance placed in trade, while another has it in leadership, while yet another in farming, etc. Absence of satisfaction with respect to the share allotted and lack of contentment, strengthens the vices of greed and covetousness within man leading him towards sins in order to procure an increased sustenance – a state that only stems from a lack of trust in Allah.

1 – They should witness the wisdom!

Prophet Mūsā ﷺ came across a poor person who, due to his abject poverty, lay bare-bodied on the desert sand. When he came nearer, the person requested: 'O Mūsā! Pray to Allah that he grants me a little sustenance for I am on the verge of dying.' Prophet Mūsā ﷺ prayed for him and then proceeded from there to Mount Sinai to converse with Allah.

A few days later, Prophet Mūsā ﷺ, on his return, happened to pass by that very place when he witnessed that the same poor man had been arrested and a large crowd had gathered around him. He enquired: 'What has happened?'

The people present there said: 'Until recently he was penniless, but of late he had managed to acquire some money; having consumed wine, he got involved in a brawl and killed a person. He has now been arrested so that he can be subjected to retributory punishment and put to death!'

Allah says in the Holy Qur'an:

Were Allah to expand the provision for His servants, they would surely create havoc on the earth. (42:27)

Prophet Mūsā ﷺ acknowledged the divine wisdom and, expressing repentance over his request, sought Allah's forgiveness.[1]

2 – Incorrect deduction from the Qur'an

'Umar ibn Muslim was one of the companions of Imam al-Ṣādiq ﷺ and used to visit him frequently.

---

[1] *Ḥikāyat-hā-yi Gulistān*, p. 161.

Once, when he did not visit the Imam for a long time, the Imam enquired about him from 'Alī ibn 'Abd al-'Azīz, who said: 'May I be made your ransom! He has stopped working for his livelihood and has engaged himself in worship and asceticism instead.'

Hearing this, Imam al-Ṣādiq ﷺ said: 'Woe unto him! But does he not know that the prayers of one who stops working go unanswered?!'

During the time of the Holy Prophet, when this verse was revealed: And whoever is wary of Allah, He shall make a way out for him, and provide for him from whence he does not reckon. (65:2-3), a group from amongst the Muslims abandoned their professions, adopted seclusion, and engaged themselves in worship, saying: 'Allah Himself provides the sustenance and shall never permit the religious ones to become distressed and destitute; hence why do we need to toil in order to procure our sustenance?'

When the Holy Prophet was informed of this he summoned them, and, objecting at this attitude of theirs, asked: 'Why have you abandoned your professions?'

They replied: 'Allah has undertaken to provide us our sustenance.'

When he heard this, he explained: 'It is not as you think. Allah does not answer the prayers of a person who, despite possessing the ability to work and exert himself, fails to do so. You must continue to engage yourselves in your respective professions.'[1]

3 – Sustenance in the measure of sufficiency

Once, passing through a desert, the Holy Prophet and his companions happened to come across a person tending camels and requested him to provide them with some milk. The man excused himself, saying: 'The milk that is in the breasts of these camels is for the breakfast of the people of the tribe, and that which lies in the container is for their evening meals.'

When he heard this the Holy Prophet prayed for him, saying: 'O Lord! Increase this person in wealth and children.' The group continued on its way. A little later they came across another person who was also engaged

---

[1] *Bā Mardūm Īn Gūnih Barkhūrd Kunīm*, p. 163; *al-Wāfī*, vol. 10, p. 15.

in feeding camels. When they requested him to provide them with some milk, he immediately milked the she-camels and poured all of the milk into the vessels of the Holy Prophet's [company]. In addition to the milk, he even presented them with a sheep, and said: 'At the moment this is all I can offer but if you desire I shall arrange for more.'

The Holy Prophet raised his holy hands and prayed: 'O Lord! Grant him sustenance in a measure that is sufficient for him.'

Astonished, his companions said: 'O Prophet of Allah! For the person who rejected your request you sought something which all of us long for, whereas for the one who fulfilled your desire you prayed for something which none of us prefer!'

The Holy Prophet said: 'A livelihood that is less but sufficient for [the needs of] one's life is better than great riches that divert man away from Allah.' He then supplicated: 'O Lord! Grant Muḥammad and his progeny a sustenance in the measure that is just sufficient.'[1]

4 – Charity increases sustenance

Imam al-Ṣādiq ﷺ had many sons, one of whom was named Muḥammad. Occasionally, it would so happen that his income would exceed his expenses. Once, Imam al-Ṣādiq ﷺ enquired: 'How much have you managed to save?'

He replied: 'Forty dinars.'

The Imam said: 'Give it as charity in the way of Allah.'

He said: 'This is all that I have with me and if I were to give this in charity there would be nothing left for me.'

The Imam insisted: 'Go and give it in charity and Allah shall compensate it for you. Do you not know that for everything there is a key, and the key to sustenance is charity?'

Muḥammad, heeding his father's advice, gave the forty dinars in charity. Hardly ten days had passed when a sum of 4000 dinars was presented to the Imam. Turning to Muḥammad, he said: 'My son! We gave forty dinars

____

[1] *Dāstān-hā Wa Pand-hā*, vol. 2, p. 72; *Anwār al-Nuʿmāniyyah*, p. 342.

in the path of Allah and He gave us 4000 dinars in return.'[1]

5 – Wealth from unknown places

The Buyids, whose sultanate had commenced in the year 322 AH, ruled for a period of 126 years. The greatest of the Buyid rulers and the most compassionate of them all with respect to the Shi'a faith and to his subjects was 'Imād al-Dawlah, who ruled for nine years (d. 338 AH). During his lifetime, several strange incidents occurred with him in connection with riches and treasures:

1. When 'Imād al-Dawlah arrived in Shiraz, Yāqūt, whom al-Muqtadir Billāh the Abbasid had placed there as the governor, took to flight. In the circumstances, 'Imād al-Dawlah did not possess anything to pay for the expenditure of his army. Distressed and lost in thought he set out for hunting. On the way, the foot of his horse plunged into a hole. As 'Imād al-Dawlah extracted the animal's foot, the hole widened, revealing a treasure which Yāqūt had concealed there. He extracted the treasure and used it to pay for his army's expenses.

2. Once, as he lay down and reflected about his army and subjects, his eyes suddenly fell upon a snake that had emerged from one corner of the roof and disappeared into another. As a precautionary measure he ordered the roof to be taken apart and the snake killed so that it did not bite anyone.

When a portion of the roof was broken a second roof became manifest and the intervening region between the two roofs was found to house chests containing a total of 500,000 dinars. The chests were brought down and 'Imād al-Dawlah distributed the money amongst his subjects.

3. Once, having decided to have some clothes stitched for the elders of his army, his soldiers, and himself, he called for a tailor. The special tailor of Yāqūt, the erstwhile governor of the city, was recommended to him. Incidentally, this tailor happened to be deaf, but 'Imād al-Dawlah said: 'The faculty of sight is what a tailor ought to necessarily possess; as for hearing, it is not a necessity.'

---

[1] *Ḥikāyat-hā-yi Shanīdanī*, vol. 4, p. 92; *al-Kāfī*, vol. 4, p. 9

When the tailor was brought before him, he ordered: 'I want you to stitch clothes for my servants, soldiers, officers, generals, and myself.'

The tailor – deaf that he was – imagined that someone had spoken ill of him, and, complaining that he had money in his possession, said: 'There are only four chests of the governor Yāqūt in my custody and I am unaware of what is contained within them!'

'Imād al-Dawlah ordered the chests to be brought before him; when they were opened they were found to contain great riches, beautiful clothes, and valuable stones.[1]

45. Being Pleased With The Divine Decree

Allah, the Wise, says:

$$رَضِيَ اللّٰهُ عَنْهُمْ وَرَضُوا عَنْهُ$$

Allah is pleased with them, and they are pleased with Him. (58:22)

Imam al-Sajjād has said:

$$الصَّبْرُ وَالرِّضَا رَأْسُ طَاعِةِ اللّٰهِ$$

Patience and pleasure [over divine acts] constitute the pinnacle of Allah's obedience.[2]

Short explanation

The attribute of being pleased with respect to the divine decree is that a person remains pleased with occurrences, irrespective of whether they are to his liking or otherwise. This characteristic is a ray from the light of divine cognisance, such that a person possessing this attribute turns away from his own desires and seeks that which Allah has decreed for him instead. This is because attachment of the heart to worldly and material things is polytheism, and therefore inconsistent with the attribute of pleasure over divine acts.

It is amazing to observe those who vociferously claim to be the servants

---

[1] *Jāmiʿ al-Nūrayn*, p. 323.

[2] *Jāmiʿ al-Saʿādāt*, vol. 3, p. 203.

and worshippers of Allah complaining and grumbling over divine decrees and acts. However, those who are truly cognisant are in total submission and subservience to Allah – pleased and satisfied with divine destinies, uncomplaining in the face of adversities, shortages, and severity of trials, and content and happy over things bestowed to them as well as those not granted to them.[1]

1 – Complete contentment with Allah

Jābir ibn ʿAbd Allāh Anṣārī, who had been of the companions of the Holy Prophet, had remained alive till the time of Imam al-Bāqir ﷺ, but had become old and blind by then.

Once, when he had arrived in the presence of the Imam, the Imam enquired after his health, whereupon he said: 'I find myself in a state such that I give preference to old age over youth, to sickness over soundness of health, and to death over life!'

The Imam responded by saying: 'However, for me, if Allah makes me old, I prefer old age; if He desires to give me youth, I prefer youth; if He afflicts me with sickness, I desire sickness; and if He desires to favour me with sound health, I prefer soundness of health. If Allah wishes to give me death, I prefer death, and if He wills to keep me alive, I desire to live.'

As soon as Jābir heard the Imam's speech he kissed his face and said: 'The Noble Prophet ﷺ had spoken the truth. He had said: "O Jābir! You shall continue to live till you meet one of my children whose name shall be Bāqir. He shall split open knowledge just as a cow splits open the earth."'[2]

2 – Pleased with three calamities

Prophet ʿĪsā ﷺ happened to come upon a blind and paralytic leper whose disease had caused his very flesh to fall out of his body, and overheard him say: 'Thanks to Allah who has cured me from the affliction that has seized numerous persons in its grasp!'

---

[1] *Tadhkirat al-Ḥaqāʾiq*, p. 85.

[2] *Pand-i Tārīkh*, vol. 5, p. 186.

Prophet ʿĪsā 🙶 said to him: 'O man! What is that affliction from which He has protected you?'

The man replied: 'O Spirit of Allah! I am better off than one whose heart does not possess the cognisance of Allah – that cognisance which He has placed in mine.'

Hearing this, Prophet ʿĪsā 🙶 said to him: 'You have spoken correctly. Now give me your hand.' Then, taking hold of his hand, Prophet ʿĪsā 🙶 moved his holy hand over the leper's body, whereupon the leper was immediately cured of his afflictions and was transformed into a man of charming appearance and good physique. Since he had remained pleased over the tribulations that had afflicted him, Allah cured him of his ailments. Later, he went on to become one of the companions of Prophet ʿĪsā 🙶, and engaged in worship along with him.[1]

3 – One of the inmates of paradise

Imam al-Ṣādiq 🙶 relates:

'Once, Allah revealed to Prophet Dāwūd 🙶 to give glad tidings to Khallādah, the daughter of Aws, that she was of the inmates of paradise and would be one of his companions in it. Prophet Dāwūd 🙶 went to her house and knocked at her door, and it was Khallādah herself who opened it. She recognised him the moment she set her eyes upon him and enquired: "Has something been revealed about me to make you come here?" When he 🙶 had replied in the affirmative, she said: "The revelation is probably for someone else who resembles me in name."

'He 🙶 said: "No; the revelation has been for you. Tell me something about yourself."

'She replied: "Whenever any pain, injury, or misfortune would come to afflict me I would exhibit patience and submit myself to Allah's pleasure. Neither would I desire any of the adversities to be warded away from me nor would I aspire for anything in exchange; I was always thankful to Him, and His pleasure was the only thing that I coveted."

---

[1] *ʿIlm-i Akhlāq-i Islāmī*, vol. 3, p. 262; *Jāmiʿ al-Saʿādāt*, vol. 3, p. 208.

'When he heard this, Prophet Dāwūd 🕮 said: "It is because of this that you have reached such a rank that Allah has sent down this revelation about you."'

Having related this incident, Imam al-Ṣādiq 🕮 said: 'This is that very religion which Allah has chosen for His righteous servants.'[1]

4 – 'Ammār in the Battle of Ṣiffīn

'Ammār Yāsir was one of the special companions of the Holy Prophet. He possessed such a high degree of faith that the Holy Prophet had stated: ''Ammār is replete with faith from head to toe, and faith has blended with his flesh and blood.'[2]

After the death of the Holy Prophet he continued to be of those who fiercely supported Imam 'Alī 🕮, and when the Battle of Ṣiffīn commenced he fought on the side of the Imam. One day, coming out of the ranks of the Imam's army, he stationed himself before the enemy forces and said: 'O Lord! You are aware that if I were to realise that Your happiness lies in my hurling myself into the seas, I would surely do so; and if I were to know that Your happiness lies in that I fling myself upon the point of a sword so that it enters into my stomach and emerges from the back of my neck, I would certainly do so. I know that today Your happiness lies in waging a battle with these sinning and corrupt people, and had I known of an act that would have pleased You more, I would have surely opted for it.' Then, raising his voice, he said: 'Whoever desires Allah's pleasure and does not desire to return to his wealth and children should come to me.'

He was eventually martyred after displaying great valour and courage in the battlefield. Reaching his dead body, the Commander of the Faithful sat down, placed his head upon his thighs and, as he wept, said: 'O death! It appears that you are totally familiar with those whom I love; you come and take them away from me.'[3]

---

[1] *Dāstān-hā Wa Pand-hā*, vol. 3, p. 37; *Biḥār al-Anwār*, vol. 71, p. 89.

[2] *Safīnat al-Biḥār*, vol. 2, p. 275.

[3] *Payghambar Wa Yārān*, vol. 5, pp. 24-28; *Biḥār al-Anwār*, vol. 8, p. 524.

5 – The best creation

Prophet Mūsā 🕮 requested Allah: 'O Lord! Show to me who from amongst all Your creations is the best in worship to You.'

Allah revealed to him: 'Proceed towards the village situated near the seashore and you shall find the person there.'

Reaching there, Prophet Mūsā 🕮 found a leper who was engaged in praising and glorifying Allah. He asked Jibrīl: 'Where is the person I had sought from Allah?'

Jibrīl pointed to the sick person and said: 'This is the person. I am under instructions to take away his eyes; pay careful attention to what he shall say.' Having said this, he pointed towards the leper's eyes and they suddenly popped out of their sockets.

As soon as this happened, the leper said: 'O Allah! Till You desired you let me benefit from my eyes, and now You have desired to take them away from me. O the one who does good to me and provides me with goodness!'

Approaching him, Prophet Mūsā 🕮 said: 'O servant of Allah! I am a person whose prayers are always accepted; if you desire, I shall pray to Allah so that He returns your eyes to you.'

The man said: 'No, I do not desire it. Allah has desired this state for me and I am pleased with all that pleases Him.'

Prophet Mūsā 🕮 said: 'I heard you say "O the one who does good to me and provides me with goodness". What did you mean by these words?'

He said: 'In this village I am the only one who is cognisant of Allah and worships Him [and this is the greatest goodness].'

Prophet Mūsā 🕮 was overcome by astonishment and amazement, and as he turned back he said to himself: 'He is the greatest worshipper of Allah in the world.'[1]

46. Showing Off

Allah, the Wise, has said:

---

[1] *Namūnah-i Maʿārif*, vol. 5, p. 373; *Shayṭān*, vol. 1, p. 524.

$$\text{وَلَا تَكُونُوا كَالَّذِينَ خَرَجُوا مِنْ دِيَارِهِم بَطَرًا وَرِئَاءَ النَّاسِ}$$

Do not be like those who left their homes vainly and to show off to the people. (8:47)

The Holy Prophet said:

$$\text{لَا يَقْبَلُ اللّٰهُ تَعَالَى عَمَلًا فِيهِ مِثْقَالُ ذَرَّةٍ مِنْ رِيَاءٍ}$$

Allah shall not accept a deed which has [even] an atom's weight of showing off in it.[1]

Short explanation

Showing off is a tree that comes into existence as a result of hypocrisy and whose fruit is nothing but concealed polytheism. It is exhibited before entities that neither have the ability to grant life and death, nor the authority to fulfil the needs of any person.

On the Day of Judgement, at the time of reckoning, it will be said to a person who showed off: 'Collect the rewards of your deeds from those you had made partners to Me and for whom you had performed your deeds!'

Showing off usually occurs in gatherings and with respect to clothes and acts of worship. Thus, it is essential to remain attentive towards and heedful of Allah in order to purge our interiors of this satanic vice.[2]

1 – The proud monk

Ibrāhīm Adham narrated:

'I acquired wisdom and enlightenment from a monk by the name of Sama'ān. One day I entered his monastery and asked him: "O Sama'ān! How long have you been in this monastery?"

'He replied: "Seventy years."

'I enquired: "What has been your food during this period?"

'He asked: "Why do you ask such a question?"

'I said: "I am curious to know."

'He said: "Every night I eat just one hazelnut!"

---

[1] *Jāmiʿ al-Saʿādāt*, vol. 2, p. 376.

[2] *Tadhkirat al-Ḥaqāʾiq*, p. 48.

'I enquired: "What is it that keeps your mind so engrossed so as to make one hazelnut sufficient for you?"

'He replied: "Every year, on an appointed day, a group of my followers come here, revere me, decorate the monastery, circumambulate it, and then depart. Whenever I get exhausted of worship and I experience hunger and loneliness, I overcome it by bringing to mind that day, and the honour and esteem that I come to acquire in it. Thus, my entire year's exertion and efforts are motivated by the grandeur of that one day!"'[1]

2 – The congregational prayers

One of the distinguished scholars who had journeyed the path of spiritual cleansing and possessed sublime ethics, was Mullā ʿAbd Allāh Shūshtarī. He was the tutor of Muḥammad Taqī Majlisī and has numerous books to his name, one of them being *Majāmiʿ al-Fawāʾid*, which runs into seven volumes.[2]

He was a contemporary of Shaykh Bahāʾī and one day proceeded to pay him a visit. They sat in conversation until the sound of *adhān* was heard, whereupon Shaykh Bahāʾī said to him: 'Offer your prayers here so that we can follow you and acquire the rewards of the congregational prayers.'

Mullā reflected for a few moments after which, excusing himself, he got up and left for his house. He was asked: 'Why did you turn down the Shaykh's offer when you yourself attach great importance to offering the prayers as soon as its time sets in?'

He replied: 'I reflected within myself and perceived that I was not of the kind that if a person like Shaykh were to pray behind me, I would not experience a change of state. I realised that some form of showing off might creep into me and so turned down his request.'[3]

---

[1] *Shanīdanī-hā-yi Tārīkh*, p. 362; *al-Maḥajjah al-Bayḍāʾ*, vol. 6, p. 207.

[2] *Qaṣaṣ al-ʿUlamāʾ*, p. 336.

[3] *Sīmā-yi Farzānigān*, p. 147; *Bīdādgarān-i Aqalīm-i Qibleh*, p. 14.

3 – The two apparels

Sufyān Thawrī happened to pass by Masjid al-Ḥarām and there he witnessed Imam al-Ṣādiq ☙ wearing costly and expensive clothes. He said to himself: 'By Allah! I shall go to him and reprimand him.' Approaching the Imam, he said: 'O son of the Prophet of Allah! By Allah! You have attired yourself in a clothing the like of which had neither been worn by the Noble Prophet ☙ nor by 'Alī ☙, or any of your forefathers!'

Hearing this, the Imam said: 'During the era of the Noble Prophet ☙ the people were troubled with poverty and paucity, but later the circumstances improved and things changed for the better. Of the inhabitants of the world, those who most deserve to taste the benefits of abundance, ease, and comfort, are the righteous ones.'

Having said this he recited the following verse: Say: 'Who has forbidden the adornment of Allah which He has brought forth for His servants, and the good things of [His] provision?' [7:32]

And then he said: 'Thus, we are the ones who most deserve to utilise that which Allah has provided. O Sufyān! The apparel that you presently observe me wearing is for the people and for preserving my reputation and esteem.' Then, taking hold of Sufyān's hand, the Imam drew back his dress, revealing his inner clothing which was coarse and rough. He then said: 'This, I have worn for myself while the other I have worn for the people.' Then, taking hold of Sufyān's clothing, he pulled it up to reveal a soft inner clothing, and said: 'You have worn this exterior clothing for the people and the concealed soft inner clothing for your ease and comfort!'[1]

4 – The dissembled worship

There once lived a worshipper who could never get himself to perform any of his deeds sincerely and free from showing off. Once, attempting to redress his problem, he said to himself: 'In the corner of the city there lies an abandoned mosque which is never frequented by anyone. It would be better if I go there in the night so that there is none to see me and engage

---

[1] *Bā Mardūm Īn Gūnih Barkhūrd Kunīm*, p. 169; *Biḥār al-Anwār*, vol. 47, p. 360.

myself in worshipping Allah in total sincerity.'

At midnight, in the darkness of the night, he stealthily set out for the mosque. The night was a rainy one with severe lightning and thunder.

Once inside, he engaged himself in worship. A short while later he suddenly happened to hear a sound and ecstatically said to himself: 'Surely, a person has entered the mosque.' With this in mind he increased the quality and quantity of his prayers and continued his acts of worship till daybreak. In the morning, as he was about to go out of the mosque, he looked behind with the corner of his eyes only to realise that there was no one there save a black dog that had sought shelter in the mosque from the rains, lightning, and thunder.

This distressed him immensely, and repentant and shameful for having worshipped for hours for a dog, he rebuked himself: 'Woe unto me! I fled and came to this abandoned mosque so that I could worship Allah with sincerity, but I have ended up performing my acts of worship for a black dog instead.'[1]

5 – Informing people of worship

In the tribe of Banī Isrā'īl, there lived a worshipper who, after years of worship, requested Allah to manifest to him his rank and status, and prayed: 'O Lord! If my deeds are to Your liking I would strive further in performing good deeds, but if not, then I would want to make amends for it before death overtakes me, and engage myself in [more] acts of worship.'

In his dreams he was informed: 'In the eyes of Allah, you do not possess any good deed.'

Perturbed, he exclaimed: 'O Allah! Where then have my deeds gone?'

It was said to him: 'You do not possess any deed, for whenever you performed a good deed you informed the people of it. Therefore, the pleasure that you derived out of informing them of your acts is your reward for those acts.' This disturbed him immensely and left him greatly saddened.

---

[1] *Dāstān-hā Wa Pand-hā*, vol. 9, p. 173; *Muntakhab Qawāmīs al-Durar*, p. 144.

For the second time, he was informed in his dreams: 'Now purchase your life from Us. Give charity equivalent to the number of veins in your body, every day!'

He pleaded: 'O Lord! How can I give such a large amount in charity when I do not possess anything?'

He heard: 'We do not impose any duty on a soul except in the measure of its ability. Recite the following 360 times daily; every word of it is charity for a vein of your body: *Subḥān allāhi wa al-ḥamdu lillāhi wa lā ilāha ill-allāhu wallāhu akbar, wa lā ḥawla wa lā quwwata illā bi-llāh.*'

The worshipper, who was overjoyed to hear these words, said: 'Grant me more than this.'

It was said to him: 'The more you recite the more reward you shall earn.'[1]

47. Fornication

Allah, the Wise, has said:

الزَّانِيَةُ وَالزَّانِي فَاجْلِدُوا كُلَّ وَاحِدٍ مِنْهُمَا مِائَةَ جَلْدَةٍ

As for the fornicatress and the fornicator, strike each of them a hundred lashes. (24:2)

The Holy Prophet has said:

إِذَا ظَهَرَ الزِّنَا مِنْ بَعْدِي كَثُرَ مَوْتُ الْفُجْأَةِ

After my death, when fornication increases, sudden deaths shall [also] increase.[2]

Short explanation

Fornication is considered to be one of the great sins. A person, as a result of being overcome by lust and due to lack of faith, audaciously transgresses the sexual boundaries of other people.

In this world, fornication reduces sustenance and shortens the lifespan,

---

[1] *Pand-i Tārīkh*, vol. 1, p. 35; *Biḥār al-Anwār*, vol. 18, p. 523 (old publication).

[2] *Tafsīr Muʿīn*, p. 366.

while on the Day of Judgement, a fornicator shall suffer the wrath of Allah and an evil reckoning.

The murderers of prophets, such as Prophet Yaḥyā ﷺ, and the close friends of Allah such as Imam al-Ḥusayn ﷺ, were mostly illegitimate children – a consequence of Shayṭān's invitation to a male and female to commit this sin.

Prophet 'Īsā ﷺ said to his disciples: 'Prophet Mūsā ﷺ had advised his people: "Do not commit fornication," but I advise you: do not even think of committing fornication.'[1]

1 – Five fornicators and five rulings

Five persons who had committed fornication were brought before 'Umar, who ordered them to be subjected to the legal punishment for the crime. At that moment the Commander of the Faithful arrived and said: 'O 'Umar! Allah's ruling in their case is not as you have ruled!'

'Umar requested: 'You issue the ruling for them and implement the legal punishment.'

The Imam beheaded the first person, stoned the second, subjected the third to the full punishment of eighty lashes, the fourth to half the punishment, and ordered the discretionary punishment for the fifth.

'Umar was amazed and the people astounded over the Imam's ruling. 'Umar asked him: 'O Abū al-Ḥasan! Five persons were involved in one crime and you have issued different rulings for all of them?!'

The Commander of the Faithful explained: 'The first person was a *dhimmī*[2] who had transgressed [the honour of] a Muslim woman and so had fallen out of the *dhimmah*[3] – as such, his punishment could only be death. The second person who had committed fornication possessed a spouse and so I had him stoned. The third one to have been involved in the crime did not have a wife and so I punished him with eighty lashes. The fourth was

---

[1] *Shayṭān*, vol. 1, p. 560.

[2] A free non-Muslim subject living in a Muslim country. (Tr.)

[3] Covenant of protection. (Tr.)

a slave and therefore I subjected him to half the legal punishment, while the fifth one was poor of intellect due to which I subjected him to the discretionary punishment [a few lashes].'

Hearing the explanation, 'Umar exclaimed: 'O Abū al-Ḥasan! May it never happen that I have to live with the people when you are not around [to help me]!'[1]

2 – Interpretation of the dream

Ibn Sīrīn was an extremely good-looking and elegant youth, and a cloth-merchant by profession. Once, it so happened that a woman became enchanted with his looks; she expressed her desire to purchase cloth from him upon the condition that he should deliver it to her house, whereupon she would hand him the money.

As he reached her house and entered it, she immediately bolted the door and invited him to commit fornication. Aghast, the youth said: 'I seek refuge in Allah,' and then proceeded to lecture her about the reproach associated with the obscene act.

However, when he observed that his words failed to have any effect upon the woman, he decided to resort to deception in order to extricate himself from his quandary.

He sought her permission to use the lavatory. Procuring her permission he entered the lavatory, he dirtied himself with excrement and then approached her.

The woman, seeing him in that odious state, felt revolted and promptly turned him out of her house.

Due to this abstinence on his part with respect to fornication, Allah graced him with the science of interpretation of dreams.[2]

3 – Prophet Yaḥyā's 🕮 murderer was an illegitimate child

During the time of Prophet Yaḥyā 🕮, there lived a king by the name of

---

[1] *Qaḍāwat-hā-yi Muḥayyir al-ʿUqūl*, p. 45; *Dāstān-hā-yi Zindagī-yi ʿAlī*, p. 145.
[2] *Shayṭān*, vol. 1, p. 678.

Herod who was fond of him and considered him to be a just and righteous person.

There was an adulteress with whom this king had been having an illicit relationship; as she became old, she began to ornament her daughter and present her before the king, who eventually fell in love with her and desired to marry her.

He questioned Prophet Yaḥyā ﷺ about the issue who, on the basis of the religion of Prophet 'Īsā ﷺ, declared it to be unlawful. Consequently, the adulteress harboured resentment and malice towards Prophet Yaḥyā ﷺ.

One day, observing the king to be in a state of intoxication, she adorned her daughter and sent her before him. Seeing her, the king sought to gratify himself but the daughter said: 'I shall submit myself to you only upon the condition that you sever Yaḥyā's head from his body.' The king, in his state of inebriation, agreed, and upon his instance, and Prophet Yaḥyā ﷺ was beheaded.

According to another tradition, the king desired to enter into marriage with his niece by the name of Herodia, but Prophet Yaḥyā ﷺ prohibited such a marriage as a result of which the lady coveted his death.

Imam al-Bāqir ﷺ said: 'Yaḥyā's ﷺ killer was an illegitimate child, as were the killers of 'Alī and Ḥusayn ibn 'Alī ﷺ.'

When Prophet Yaḥyā ﷺ was murdered, Allah made Nebuchadnezzar, one of the Babylonian kings, dominant over the people, who initiated a massacre in the city. It was only when he had killed 70,000 of the inhabitants of the city that Prophet Yaḥyā's ﷺ blood stopped oozing out.[1]

4 – The bath of Minjāb

Once, a wealthy person who was unmindful of Allah and always engaged in pleasure and enjoyment, happened to be sitting near the door of his house. A woman wanting to go to a bath, popularly known by the name of Minjāb, had lost her way to it. Exhausted, she looked around if she could

---

[1] *Tārīkh-i Anbiyā'*, vol. 2, p. 284.

find someone who could guide her to the place when her eyes fell upon the man. Approaching him, she enquired: 'Where is the Minjāb bath?'

Pointing to his house, he said: 'This is the Minjāb bath.' Taking it to be the bath, she entered the house and the man quickly entered into it behind her. Once inside, he bolted the door and approaching the lady, sought to commit adultery.

The woman, perceiving that she had walked into the clutches of an immoral person and realising that deception was the only means of escape, said to him: 'I am ardently desirous too; however I am hungry and covered with dirt. Bring some perfume and some food; we can have food together after which I shall place myself at your disposal.'

The man agreed and went out of the house. Having procured some food and perfume he returned home only to find the lady missing. Her escape upset him immensely and the craving for committing adultery with the lady remained so deeply embedded in his heart that he would always recite the following verses: 'What happened to the lady, who had become exhausted? And had asked: "Where is the way to the Minjāb bath?"'

The time passed until it so happened that one day he lay on his deathbed. His acquaintances approached him and asked him to recite *lā ilāha ill-allāh, muḥammad al-rasūl allāh*, but instead he would only recite those verses; eventually he passed away in that very state.[1]

5 – The Holy Prophet and the youth

One day, a youth approached the Holy Prophet and with utmost disrespect and discourtesy, said: 'O Prophet of Allah! Do you permit me to commit fornication?'

These words created a great uproar amongst the people and objections could be heard from every nook and cranny. The Holy Prophet, exhibiting sublime ethics and speaking with absolute gentleness, said: 'Come near.' The youth stepped forward and sat down beside him, whereupon the Prophet asked: 'Would you like someone to commit the act with your

---

[1] *ʿĀlam-i Barzakh*, p. 41; *Kashkūl of Shaykh Bahāʾī*, vol. 1, p. 232.

mother?'

The youth replied: 'May I be made your ransom! Never!'

The Holy Prophet said: 'Similarly, the people also do not approve of this with respect to their daughters.' The Holy Prophet continued: 'Tell me: would you approve of this act for your sister?' Once again the youth denied [and repented having asked the question].

The Holy Prophet placed his hands upon the youth's chest and prayed for him, saying: 'O Lord! Purify his heart, forgive his sins, and protect him from the pollution of depravity.' From then on, fornication became the worst of deeds in the eyes of that youth.[1]

48. Generosity

Allah, the Wise, has said:

فَأَمَّا مَنْ أَعْطَى وَاتَّقَى ۞ وَصَدَّقَ بِالْحُسْنَى ۞ فَسَنُيَسِّرُهُ لِلْيُسْرَى

As for him who gives and is God-wary, and confirms the best promise, We shall surely ease him into facility. (92:5-7)

The Holy Prophet said:

لَا يُصْلِحُ دِينَكُمْ إِلَّا السَّخَاءُ وَحُسْنُ الْخُلُقِ

Nothing shall ensure the welfare of your religion except generosity and good disposition.[2]

Short explanation

Generosity is one of the ethics of the prophets, a pillar of faith, and a ray of the light of firm faith. The Holy Prophet has said: 'The close friends of Allah are essentially and inherently generous.' Hence, in order to acquire this attribute, a believer should greatly endeavour to be munificent and generous towards relatives, the needy, and the like, for the pleasure of Allah.

---

[1] *Dāstān-hā Wa Pand-hā*, vol. 3, p. 138; *Tafsīr al-Manār*, under the discussion relating to 3:104.

[2] *Jāmiʿ al-Saʿādāt*, vol. 1, p. 308.

It is better that a person's generosity is associated with a thing that is dear to him – eatables, clothes, money, etc. – and that no obligation is placed upon the person towards whom generosity has been exhibited; man should only view himself as a trustworthy person whose responsibility is to pass on Allah's things to deserving and needy individuals. As such, he should stay away from frugality and refrain from withholding divine trusts; this is because it is not known whether or not they would yield any benefit, if given after his death, and whether or not his inheritors would expend them in a correct and appropriate manner.

1 – What shall I answer Imam al-Zamān ?

Shaykh Zayn al-ʿĀbidīn Māzandarānī, a student of the author of *Jawāhir* and of Shaykh Anṣārī, lived in the city of Karbala. In connection with his generosity and alms-giving, it has been recorded that he would borrow as much money as he could and then distribute it amongst the needy, and his debts would then be repaid by those coming to Karbala from India.

One day, a destitute person arrived at his door and asked for alms. Not having any money with him, the Shaykh picked up his copper jar, handed it to him, and said: 'Take this and sell it.'

A couple of days later when his family members realised that the jar was missing, they created an uproar, shouting: 'A thief has taken away our jar.'

When the Shaykh, who was in his library, heard the outcry, he said to them: 'Do not accuse the thieves for I am the one who has taken the jar.'

Once, on one of his trips to Samarra, he fell seriously ill. Mīrzā Shīrāzī paid him a visit and began comforting him, whereupon the Shaykh said to him: 'I am not at all fearful of death; my uneasiness is due to the fact that according to our beliefs when we die our souls are taken in the presence of Imam al-ʿaṣr . If at that time the Imam were to question me: "O Zayn al-ʿĀbidīn! With the credibility and esteem that we had bestowed upon you, you could have borrowed a greater amount of money for helping the needy than what you used to; why then did you not do so?" What shall I answer him 🖾?'

It is reported that Mīrzā Shīrāzī was greatly affected by these words; returning home, he brought out all the religious taxes that lay in his house and distributed them amongst the needy.[1]

2 – More generous than Ḥātim

Ḥātim Ṭāʾī was questioned: 'Have you come across anyone more generous than yourself?'

He replied: 'Yes, I have.'

He was asked: 'Where?'

He said: 'I had been travelling in the desert when I came across a tent. Inside it there was an old lady, while behind the tent a goat lay tied. When the old lady saw me she approached me and held the reins of my horse so that I could dismount. A little later, her son arrived and was immensely pleased to have me as their guest. The old lady said to him: "Commence the preparations to entertain our guest. Go and slaughter the goat and prepare some food."

'The son said: "First I shall go and collect some firewood," but the old lady said: "Going to the desert and bringing the firewood shall take a lot of time due to which our guest would have to remain hungry for long, and this would be contrary to etiquette."

'So the son, breaking the only two lances that he possessed, slaughtered the goat, prepared the food, and presented it before me. When I investigated about their condition I realised that the goat had been their only possession and despite this, they had slaughtered it for me. I said to the old lady: "Do you recognise me?" When she replied in the negative, I said: "I am Ḥātim Ṭāʾī. You must come with me to my tribe so that I can entertain you and shower you with gifts and presents!"

'The old lady said: "We do not seek any reward from our guests nor do we sell bread for money."

'She refused to accept anything from me. Witnessing this generosity, I

---

[1] *Sīmā-yi Farzānigān*, p. 357.

realised that they were far more generous and munificent than me.'[1]

3 – Allah loves generosity

Once, a group of people from Yemen arrived in the presence of the Holy Prophet. Amongst them was a person who, despite being eloquent in speech, spoke with the Holy Prophet more harshly and discourteously than the rest, such that eventually the Prophet became enraged – the vein of his forehead swelled up and the colour of his face transformed.

At that moment Jibrīl descended and said: 'Your Lord sends His greetings and says: "This man is generous by nature and feeds people."'

As soon as he heard this, his anger subsided and he said: 'Had it not been for the fact that Jibrīl had informed me on behalf of Allah – the Mighty, the Glorious – that you are a person who is generous and feeds people, I would have expelled you from my presence such that your instance would have served as an example for the others!'

The man from Yemen said: 'Does your Allah love generosity?'

When the Holy Prophet replied in the affirmative, the Yemeni declared: 'I bear witness that there is no creature or entity worthy of worship except for Allah and that you are His Messenger.' Then, he continued: 'By Allah who has sent you in truth, I have never turned away anyone from my wealth.'

4 – 300 gold coins

Ibn ʿAbbās narrates:

'Once, 300 gold coins were gifted to the Noble Prophet ﷺ, which he in turn gifted to the Commander of the Faithful ؏. As the Imam ؏ took them, he declared: "By Allah! I shall surely give this amount in charity in a manner such that it shall be accepted by Allah."'

Later, Imam ʿAlī ؏ narrates: 'That night, after having offered the ʿishāʾ prayer, I picked up 100 gold coins and came out of the mosque. As I did so, I happened to encounter a woman and so handed over the money to her.

---

[1] *Jawāmiʿ al-Ḥikāyāt*, p. 214.

In the morning the people were found to be talking amongst themselves, saying: "Last night 'Alī gave 100 gold coins in charity to an adulteress." I was greatly distressed to hear this.

'The following night, after the *'ishā'* prayer, I picked up another hundred gold coins and came out of the mosque, saying to myself: "By Allah! Tonight I shall give this in charity such that Allah shall accept this act from me." As I emerged from the mosque, I found myself face to face with a man and handed over the money to him.

'At daybreak, the talk amongst the inhabitants of Medina was: "'Alī has given 100 gold coins to a thief," and I became immensely despondent.

'The third night I picked up another hundred gold coins and said to myself: "By Allah! I shall surely give these hundred gold coins in charity to such a person, that Allah shall accept my charity." After the *'ishā'* prayer, coming out of the mosque, I ran into a man and handed him the money. In the morning, the people of Medina were found saying: "Last night 'Alī ﷺ gave 100 gold coins to a rich and wealthy person."

'I was extremely pained to hear this and so, approaching the Noble Prophet ﷺ, I informed him of the incidents that had taken place. Having heard me, he ﷺ said: "O 'Alī! Jibrīl says: 'Allah, the Exalted, has accepted your charities and considers them to be pure. The hundred gold coins that you had given to the immoral lady on the first night – returning home she turned to Allah in repentance over her past misdeeds and mended her ways. She has set aside the gold coins as her capital and is on the lookout for a husband. The hundred gold coins of the second night had reached a thief who, upon reaching home, repented over his wrongdoings and utilised the amount for engaging in trade. The hundred gold coins of the third night had reached the hands of a wealthy person, who had not been paying his zakat for years. Reaching home he began to censure himself, saying: "How lowly and base can you be? While you have been violating Allah's law and not paying the obligatory zakat for several years, 'Alī ibn Abī Ṭālib, despite not possessing anything, has given you 100 gold coins." Having rebuked himself, he then calculated his unpaid zakat of several years and disbursed it.'"'

It was due to this act on the part of Imam ʿAlī 🕮 that Allah revealed the following verse in his praise:

Men whom neither trading nor bargaining distracts from the remembrance of Allah, and the maintenance of prayer and the giving of zakat. They are fearful of a day wherein the heart and the sight will be transformed. (24:37)[1]

5 – The extremely generous companion

Qays was the son of Saʿd ibn ʿUbādah, the chief of the tribe of Khazraj and one of the companions of the Holy Prophet. He never reneged his pledge of allegiance to the Commander of the Faithful and supported him through thick and thin, and transferred his loyalties to Imam al-Ḥasan 🕮 after the martyrdom of the Commander of the Faithful.

Qays, his father Saʿd, and his grandfather ʿUbādah, had possessed a public rest-house. In one of the battles during the time of the Holy Prophet, he was part of the army in which Abū Bakr and ʿUmar were also present. Saʿd would borrow money from his friends and spend it over his fellow companions. Abū Bakr and ʿUmar discussed amongst themselves: 'If we allow him to act in this fashion he shall soon squander away his father's property.' So they announced in public: 'No one should lend money to Qays.'

When his father came to know of this, he, after having recited the congregational prayers behind the Holy Prophet, stood up and said: 'I complain before the Holy Prophet and the people that Abū Bakr and ʿUmar shall turn my son into a miser!'

In one of the battles he was appointed commander of the army. In that expedition, which lasted for a few days, he sacrificed nine camels for his fellow companions, who were very few in number. When the Holy Prophet was informed of this, he said: 'Generosity is the conduct of this family!'

When he fell ill, very few people came to visit him. This surprised him and he sought to know the reason for this, whereupon he was informed:

---

[1] *Islām Wa Mustamandān*, p. 90; *Dāstān-hā-yi Zindagī-yi ʿAlī*, p. 165.

'The reason for this is that a lot of your wealth lies with the people. Being indebted to you, they are ashamed to present themselves before you.'

Hearing this, Qays said: 'May destruction strike the wealth that brings about separation amongst the brethren-in-faith!' Then, upon his instructions, it was announced in Medina: 'Whoever possesses any money belonging to Qays is henceforth the owner of that money for Qays has gifted the money to him.'

After this announcement the crowd that had flocked to his house was so great that the stairs leading up to Qays's room broke down and collapsed.[1]

49. Polytheism

Allah, the Wise, has said:

$$\text{لَا تُشْرِكْ بِاللهِ إِنَّ الشِّرْكَ لَظُلْمٌ عَظِيمٌ}$$

Do not ascribe any partners to Allah. Polytheism is indeed a great injustice.

(31:13)

Imam al-Bāqir 🕮 said:

$$\text{الْمَعَاصِي الَّتِي يَرْتَكِبُونَ فَهِيَ شِرْكُ طَاعَةٍ أَطَاعُوا فِيهَا الشَّيْطَانَ}$$

The commitment of sins on the part of people is polytheism with respect to obedience [of Allah], in which they obey Shayṭān.[2]

Short explanation

One of the vices of the soul is polytheism, in which a person, as a result of ignorance, poverty, scepticism, and the like, attributes god-ship to certain things that do not possess the merit and the ability to be Allah; or regards someone, other than Allah, to be inherently and independently efficacious; or invokes someone, other than Allah, during worship; or intermingles some other intention and objective with his acts of worship.

---

[1] *Payghambar Wa Yārān*, vol. 5, p. 165; *Qāmūs al-Rijāl*, vol. 7, p. 399.

[2] *Shayṭān*, vol. 1, p. 697.

A polytheist's act of resorting to someone other than Allah is a sin; increase in polytheistic beliefs is brought about by the deceptions of Shayṭān, and the persistence of such views leads to hypocrisy and the nullification of deeds, which in turn bring about damnation in this world and the Hereafter.[1]

1 – The extremist who considered himself a Shiʿa

Sahl ibn Ziyād Ādamī relates:

'Some of our friends wrote a letter to Imam al-ʿAskarī ☙ saying: "ʿAlī ibn Ḥasakah claims to be one of your friends and followers, but is of the belief that you are Allah and he is the 'door' that leads to you and the Noble Prophet ☙. He is of the opinion that prayers, fasts, zakat, and hajj are nothing but your *maʿrifah*, and according to him whoever holds this belief is a true and perfect believer and is then relieved of the responsibility of performing the other acts like prayers and fasts."

'In reply, the Imam ☙ wrote: "ʿAlī ibn Ḥasakah lies. May the curse of Allah be upon him! I do not consider him to be of my friends. By Allah! Muḥammad ☙ and the prophets before him had been sent to preach monotheism and invite the people towards prayers, fasts, zakat, hajj, and *wilāyah*. Never did Muḥammad ☙ ever invite anyone towards polytheism, and all of us are the successors of the Noble Prophet ☙ and the servants of Allah, and never do we ascribe partners to Him. If you happen to see one of them, smash his head by means of a stone (due to his polytheistic views)."'

'ʿAlī ibn Ḥasakah was of the extreme Shiʿas, who possessed deviated beliefs and had nurtured students such as Qāsim Shaʿrānī, Yaqṭīnī, Ibn Bābā, and Muḥammad ibn Mūsā Sharīfī. The Imam ☙ made manifest his rejection of their polytheistic beliefs when he announced: 'I absolve myself from them; may Allah curse them!'[2]

---

[1] *Iḥyāʾ al-Qulūb Dar Darmān-i Ṣifāt-i Radhīlah*, (a work of this author), p. 22.

[2] *Shāgirdān-i Maktab-i Aʾimmah*, p. 13; *Rijāl Kashshī*, p. 435.

2 – A polytheist turns into a believer

Shabīḥ ibn ʿUthmān was a polytheist whose father and brother had been killed by the Muslims in the Battle of Uḥud. He awaited an opportunity to kill the Holy Prophet and thus avenge the death of his father and brother.

Years passed and in the year 8 AH the Battle of Ḥunayn loomed. During that crisis, Shabīḥ said to himself: 'This is an excellent opportunity,' and readied himself for battle. In the battle, he advanced forward and positioned himself behind the Holy Prophet in order to execute his sinister intention.

Allah informed the Holy Prophet of his evil designs whereupon the Holy Prophet immediately turned around, and striking Shabīḥ's chest with his fist, said: 'O Shabīḥ! I seek shelter in Allah from your evils.'

Shabīḥ relates: 'A shiver ran through my body. I looked at the face of the Noble Prophet ﷺ and at that very moment I felt as if he was the most beloved of all persons to me, to the extent that I even perceived him to be dearer to me than my very own eyes and ears. At that very moment I bore witness to the unity of Allah and the prophethood of the Noble Prophet ﷺ and became a Muslim, after which I said to him ﷺ: "I bear witness that Allah informed you of my concealed intentions."[1]

'The Holy Prophet, placing his hand upon my chest, prayed: "O Lord! Ward Shayṭān away from him."

'After the battle had concluded, he ﷺ said to me: "What Allah had desired for you is better than what you had desired for yourself."'[2]

3 – Concealed polytheism

Abū Saʿīd al-Khudrī narrates:

'We were a few individuals, who, in a difficult and dangerous period, had shouldered the responsibility of guarding the Noble Prophet ﷺ in turn and according to a pre-determined schedule. After a period, some of us had become accustomed to speaking to each other softly and in whispers, including myself. One night, the Noble Prophet ﷺ approached us and,

---

[1] *Ḥikāyat-hā-yi Shanīdanī.*

[2] *Biḥār al-Anwār*, vol. 21, p. 156.

noticing some of us talking secretly and in whispers, said to us: "What is this secret conversation? Have you not been prohibited from this act?"[1]

'We pleaded: "We seek the forgiveness of Allah and His Prophet, [however], we were discussing about Dajjāl."

'The Noble Prophet ﷺ said: "Should I inform you of one whom I regard to be more dangerous than Dajjāl?" He then said: "Concealed polytheism – that is, a person becomes a cause for the sins and evils of others. Danger from such a person is greater than that from Dajjāl.""[2]

4 – Disbelief and polytheism

After the death of Hishām ibn ʿAbd al-Malik – the Umayyad caliph – Walīd ibn Yazīd took over the reins of the caliphate in the year 125 AH. He was of those about whom the Holy Prophet had prophesised: 'From this *ummah* there shall ascend to the caliphate a person who shall be worse than how Firʿawn had been to his people.'

Walīd, who was perpetually in a state of intoxication, used to say: 'Who has ever said that prophethood has been for the Hashemites? Essentially, there has neither been any revelation nor any book from Allah.'

Once, the muezzin's recitation of the *adhān* for the morning prayers aroused the inebriated Walīd who had been sleeping with his slave-girl, who was also in a state of intoxication. Waking up, he had sexual intercourse with her and then swore that he would make her lead the congregational prayers that morning. Attiring her in his clothes, he sent her to the mosque in the state of ceremonial uncleanness where she led the congregation and the people offered their prayers behind her!

One day, seeking an *istikhārah* from the Holy Qur'an, the following verse came before Walīd:

They prayed for victory [against the infidels], and every obdurate tyrant has failed. (14:15)

Closing the Qur'an, he suspended it as a target and then began shooting

---

[1] A reference to Qur'an, 58:9.

[2] *Dāstān-hā Wa Pand-hā*, vol. 10, p. 65, *Tafsīr Qurṭubī*, vol. 9.

arrows at it, striking it with so many arrows that it eventually tore into pieces. Having done this, he shouted: 'O Qur'an! Do you threaten me and refer to me as an obstinate transgressor? When the Day of Judgement comes to pass, tell Allah: "Walīd tore me into pieces."'

The consequence of his disbelief and rebelliousness was that he could only rule for one year; he was killed in an extremely horrendous fashion: his head was suspended from atop the palace and his impure body buried outside the city.[1]

5 – Debate with the polytheists

Prophet Ibrāhīm ☙, in explaining and propagating the concept of monotheism, found himself in persistent conflict with the idolaters – who possessed idols and statues – and star-worshippers – who claimed god-ship for the sun, moon, and the stars, and ascribed them as partners to Allah.

In Babylon and Carrhae – Prophet Ibrāhīm's ☙ second place of migration – they had even constructed temples and figures in the names of stars and used to worship them!

In connection with his debate with the star-worshippers, it has been narrated that once, when the darkness of the night had spread itself over the horizon and Venus had manifested itself, he said: 'This is my Lord!' When it had set he started out in search of it, but when he failed to find it he said to the star-worshippers: 'I do not love the gods that set.'

Then he saw the moon rise whereupon he said to the people: 'This is my Lord,' but when it disappeared from sight, he said: 'If my Lord does not guide me I shall surely be of the deviated ones.'

When the sun rose he said: 'This is my Lord,' but when it also set he distanced himself from the beliefs of the disbelievers and polytheists and declared: 'I turn my heart and direct my worship towards He who has created the heavens and the earth and I am not of the polytheists. Do you dispute me with respect to the One Allah, who has guided me aright? I fear

---

[1] *Tatimmat al-Muntahā*, p. 90.

not those whom you regard as partners to Him.'[1]

50. Shayṭān

Allah, the Wise, has said:

$$إِنَّ الشَّيْطَانَ لِلْإِنْسَانِ عَدُوٌّ مُبِينٌ$$

Shayṭān is indeed man's manifest enemy. (12:5)

Imam al-Ṣādiq ﷺ said:

$$لَيْسَ لِإِبْلِيسَ أَشَدُّ مِنَ النِّسَاءِ وَالْغَضَبِ$$

Iblīs does not possess weapons more dangerous than women and anger.[2]

Short explanation

In opposition to divine guidance there exists satanic deviation. Within the human there is a continuous and persistent combat between the divine forces, meaning intellect, and the satanic forces, meaning ignorance.

It is only when the human gains a cognisance of the weapons of Shayṭān and his forces and protects himself from their whisperings that he can escape from their snares. And if, at times, Shayṭān happens to overcome him, he should turn to Allah in repentance and plead for His forgiveness lest his heart gets imprinted with a black blemish, and seek refuge in Him from his evils.

1 – Prophet Nūḥ ﷺ and Shayṭān

After Prophet Nūḥ ﷺ had disembarked from his ark, Shayṭān approached him and said: 'You have greatly obliged me and I wish to thank you for your obligation and give you something in exchange!'

Prophet Nūḥ ﷺ said: 'I am indisposed to the fact that I oblige you and you recompense me for it. Anyway, go on and tell me the truth.'

Shayṭān said: 'Indeed I have to strive hard and exert myself before I can lead one person astray, but you cursed the people and all of them were

---

[1] *Tārīkh-i Anbiyā'*, vol. 1, p. 134.

[2] *Biḥār al-Anwār*, vol. 78, p. 246.

destroyed, and so, at least at present, I am at ease until another community is born and reaches the age of responsibility before I invite them towards disobedience [of Allah]. Now, in reciprocation of your good deed, I shall give you a word of advice: stay away from three attributes: firstly, never exhibit arrogance, for it was because of this vice that I did not prostrate before your father, Ādam, and was expelled from the presence of Allah. Secondly, stay away from greed, for it was due to this that Ādam consumed the wheat and was deprived of paradise. Thirdly, distance yourself from envy, for it was because of this vice that Qābīl killed his brother Hābīl and eventually perished as a result of divine punishment.'[1]

2 – Prophet Mūsā ☜ and Shayṭān

Once, Shayṭān approached Prophet Mūsā ☜ and said to him: 'You are the Prophet of Allah while I am one of His sinning and disobedient creations. It is my desire that I repent before Him, so request Him to accept my repentance.'

Prophet Mūsā ☜ agreed and prayed for him, whereupon Allah said: 'O Mūsā! I shall accept your intercession for him. Tell him to prostrate upon Ādam's grave in order that I accept his repentance.'

Prophet Mūsā ☜ met Shayṭān and said: 'Prostrating upon Ādam's grave shall cause your repentance to be accepted.'

Hearing this, Shayṭān said: 'I did not prostrate before Ādam when he was alive, how can I prostrate upon his grave now that he is dead? I shall never do such a thing!' Then, continuing, he said: 'O Mūsā! Since you interceded for me before Allah you have obliged me. I shall advise you to be wary of me in three places in order that you do not face damnation and ruin; firstly, during anger; for in that state my soul is in your heart and my eyes in yours. Secondly, during a battle; for in that state I cause the soldiers to bring their wives, children, and relatives to mind in order that they turn back from the battle and flee away. Thirdly, never sit with a non-*maḥram*

----

[1] *'Unwān al-Kalām*, p. 167.

woman in one place for I shall whisper temptations into both of you.'[1]

3 – Firʿawn

Once, an inhabitant of Egypt brought a bunch of grapes before Firʿawn and asked him to transform them into pearls. Firʿawn took the grapes inside his chamber and sat down, pondering as to how he could transform them into pearls. In the meantime Shayṭān arrived and knocked at his door. Firʿawn asked: 'Who is it?'

Shayṭān replied: 'Woe unto that god who knows not who stands behind the door.' Having said this he stepped into the chamber, took the grapes from Firʿawn, and recited one of the holy names of Allah upon them, whereupon they were immediately transformed into pearls. Then, turning to Firʿawn, he said: 'O Firʿawn! Judge with fairness and justice! Despite possessing such virtues and powers I am not worthy of being worshipped, but you, with the ignorance that you possess, claim god-ship for yourself and say: "I am the great god of the people"!'

Firʿawn enquired: 'Why did you not prostrate before Ādam so as not to be expelled from the presence of Allah?'

Shayṭān retorted in disgust: 'Because I knew that a dirty entity like you would come into existence from his loins.'[2]

4 – Muʿāwiyah

It has been reported that Muʿāwiyah had been asleep in his palace when he was suddenly awakened by someone. When Muʿāwiyah looked towards him, the person immediately concealed himself behind the curtains. Muʿāwiyah shouted: 'Who are you that have entered the palace without my permission and exhibited such impertinence?'

The man said: 'I am Shayṭān.'

Muʿāwiyah asked: 'Why did you wake me up?'

---

[1] *Shanīdanī-hā-yi Tārīkh*, p. 258; *al-Maḥajjah al-Bayḍāʾ*, vol. 5, p. 59.

[2] *Pand-i Tārīkh*, vol. 1, p. 23; *Anwār al-Nuʿmāniyyah*, p. 80. This incident has been narrated slightly differently in *Jawāmiʿ al-Ḥikāyāt*, p. 21.

He replied: 'It is time for prayers and I have aroused you so that you can proceed to the mosque in time for the prayers!'

Mu'āwiyah said: 'You are Shayṭān, and Shayṭān is an entity who never desires any good for people. Is it correct to accept a thief's claim that he had come to the house for the purpose of guarding it?'

Shayṭān said: 'I woke you up lest you continue to sleep and your prayers become lapsed thereby causing you to sigh in regret and your heart to grieve that the time for prayers had passed away and you did not go to the mosque for offering your prayers! This sigh is more significant and important than hundreds of prayers, and I did not want you to engage yourself in such sighing and lamentations, for then you would have been graced by Allah's mercy.'

Having heard this, Mu'āwiyah attested the veracity of his words.[1]

5 – Prophet Yaḥyā 🕮 and Shayṭān

Once, the accursed Shayṭān manifested himself before Prophet Yaḥyā 🕮, the son of Prophet Zakariyyā 🕮. Observing that he had in his possession numerous ropes, Prophet Yaḥyā 🕮 enquired: 'O Iblīs! What are these ropes that you hold in your hand?'

Shayṭān replied: 'These ropes are the various attachments, inclinations, and lusts that I have found in the children of Ādam.'

Prophet Yaḥyā 🕮 asked: 'Does there exist a rope for me too?'

Shayṭān said: 'Yes. When you satiate yourself with food you experience weightiness, and it is for this reason you become disinclined with respect to your prayers, remembrance, and supplications.'

Hearing this, Prophet Yaḥyā 🕮 vowed: 'By Allah! Never shall I eat to my fill, ever again.'

Iblīs responded by pledging: 'By Allah! Never shall I advise anyone, ever again.'[2]

---

[1] *Dāstān-hā-yi Mathnawī*, vol. 2, p. 15.

[2] *Iblīs Nāmih*, vol. 1, p. 35; *Maḥāsin Barqī*, p. 439.

51. Patience

Allah, the Wise, has said:

فَٱصْبِرْ كَمَا صَبَرَ أُوْلُوا الْعَزْمِ مِنَ الرُّسُلِ

So be patient just as the resolute among the apostles were patient. (46:35)

Imam ʿAlī said:

حَلَاوَةُ الظَّفَرِ تَمْحُوا مَرَارَةَ الصَّبْرِ

The sweetness of success erases the bitterness of patience.[1]

Short explanation

For some, the initial phase of patience is bitter while its final phase is sweet, while for others, its initial as well as its final phase is bitter, while for yet others, patience, in all phases, is sweet.

One who exhibits patience willingly, refrains from complaining before others and does not fret and fume, is of the patient ones. And one, who is not forbearing in the face of misfortunes and does not beseech and supplicate to Allah, is regarded as being of the impatient ones.

It is in the face of misfortune and calamity that a truly patient person is differentiated from a false claimant. A patient person is submissive in the face of adversities while one who claims falsely is overcome with perturbation, anguish, and sorrow.[2]

1 – Survival of religion lies in patience

One day, the Holy Prophet, accompanied by the Commander of the Faithful, was heading towards the Mosque of Quba when they happened to come across a lush-green garden. Witnessing it, Imam ʿAlī commented: 'O Prophet of Allah! It is a nice garden.'

The Holy Prophet responded: 'Your garden in paradise is nicer!'

They passed by the garden and continued on their way; in the course of their walk they passed by seven gardens and on each occasion the same

---

[1] *Ghurar al-Ḥikam*, h. 4882.

[2] *Tadhkirat al-Ḥaqāʾiq*, p. 86.

conversation ensued between the two. Then, the Holy Prophet took Imam 'Alī ﷺ into his arms and began weeping intensely, causing the Imam to weep as well. When Imam sought to know the reason for the Holy Prophet's weeping, he replied: 'I suddenly recollected the malice that has taken root in the breasts of the people towards you and which they shall make manifest after my death.'

The Imam enquired: 'O Prophet of Allah! What should I do?'

He advised: 'Patience and fortitude. If you fail to exhibit patience you shall fall into far greater difficulties.'

The Imam said: 'Do you fear the destruction of my religion?'

The Holy Prophet replied: 'The survival of your religion lies in patience.'[1]

2 – Ease after patience

The only son of an indigent woman had gone on a journey which had transformed into a protracted one. Extremely worried, she approached Imam al-Ṣādiq ﷺ and complained: 'My son has been away on a journey which has turned into a very long one and I am terribly distressed.'

The Imam said: 'O lady! Be patient and control yourself.'

The lady left, but after having waited for a few more days and with no sign of her son's arrival she was not able to withstand it any longer. She approached the Imam again and said: 'My son has still not returned. What should I do?'

The Imam said to her: 'Did I not advise you to be patient and exhibit fortitude?'

She lamented: 'By Allah! I have reached the limit of my patience and do not possess the strength to bear this separation anymore!'

Hearing this, the Imam said: 'Return home for your son has arrived.'

Confounded, she returned to her house only to find her son back from his journey. Even as she was overjoyed at seeing him, she thought to herself: 'How did the Imam know that he had returned? Does revelation

---

[1] *Dāstān-hā-yi Zindagī-yi ʿAlī*, p. 97; *Manāqib* of Ibn Shahr Āshūb, vol. 1, p. 322.

descend upon him? Let me go and ask him about this issue.' Approaching the Imam, she asked: 'Just as you had said, my son has returned from his journey. But tell me, do you receive revelation that you were able to inform me of the unseen?'

He said: 'I deduced this from one of the traditions of the Noble Prophet ﷺ. He ﷺ had said: "When man's patience reaches its end, ease and relief sets in upon him." When I observed that your patience had reached its termination I realised that relief had arrived and so informed you that your son had arrived, and my deduction proved to be correct.'[1]

3 – Bilāl

Bilāl was originally from Abyssinia, and in Medina he was a slave. After he had embraced Islam he had to suffer intense hardships at the hands of his owners.

During the onset of Islam, those in Mecca who had embraced the faith had to face great adversities, especially those who did not possess any familial or tribal support, or were slaves and servants. Some, due to the intensity of sufferings, even backtracked from their religion; but Bilāl, exhibiting great patience, increased in steadfastness, and due to this his owners increased their torture upon him.

Abū Jahl would force him to lie on his stomach on the hot sands of Hijaz, pin him down by means of a millstone until his brains would almost come to a boil due to the intensity of the heat, and then say to him: 'Deny the god of Muḥammad!' However, all that Bilāl would say was: '*Aḥad, aḥad,*' meaning Allah is one.

One of those who greatly persecuted him was Umayyah ibn Khalaf, who used to torture him repeatedly. However, as divine decree would have it, he was killed in the Battle of Badr at the hands of Bilāl.

During one of those occasions when Bilāl was being tortured, the Holy Prophet happened to pass by. Witnessing him, he said to Abū Bakr: 'Had I possessed money, I would have purchased Bilāl.' Later, he approached his

---

[1] *Ḥikāyat-hā-yi Shanīdanī,* vol. 5, p. 147; *La'ālī al-Akhbār,* vol. 1, p. 266.

uncle ʿAbbās and said: 'Purchase Bilāl for me.'

Even as ʿAbbās went in search of the woman who owned him, Bilāl was being subjected to torture and persecution, pinioned under the weight of heavy stones and almost on the verge of death. ʿAbbās approached the woman and expressed his desire to purchase Bilāl, whereupon she began to criticise and speak ill of him, but eventually sold him. Thus, Bilāl, as a result of his patience in the face of torture and persecution, became free, and entering into the services of the Holy Prophet, he became his muezzin.[1]

4 – The wedding night

Sibṭ al-Shaykh has narrated:

'One of the elders of Arabia – the chief of a tribe that dwelled in the environs of Baghdad – decided to marry his son to a maiden from amongst his relatives. As per the custom prevalent there, the marriage and its consummation was supposed to take place on the same night. On the appointed night, preparations were made for feast and entertainment, and the supreme religious authority of the Arab world – Shaykh Mahdī Khāliṣī – was invited to recite the marriage formula.

'Some of the youths proceeded towards the bridegroom in order to bring him to the marriage gathering in a special ceremony and with special formalities. As was their custom, they began firing bullets into the air, and in the process a bullet from the gun of one of the youths – a sayyid – accidentally struck the bridegroom in the chest and killed him.

'Witnessing this, the sayyid youth ran away and the episode was brought to the attention of the bridegroom's father. The late Shaykh Mahdī Khāliṣī, coming to know of the incident, instructed the father to exhibit patience, and advised: "Do you know that the Noble Prophet ﷺ has a great obligation upon us and all of us are in need of his intercession? This youth did not do this intentionally, but it was by providence that the bullet happened to strike your son, killing him. Forgive this youth for the sake of his grandfather ﷺ, and exhibit patience over this misfortune so that Allah

---

[1] *Payghambar Wa Yārān*, vol. 2, p. 66; *Asad al-Ghābbah*, vol. 1, p. 206.

grants you the rewards of the patient ones!"

'Upon hearing the Shaykh's counsel, the father of the bridegroom became silent, and after little reflection, said: "We have numerous guests now and the occasion of joy has been transformed into an occasion of grief. For completing the right of the Noble Prophet ﷺ, call the sayyid youth and instead of my son, marry him to the maiden and lead them to the bridal chamber!"

'The Shaykh praised and commended him. When the people went after the sayyid youth and informed him that he was to get married in place of the chief's son, he initially refused to believe it, thinking it to be a ploy to seize him and kill him. However, ultimately the Shaykh married the maiden to the sayyid youth on that night, while the dead son was buried the next day.'[1]

52. Charity

Allah, the Wise, has said:

$$\text{إِنْ تُبْدُوا الصَّدَقَاتِ فَنِعِمَّا هِيَ}$$

If you disclose your charities, that is well. (2:271)

The Holy Prophet said:

$$\text{تَصَدَّقُوا وَلَوْ بِتَمْرَةٍ}$$

Give charity, even if it happens to be a date.[2]

Short explanation

Charity is of two kinds: the first is concealed charity – one that had been the conduct of the Imams and which wards away poverty, lengthens the life, does away with seventy kinds of evil deaths, and smothers the divine wrath. And the second is manifest charity – one that increases the sustenance and breaks Shayṭān's back.

An important point in connection with charity is that quantity and

---

[1] *Dāstān-hā-yi Shigift*, p. 255.

[2] *Jāmiʿ al-Saʿādāt*, vol. 2, p. 145.

immenseness of money, clothes, or food, is not the criterion for perfection; rather, it is the purity and sincerity of intention which is the requisite for perfection.

At times, when the Holy Prophet did not possess any money, he would give his clothes in charity and would recommend: 'Commence your day with charity, for it serves to insure you.'

1 – Auspicious and inauspicious times

Imam al-Ṣādiq ﷺ relates:

'There was a piece of land that I owned in partnership with an astrologer and it was mutually decided that it should be divided between us. He made preparations so that his arrival should be in an auspicious hour while I should arrive in an inauspicious hour so that the better portion of the land fell in his hands. The land was divided, but it so happened that the better portion came into my share of the land. The man slapped his right hand over his left in regret and said ruefully: "Oh! Had I never lived to see such a day!"

'I said to him: "Why are you so upset today?"

'He said: "I am an astrologer and I brought you out of your house in an inauspicious hour while I myself came out in an auspicious hour. However, now that the land has been divided, you have come to acquire the better portion of it."

'I said: "I shall inform you of a tradition of the Noble Prophet ﷺ wherein he said: 'If one desires that Allah wards away from him the inauspiciousness of a day, he should start his day by giving charity, and if one desires to ward away the inauspiciousness of the night, he should commence his night by giving charity.'"'

The Imam then said: 'I gave charity as I came out today; charity is better for you than astrology.'[1]

---

[1] *Bā Mardūm Īn Gūnih Barkhūrd Kunīm*, p. 135; *al-Kāfī*, vol. 4, p. 6.

2 – Ḥātim's mother

'Atbah bint 'Afīf, the mother of Ḥātim Ṭā'ī, was an open-hearted and generous lady, who used to distribute all her wealth amongst the needy.

When her brothers saw her giving her wealth in charity, they prevented her from accessing it, and said: 'You are indulging in extravagance and ruining your property.'

For a period of one year they did not provide her with any money. When the year had passed, they spoke amongst themselves and said: 'She has suffered much in this year as a result of scarcity and perhaps now, after this prohibition, she would spend her wealth moderately and not exhibit extravagance.' They gave her a herd of camels so that she could make use of them.

At that juncture, a woman from the tribe of Hawāzin approached her and, as in the past, sought food and assistance from her. Ḥātim's mother gifted the entire herd of camels to her, saying: 'In this period [of one year], I have tasted the sufferings of poverty and have promised myself that whatever I come to possess I shall give in charity to the needy and the deprived ones!'[1]

3 – In the darkness of the night

Mu'allā ibn Khunays narrates:

'One rainy night, Imam al-Ṣādiq ⁣ started out from his house with the intention of proceeding towards the tent of the tribe of Banī Sā'idah (under which they used to gather in the heat of the day, while it would be utilised as a sleeping place by the travellers and the indigent ones, during the night).

'I followed the Imam ⁣ when I noticed that something had suddenly fallen out of his hands. He ⁣ supplicated: "O Allah! Return to me that which has fallen." I advanced nearer and saluted him at which he questioned: "Mu'allā?"

'I said: "Yes; may I be made your ransom."

---

[1] *Jawāmi' al-Ḥikāyāt*, p. 248.

'The Imam ﷺ said to me: "Move your hand over the ground and hand over to me whatever you happen to find."

'As I moved my hand over the ground I found some pieces of bread scattered around; gathering them all, which eventually became a sack-full, I handed them to him ﷺ and said: "May I be made your ransom; allow me to carry the sack upon my back."

'He ﷺ said: "No; I am more deserving of carrying the sack, but yes, I do permit you to accompany me."

'Thus, together with the Imam ﷺ I reached the tent of Banī Sāʿidah where a group of poor people lay asleep. The Imam ﷺ began placing one or two pieces of bread below their garments till all the pieces of bread were used up. As we turned back, I said to him: "May I be made your ransom, are they Shiʿas?"

'The Imam ﷺ replied: "Had they been Shiʿas I would have provided them with all that they needed – even their salt."'[1]

4 – The mother of the devils

Sayyid Niʿmat Allāh Jazāʾirī narrates in his book:

'One year, a famine struck. During that period a preacher, from atop the pulpit in the mosque, preached: "When one desires to give charity, seventy devils cling onto his hands to prevent him from giving it."

'Hearing this, a person said to his friends in amazement: "Giving charity has no such thing associated with it. I have some wheat present in my house which I shall immediately bring to the mosque and distribute amongst the poor."

'With this in mind he set off for his house. When he reached home and informed his wife of his intention, she began to reprimand him, saying: "In this period of drought do you have no consideration for your wife and child? Maybe the drought will extend for a long time, in which case we shall die of hunger and …" In short, she rebuked him to such an extent that eventually the man returned to the mosque empty-handed.

____

[1] *Muntahā al-Aʿmāl*, vol. 2, p. 127.

'His friends asked him: "What happened? Did you see how seventy devils clung to your hand and prevented you?"[1]

'The man said: "Honestly speaking, I did not see the devils but I certainly saw their mother, who prevented me from performing this good deed."[2]

5 – The widely respected Shi'a government minister

Perhaps the only Shi'a minister to have been widely popular amongst the people of all classes was Ṣāḥib ibn 'Abbād (326 AH to 385 AH). He had initially been the minister of Mu'ayyad al-Dawlah Daylamī (d. 373 AH), after whose death he became the minister of Mu'ayyad's brother, Fakhr al-Dawlah.

Shaykh Ṣadūq compiled the book 'Uyūn Akhbār al-Riḍā for him, while Ḥusayn ibn Muḥammad Qummī authored the book Tārīkh Qum upon his orders.

During the period when he was the minister, it was not possible for one who came to him in the afternoon of the month of Ramadan to leave except after consuming iftār, and at times the people breaking their fast at his place totalled 1000 in number. His charity in this holy month would equal that of all the other months combined as it was from his infancy that his mother had trained him to act in such a manner.

During his childhood, when he would start out for his classes, his mother would give him a dinar and a dirham every day and advise him: 'Give charity to the first needy you come across!' This act transformed itself into a habit for him.

From his childhood to youth and then on until he became a minister, he never disregarded the recommendation and training of his mother. Fearful of forgetting this recommendation, he instructed the slave who was in charge of his quarters to place one dinar and one dirham under his mattress every night. Upon waking up in the morning, he would give them

---

[1] The Holy Prophet said: 'O 'Alī! Do you know that alms does not go out of the hands of a believer except that seventy devils attempt to dissuade him by various means from giving it.' Wasā'il al-Shī'ah, vol. 6, p. 257.

[2] Iblīs Nāmih, p. 60; Anwār al-Nu'māniyyah, vol. 3, p. 96.

in charity to the first needy he encountered.

It so happened that one night the servant forgot to place the money. The next morning, Ṣāḥib ibn ʿAbbād, upon waking, thrust his hand under the mattress to collect the money only to realise that the servant had forgotten to place the money there. He took this to augur ill for himself and thought: 'Surely, my end has drawn nigh that the servant forgot to place the charity.'

He ordered the blanket, mattress, and pillows that lay in his bedroom to be given in charity to the first destitute that came his way as an expiation for the forgetfulness. Having collected all the items – all of which were costly and expensive – he set out of his house, only to encounter an old blind sayyid who was shedding tears as his wife led him by the hand. Ṣāḥib's servant went forward and asked him: 'Will you accept these items?'

The man asked: 'What are the items?'

The servant replied: 'A blanket, mattress, and some brocaded pillows.'

As soon as he heard this the destitute fell down unconscious. When Ṣāḥib ibn ʿAbbād was informed of this he approached the man and ordered water to be sprinkled over his face. When the man had regained his consciousness, Ṣāḥib asked him: 'What caused you to lose consciousness?'

He answered: 'I am a respectable person. It is of late that I have fallen into bad times. I have a daughter from this wife who had reached the age of marriage; a person sought her hand in marriage and they were married. It has been two years now that we have been collecting items for her marriage. Last night my wife said to me: "We must make arrangements for a blanket and brocaded pillows for my daughter." Try as much as I could, I could not get her to change her mind until there ensued a dispute between us over this issue. Finally I said to her: "Tomorrow morning, hold my hand and take me out of the house," so that I could pass in front of you. Then, when your servant spoke those words to me, it was but natural that I should fall down unconscious.'

Ṣāḥib was greatly affected by this speech. Summoning the daughter's husband he gave him sufficient wealth so that he could engage himself in a respectable profession, after which he gave the entire dowry of the daughter in a measure befitting a minister's daughter.[1]

53. Establishing Bonds Of Kinship

Allah, the Wise, has said:

$$\text{فَهَلْ عَسَيْتُمْ إِنْ تَوَلَّيْتُمْ أَنْ تُفْسِدُوا فِي الْأَرْضِ وَتُقَطِّعُوا أَرْحَامَكُمْ}$$

May it not be that if you were to wield authority you would cause corruption
in the land and ill-treat your blood relations? (47:22)

Imam al-Bāqir ﷺ said:

$$\text{صِلَةُ الْأَرْحَامِ تُطَيِّبُ النَّفْسَ وَتَزِيدُ فِي الرِّزْقِ}$$

Establishing the bonds of kinship freshens the soul and increases the
sustenance.[2]

Short explanation

The term *rahim* is used to denote those who are one's relatives by birth,
and it is forbidden to sever one's relationship with them.

Those who associate with their relatives in a goodly manner and seek
to help them, Allah shall lengthen their lives, grant them an increase in
their livelihood, and subject them to an easy reckoning on the Day of
Judgement.

On the other hand, those who distance themselves from their relatives
and seek to trouble them shall have to face detrimental consequences for
such acts of theirs – destruction of their faith, ruining of their Hereafter,
lessening of their lifespan, diminution in sustenance, and, the worst of all,
the termination in the bestowal of divine grace and favour upon them.
Allah has mentioned in Ḥadīth al-Qudsī: 'I am the All-beneficent. One who
severs his relation with his relatives, I shall sever My relation with him.'[3]

---

[1] *Pand-i Tārīkh*, vol. 4, p. 112; *Rawḍāt al-Jannāt*, p. 105.

[2] *Jāmiʿ al-Saʿādāt*, vol. 2, p. 260.

[3] *Iḥyāʾ al-Qulūb*, p. 127.

1 – Plague

Once, one of the companions of Imam al-Ṣādiq ﷺ said to him: 'My brothers and cousins have made life very difficult for me in my house to the extent that I lead my life in only one room. If I were to even attempt to complain to them or the governor, they shall take away all the wealth and property that I possess.'

The Imam said: 'Be patient, for after adversity you shall be in ease and comfort.'

Later, narrating the incident, the man said: 'I decided against initiating legal proceedings against them.'

Before long, plague struck the region in the year 131 AH, and all those relatives who used to trouble him died as a result of it.

After a period he presented himself before the Imam, who enquired: 'How are your relatives?'

The man replied: 'All of them are dead!'

The Imam said: 'They died as a result of the inconveniences that they had subjected you to; a punishment for their deeds [i.e. severing the bonds of kinship] with respect to you, their relative.' The Imam then asked: 'Did you want them to stay alive and inconvenience you?'

Whereupon the man replied: 'By Allah, no.'[1]

2 – The Imam's bonds of kinship

Ḥasan ibn ʿAlī, a cousin of Imam al-Ṣādiq ﷺ, was a courageous, robust, and physically powerful person such that he was referred to as the 'lance of the family of Abū Ṭālib'. Possessing a wide nose, he was popularly known as Ḥasan Afṭas.

He was the standard-bearer in the uprising initiated by ʿAbd Allāh Maḥḍ (the grandson of Imam al-Ḥasan ﷺ) against Manṣūr Dawānīqī. His relations with Imam al-Ṣādiq ﷺ turned sour over the issue and he even went to the extent of attacking the Imam with a large knife with the intention of killing him.

---

[1] *Shayṭān*, vol. 1, p. 515; a*l-Kāfī*.

Sālimah, one of Imam's slave-girls, relates: 'The Imam ﷺ was on his deathbed and I was at his bedside nursing him when he suddenly dropped into unconsciousness. As soon as he had regained his consciousness, he instructed me: "Give seventy dinars to Ḥasan Afṭas and such and such sums to such and such individuals."

'I said to him: "Should we give seventy dinars to the person who had lunged at you with a knife and desired to kill you?"

'He said: "Do you not desire that I should be one of those about whom Allah says: Those who join what Allah has commanded to be joined, and fear their Lord, and are afraid of an adverse reckoning – those who are patient for the sake of their Lord's pleasure, maintain the prayer, and spend out of what We have provided them, secretly and openly, and repel evil [conduct] with good. For such will be the reward of the [ultimate] abode [13:21-22]?"

'He then continued: "Yes, O Sālimah! Allah has created paradise and made it pure and fragrant such that its fragrance can be perceived at a distance of 2000 years; but this fragrance shall not reach the person who has severed ties with his relatives and one who has been disowned by his parents."'[1]

3 – 'Abbās – the Holy Prophet's uncle

'Abbās, the uncle of the Holy Prophet, was a person who exhibited great kindness towards his relatives and thus found himself to be an object of praise and commendation of the Holy Prophet, who lauded him by saying: ''Abbās ibn 'Abd al-Muṭṭalib is the most generous and benevolent towards his relatives from amongst all the Quraysh.'

During one of the battles, the Holy Prophet ordered: 'Whoever happens to encounter anyone from the Banī Hāshim should not kill him, for the Banī Hāshim have been made to participate in the battle under compulsion.'

During the Battle of Badr, a person by the name of Abū Yasīr captured 'Abbās, who, not intending to resist the capture, stood firm and unmoving

---

[1] *Ḥikāyat-hā-yi Shanīdanī*, vol. 5, p. 30; *al-Ghunyah* of Shaykh Ṭūsī, p. 128.

like a staff. When the battle had concluded, the Holy Prophet, for the sake of equity, did not exhibit any discrimination between ʿAbbās and the other captives. At night, all the captives were tied by means of ropes and ʿAbbās was seated near the tent of the Holy Prophet. The moans and groans of ʿAbbās kept reaching his ears as a result of which he could not sleep until midnight, and kept turning from one side to another. One of the Muslims who was near the Holy Prophet, enquired: 'O Prophet of Allah! Why do you not sleep?'

He replied: 'The moans of my uncle ʿAbbās distress me and prevent me from sleeping.' A little later the moans subsided and could no longer be heard. The Holy Prophet enquired: 'What has happened that I do not hear the moans of my uncle ʿAbbās anymore?'

The man said: 'I have loosened the ropes that bound him.'

Hearing this, the Holy Prophet instructed: 'Loosen the ropes of all the other captives too.'[1]

4 – Non-observance of kinship bonds and death

Shuʿayb ʿAqarqūfī narrates:

'Imam Mūsā ibn Jaʿfar 🕮 said to me: "Tomorrow, a person by the name of Yaʿqūb – an inhabitant of Maghreb – shall meet you and enquire about me; guide him to my house."

'I found the person performing the *ṭawāf*, and as I enquired about his health I realised that he appeared to know me; I asked him: "How do you know me?"

'He said: "A person appeared to me in my dreams and said: 'Meet Shuʿayb and ask him whatever you desire to know.' Upon waking I enquired about you and the people pointed you to me."

'I found him to be an intelligent person and upon his request took him to the Imam's house. Reaching there, I sought permission to enter the house and the Imam obliged. As soon as the Imam's eyes fell upon him, he said: "O Yaʿqūb! You arrived here yesterday, but on the way, at such

---

[1] *Payghambar Wa Yārān*, vol. 4, p. 85; *Ṭabaqāt*, vol. 4, pp. 2-7.

and such a place, there ensued a quarrel between you and your brother to the extent that both of you hurled abuses and insults at each other. This is neither our conduct nor that of the religion of our forefathers. We do not approve of such a conduct from anybody; fear Allah, who is one and has no partners. Very soon death shall cause a separation between both of you – a consequence of having broken the bond of kinship!"

'He said: "May I be made your ransom! When am I going to die?"

'The Imam replied: "Verily, your end had neared too, but since you resolved your differences with your aunt and re-established your bonds of kinship at such and such place, your life has been increased by twenty years."

'A year later I met Ya'qūb during the season of hajj and enquired after his health, whereupon he said: "On the return journey my brother died before he could reach home and was buried on the way."'[1]

5 – The painful consequence of breaking family ties

The intense slandering with respect to Imam Mūsā ibn Ja'far ﷺ that reached the ears of Hārūn al-Rashīd, the Abbasid caliph, provoked him to say: 'Present before me someone from the descendants of Abū Ṭālib so that I can become aware of his activities.'

Hārūn's minister, Yaḥyā Barmakī, and some others suggested the name of 'Alī ibn Ismā'īl – the Imam's nephew.

Upon Hārūn's orders a letter was dispatched to him asking him to present himself before the caliph in Baghdad. When the Imam came to know of this, he called for him and questioned: 'Where do you intend to go?'

'Alī ibn Ismā'īl answered: 'Baghdad.'

The Imam enquired: 'For what purpose?'

He replied: 'I am burdened by great debts.'

The Imam said: 'I shall repay your debts and arrange for your expenses.'

However, 'Alī ibn Ismā'īl refused the offer, and instead said: 'Advise

---

[1] *Muntahā al-A'māl*, vol. 2, p. 206.

me!'

The Imam said: 'I advise you that you do not associate yourself in shedding my blood and do not make my children fatherless.' Repeating this three times, Imam presented him with 300 dinars and 4000 dirhams. Later, when Ismāʿīl had left, the Imam said to those around him: 'His slandering and vilification shall contribute to my murder.'[1]

Arriving in Baghdad, ʿAlī ibn Ismāʿīl went to Yaḥyā ibn Khālid Barmakī. That night, Yaḥyā said to him: 'Tomorrow, in the presence of the caliph, when you are questioned about Mūsā ibn Jaʿfar ﷺ, you must say: "I have never witnessed two caliphs exercising authority at one time – you in Baghdad and Mūsā ibn Jaʿfar ﷺ, in Medina. He is about to incite the people into rebelling against you!"'

The next morning, arriving in the presence of the caliph, ʿAlī ibn Ismāʿīl maligned and slandered the Imam as much as he could. In the course of his talks he even said that people from distant places brought money for him and armed him with weapons, and that he was taking the pledge of allegiance from the people and intended to establish a separate state and government.

Hearing this, Hārūn appeared to have been jolted out of sleep; he dismissed him from his presence and sent a sum of 4000 dirhams for him to the place where he had been staying.

When the money was brought before him, an intense pain rose up inside his throat and he died then and there – a consequence of having severed the bond of kinship with his uncle, Mūsā ibn Jaʿfar ﷺ.

The bags of money were carried back to Hārūn's coffers while sorrow and regret was the only thing that Ismāʿīl carried to his grave.[2]

54. Oppression And Injustice

Allah, the Wise, has said:

---

[1] *Muntahā al-Aʿmāl,* vol. 2, p. 213.

[2] *Jāmiʿ al-Nūrayn,* p. 24.

$$\text{وَسَيَعْلَمُ الَّذِينَ ظَلَمُوا أَيَّ مُنْقَلَبٍ يَنْقَلِبُونَ}$$

And the wrongdoers will soon know at what goal they will end up. (26:227)

Imam al-Bāqir ﷺ said:

$$\text{مَا مِنْ أَحَدٍ يَظْلِمُ بِمَظْلِمَةٍ إِلَّا أَخَذَهُ اللهُ تَعَالَى بِهَا فِي نَفْسِهِ أَوْ مَالِهِ}$$

There is none who commits oppression by means of an injustice, except that Allah afflicts him or his wealth because of it.[1]

Short explanation

Oppression and injustice are, in reality, insubordination to the orders of Allah, acts of transgression, and a consequence of transcending the limits of the shariah and the intellect.

Throughout history, that which has befallen the weak and the oppressed has been due to the oppression of the oppressors. Power and craving for dominance serve as a prelude for a disobedient soul to oppress the vulnerable and weak individuals.

One who transgresses divine limits and is uninhibited with respect to every kind of oppression and injustice such as murder, abuse, vilification, fornication, rape, usurpation of the property of others, etc., has, in effect, gone out of the bounds of Allah's obedience, drowned himself in carnal desires, and become afflicted with the disease of rebelliousness. Such a person, sooner or later, shall be seized by punishment and retribution since the lamentations of the weak, oppressed, and the orphaned ones possess negative overtones which manifest themselves in this world and the Hereafter.[2]

1 – The oppression of Dadhanah

In Syria there lived a king by the name of Dadhanah, who was an idol worshipper. Allah sent a prophet to Dadhanah to advise him and invite him to monotheism, but instead Dadhanah responded by asking him: 'Which city do you come from?'

---

[1] *Jāmiʿ al-Saʿādāt*, vol. 2, p. 220.

[2] *Iḥyāʾ al-Qulūb*, p. 76.

He replied: 'I am of Roman origin and have come from Palestine.'

Upon Dadhanah's orders, the prophet was imprisoned, his holy body subjected to injuries by means of iron spikes till his flesh fell apart, and vinegar was poured over the wounds. After this, his thighs, knees, soles of his feet, and head were pounded by means of red-hot iron skewers to such an extent that he was on the verge of death. Allah sent an angel to him, who said: 'Allah says: "Be patient and happy and fear not, for I am with you and shall deliver you from them. They shall attempt to kill you four times, but I shall ward away the pain and agony of the sufferings from you."'

The second time, Dadhanah ordered that this Prophet's back and stomach should be lashed after which he should be hurled into prison. He then summoned every sorcerer and magician before him and ordered them to use their magic to his benefit against the prophet, but despite their best efforts their magic failed to have any effect on him. Having failed in this they tried to poison him, but the prophet recited Allah's name and the poison caused him no harm. One of the magicians said: 'Had I fed this poison to all of the inhabitants of the earth they would have turned blind, their appearances would have changed, and all of them would have perished!' Then, repenting over his past misdeeds, he declared his faith in the prophet, whereupon Dadhanah had him killed.

For the umpteenth time, Dadhanah hurled the prophet into prison and on this occasion ordered his body to be cut into pieces and thrown into a well.

With the objective of admonishing him, Allah sent down lightening and earthquake, but he refused to heed the warning. Allah sent angel Mīkā'īl who brought the prophet out of the well and said to him: 'Be patient,' and then conveyed to him glad tidings of the divine rewards.

The prophet again approached the king and invited him towards monotheism, but once again he refused. However, on this occasion, the commander of his army together with 4000 people accepted the faith. Witnessing this, Dadhanah ordered all of them to be put to death.

This time, he prepared a tablet out of molten copper and forced the prophet to lie upon it. He then poured molten lead down his throat and then, lighting up an inferno, hurled him into it in order that he be burnt to death.

This time again, Allah sent Mīkāʾīl to grant him soundness of health. Having regained his health, the prophet approached the king yet again and advised him to abandon idolatry and invited him towards monotheism.

On this occasion, Dadhanah hurled him into a cauldron containing molten lead and sulphur, and ignited a fire under him in order to melt his body with the molten lead and sulphur. Allah sent down the angel Isrāfīl who issued a shriek, causing the cauldron to topple over, leaving the prophet safe and unharmed.

Having regained his health by the power of Allah, he again approached Dadhanah and invited him towards the worship of Allah. Frustrated and desperate, Dadhanah ordered all the people to gather together in the desert and kill him in unison, whereupon the prophet supplicated to Allah and pleaded for patience and fortitude.

The people beheaded him and were on their way back when all of them were seized by an onslaught of divine chastisement.[1]

2 – Working for the oppressors

A person by the name of Muhājir narrates as follows:

'I had gone to Imam al-Ṣādiq and said to him: "Such and such persons have sent you their salutations." The Imam responded in kind, whereupon I said: "They have also requested you to pray for them."

'He enquired: "What is their problem?"

'I said: "Manṣūr Dawānīqī has flung them into prison."

'He asked: "What did they have to do with Manṣūr?"

'I replied: "They used to work for him and one day, in a fit of anger, he hurled them behind bars."

'The Imam said: "But had I not prohibited them from working for him? Such work entails great danger." Having said this, the Imam then prayed:

---

[1] *Ḥayāt al-Qulūb*, vol. 1, p. 477.

"O Allah! Repel from them the evils and grant them deliverance."'

Muhājir says: 'I returned from Mecca and enquired about my friends whereupon I was informed that they had been set free.' According to the dates, they had been released three days after the Imam had prayed for them.[1]

3 – Retaliation

Once, Prophet Mūsā ☙ was passing by a region when he came across a spring which flowed alongside a mountain. Performing ablution with the water, he proceeded to the top of the mountain to offer prayers. Meanwhile, a person on horseback reached the spring and dismounted the horse with the intention of quenching his thirst. When he had satiated himself, he mounted his mount and galloped away, dropping his money pouch in the process.

A short while later, a shepherd arrived there; noticing the money pouch, he picked it up and left.

After the shepherd had left, an old man – a bundle of firewood on his head and possessing an appearance that manifested his destitution and poverty – reached there. Placing his load on the ground he stretched himself out near the spring and went to sleep. Before long, the rider returned to the spring and began searching for his lost money pouch. Failing to locate it, he questioned the old man, who pleaded ignorance about it. There ensued an altercation between the two and very soon they began trading blows. In the resulting brawl, the rider beat the old man so severely that he died.

Witnessing this, Prophet Mūsā ☙ said: 'O Lord! What kind of incident was this and what kind of justice exists in this episode? The money was taken by the shepherd but it was the old man who had to face oppression and injustice!'

He was told: 'O Mūsā! This old man had killed the rider's father and so retaliation was achieved between them. The rider's father had owed the shepherd's father the same amount that was contained in the money

---

[1] *Shanīdanī-hā-yi Tārīkh*, p. 57; *al-Maḥajjah al-Bayḍā'*, vol. 3, p. 256.

pouch, and in this way the shepherd acquired his right. O Mūsā! I pass My judgement on the basis of justice and fairness.'[1]

4 – The oppression of Ḍaḥḥāk Ḥimyarī

Having ruled Iran for years, Jamshīd slowly came to be filled with pride, ultimately claiming god-ship for himself and inviting the people to worship him. The people, out of fear of his sword, submitted to his demand; this continued until Ḍaḥḥāk initiated a military expedition against him and eventually killed him.

Placing himself at the helm of affairs of the sultanate, Ḍaḥḥāk adopted a policy of oppression and persecution, killing his father and subjecting his people to various forms of brutality and tribulation.

One day, he happened to experience discomfort in his head and shoulders. An evil cook suggested a remedy, saying: 'The thing that can cure you is [eating] the brains of the youths.'

Upon Ḍaḥḥāk's orders, two youths from the prison were killed; eating their brains, he felt a slight comfort in his state and so went to sleep. The next day onwards, two youths would be killed every day and their brains utilised for his treatment.

He committed great brutalities, never gave ear to any petition, and never meted out justice to any oppressed, and so, when he murdered two sons of Kaveh the ironsmith, it turned out to be the final straw and provoked a rebellion against him.

He was ultimately killed in an extremely gruesome manner – his head bludgeoned by a mace (or hurled into the depths of a well, according to another report), and it was Farīdūn who later took the reins of the sultanate.[2]

5 – The incident of Ḥarrah

After the incident of 'Āshūrā' and two and a half months before his death, Yazīd initiated yet another horrendous act on the twenty-eighth of Dhū al-

---

[1] *Pand-i Tārīkh*, vol. 3, p. 161; *Shayṭān*, vol. 2, p. 424.

[2] *Jawāmiʿ al-Ḥikāyāt*, p. 52.

Ḥijjah in the year 63 AH, which was the looting and killing of the people of Medina, and sacrilege with respect to the shrine of the Holy Prophet at the hands of an old, sick, brash, and impudent man by the name of Muslim ibn ʿAqabah, notoriously known as Musrif.

When the news of Yazīd's oppression and depravity reached the ears of the people of Medina, a group from amongst them proceeded to Syria to obtain first-hand information regarding the situation.

Witnessing his sacrilegious behaviour, they returned to Medina and drove his governor, ʿUthmān ibn Muḥammad, together with Marwān ibn Ḥakam and the other Umayyads, out of the city. The people then flocked to ʿAbd Allāh ibn Ḥanẓalah – known as Ghasīl al-Malāʾikah[1] – and pledged allegiance to him. Coming to know of this, Yazīd dispatched a force under the command of Musrif towards Medina.

In order to defend themselves, the people of Medina took up position in a region outside of the city where a fierce battle ensued between the two forces. Some of the inhabitants of Medina were killed while others fled and sought shelter in the holy shrine of the Holy Prophet.

Musrif's soldiers advanced into Medina, entered the holy shrine on horseback, and began their carnage, killing so many people that the mosque and the holy tomb were covered with blood; the number of people that were killed have been reported to be around 11,000!

Here is one example of the numerous brutalities committed by the forces of Musrif: one of the soldiers of the army of Yazīd, an inhabitant of Egypt, entering the house of a lady from the Anṣār who had recently given birth to a child which was in her arms, said to her: 'Bring me all your wealth.'

The lady said: 'By Allah! They have not left behind anything that I can give you.'

He said: 'I shall kill you and your child.'

The lady pleaded: 'Fear Allah, for this infant is the child of Ibn Abī Kabshah Anṣārī, the companion of the Noble Prophet ﷺ.' The name seemed

---

[1] One whose ghusl has been performed by the angels. (Tr.)

to have no effect upon the merciless man, who, picking up the innocent child by its legs even as it was being suckled, flung him against the wall, scattering his brains upon the floor.[1]

In the face of such atrocities,[2] all the people of Medina were forced to pledge allegiance to Yazīd with the exception of two: Imam Zayn al-ʿĀbidīn ﷺ and ʿAlī ibn ʿAbd Allāh ibn ʿAbbās.

The Imam arrived before Musrif after reciting a supplication as a result of which he was so was overcome with dread and awe that he could not get himself to kill the Imam. As for ʿAlī ibn ʿAbd Allāh, some of his maternal relatives were present in Musrif's army and they prevented him from being killed.[3]

55. Worship

Allah, the Wise, has said:

$$\text{وَمَا خَلَقْتُ الْجِنَّ وَالْإِنْسَ إِلَّا لِيَعْبُدُونِ}$$

I did not create the jinn and the humans except that they may worship Me.

(51:56)

Imam al-Sajjād ﷺ said:

$$\text{مَنْ عَمِلَ بِمَا افْتَرَضَ اللّٰهُ فَهُوَ مِنْ أَعْبَدِ النَّاسِ}$$

One who performs [all] that Allah has made obligatory, is of the most worshipful of people.[4]

---

[1] There are reports that in the aftermath of the incident of Ḥarrah, thousands of unwed maidens gave birth to illegitimate children, who were referred to as 'children of Ḥarrah' – a consequence of the transgressions committed by Musrif's soldiers with the maidens and women of Medina. *Tatimmat al-Muntahā*, p. 39.

[2] The incident of Ḥarrah has been reported, in addition to Shiʿa sources, by Sunni sources such as *Kāmil* of Ibn Kathīr, *Maqātil al-Ṭālibīn*, *Kashf al-Astār*, *al-Imāmah Wa al-Siyāsah*, *Akhbār al-Duwal*, *Tārīkh Masʿūdī*.

[3] *Muntahā al-Aʿmāl*, vol. 2, p. 34.

[4] *Shayṭān*, vol. 2, p. 113.

Short explanation

A believer performs the obligatory and the recommended acts, for these are the basis for Allah's obedience and subservience. If one performs these it is as if he has exhibited his devotion and subservience in entirety.

The best worship is that which is protected from external influences and shielded from internal catastrophes.

Should the deeds of a person be continual and flawless, the person shall be successful in his worship, however meagre the deeds might be.

Those who seek plain knowledge and mere external excellences but remain heedless of the soul and the reality of worship, do not achieve anything except a mould, as far as the worship of the Beneficent Allah is concerned.[1]

1 – The outcome of 'dry' worship

The Kharijites were individuals who, as a result of their fanaticism and extremism, had gone greatly astray. Their leader was a person by the name of Ḥurqūṣ ibn Zuhayr, who, during the time of the Holy Prophet, had drowned himself in prayers, fasts, and other acts of worship, causing many of the Muslims to become fascinated with him.

When the Holy Prophet had been distributing the spoils of war after the Battle of Ḥunayn, this person, who was just an arid and ceremonial worshipper, said to him with great impudence: 'O Muḥammad! Conduct yourself with fairness and equity,' and repeated the sentence three times.

When he had repeated it for the third time, the Holy Prophet became greatly disturbed and said: 'If I do not behave with fairness and equity then who shall behave so?'

This 'dry' worshipper eventually set out for battle against Imam ʿAlī in the Battle of Nahrawān and was killed. When the Imam's eyes fell upon his inauspicious corpse lying amongst the dead, he offered a prostration of thanksgiving and said [to his companions]: 'You have killed the worst of

---

[1] *Tadhkirat al-Ḥaqāʾiq,* p. 28.

men.'[1]

2 – Worship out of love

Saʿdī recounts:

'During one of my travels to Mecca, I found myself in the company of a group of pure-hearted and sincere youths who used to chant supplications and recite poems befitting men of letters, and engage themselves in acts of worship with an extraordinary presence of heart.

'On the way, we were joined by a 'dry' and 'soulless' worshipper, who did not approve of this mystical state of theirs and, being unaware of the inner fervour of the devoted youths, persistently criticised their behaviour.

'We continued on our way till we reached a place known as Banī Hilāl, where a black-faced Arab child approached us and began chanting for us in a manner so melodious that it even enraptured the birds and caused them to descend from their flight. The enchanting melody instilled such fervour in the worshipper's camel that it flung the worshipper to the ground and frantically rushed out into the desert.

'Turning to the worshipper, I said: "O old worshipper! You observe how a pleasant melody tends to affect even the animals whereas you are apathetic and indifferent [to spiritual melodies, not submitting your heart to Allah and not acquiring purity, unlike the pious and the pure-hearted ones]."'[2]

3 – The long worshipper

Uways Qaranī was of those individuals who had become completely enraptured with worship, such that, at times, he would pass the entire night in the state of *rukūʿ*, while at other times he would say: 'Tonight is the night for prostration,' and would remain in prostration till dawn.

He was told: 'What is this inconvenience that you impose upon

---

[1] *Dāstān-hā Wa Pand-hā*, vol. 9, p. 77; *ʿAlī Wa Farzandān* by Dr. Taha Husain, p. 123.

[2] *Ḥikāyat-hā-yi Gulistān*, p. 128.

yourself?'

He replied: 'Oh how I wish that the entire eternity were one night which I could pass in one prostration.'

Rabī' ibn Khathīm (who is buried in Mashhad and is popularly known as Khwājah Rabī') relates: 'I was in Kufa and my prime objective was to meet Uways Qaranī. When I eventually found him he was engaged in his afternoon prayers near the Euphrates. I said to myself: "I shall wait till he completes his prayers."

'Completing his afternoon prayers, he began reciting supplications and continued to do so till it became time for the *maghrib* and *'ishā'* prayers. Having offered them, he engaged himself in offering the recommended prayers – at times in *rukū'* while at other times in *sajdah*, and this continued till the night reached its termination. He offered his morning prayers and once again engaged himself in reciting supplications until the sun rose above the horizon, whereupon he permitted himself some rest. Waking up, he performed his ablution and was about to start his worship when I approached him and said: "How greatly you trouble yourself!"

'He said: "It is for achieving comfort that I endure such effort."

'I said to him: "I did not see you eat anything. How do you manage to arrange for your expenses?"

'He said: "Allah has taken it upon Himself to provide sustenance to His servants. Now do not indulge in any more of such talk." Having spoken thus, he left.'[1]

4 – The worship of Iblīs

The Commander of the Faithful said: 'Take lesson from Allah's action with respect to Iblīs, for He annulled all his acts of worship (because of his arrogance); he had worshipped Allah for 6000 years, and it is not known whether they were of the years of the world or those of the Hereafter. And this was a consequence of a moment's disobedience [in that he considered himself to be superior to Ādam and refused to prostrate before

---

[1] *Payghambar Wa Yārān*, vol. 1, p. 350; *Nāsikh al-Tawārīkh – 'Alī*, p. 176.

him]. So, after Shayṭān, is there anyone who can remain safe from Allah's punishment by being disobedient to Him?'[1]

Imam al-Ṣādiq ﷺ was asked: 'For what reason did Allah respite Iblīs till the 'appointed time'?'

The Imam replied: 'Because of his praise and thanksgiving to Allah.'

He was asked again: 'What was his praise and thanksgiving?'

He replied: 'His 6000 years of worship in the heavens.'

On another occasion he said: 'Iblis offered a two-unit prayer which extended for a period of 6000 years.'[2]

5 – Imam al-Sajjād ﷺ

The reason why Imam al-Sajjād ﷺ was given the title of Zayn al-ʿĀbidīn ﷺ is because one night, as he stood for prayers in his place of worship, Shayṭān manifested himself in the form of a huge serpent with the intention of distracting him from his prayers. When the Imam took no notice of him, Shayṭān approached him and bit his big toe causing pain to run through him, but despite this act of his the Imam continued to remain oblivious of him and carried on with his prayers.

When, after the completion of his prayers he realised it was Shayṭān, he cursed him, saying: 'O accursed! Go away!' and once again engaged himself in worship. It was at this moment that he heard an angel call out three times: 'You are the embellishment of the worshippers.'[3]

56. Covenants And Promises

Allah, the Wise, has said:

$$\text{وَأَوْفُوا بِعَهْدِ اللهِ إِذَا عَاهَدْتُمْ}$$

Fulfil Allah's covenant when you pledge. (16:91)

---

[1] *Nahj al-Balāghah* of Fayḍ al-Islam, p. 780, Sermon 234.

[2] *Iblīs Nāmih*, p. 165; *ʿIlal al-Sharāʾiʿ*, vol. 2, p. 243.

[3] *Muntahā al-Aʿmāl*, vol. 2, p. 3.

The Holy Prophet said:

$$\text{لَا دِينَ لِمَنْ لَا عَهْدَ لَهُ}$$

One who does not adhere to his covenants has no religion.[1]

Short explanation

In the Holy Qur'an, Allah has made many promises and has ordered that covenants and promises should be fulfilled.

One who enters into a covenant must adhere to it and not violate it irrespective of whether the covenant is with Allah and the Prophet, or with the creations of Allah. Non-adherence to one's covenant and promise shall cause one to become ostracised, its burden shall remain upon his neck like a necklace till the Day of Judgement, and Allah shall cause the person's enemies to gain ascendancy over him.

Even if the opposite party happens to be a disbeliever or an immoral person, one must not break one's covenant with him and cause his life to fall into disarray.

1 – The conquered king of the Sasanian Empire

The Sasanian period saw the rule of seven kings with Khusrow being regarded as the greatest of them, and referred to as Mālik al-Mulūk (the King of kings). One of the seven kings was Hormuzan, who ruled in Ahwaz. When the Muslims conquered Ahwaz, Hormuzan was taken captive and brought before 'Umar, who said to him: 'If you truly desire to remain safe, accept Islam or else I shall surely kill you.'

Hormuzan said: 'Now that you shall eventually kill me, order for some water to be given to me for I am intensely thirsty.'

Upon 'Umar's order, some water was brought for him in a wooden bowl, but Hormuzan said: 'I shall not drink from this bowl for I am used to drinking water in bowls studded with jewels.'

At this point the Commander of the Faithful said: 'This is not an extravagant request; bring for him a crystalline bowl.'

---

[1] *Shayṭān*, vol. 2, p. 294.

Water was poured into a crystalline bowl and presented to him but, instead of drinking it, he kept holding the bowl in his hands. 'Umar said: 'I have taken a covenant with Allah that I shall not kill you until you have drunk the water.'

Having heard this, Hormuzan smashed the bowl on the ground and spilled all the water in the process. 'Umar stood aghast over this deception and, turning to the Commander of the Faithful, asked: 'What should be done now?'

He replied: 'Since you had made his death contingent to his drinking the water and had entered into a covenant in this regard, you cannot put him to death now; impose upon him the *jizyah* tax instead.'

Hormuzan said: 'I refuse to pay the tax; however, now with serenity of mind and without any fear, I shall become a Muslim.' Saying this, he testified to the unity of Allah and the prophethood of the Holy Prophet and became a Muslim.

'Umar was delighted, and seating Hormuzan beside himself he granted him a house in Medina and allotted for him an annual sum of 10,000 dinars.[1]

2 – The oath of *fuḍūl*

Twenty years before the Holy Prophet's proclamation of prophethood and at a time when he was exactly twenty years of age, an incident transpired as follows: one day, a person from the tribe of Banī Zubayd sold some goods to 'Āṣ ibn Wā'il. 'Āṣ took possession of the goods but refused to pay him the money for it. In desperation, the man climbed atop the mountain of Abū Qubays and shouted: 'O people! Rush to the help of an oppressed one who happens to be far from his tribe and relatives. Surely, reverence befits one who possesses integrity, whereas there is no esteem for a cheat.'

The people, who were around the Ka'bah, were inspired and motivated by this speech, and so a group consisting of some individuals from various tribes gathered in the house of 'Abd Allāh ibn Jad'ān and made a pact amongst themselves to provide assistance to the oppressed ones and

---

[1] *Pand-i Tārīkh*, vol. 2, p. 42; *al-Kalām Yajurru al-Kalām*.

prevent anyone from being oppressed in Mecca. The Holy Prophet was also a party to this agreement. Later, all of them set out and handed the person his money.

Years later, after the Holy Prophet had proclaimed his prophethood, he said: 'In the house of 'Abd Allāh ibn Jad'ān I had participated in a covenant such that had I been invited to the like of it in Islam, I would have surely accepted.'[1]

3 – Standing up for Islam until the end

Anas ibn Naḍar was the uncle of Anas ibn Mālik – the slave of the Holy Prophet. As he had not participated in the Battle of Badr, he said to the Holy Prophet: 'O Prophet of Allah! I could not participate in the battle that had loomed up before you; nonetheless, I promise that should there ensue another battle, I shall surely participate in it.'

When the Battle of Uḥud came to pass he presented himself and fought in it. In the course of the battle, when rumours were making round amongst the Muslim forces that the Holy Prophet had been killed, some said: 'O how we wish we had a representative whom we could send to 'Abd Allāh ibn Ubayy, so that he could procure a pardon for us from Abū Sufyān!'

Some sat at a distance, hand upon hand, and worried and anxious, wondering about what would happen. Some others said: 'Now that Muḥammad has been killed, revert back to your original faith.'

Hearing these words, Anas ibn Naḍar announced: 'I absolve myself from what these people recommend.' He then asserted: 'If Muḥammad has been killed, the Allah of Muḥammad is still alive. What is the purpose of life now that Noble Prophet has died? Continue fighting for the very purpose that the Noble Prophet fought!' Then, unsheathing his sword and in accordance with his covenant, he battled with the enemies till he tasted martyrdom, suffering around eighty injuries of arrows and lances. His wounds were so numerous that when his sister Rabī' arrived she managed

----

[1] *Dāstān-hā-yi Zindagī-yi Payāmbar*, p. 36; *Ṭabaqāt al-Kubrā*, vol. 1, p. 128.

to identify him only by means of his fingertips.[1]

4 – The Muslim slave

Fuḍayl ibn Zayd, one of the Muslim officials, along with his soldiers, laid siege to a fort, with the objective of conquering it. After some hours of battle, he returned to his camp for some rest.

In those days, slaves who came into the captivity of the Muslims were put up for sale in the market. If they happened to be Muslims, they would battle against the enemies alongside their Muslim brethren.

In Fuḍayl's army there was a slave soldier who happened to lag behind the main contingent. Observing him to be alone, the enemy forces spoke to him in the local dialect from atop the fort and sought pardon and safety from him; the soldier acceded to their demand and granted them the letter of pardon.

When the forces of Islam advanced upon the fort, the enemy forces opened its door before them leaving the Muslim soldiers bewildered. The enemy forces carried the letter of pardon of the slave soldier and presented it to the Muslim army. Acknowledging a pardon granted by a slave soldier was very unusual in those days, and so the issue was referred to the Second Caliph, who wrote back stating: 'The Muslim slave is also from the Muslims and his covenants deserve the same respect as yours. Honour his letter of pardon and ensure that it is implemented.'[2]

57. Justice

Allah, the Wise, has said:

$$\text{اِعْدِلُوا هُوَ أَقْرَبُ لِلتَّقْوَى}$$

Be fair; that is nearer to God-wariness. (5:8)

---

[1] *Payghambar Wa Yārān*, vol. 1, p. 334.

[2] *Dāstān-hā-yi Mā*, vol. 1, p. 111; *Kūdak-i Falsafī*, vol. 2, p. 17.

Imam ʿAlī has said:

اَلْعَدْلُ يَضَعُ الْأُمُورَ مَوَاضِعَهَا

Justice places issues in their appropriate position.[1]

Short explanation

Justice means to act with equality and fairness to the maximum extent possible for a person. Fulfilment of mutual rights, payment of that which is due to a person – whatever be its measure – and fairness and even-handedness with respect to partners, are all examples of justice. A person's esteem is reliant upon his justice and fairness. If a king is just, his subjects shall be the beneficiaries of divine grace and blessings.

Allah sent the prophets with manifest proofs in order to establish justice within society and to prevent it from being led towards decadence.

Dependence of people with respect to one another necessitates that moderateness and fairness is taken into regard with respect to discipline, morals, covenants, and even children.

Deviating from moderation and going towards extremes weakens the foundations of justice and serves to inflame discord among people.

1 – Shadīd's governance

After the death of ʿĀd, his two sons – Shaddād and Shadīd – became kings.

Although a polytheist, Shadīd exhibited justice to such an extent that it became well-known that during his reign a wolf would not attack a sheep nor would an eagle attack a pigeon.

With the objective of resolving the disputes of his subjects, Shadīd nominated a judge in his kingdom and provided him with a monthly allowance. However, despite sitting in the court for a period of one year, no one came with a dispute for him to resolve! Therefore, he said to Shadīd: 'It is unbecoming for me to take my monthly allowance for I have not resolved any dispute.'

However, Shadīd ordered: 'You must take your allowance and continue

---

[1] *Shayṭān*, vol. 2, p. 166.

to fulfil the responsibilities entrusted unto you.'

After a period, two persons approached the judge and one of them said to him: 'I had purchased a piece of land from this person and have stumbled across a treasure in it. Despite my repeated requests, this seller is unwilling to accept it.'

On his part, the seller said: 'I had sold the land to the purchaser together with everything that existed within it.'

Conducting his investigations, the judge came to realise that the seller had a son while the purchaser had a daughter, and so he ruled: 'The purchaser's daughter should be married to the seller's son and the treasure should be given to them; and in this manner put an end to their dispute.'[1]

2 – Impartiality between children

Once, a lady entered the house of ʿĀʾishah, the wife of the Holy Prophet, with her two children. ʿĀʾishah presented three dates to the lady who gave one date to each of her two children, and taking the third date she halved it and once again distributed it evenly amongst them.

When the Holy Prophet returned, ʿĀʾishah narrated the episode to him, whereupon he said: 'Did the lady's act leave you astonished? Due to her fairness and even-handedness Allah shall place her in paradise.'

It has also been reported that once, a father arrived in the presence of the Holy Prophet accompanied by his two children. In his presence he kissed one child and ignored the other. Noticing this incorrect act, the Holy Prophet commented: 'Why do you not treat your children equally?'[2]

3 – The red apparel

Once, a pious and abstemious person came to Manṣūr Dawānīqī, the second Abbasid caliph, and began preaching and advising him. In the course of his dialogue, he said: 'In the course of my travels I had gone to China, which was ruled by a just ruler. One day, he was afflicted by

---

[1] *Rāhnumā-yi Saʿādat*, vol. 2, p. 451.

[2] *Riwāyat-hā Wa Ḥikāyat-hā*, p. 73; *al-Ḥadīth*, vol. 2, p. 267.

sickness which weakened his faculty of hearing. He called his ministers and said: "I have fallen sick and have lost my hearing," and he then began weeping profusely.

'They consoled him, saying: "Although your hearing has weakened, Allah shall grant you a long life due to your justice and equity."

'The king said: "You are in error and you reflect on something which is away from reality. I do not weep for my hearing, for a learned one knows that all the limbs and organs shall eventually perish. I weep because if an oppressed one were to seek justice and clamour for help, I would not hear him and thus would not be able to strive towards providing him with justice."

'He then issued instructions that it should be announced in all cities that whoever happens to suffer oppression should wear a red apparel so that the king's soldiers recognise him from afar and endeavour to provide justice to him.'[1]

4 – Equality in the spoils of war

When the Battle of Ḥunayn concluded and the spoils of war were about to be distributed, some of the Bedouins who had participated in the battle approached the Holy Prophet and said: 'O Prophet of Allah! Grant us a share as well.'

They created such a commotion that he had to retreat towards a tree, and in the tumult his cloak was pulled off his shoulders. He said: 'Hand me back my cloak. By Allah in whose power lies my soul! Had there been camels, cows, and sheep equivalent to the number of trees on the face of the earth I would have surely distributed them amongst you.' As he said this he plucked out a hair from the hump of a camel and said: 'By Allah! From the spoils of war I shall not take anything more than the *khums*, even in the measure of this hair, and that too I shall gift to you. You also, with respect to the spoils of war, should not be unfaithful – not even in the measure of a needle or a yarn – for theft with regards to it only merits

____
[1] *Jawāmiʿ al-Ḥikāyāt*, p. 73.

ignominy and the fire of hell.'

A person from amongst the Anṣār stood up, brought out a woven yarn, and said: 'I had taken this to weave a saddle for my camel.'

The Holy Prophet said: 'I gift to you my share that exists in this yarn.'

Hearing this, the man said: 'If the accounting and distribution has to be so accurate and severe, then I do not need this yarn.' Saying this, he dropped the yarn onto the ground.[1]

5 – The name of ʿAlī ﷺ is synonymous with justice!

On one of the occasions when Muʿāwiyah had gone for hajj, he made enquiries about a woman by the name of Dārmiyyah Ḥajūniyyah, who was well-known for her long-standing support for Imam ʿAlī ﷺ and her enmity towards Muʿāwiyah. Having been informed that she was alive, he ordered her to be brought before him. When she had arrived, he asked her: 'Do you have any idea as to why I have summoned you before me? I have brought you here to know why you love ʿAlī and harbour animosity towards me.'

The woman said: 'It is better if you refrain from such talk.'

Muʿāwiyah insisted: 'You must answer me.'

She said: 'For the simple reason that ʿAlī ﷺ was a just person and supported equality, whereas you needlessly fought him. I approve of ʿAlī ﷺ because he loved the poor, whereas I detest you because you shed unwarranted blood, spread dissension and discord amongst the Muslims, adjudicate oppressively and unfairly, and act in accordance with your carnal desires!'

Muʿāwiyah was infuriated and an impolite dialogue ensued between the two, but eventually Muʿāwiyah stifled his anger and as per his habit, exhibiting gentleness, he asked: 'Did you see ʿAlī with your own eyes?'

She replied: 'Yes.'

He then asked: 'How?'

____

[1] *Dāstān-hā Wa Pand-hā*, vol. 2, p. 40; *Nāsikh al-Tawārīkh* (Ḥaḍrat Rasūl), vol. 3, p. 150.

She said: 'By Allah! I had seen him in a state such that this kingdom and sultanate which has deceived you and made you heedless, had neither deceived him nor made him heedless.'

Mu'āwiyah said: 'Have you heard his voice?'

She replied: 'Yes; a voice that would burnish the heart and clear the turbidity from it just as olive oil clears away the rust.'

Mu'āwiyah said: 'Do you desire anything?'

She said: 'Will you give me whatever I ask for?' When he had replied in the affirmative, she said: 'Give me 100 red-haired camels.'

Mu'āwiyah said: 'If I give them to you would you look upon me as you look upon 'Alī?'

Defiantly, she said: 'Never.'

However, Mu'āwiyah ordered 100 red-haired camels to be given to her and then commented: 'Had 'Alī been alive, he would not have given you even one of these.'

Hearing this, the woman retorted: 'By Allah! He would not have given me even one single hair of these camels, for he considered them to be the property of all the Muslims.'[1]

58. Chastisement

Allah, the Wise, has said:

$$\text{إِنَّ عَذَابَ رَبِّكَ لَوَاقِعٌ}$$

Indeed your Lord's punishment will surely befall. (52:7)

The Holy Prophet said:

$$\text{لَا يُعَذِّبُ اللهُ قَلْبًا وَعَى الْقُرْآنَ}$$

Allah shall not chastise the heart that contains the Qur'an.[2]

Short explanation

In order to prevent the people from committing crimes and offences – an

---

[1] *Dāstān-hā-yi Ustād*, vol. 2, p. 97; *Bīst Guftār*, p. 67.

[2] *Shayṭān*, vol. 2, p. 415.

excess of which would result in the disintegration and destruction of the society – Allah ordered all the prophets to warn their people: 'Chastisement awaits you'.

The kind of chastisement depends upon the kind of offence and the type of vice. The Arabs would be punished because of fanaticism, the rulers due to oppression, scholars because of envy, the traders due to unfaithfulness, and the villagers as a result of ignorance.

Since the levels of hell vary, consequently the intensity and severity of the chastisement also vary. Some shall remain eternally within it while others, as a result of intercession or upon completion of their term, shall attain deliverance and then go on to enter paradise. The worst of the chastisements is that a person suffers from hard-heartedness in the world and finds himself in the lowest rank of hell in the Hereafter.

1 – The chastisement of the people of ʿĀd

When Prophet Hūd ﷺ was forty years of age Allah revealed to him: 'Go to your nation and invite your people towards monotheism and My worship.'

The nation of Prophet Hūd ﷺ was ʿĀd, which consisted of thirteen tribes. The people possessed a tall physique and a long lifespan. They engaged themselves in farming and possessed excellent date palms, and their cities were the most prosperous of the Arabian cities.

For years on end, Prophet Hūd ﷺ strived to guide his nation, but when it yielded no result, he said to them: 'I shall curse you.'

His people said: 'O Hūd! The people of Nūḥ possessed a frail and weak physique but our gods are strong and so are our bodies. We do not fear the punishment.'

Allah sent down upon them a devastating wind (about which the Commander of the Faithful said: 'I seek refuge in Allah from the devastating wind.')

When the chastisement came upon them it plucked their castles, forts, cities, and all the other structures, tossed them into the air as if pebbles, and then grounded them into fine powder. For seven nights and eight days it blew over them – picking up the men and the women and annihilating them.

The people of Prophet Hūd ﷺ were referred to as 'the possessors of pillars' for they would carve out gigantic pillars from the mountains and then construct their palaces atop these pillars. In the wake of the chastisement all of them were ground into dust. According to the Holy Qur'an,[1] their chastisement was a furiously raging cold wind, which plucked them up from the ground, tossed them into the air like locusts, and then dashed them against the mountains till their bones crumbled into powder.[2]

2 – Ibn Muljim and the chastisement in barzakh

Ibn Raqa narrates:

'I was near Masjid al-Ḥarām in Mecca when I noticed that a group of people had gathered near Maqām Ibrāhīm ﷺ whereupon I enquired: "What is the matter?"

'I was told: "A Christian monk has accepted Islam."

'I pushed myself into the crowd and witnessed a tall, old man, dressed in woollen clothes and wearing a woollen cap, seated opposite Maqām Ibrāhīm and delivering a speech. I heard him say: "One day I was seated in the monastery and was looking out of it when, as a result of mystical intuition, I suddenly witnessed a gigantic bird resembling a hunting-hawk descend upon a slab of stone near the sea and vomit out something. I observed that one-fourth of a human body had come out of its mouth. The bird then flew off and disappeared from view. A little later it returned and vomiting out something, it once again flew out of sight. I saw that once again one-fourth of a human body had come out of its mouth. It returned for the third time and threw out another fourth of a human body, and yet again for the fourth time till an entire human figure was formed. After some time it returned, and striking its beak it took away one fourth of

---

[1] 54:19.

[2] *Ḥayāt al-Qulūb*, vol. 1, p. 99.

the body. It repeated this act three more times till it had taken away the person completely. I was stunned and exclaimed: 'O Allah! Who is this person, who is being subjected to this chastisement?' I was greatly upset with myself as to why I did not go and question him but it was not long before the hunting bird returned and vomited out one fourth of the human body and repeated the act three more times till the entire human body was formed again. I hastened towards the person and enquired: 'Who are you and what have you done?' He replied: 'I am Ibn Muljim and I am the person who killed 'Alī ibn Abī Ṭālib. Allah has commanded this bird to kill, eat, and chastise me in this manner every day.' I asked him: 'Who is 'Alī ibn Abī Ṭālib?' He replied: 'The cousin of the Prophet of Islam.' Thus, it was this strange incident that prompted me to become a Muslim.'"[1]

3 – The recompense of deeds

When the forces of Genghis Khan, the Mongol, had barbarically attacked Iran, there was a bloodbath everywhere. Every city that he would enter, Genghis would question the people: 'Who kills you – Allah or I?' If they answered: 'You kill us,' he would kill them all, and if they answered: 'Allah kills us,' he would still kill them all.

Once, upon entering the city of Hamadan, he sent some persons to the elders of the city asking them to present themselves before him as he desired to speak to them. All were perplexed as to what could be done, when a brave and intelligent youth said: 'I shall go to him.'

The others said: 'We fear for your life.'

He replied: 'I too am like the others,' and he prepared to go.

Taking along with him a camel, a rooster, and a goat, he approached Genghis's camp and, presenting himself before him, said: 'If you want someone big, here is a camel; if you are looking for a long-bearded one, then here is a goat for you; and if you desire someone talkative, there is a rooster for you here; however, if you need to converse with someone, I stand here before you.'

---

[1] ʿĀlam-i Barzakh, p. 178; Biḥār al-Anwār, vol. 42, p. 307.

Genghis said: 'Tell me, who shall kill these people, Allah or I?'

The youth said: 'It is neither Allah who shall kill them, nor you.'

Hearing this, Genghis asked: 'Then who is it that shall kill them?'

The youth replied: 'The retribution of their deeds.'[1]

4 – The cause for the descent of chastisement

The first person to devise a balance for people to use for measurement was Prophet Shuʿayb ﷺ. However, as time passed, his people began to indulge in weighing less than the weights, and this sin was in addition to their other sins of not believing in Allah and rejecting the prophets.

When weighing for themselves they would weigh correctly, but when they would sell their products they would sell less than the weights and would indulge in fraud.

They were leading a life of ease, comfort, and abundance until their king ordered them to hoard goods and commit cheating in weights. Prophet Shuʿayb ﷺ advised the king and the people to refrain from these evils but it was to no avail; on the contrary, upon the king's orders, Prophet Shuʿayb ﷺ and his followers were thrown out of the city. When this happened, divine chastisement descended upon them.[2]

A wave of intense heat overtook the people – so severe that neither shade nor water could provide any relief. Subsequent to this intense heat a cloud appeared over their heads and a cool breeze began to blow, prompting all the people to gather under the cloud to escape the severe heat. When all the people had gathered under it, sparks of fire began to rain down from it while simultaneously the ground beneath them began to shake vigorously, leaving all of them crumpled and burnt. The duration of this sequence of chastisement has been reported to be nine days and consisted of a scorching wind, hot water, and a severe earthquake.[3]

---

[1] *Dāstān-hā Wa Pand-hā*, vol. 6, p. 105.

[2] This is referred to in Sūrat al-Aʿrāf as 'earthquake', and in Sūrat al-Shuʿarāʾ as 'day of overshadowing gloom'.

[3] *Tārīkh-i Anbiyāʾ*, vol. 2, p. 34.

5 – Chastisement of those who conceal the truth

Jābir ibn ʿAbd Allāh Anṣārī relates:

'Imam ʿAlī 🖼 had been delivering a sermon for us, and after he had praised and glorified Allah, he said: "In the forefront of this gathering there are some companions of the Noble Prophet 🖼: Anas ibn Mālik, Barrāʾ ibn ʿĀzib Anṣārī, Ashʿath ibn Qays, and Khālid ibn Yazīd Bajallī." Then, turning towards them, he first said to Anas ibn Mālik: "O Anas! If you had heard the Noble Prophet 🖼 say about me: 'Of whomsoever I am the master, this ʿAlī is his master too,' and refuse to testify to my leadership today, Allah shall afflict you with leprosy such that white spots shall become manifest upon your head and face and even your turban would fail to conceal them."

'Then, addressing Ashʿath, he said: "As for you, O Ashʿath! If you had heard the Noble Prophet 🖼 say it about me and refrain from bearing witness to it, you shall become blind in both eyes towards the end of your life. And you, O Khālid ibn Yazīd! If you had heard it about me and now conceal it and refrain from testifying in my favour, Allah shall afflict you with a pagan death. And you, O Barrāʾ ibn ʿĀzib, if you have heard the Noble Prophet 🖼 say this and refuse to bear witness for my *wilāyah*, you shall die in the same place from which you had migrated (towards Medina)."

'Of course, all four of them had been present on the day of Ghadīr and had heard this well-known sentence from the Noble Prophet 🖼, but later concealed it and denied the event!'

Jābir ibn ʿAbd Allāh Anṣārī states: 'By Allah! After a period, I witnessed Anas ibn Mālik such that he had been afflicted with leprosy to the extent that he could not conceal the white spots of the disease which had erupted on his face and head, even by means of his turban. I saw Ashʿath such that he had become blind in both eyes and used to say: "Thank Allah that ʿAlī cursed me about being blinded in my eyes in this world and did not curse me with chastisement in the Hereafter, for had he done so I would have suffered eternal chastisement in the Hereafter." I witnessed Khālid ibn Yazīd who died in his house; his family members desired to bury him in the house but the tribe of Kindah came to know of their intention and attacked them and buried him, according to pagan rites, near the door of the house, and he died a death of the pre-Islamic era. As for Barrā', Muʿāwiyah appointed him the ruler of Yemen and he died there, the very place from where he had previously migrated to Medina.'[1]

59. Forgiveness

Allah, the Wise, has said:

$$\text{وَأَنْ تَعْفُوا أَقْرَبُ لِلتَّقْوَى}$$

And to forgo is nearer to God-wariness. (2:237)

The Holy Prophet said:

$$\text{الْعَفْوُ لَا يَزِيدُ الْعَبْدَ إِلَّا عِزًّا}$$

Forgiveness increases a person in esteem.[2]

Short explanation

Forgiving, despite possessing the strength to retaliate, is of the conduct of the prophets. Pardon is when a person commits an offence or sin with respect to another, who in return not only forgives him from within his heart but also manifests his beneficence and kindness externally.

How can one who does not forgive others, expect to be forgiven by the Almighty Lord?

Allah cloaks every servant of His with forgiveness in this world and in the Hereafter, and hence it becomes imperative for them to forgive and pardon one another. And if it so happens that someone – intentionally or unintentionally – does commit a malevolent deed, one should magnanimously and graciously disregard it in order that Allah, by His favour, disregards one's own malevolence.[3]

---

[1] *Ḥikāyat-hā-yi Shanīdanī*, vol. 1, p. 102.

[2] *Jāmiʿ al-Saʿādāt*, vol. 1, p. 368.

[3] *Tadhkirat al-Ḥaqāʾiq*, p. 56.

1 – Beating the servant

Once, a companion of the Holy Prophet began hitting his slave. The slave kept pleading: 'By Allah! Do not beat me. For Allah's sake forgive me.' The master, however, refused to pardon him and continued to shower beatings upon him.

Some people informed the Holy Prophet of the slave's predicament whereupon he got up and started out towards the scene of this incident. As soon as the companion's eyes fell upon the Holy Prophet, he stopped his beatings; the Holy Prophet said to him: 'He placed you under the oath of Allah but you refused to pardon him, and now that you have set your eyes upon me, you have restrained yourself?'

The man, in order to make amends for his deplorable behaviour, said: 'I now free him for the sake of Allah!'

The Holy Prophet said: 'Had you not freed him you would have dropped face down into the fire of hell.'[1]

2 – Pardon for the killer

During the period of the leadership of the late Grand Ayatollah Sayyid Abū al-Ḥasan Iṣfahānī, one night, as he led the congregation for the *maghrib* prayers in Najaf, a person knifed his son – who was an extremely admirable and exemplary person – to death.

When Sayyid Abū al-Ḥasan Iṣfahānī was informed of his son's martyrdom, exhibiting great patience and forbearance, he said: 'There is no power or strength save with Allah.' And then, standing up, he led the *'ishā'* prayers.

Later, when the people approached him and sought to know of the action he desired to initiate against his son's murderer, he simply said: 'I have forgiven him.'[2]

---

[1] *Shanīdanī-hā-yi Tārīkh*, p. 98; *al-Maḥajjah al-Bayḍā'*, vol. 3, p. 445

[2] *Sīmā-yi Farzānigān*, p. 336; *Ganjīnah-i Dānishmandān*, vol. 1, p. 221.

3 – Freedom of the slave-girl

One day, some people had come to the house of Imam al-Sajjād 🕮 as guests. Preparing the meals, one of Imam's servants hastily pulled out the kebabs from the oven; as he did so, the skewers of the kebabs slipped from his grasp, fell upon the head of Imam al-Sajjād's 🕮 child who had been standing below the ladder, and caused his death. The servant stood aghast and terribly perturbed, but the Imam said: 'You have not done it on purpose; go away, for I have freed you in the way of Allah.' He then ordered that the child be given *ghusl*, shrouded, and buried.[1]

Sufyān Thawrī relates: 'One day, arriving in the presence of Imam al-Ṣādiq 🕮, I found him to be disturbed and unsettled. I sought to know the reason for it whereupon he said: "I had prohibited everyone from climbing atop the roof of the house, however when I entered the house I observed one of the slave-girls, who had been entrusted the responsibility of educating one of my children, standing atop the ladder with my infant in her arms. As soon as she saw me she was left dumbfounded and began to tremble, as a result of which my son dropped out of her hands onto the ground, and died. I am disturbed and uneasy over the fear that overtook the slave-girl because of me. Nevertheless, I told her: 'There is no sin upon you and I have set you free for the pleasure of Allah.'"'[2]

4 – The son's pardon for the killer

When the caliphate fell into the hands of the Abbasids, the Umayyad elders took to flight and concealed themselves. One of them was Ibrāhīm ibn Sulaymān ibn 'Abd al-Malik, an old but wise and erudite person, who was eventually pardoned and granted protection by Abū al-'Abbās Saffāḥ, the first Abbasid caliph. One day, Saffāḥ said to him: 'I would like to know

---

[1] *Muntahā al-A'māl*, vol. 2, p. 4. It has been mentioned in *Biḥār al-Anwār*, vol. 11, that Imam al-Sajjād 🕮 would summon all his slaves and slave-girls before him on the day of Eid al-Fiṭr, forgive their misdeeds, grant them gifts, and free some of them, after which he would say to them: 'Say to Allah: forgive 'Alī ibn Ḥusayn just as he has forgiven us!'

[2] Ibid., p. 128.

what transpired with you during your period of concealment.'

Ibrāhīm said: 'I had concealed myself in Herah, in a place close to the desert. One day, from the rooftop I witnessed black flags advancing from the direction of Kufa. I assumed that they were coming for me and so I fled from my hideaway and arrived in Kufa. There, perplexed and distressed, I wandered through the streets till I reached a large house. As I stood there, I witnessed a person seated on his horse and accompanied by a few servants, enter the house. The servants asked me: "What is it that you desire?" I said: "I am a person who is fearful and alarmed, and have come to you for shelter." They took me into the house, accommodated me in one of the rooms, and hosted me in the most excellent of manners. Neither did they question me about myself and nor did I ask them about the owner of the house, however, I observed that every day the owner of the house would go out in the company of his slaves and return home after a period, and so, one day, I enquired: "Are you in search of someone for which you go out every day?"

'He said: "We are on the lookout for Ibrāhīm ibn Sulaymān who has killed my father so that I can extract revenge for my father's murder." I realised that he spoke the truth for I had indeed killed his father. I said to him: "Since you have accommodated and hosted me, I shall guide to you your father's killer." With great urgency and impatience he asked: "Where is he?"

'I said: "I am Ibrāhīm ibn Sulaymān!"

'Hearing this, he said: "You lie!"

'I said: "By Allah! No, I do not. I killed your father on such and such day."

'Realising that I spoke the truth, his complexion changed and his eyes began to spew blood. He lowered his head towards the ground and then raising it after some time, said: "Since I had granted you shelter I shall not kill you, however, in the presence of the just God, I shall surely seek revenge for my father's murder. Hasten away from here for I fear lest you may suffer harm from me."

'He offered me 1000 dinars but I declined and departed from there. O

Caliph! I declare with complete candidness that excepting you, I have not witnessed a person more beneficent than him.'[1]

5 – The conquest of Mecca

When the Holy Prophet conquered Mecca he announced a general amnesty for all the people, except a few individuals who were to be killed whenever found. Amongst these were 'Abd Allāh ibn Zab'arī, who used to satirise him, Waḥshī, who had killed his uncle Ḥamzah in the Battle of Uḥud,[2] 'Ikramah ibn Abī Jahl, Ṣafwān ibn Umayyah, and Habbār ibn al-Aswad, all of whom he eventually pardoned after they were brought before him.

As for Habbār ibn al-Aswad, he was the person who frightened Zaynab – who had been sent towards Medina by her husband, Abū al-'Abbās ibn Rabī', on the way to Medina, as a result of which she suffered a miscarriage. Subsequent to this act of his, the Holy Prophet had declared it permissible to shed his blood.

After the conquest of Mecca he approached the Holy Prophet, expressed regret over his misdeed, and, seeking forgiveness, said: 'O Prophet of Allah! We were of the polytheists, however, Allah, by means of you, guided us aright and delivered us from perdition, so disregard my ignorance and that which you have heard about me, and pardon me!'

The Holy Prophet said: 'I pardon you. Allah has exhibited kindness towards you in that He has guided you into Islam; with the acceptance of Islam, bygones become bygones.'[3]

60. Intellect

Allah, the Wise, has said:

$$\text{وَمَا عِنْدَ اللهِ خَيْرٌ وَأَبْقَى أَفَلَا تَعْقِلُونَ}$$

---

[1] *Pand-i Tārīkh*, vol. 2, p. 92.

[2] When Waḥshī recounted the episode of the killing of the Prophet's uncle, Ḥamzah, he wept profusely but then pardoned him and said: 'Disappear from my sight.'

[3] *Shayṭān*, vol. 1, p. 412.

And what is with Allah is better and more lasting. Will you not apply reason? (28:60)

Imam al-Ṣādiq ﷺ said:

وَلَا بَلَغَ جَـمِيعُ الْعَابِدِينَ فِي فَضْلِ عِبَادَتِهِمْ مَا بَلَغَ الْعَاقِلُ

And no worshipper can achieve a value of worship greather than what a person with intellect can.[1]

Short explanation

O Lord! What have You not granted those to whom You have granted intellect?! And what have You granted those to whom You have not granted intellect?![2]

The personality of a person is founded upon his intellect and one who does not seek the assistance of this faculty in his affairs shall suffer loss and harm.

Intellect is one of the divine soldiers and an internal argument and proof. Intellect, irrespective of whether it is inherently possessed or empirically achieved, brings about progress and advancement of man.

The prophets used to guide the people by speaking to them in accordance with their intellectual capabilities, and on the Day of Judgement Allah shall reckon the deeds of His servants according to the measure of their understanding and intellect. Blind following brings about eternal damnation in the Hereafter, as was the case with the Banī Isrā'īl who, in a fit of fanaticism and foolishness, killed seventy divine prophets in one day!

1 – Slaughtering the gourd

After Muʿāwiyah had embarked upon his policy of opposition towards the Commander of the Faithful, he once resolved to test the measure of obedience of the people of Syria towards him, and so consulted ʿAmr ibn ʿĀṣ in this regard. ʿAmr said: 'Command the people to slaughter the gourd before eating it just as they slaughter a sheep. If they act in accordance

---

[1] *Jāmiʿ al-Saʿādāt*, vol. 1, p. 111.

[2] Khwājah ʿAbd Allāh Anṣārī.

with your order then they are your allies, but if not then they are not yet fully obedient to you.'

Mu'āwiyah ordered that henceforth the people should slaughter the gourds just as they slaughtered the sheep; the people too, without the slightest of objections, acted in compliance, and subsequently this innovation became a customary practice throughout Syria.

It was not long before the news of this innovation reached the ears of the people of Iraq prompting some of them to question the Commander of the Faithful about it, whereupon the Imam replied: 'It is not required to slaughter a gourd in order to eat it. Be wary, lest the Shayṭān takes away your intellect and satanic ideas leave you confused and lead you astray.'[1]

2 – Mature in intellect

With the intention of suppressing a group of rebellious enemies existing around Mecca and Medina, the Holy Prophet readied an attack unit for the purpose of advancing secretly upon the enemies in the darkness of the night and overcoming them; he appointed a youth from the tribe of Hudhayl as the commander of this unit.[2]

A shallow-minded person remonstrated, saying: 'Why have you appointed a youth as our chief? We refuse to obey his orders. You ought to have appointed an elderly person as the chief and commander.'

The Holy Prophet said: "O shallow-minded person! Although he is a youth, nevertheless he possesses a strong heart and a sound intellect, whereas the elders that you talk about, although they possess white beards and apparently should be given the leadership, however, their hearts are dark as pitch. On numerous occasions I have put this youth to test and found him to be mature in intellect. Elderly in age but lacking in intellect yields no benefit. Strive to the maximum extent possible to be elderly

---

[1] *Dāstān-hā Wa Pand-hā*, vol. 1, p. 92; *al-Kāfī*, vol. 6, p. 370.

[2] Historical accounts have reported many such appointments on the part of the Holy Prophet, amongst them being the appointment of a twenty-one year old youth, as the ruler of Mecca, and the appointment of the youth Usāmah ibn Zayd as the commander of his army.

in intellect and religion, for leadership is determined not by age but by intelligence, reflection, and a pure, luminous heart.'[1]

3 – The consequence of foolishness

In the biography of Ḥajjāj ibn Yūsuf Thaqafī – the bloodthirsty Umayyad – it has been reported that his mother had initially been the wife of Ḥārith, a well-known doctor, who divorced her when she picked her teeth at an inopportune time; it was later that she entered into the wedlock of Yūsuf ibn ʿAqīl Thaqafī.

Ḥajjāj, at the time of his birth, did not possess an excretory opening; left with no other option, his parents were forced to create an opening in his rear.

In addition to this, he would also not drink the milk from the breast of his mother and this left the parents worried and wondering as to what should be done.

One day, an evil person approached them and instructed them that in order to remedy this problem they should kill a black goat and make Ḥajjāj drink its blood. When the goat was killed and the blood put into his mouth, Ḥajjāj began sucking and licking it. The following day, the person directed them to kill a goat and pour its blood into his mouth. On the third day, he ordered them to kill a black snake, pour its blood into his mouth, and rub it upon his face as well, whereupon from the fourth day onwards Ḥajjāj began feeding himself with the milk of his mother.

As a result of this ignorant act, he grew up into such a savage and bloodthirsty individual that he would say: 'I derive maximum pleasure by shedding blood – especially the blood of the descendants of the Noble Prophet.'

He was appointed governor and the commander of the army by ʿAbd al-Malik ibn Marwān and ruled for twenty years until he died in the year 95 AH, at the age of fifty-four.

In the course of this period he killed 120,000 people, and at the time

______
[1] *Dāstān-hā-yi Mathnawī*, vol. 3, p. 64.

of his death his roofless prison contained 50,000 male and 30,000 female prisoners – the majority of them bare and unclothed.

Amongst those killed by this cruel tyrant were Kumayl ibn Ziyād Nakha‘ī – the companion of Imam ‘Alī ﷺ, Qambar – the slave of Imam ‘Alī ﷺ, Yaḥyā ibn Umm al-Ṭawīl – a companion of Imam al-Sajjād ﷺ, Sa‘īd ibn Jubayr – who has been greatly praised and commended by Imam al-Sajjād ﷺ, and numerous other celebrated personalities.[1]

4 – Imam ‘Alī ﷺ and the astrologer

There are some who are heedless with respect to reflection, reasoning, and trusting in Allah, and instead turn to soothsayers and astrologers who have cleverly started a business in order to swindle the people of their money.[2] As an example, we shall present an incident that transpired during the time of Imam ‘Alī ﷺ.

The Commander of the Faithful and his army had started out for the Battle of Nahrawān against the Kharijites, and having reached the city of Madain they pitched their tents. The next morning, as they were about to commence their journey, an astrologer approached them and said: 'My astrological calculations reveal that it is not in your interest to advance in this hour. Commence your journey after three hours and you shall be victorious.'

Hearing this, the Imam said: 'Whoever upholds your words has rejected the Qur'an of Allah.'[3] He then asked: 'Do you possess knowledge as to which family has taken over the reins of leadership in China?'

The astrologer replied: 'I have no knowledge.'

The Imam questioned: 'What is that star which when rises stirs up lust within the camels?'

---

[1] *Tatimmat al-Muntahā*, p. 66

[2] Of course, the issue of the close friends of Allah and those who have strived towards spiritual purification, differ vastly from the others, for their words are light; and if, at times, they were to say something to someone, it would surely occur, and hence such personalities should not be compared to others.

[3] 31:34.

The astrologer confessed: 'I have no idea.'

The Imam asked: 'The rise of which star stirs up passion within the cats?'

He said: 'I do not know!'

He asked: 'Inform me of the thing that is concealed beneath the hoofs of my horse.'

When the astrologer had once again pleaded ignorance, the Imam said to him: 'Within the earth, below the feet of my horse, lies a jar filled with gold coins, beneath which a serpent lies asleep.' When the place was dug up, the people witnessed that the scenario was exactly as it had been described by the Imam. Observing this, the astrologer was totally bewildered; the Imam took possession of his books, ordered them to be destroyed, and then said to him: 'The next time you try to attract the people towards yourself by means of astrology, I shall put you behind bars.'[1]

5 – The insanity-exhibiting wise person

Every thing is recognised by means of its attributes and effects; the sagaciousness and intelligence of a person become manifest by means of his words and deeds.

Buhlūl (d. 190 AH), despite the fact that his father was the uncle of Hārūn al-Rashīd, exhibited himself as a lunatic in order to abstain himself from accepting the post of judge and issuing the death sentence for the seventh Imam. One of the most evident examples of his rationality and intellect was the incident of his entry into the class of Abū Ḥanīfah, one of the leaders of the Sunnis.

Once, as he happened to pass by the class of Abū Ḥanīfah, he heard him say: 'Ja'far ibn Muḥammad has said to his students three things, which I do not approve of. He has said: "Shayṭān shall be chastised in the fire of hell." But how can he be punished by means of fire when he has himself been created out of fire? He also says: "Allah cannot be seen," whereas every entity can be perceived by means of vision. He also says: "Man, in

---

[1] *Jāmi' al-Nūrayn*, p. 15; *Biḥār al-Anwār*.

performing his actions, is free and has a choice," whereas in reality, Allah is the Creator and His servants have no discretion and freedom.'

Having heard this from Abū Ḥanīfah, Buhlūl picked up a clod of earth and hit him on the head, injuring him and prompting lamentations from him. His students rushed towards Buhlūl, and seizing him, presented him before the caliph. Abū Ḥanīfah said to the caliph: 'Buhlūl has struck me with a clod of earth and injured me.'

Buhlūl retorted: 'If he speaks the truth ask him to show the pain.' Then, turning to Abū Ḥanīfah, he said: 'Have you not been created from earth? How then can earth harm and injure you? What wrong have I done? Are you yourself not of the opinion that it is Allah who performs all the acts and deeds and man has no discretion and freedom? Thus, you should register a complaint against Allah and not against me.'

Abū Ḥanīfah, having received the answers to his objections, withdrew his complaint and went his way.[1]

61. Knowledge

Allah, the Wise, has said:

$$وَعَلَّمَكَ مَا لَمْ تَكُنْ تَعْلَمُ$$

And He has taught you what you did not know. (4:113)

The Holy Prophet said:

$$لَا يُحِبُّ الْعِلْمَ إِلَّا السَّعِيدُ$$

None loves knowledge except one who is fortunate [and prosperous].[2]

Short explanation

The way to attain cognisance of Allah and the shariah is by means of knowledge. Knowledge not only provides man with status and respect in society, it elevates his spiritual station to one who is the beneficiary of Allah's pleasure and honour.

---

[1] *Shāgirdān-i Maktab-i Aʾimmah*, p. 262; *Qāmūs al-Rijāl*, vol. 2, p. 252.

[2] *Jāmiʿ al-Saʿādāt*, vol. 1, p. 104.

One who possesses knowledge must realise that the acquisition of an hour of knowledge demands a lifetime of practice in accordance with the knowledge attained. Hence, when a person seeks to acquire knowledge he should bear in mind that he must practice what he learns. Regarding a scholar who does not act in accordance with the knowledge that he possesses, Allah has warned: 'From seventy of my punishments the least that I would do to him is to remove the sweetness of My remembrance from his heart.'[1]

True knowledge is not the mere memorisation of facts and terms, nor the acquisition of information that provides little or no spiritual benefit, nor is it motivated by base intentions such as arrogance and ostentation. Rather, true knowledge refers to the awareness and realisation of piety, cognisance of the divine, and the attainment of certainty.

1 – Al-Ḥājj Shaykh ʿAbbās Qummī

The author of *Mafātīḥ al-Jinān*, the late Shaykh ʿAbbās Qummī, narrates:

'Once I had compiled and published the book *Manāzil al-Ākhirah*, it reached the hands of Shaykh ʿAbd al-Razzāq who used to explain Islamic rulings daily before midday in the holy courtyard of Lady Maʿṣūmah (A). My father, Karbalāʾī Muḥammad Riḍā, was greatly fond of Shaykh ʿAbd al-Razzāq and would attend his sessions every day. Having procured the book *Manāzil al-Ākhirah*, the Shaykh would read from it for his audience. One day, my father returned home and said to me:

"O Shaykh ʿAbbās! I wish you would be like the person [ʿAbd al-Razzāq] who explains Islamic rulings, climbs onto the pulpit, and recites from the book in the manner he did for us today." I often felt the urge to tell him that I had actually authored the book but I restrained myself and merely said to him: "Pray to Allah that He grants [me] grace and success [for such a venture]."'[2]

---

[1] *Tadhkirat al-Ḥaqāʾiq*, p. 58.

[2] *Sīmā-yi Farzānigān*, p. 153; *Mard-i Taqwā Wa Faḍīlat*, p. 48.

2 – The tutor of Jibrīl

Jibrīl was once engaged in a conversation with the Holy Prophet when Imam ʿAlī ﷺ entered. As soon as Jibrīl's eyes fell upon Imam ʿAlī ﷺ, he stood up in respect and reverence. Witnessing this, the Holy Prophet asked: 'O Jibrīl! Why did you show such respect for this young man?' Jibrīl replied: 'How could I not exhibit deference towards him when I am under his obligation by virtue of the fact that he has taught me!' The Holy Prophet enquired: 'What has he taught you?' Jibrīl replied: 'After Allah created me, He asked me: "Who are you and who am I?" I did not know how to respond and so I remained silent for some time whereupon this youth appeared before me in a state of light and taught me to say: "You are the Glorious and Beautiful Lord while I am Jibrīl, a lowly servant." And it is for this reason that when I saw him now, I paid my respects to him.' The Holy Prophet then asked: 'How old are you, Jibrīl?' He replied: 'O Prophet of Allah! In the heavens there is a star that rises once every 30,000 years and I have witnessed it 30,000 times.'[1]

3 – The practicing scholar

Shaykh Aḥmad Ardabīlī, popularly known as Muqaddas Ardabīlī (d. 993 AH), was a practicing scholar and a contemporary of Shaykh Bahā'ī, Mullā Ṣadrā, and Mīr Dāmād. His grave lies in the vicinity of the holy shrine of Imam ʿAlī ﷺ in the city of Najaf. It has been reported that a person once came to Najaf for pilgrimage, and not recognising Shaykh Ardabīlī requested him to wash his clothes. The Shaykh agreed, and after washing the clothes, brought them to the pilgrim.

It was at this point that the pilgrim suddenly recognised who the Shaykh was and felt greatly embarrassed on account of his irreverent behaviour. Having witnessed the interlude, the surrounding people also rebuked him for his conduct. However, Shaykh Ardabīlī said: 'Why do you censure him? Nothing has happened. The rights of brethren-in-faith

---

[1] *Tuḥfat al-Majālis*, p. 80.

extend far beyond that which I have done for him.'[1]

4 – The dangers of possessing knowledge without prior purification of the soul

'Alī ibn Muḥammad al-Māwardī, an inhabitant of Basra, was a judge, teacher of Shafi'i jurisprudence, and a contemporary of Shaykh Ṭūsī. He narrates:

'I had expended great effort in writing a book on Islamic rulings relating to business transactions and had memorised all the details with regards to this subject to such an extent that when the book reached completion, it crossed my mind that my knowledge superseded all others with regards to this topic; I was overcome with pride, conceit, and vanity.

'One day, two Arab Bedouins came to my assembly seeking a ruling in connection with a transaction that had transpired in their village. The issue also prompted four further queries; however, I was unable to provide answers to any of them. For a while, I was lost in thought.

'I then said to myself: "You claim to be the most learned of all your contemporaries in this chapter of jurisprudence; how is it [then] that you are unable to answer the questions of the inhabitants of the village?" Turning to them, I confessed: "I do not know the answers."

'Astonished, they responded: "You should study more so that you are able to answer the questions [placed before you]." They left me and proceeded to refer their queries to a person who, in terms of knowledge, was inferior to even some of my students. However, when the Bedouins presented their questions to him he was able to provide them with suitable answers. The Bedouins were delighted to hear the rulings, and, praising him, returned to their village. This incident caused me to come to my senses and remove the conceit and vanity from my soul, such that I would not incline towards self-praise in the future.'[2]

---

[1] *Muntakhab al-Tawārīkh*, p. 181.

[2] *Safīnat al-Biḥār*, vol. 2, p. 162.

5 – Aṣmaʿī and the intrusive grocer

Aṣmaʿī[1] narrates:

'The initial period of my education was endured in poverty and indigence. Moreover, every morning upon leaving my house to acquire knowledge, I would pass an intrusive grocer who would question me: "Where are you going?"

'I would reply: "I am going to gain knowledge."

'On my way home, he would repeat the same question. At times he would say: "Don't waste your life. Why don't you study a profession so that you can become wealthy and affluent? Give me these books and papers of yours; I shall put them in the wine-jar and you will see that nothing shall remain of them." He would constantly reproach me as a result of which I became gravely distressed.

'The passing days brought further financial hardship; I became too poor to even afford a new garment to clothe myself. For years, I persisted in my education while living in destitution. One day, [my fortunes changed when] a messenger of the ruler of Basra approached me and asked me to present myself before the ruler. I said to him: "How can I present myself before him in this torn garment?"

'The messenger departed only to arrive again with some clothes and money. I wore the clothes and arrived before the ruler. He said: "I have selected you to educate the caliph's son and so you must proceed to Baghdad."

'I set off for Baghdad and approached the Abbasid caliph, Hārūn al-Rashīd, who ordered me to educate his son, Muḥammad Amīn. Thereafter, my financial state gradually improved until I was quite wealthy. When Muḥammad Amīn had attained a high level of knowledge, Hārūn desired to test him and so asked him to deliver a sermon. One Friday, Muḥammad delivered a highly eloquent sermon that greatly pleased Hārūn. Hārūn turned to me and asked: "What do you desire?"

---

[1] ʿAbd al-Malik ibn Qarīb Baṣrī (d. 828 CE) was a great narrator of poems and Arab traditions and has authored several books.

'I replied: "I wish to return to my birthplace, Basra." He accepted my request and arranged for me to return with dignity and honour to Basra.

'The people of Basra came to meet me and amongst them was the intrusive grocer. As soon as my eyes fell upon him, I asked: "Do you observe the fruits that knowledge and learning have yielded?"

'Apologetic and rueful, the grocer admitted: "I uttered those accusations out of ignorance. While they may be delayed, knowledge indeed yields [both] worldly and spiritual returns."'

62. Deeds

Allah, the Wise, has said:

$$مَنْ عَمِلَ صَالِحًا فَلِنَفْسِهِ وَمَنْ أَسَاءَ فَعَلَيْهَا وَمَا رَبُّكَ بِظَلَّامٍ لِلْعَبِيدِ$$

Whoever acts righteously, it is for his own soul, and whoever does evil, it is to its detriment, and your Lord is not tyrannical to the servants. (41:46)

Imam al-Ṣādiq ﷺ states:

$$كُونُوا دُعَاةَ النَّاسِ بِأَعْمَالِكُمْ وَلَا تَكُونُوا دُعَاةً بِأَلْسِنَتِكُمْ$$

Invite people [towards guidance] by means of your deeds and not by means of your tongues.[1]

Short explanation

Whilst many people may be well-versed in Islamic laws and legal rulings, unfortunately many fail to apply what they know. A person's good and evil actions are recorded in his book of deeds and only his deeds shall accompany him after his death. If a person dedicates his deeds solely for the pleasure of Allah whilst also ensuring that the rights of others are not trampled upon, Allah will safeguard his affairs in this world and the Hereafter, regard him with love and affection, and praise and exalt his station before the angels.

---

[1] *Safīnat al-Biḥār*, vol. 2, p. 278.

1 – The lawful work

Ḥasan ibn Ḥusayn Anbārī narrates:

'Over a period of fourteen years I kept writing letters to Imam al-Riḍā , seeking permission from him to allow me to work within the local ruling administration. Since the Imam did not reply, I wrote in my final letter: "I fear oppression and persecution. Those working with the ruler say: 'You are of the Shi'as and this is why you do not co-operate with us and are evasive.'"'

'In reply, the Imam wrote: "From your letter I sense that you fear for your life. You are aware that if you are placed in a position of responsibility, you should adhere to and act upon the teachings and traditions of the Holy Prophet; this would encourage your subordinates to also follow the dictates of your faith. If you come across instances whereby you have to deal with poor and indigent believers, ensure that you exhibit consideration, tolerance, and forbearance towards them. And since you are now working with them it would be deemed that you are one of them, [and thus] you must strive hard to perform deeds pleasing to Allah, since these deeds would then serve to compensate for your co-operation with the illegitimate ruling apparatus. However, if you are unable to act in this manner then it is not permissible for you to take up this employment."'[1]

2 – The practicing ones will enter heaven

Imam al-Bāqir relates:

'Once, my father was seated with his companions and he asked them: "Which of you is willing to hold flaming fire in his hand until the flames die out?" All those present, in admission of their inability to do so, lowered their heads and remained silent.

'I asked: "Dear father! Do you permit me to do it?"

'He said: "No, dear son! You are from me and I am from you. It is these people whom I was addressing."

'He then repeated his request three times, but when no one responded,

---

[1] *Bā Mardūm Īn Gūnih Barkhūrd Kunīm*, p. 65.

he said: "How numerous are those who talk and how few are those who act! I only wanted to test you." By Allah! At that moment I observed that they were overcome with such embarrassment that it appeared as if the earth was pulling them towards itself. Perspiration flowed from the foreheads of some, but they did not raise their lowered eyes. When my father observed their embarrassment, he said to them: "May Allah forgive you! I did not intend anything [towards you] except goodness. Heaven has many ranks, one of which will be the abode of none except those who practice and act." Thereafter, they appeared calmer and seemed relieved of a heavy and weighty burden.'[1]

3 – The working youth

The Holy Prophet was once seated with a group of his companions when he observed a strong and robust youth hard at work since the early morning. Those around him remarked: 'Had this youth expended his strength and energy in the way of Allah, he would have been worthy of immense commendation and praise.'

Hearing this, the Holy Prophet said: 'Do not utter such words for there are several probabilities that exist; he may be working to earn his sustenance so that he does not have to depend upon others, in which case he is striving in the way of Allah. He may be working to look after the needs of his feeble parents and weak children so that they are not dependent upon other people, in which case he is again striving in the way of Allah. However, if by means of this work he seeks to increase his wealth and manifest his superiority over those who are less privileged, he has travelled on the path of Shayṭān and deviated from the right path.'[2]

4 – Good deeds prompt a Jew to become a Muslim

The Holy Prophet once owed a few dinars to a Jew. The Jew sought the repayment of his debt from the Holy Prophet, who replied: 'At present I do

---

[1] *Dāstān-hā Wa Pand-hā*, vol. 2, p. 140; *Kashkūl* of Baḥrānī, vol. 2, p. 93.

[2] *Dunyā-yi Jawānān*, p. 316; *al-Maḥajjah al-Bayḍā'*, vol. 3, p. 140.

not have any money.'

The Jew responded: 'I shall not leave you until you repay what is owed to me.'

The Holy Prophet said: 'If that is the case, then I too shall sit by you here.' The Holy Prophet sat beside the Jew and remained with him, performing the *ẓuhr*, *ʿaṣr*, *maghrib*, *ʿishāʾ*, and the *fajr* prayers of the following day, next to the Jew.

Distressed by the situation, the companions of the Holy Prophet asked him: 'What are you doing? How can a Jew hold you captive?'

The Holy Prophet explained: 'Allah has not sent me as a prophet in order that I permit those who have established a religious covenant with me to be oppressed.'

The Holy Prophet remained seated next to the Jew until the following sunrise whereupon the Jew said to him: 'O Prophet of Allah! By Allah! It was not impertinence and audacity that prompted me to behave in the manner I did with you; rather, I desired to know whether your character conformed to the traits mentioned in the Torah about the Final Prophet. This is because I have read in the Torah that Muḥammad ibn ʿAbd Allāh would be born in Mecca, and subsequently migrate to Medina; he would neither possess a bad temperament nor would he be discourteous. He would neither speak with a loud voice nor would he be foul-mouthed and abusive. I now bear witness to the unity of Allah and to your prophethood, and I place my entire wealth at your disposal for you to utilise as Allah commands.'[1]

5 – The conduct of Muʿāwiyah and Abū al-Aswad Duʾalī

In order to attract people towards himself, Muʿāwiyah would usually send them money, honey, and other similar gifts. Destitute individuals who could not even afford curd to satiate their hunger would suddenly receive leather sacks of honey from Muʿāwiyah. Sometimes, he would even send money along with the honey. In this way, Muʿāwiyah was able buy people's

---

[1] *Dāstān-hā-yi Zindagī-yi Payāmbar*, p. 82; *Biḥār al-Anwār*, vol. 16, p. 16.

favour and redirect their support from Imam ʿAlī 🖫 to himself. Those who rejected the pay-off, refusing to abandon their loyalties to Imam ʿAlī 🖫, were few in number.

One day, Muʿāwiyah sent sacks of honey to Abū al-Aswad Duʾalī,[1] a staunch companion of Imam ʿAlī 🖫, in order to entice his support. Abū al-Aswad Duʾalī was handed a letter from Muʿāwiyah in the mosque, and told: 'Sacks of honey have been delivered to your house.'

As Abū al-Aswad entered his home, he observed that his five year old daughter was about to put a finger coated with honey into her mouth. Immediately, he shouted: 'O my daughter! Do not eat it for it is poison.'

The girl immediately wiped her finger in the mud and recited a couplet: 'O Son of Hind! Do you wish to destroy our faith and religion by means of pure honey? Never shall our support cease for ʿAlī 🖫.'

Holding Muʿāwiyah's letter in one hand and his daughter's hand in the other, Abū al-Aswad approached the Imam and recited his daughter's verses for him. Hearing them, the Imam smiled and prayed for both of them.[2]

63. Foods

Allah, the Wise, has said:

$$وَيُطْعِمُونَ الطَّعَامَ عَلَى حُبِّهِ مِسْكِينًا وَيَتِيمًا وَأَسِيرًا$$

They give food, for the love of Him, to the needy, the orphan, and the prisoner. (76:8)

The Holy Prophet said:

$$إِنَّ الْإِطْعَامَ مِنْ مُوجِبَاتِ الْجَنَّةِ وَالْمَغْفِرَةِ$$

---

[1] He died due to plague in the city of Basra, at the age of eighty-five, and had witnessed the lives of the Holy Prophet, Imam ʿAlī 🖫, Imam al-Ḥasan 🖫, Imam al-Ḥusayn 🖫, and Imam al-Sajjād 🖫. He is credited with writing, upon the instructions and assistance of Imam ʿAlī 🖫, a book on Arabic grammar, and placing dots on the Arabic letters that form the words of the Qurʾan.

[2] *Khazīnat al-Jawāhir*, p. 536.

Surely, feeding [others] is one of the reasons for forgiveness [of sins] and entering heaven.[1]

Short explanation

Moderation in the consumption of food and drink is integral to the well-being of the body and soul and therefore is highly emphasised in Islamic teachings. While we require nourishment to function and perform acts of worship, gluttony hardens the heart, arouses unrestrained passions, and damages health.

It is also important to note that the food we consume must be permissible and lawfully procured. All prophets and friends of Allah scrupulously abstained from impure, unlawful, and dubious food. They were fully aware that a lawful and moderate diet was a critical step in the journey towards spiritual purification.

1 – Moderation in eating and gluttony

Two mystics from Khorasan set out on a journey together. One consumed food only once every two nights and consequently appeared weak and feeble. However, his companion ate three meals a day and seemed fit and healthy.

As fate would have it, their journey was curtailed by officials who arrested them and charged them with treason and espionage. Sentenced to imprisonment for spying, they remained in a locked house for two weeks until their innocence was determined and they were set free. Upon their release, it was discovered that one of the mystics had not survived the ordeal; the mystic who ate well had died while his frail companion remained alive.

Hearing about the strange turn of events, a learned doctor explained to bewildered observers: 'On the contrary, it would have been a matter of greater astonishment if the weak mystic had died. The self-indulgent mystic died because he could not survive fourteen days without food, whereas the ascetic, accustomed to eating less, naturally had the stamina

---

[1] *Safīnat al-Biḥār*, vol. 2, p. 83.

and strength to survive the adversity he faced.'[1]

2 – Food in the company of friends

'Abd al-Raḥmān ibn Ḥajjāj narrates:

'We were having a meal in the house of Imam al-Ṣādiq 🕮 when an additional helping of rice was brought before us. We excused ourselves from eating it, whereupon the Imam said: "He who loves us more, consumes more food in our company." Upon hearing this, we sat down again to eat the rice. The Imam observed: "This is much better." He then continued: "One day, the Holy Prophet was presented with some rice, whereupon he invited Salmān, Abū Dharr, and Miqdād to join him in eating it. They excused themselves but the Holy Prophet insisted: 'Whoever loves us more should eat more in our company.'"

'Upon hearing this, all of them ate until they were full.'[2]

3 – Selling one's faith for a morsel

Faḍl ibn Rabīʿ relates:

'Mahdī, the third Abbasid caliph, once said to Sharīk ibn ʿAbd Allāh al-Nakhaʿī: "You must perform one of the following three tasks: become a magistrate in the judiciary, educate my children, or eat my food." Considering his options, Sharīk decided that educating the caliph's children was a difficult task, and becoming a judge was even more so. The third option seemed simple and easy, and so Sharīk readily accepted it.

'Mahdī instructed the cook to prepare various delicacies and place them before Sharīk who ate until he was full. Turning to the caliph, the kitchen attendant predicted: "O Caliph! After consuming these delicacies, the Shaykh will never attain salvation."[3]

'By Allah! After consuming the food not only did Sharīk increase his

---

[1] *Ḥikāyat-hā-yi Gulistān*, p. 154.

[2] *Shanīdanī-hā-yi Tārīkh*, p. 26; *al-Maḥajjah al-Bayḍāʾ*, vol. 3, p. 22.

[3] The Arabic text of this reads:

لَيْسَ يُفْلِحُ الشَّيْخُ بَعْدَ هَذِهِ الْأَكْلَةِ أَبَدًا

association with the Banī 'Abbās and agree to educate their children, he also consented to becoming a judge.

'Once, after receiving his payslip, Sharīk demanded the treasurer immediately pay him in cash. Noting his insistence, the treasurer responded: "You have not sold linen or an expensive garment to warrant receiving immediate cash payment."

'Upon hearing this, Sharīk retorted: "By Allah! I have sold something that is more precious than linen – I have sold my faith!"'[1]

4 – The blessing is in the bread[2]

The Holy Prophet states in a hadith: 'Regard bread with great esteem for most of the entities that exist between the Throne and the earth have some form of contribution in making and preparing it.'

The Holy Prophet continues: 'Previously, there lived a prophet by the name of Dānyāl. One day, he gave a loaf of bread to a poor man. The pauper frowned and flung it towards the middle of the road, saying: "How useless is a worthless loaf of bread!"

'Upon witnessing the pauper's ingratitude, Dānyāl raised his hands towards the heavens and said: "Honour bread with a lofty rank!" Due to the pauper's reprehensible action, Allah brought severe drought and famine to the land.

'Starvation forced people to resort to cannibalism. [Amongst them] were two mothers who together decided they would eat their own children. They sacrificed and consumed one child. On the following day, the mother of the child whose turn it was to be sacrificed refused to give up her child. [Unable to resolve] the ensuing dispute, the mothers brought the case before Dānyāl. When Dānyāl realised the [dire] condition of the people,

---

[1] *Pand-i Tārīkh*, vol. 4, p. 86; *Murūj al-Dhahab*, vol. 3, p. 320.

[2] The Holy Prophet ﷺ has said:

اللّٰهُمَّ بَارِك لَنَا فِي الْخُبْزِ

and also:

أَكْرِمُوا الْخُبْزَ

he prayed to Allah who then opened the doors of His mercy upon them.'[1]

5 – The caliph's fatal desire

After the death of Mu'taṣim the Abbasid (d. 841 CE), his son Hārūn became the caliph.

Historical records note that Hārūn was immensely fond of sexual intercourse and so requested his doctor to provide him with a concoction that would increase his sexual prowess. Hārūn's doctor was reluctant to do so, advising him: 'Excessive sexual intercourse wastes away the body and I do not want your health to deteriorate.'

The advice was ignored and upon Hārūn's insistence the doctor prepared the concoction by boiling the meat of wild beasts seven times in vinegar procured from wine. He prescribed the meat to be consumed after a drink of wine in a measure equivalent to the weight of fifty-four peas.

Hārūn, however, consumed more than the prescribed quantity and was soon afflicted with dropsy. The royal doctors unanimously agreed that the disease could only be cured by splitting the caliph's stomach open and placing him in a heated furnace. The procedure was performed and Hārūn remained in a burning furnace for three hours until large boils appeared on his body, whereupon he was removed. Writhing in agony, Hārūn beseeched: 'Do not place me in the furnace again for I shall surely die.' Ignoring his pleas, the doctors placed him back in the furnace. When the boils on his body burst, they pulled his burnt and blackened body out of the oven; he died shortly afterwards.

A cloth was placed over Hārūn's body and his corpse lay forgotten and unattended by the masses who rushed to offer allegiance to his brother, Mutawakkil. Hence, Hārūn's uninhibited sexual appetite proved fatal, resulting in his torturous and undignified demise in 847 ce.[2]

---

[1] *Namūnah-i Maʿārif,* vol. 1, p. 276; *Safīnat al-Biḥār,* vol. 1, p. 375

[2] *Tatimmat al-Muntahā,* p. 231

64. Pride

Allah, the Wise, has said:

$$\text{وَمَا الْحَيَاةُ الدُّنْيَا إِلَّا مَتَاعُ الْغُرُورِ}$$

And the life of this world is nothing but the wares of delusion. (57:20)

The Holy Prophet states:

$$\text{لَمِثْقَالُ ذَرَّةٍ مِنْ صَاحِبِ تَقْوَى وَيَقِينٍ أَفْضَلُ مِنْ مِلْءِ الْأَرْضِ مِنَ الْمُغْتَرِّينَ}$$

An atom's weight of good that is performed by a pious and faithful person is better than good deeds, plentiful enough to fill the earth, performed by an arrogant person.[1]

Short explanation

In accordance with Allah's system of justice, conceit deprives a person from both maximising the material benefits of this world and reaping the rewards of virtue in the afterlife. Moreover, pride in relation to one's wealth, family, health, power, and authority, is foolish and futile, for the objects of pride are transitory and fleeting. Hence, a person entrusted with wealth or position should never fall into complacency or arrogance; poverty, deprivation, disgrace, and tribulation may soon follow.

Even virtue and spiritual growth are gifts of divine grace. Hence, if a person performs numerous acts of worship, inculcates humility and God-wariness within his soul, or repents for his misdeeds, his first inclination should be to bow in gratitude to Allah for blessing him with the spiritual capacity and strength to succeed in his endeavours. Recognising divine mercy and love as the ultimate source of all achievements humbles a person and removes his desire for praise and applause from others. He is fully aware that pride and self-importance characterise one who is heedless of his absolute dependence upon Allah. A humble person will be spared from the disgrace of the Day of Judgement, when the arrogant and conceited will be raised as the most humiliated and remorseful of all people.[2]

---

[1] *Jāmiʿ al-Saʿādāt*, vol. 3, p. 5.

[2] *Tadhkirat al-Ḥaqāʾiq.*

1 – Hidden arrogance

Some of the companions of the Holy Prophet were frequently praising a particular person in his presence. One day, they pointed him out to the Holy Prophet and said: 'That is the person we often praise.'

The Holy Prophet looked at him and said: 'I am witnessing a satanic blackness covering his face.' As the person approached and greeted the Holy Prophet, the Holy Prophet asked him: 'I place you under the oath of Allah; tell me, did you not say to yourself: "Amongst the companions of the Holy Prophet there is none who is superior to me?"'

Ashamed, the man confessed: 'Yes, the thought did cross my mind.'

By asking the companion to examine his thoughts, the Holy Prophet enabled him to recognise the conceit hidden within himself and redress it.[1]

2 – Pride with respect to wealth and children

Due to his animosity towards the Holy Prophet, 'Āṣ ibn Wā'il frequently mocked the Holy Prophet, derisively calling him 'one without a son and lineage (*abtar*)'. Ibn Wā'il's son, 'Amr ibn 'Āṣ, shared his father's enmity towards the Ahl al-Bayt and worked closely with Mu'āwiyah in plotting and scheming against Imam 'Alī 🖎.

One of the companions of the Holy Prophet reports:

"'Āṣ ibn Wā'il owed me some money and so I asked him to pay the money indebted to me. However, he refused, saying: "I shall not give you your money," to which I responded: "In that case I shall collect my dues from you in the Hereafter."

"'Āṣ ibn Wā'il defiantly retorted: "In the Hereafter, if at all it exists, I will have numerous children and immense wealth; if I go there and you happen to join me, I will return your money to you!"'

Exposing the hollowness of these arrogant claims, Allah revealed:[2]

Have you not regarded him who defies Our signs, and says: 'I will surely be given wealth and children'? Has he come to know the unseen, or

---

[1] *Shanīdanī-hā-yi Tārīkh*, p. 378; *al-Maḥajjah al-Bayḍā'*, vol. 6, p. 298.

[2] *Ḥikāyat-hā-yi Shanīdanī*, vol. 5, p. 157; *al-Maḥajjah al-Bayḍā'*, vol. 6, p. 204.

taken a promise from the All-beneficent? No indeed! We will write down what he says, and We will prolong his punishment endlessly. (19:77-79)

3 – The proud champion

After a series of competitive matches a champion wrestler emerged undefeated and renowned for his wrestling prowess. Overcome with pride in his unmatched strength, he called out to the heavens one day: 'O Lord! Now arrange to send down Jibrīl so that I can test my strength against him, for on this earth there is none that can overcome my strength.'

In response, Allah reduced him to such a state of frailty and destitution that he was forced to live in the ruins of ramshackle houses. He grew so weak that he was hardly able to move.

One day, as he placed his head upon a brick to rest, a mouse darted over his face and began nibbling his toes; the former wrestler could not even muster the strength to pull his legs away from a peckish rodent!

A holy man passing by observed his decrepit state and advised: 'Allah has made you subordinate to one of his smallest soldiers in order that you realise your mistake and repent over your arrogance. Allah is both Forbearing and Merciful, and if you seek forgiveness He will indeed restore your health.'[1]

4 – The scholar of Arabic grammar

A student of Arabic grammar acquired mastery and expertise in his subject. One day, he boarded a ship and asked its captain: 'Have you studied Arabic grammar?'

'No,' replied the captain.

The scholar sneered: 'Then you have wasted half of your life!' The captain was hurt and offended by the scholar's scorn, but he did not respond and they continued the journey in silence.

Smooth sailing was suddenly interrupted by a heavy storm that threatened to capsize the boat. Observing that the ship was about to sink,

____
[1] *Rangārang*, vol. 1, p. 411.

the captain asked the scholar: 'Do you know how to swim?'

'No,' replied the scholar, to which the captain remarked: 'Then your entire life is about to be wasted for the ship is about to sink and you cannot swim!'

At his most desperate hour the scholar realised that the best knowledge is that which enables a person to eliminate the vices within him so that he does not drown in the sea of pride and vanity.[1]

5 – The arrogance of Abū Jahl

Abū Jahl, an obstinate enemy of the Holy Prophet, once performed the *ṭawāf* of the Ka'bah in the company of Walīd ibn Mughayrah. As they walked, Abū Jahl remarked to Walīd [about the Holy Prophet]: 'By God! He speaks the truth.'

Walīd rebuked: 'Keep quiet! How do you utter such a thing?'

Abū Jahl replied: 'We knew him to be a truthful and trustworthy person from childhood. Upon reaching adulthood and intellectual maturity, how could he suddenly become a liar and traitor?'

Unable to refute Abū Jahl's reasoning, Walīd questioned: 'If this is the case, why don't you testify to his truthfulness and accept Islam?'

Abū Jahl replied: 'Do you desire the womenfolk of the Quraysh to say that I, Abū Jahl, have submitted [to Islam] in cowardice and defeat? By the idols Lāt and 'Uzzā, I shall never follow him.'

Allah refers to Abū Jahl's conceit as blinding ignorance, stating: Have you seen him who has taken his desire to be his god and whom Allah has led astray knowingly, and set a seal upon his hearing and his heart, and put a blindfold on his sight?[2] (45:23)

65. Anger

Allah, the Wise, has said:

---

[1] *Dāstān-hā-yi Mathnawī*, vol. 1, p. 52.

[2] *Dāstān-hā Wa Pand-hā*, vol. 5, p. 85; *Tafsīr Irāqī*, vol. 25, p. 27.

يَا أَيُّهَا الَّذِينَ آمَنُوا لَا تَتَوَلَّوْا قَوْمًا غَضِبَ اللهُ عَلَيْهِمْ

O you who have faith! Do not befriend a people at whom Allah is wrathful.

(60:13)

The Holy Prophet states:

الْغَضَبُ يُفْسِدُ الْإِيمَانَ كَمَا يُفْسِدُ الْخَلُّ الْعَسَلَ

Anger corrupts faith just as vinegar corrupts honey.[1]

Short explanation

When guided by the intellect, the faculty of anger empowers a person to fight in defence of Islam, protect his property, family, and reputation from the threat of harm, and to resist injustice and oppression. Courage, valour, and sacrifice in defence of Islamic principles and the rights of others is commendable, if not mandatory, in Islam.

However, when anger is inspired by self-interest and satanic temptations it can act as a destructive cancer. Chronic and excessive anger can increase blood pressure, impair brain function, impede the circulation of oxygen, and lower metabolism and immunity. More significantly, anger removes compassion and temperance, obstructs rational judgement, and induces violence, malice, and ridicule. Before anger hardens into rage, jealousy, and vengefulness, its fury should be quelled with the restraints of patience and forbearance.[2]

1 – Dhū al-Kifl

When Prophet Alyasaʿ ﷺ was on his deathbed, he gathered the people and proclaimed: 'I shall appoint as my successor the one who undertakes the performance of three tasks: fasting during the days, remaining awake during the nights, and abstaining from anger.'

A youth named ʿUwaydiyā stood up and said: 'I am willing to accept the undertaking.'

Prophet Alyasaʿ ﷺ repeated his proclamation on the following day,

---

[1] *Jāmiʿ al-Saʿādāt*, vol. 1, p. 288.

[2] *Iḥyāʾ al-Qulūb*, p. 56

and once again 'Uwaydiyā alone stood up to accept the challenge. Prophet Alyasa' ﷺ nominated 'Uwaydiyā as his successor, passing away shortly thereafter. Hence, 'Uwaydiyā, later known as Dhū al-Kifl, became the next divinely appointed prophet.[1]

Shayṭān once resolved to make Dhū al-Kifl break his pledge by rousing his anger. To this end, he appointed a devil named Abyaḍ to mastermind and activate a plan to infuriate him.

Dhū al-Kifl would usually remain awake during the nights and nap briefly during the day. Abyaḍ waited for Dhū al-Kifl to fall asleep for his daily nap before loudly shouting: 'I have been oppressed! Grant me justice from my oppressor!'

Dhū al-Kifl awoke and calmly responded: 'Go and bring the person before me,' to which Abyaḍ replied: 'I will not move from here because I know he will not come with me.' Giving Abyaḍ his ring, Dhū al-Kifl asked him to take it to the accused and request his presence to discuss the matter. Abyaḍ accepted the ring and departed.

He returned the following day, wailing: 'I have been oppressed; my oppressor disregarded your ring and refused to return with me!'

Beckoning him to leave, Dhū al-Kifl's doorkeeper said to Abyaḍ: 'Let him rest, for he did not sleep yesterday nor has he slept the entire previous night.'

Abyaḍ insisted: 'I shall not let him sleep; I have been oppressed.'

Upon hearing the commotion, Dhū al-Kifl wrote a letter and handed it to Abyaḍ to present to the so-called oppressor, in the hope that he would be persuaded to accept his request for a meeting.

The following day, Abyaḍ interrupted Dhū al-Kifl's midday nap with the same shrill complaint. Unperturbed, Dhū al-Kifl calmly took Abyaḍ's hand and asked him to direct him towards the accused so that the matter could finally be resolved. Realising he had failed miserably in his efforts to aggravate Dhū al-Kifl, a dejected Abyaḍ removed his hand from Dhū al-

---

[1] He was one of the prophets and lived after the period of Prophet Sulaymān ﷺ.

Kifl's grasp and ran away.[1]

2 – True strength

The Holy Prophet once passed a large crowd gathered around a powerfully-built man lifting a gigantic stone, popularly known as the 'stone of the strong ones' and 'weight of the champions'. The display of physical prowess prompted gasps of amazement and a flurry of praise from the impressed spectators.

When the Holy Prophet asked what had attracted such a large crowd, he was told that a weight-lifter was performing a feat of exceptional strength. The Holy Prophet responded: 'Shall I inform you as to who is a true champion of strength? He is one who does not become enraged when abused, exhibits tolerance, and prevails over his ego and the devil of his self.'[2]

3 – The best advice

A person once requested the Holy Prophet: 'Impart to me knowledge and teach me the rulings of religion.'

The Holy Prophet advised him: 'Refrain from getting angry.'

'This very sentence will suffice me,' responded the man; he then left the Holy Prophet and returned to his tribe.

Upon his return he saw that a dispute had escalated into armed conflict and a battle was about to begin. As the man wore his armour and rushed to support his friends in battle, he suddenly remembered the advice of the Holy Prophet to abstain from anger. Dropping his weapons, he appealed for peace and reconciliation, saying: 'Battle and war will not yield anything. I shall pay you from my own wealth whatever you desire!' Ashamed of their hastiness to resort to war, both sides agreed to resolve their dispute with

---

[1] *Tārīkh-i Anbiyā'*, vol. 2, p. 196.

[2] *Iblīs Nāmih*, vol. 1, p. 75; *Majmū'ah Warrām*, vol. 2, p. 10. The late Shaykh Ṣadūq has reported in his book, *Ma'ānī al-Akhbār*, that the Holy Prophet identified three qualities of a true champion of strength, one of them being that when he is enraged, his anger does not distance him from truthful and correct speech.

diplomacy and negotiation.

Hence, the restraint and forbearance advised by the Holy Prophet prevented the outbreak of a major inter-tribal conflict.[1]

4 – Imam al-Ṣādiq ﷺ and his servant

Imam al-Ṣādiq ﷺ sent his servant out to perform a task for him. As the slave did not return for some time, the Imam set out to search for him. The search proved short and the Imam soon found him sound asleep.

Without the slightest sign of irritation the Imam sat down near his head and lightly fanned him until he awoke. Once the slave had woken up, the Imam gently chided him: 'By Allah! It does not befit you to sleep during the night as well as during the day. It is advisable for you to sleep during the night and work for us during the day.'[2]

5 – Kindness towards impertinent servants

Upon the death of his brother Ṭalḥah (d. 828 CE), ʿAbd Allāh ibn Ṭāhir was appointed the governor of Khorasan, which he presided over for seventeen years until he died in the year 845 CE, at the age of forty-eight. ʿAbd Allāh ibn Ṭāhir relates:

'One day, I found myself alone in the presence of the Abbasid caliph; none of the royal servants were in the court. Upon observing this the caliph called out: "O slave! O slave!" A Turkish slave arrived before the caliph, saying in annoyance: "The servants also have their own important tasks to perform, such as eating, using the lavatory, performing ablutions, offering prayers, and sleeping; just as we attend to our own needs you raise your voice and holler: 'O slave! O slave!' How long will you cry 'O slave'?"

'Upon hearing this outburst the caliph lowered his head; I was convinced that the caliph would order the slave to be beheaded as soon as he raised his head. However, when the caliph raised his head after a few moments, he said to me: "O ʿAbd Allāh! When the masters conduct themselves in a

---

[1] *Shanīdanī-hā-yi Tārīkh*, p. 305; *al-Maḥajjah al-Bayḍāʾ*, vol. 5, p. 293.

[2] *Muntahā al-Aʿmāl*, vol. 2, p. 130.

good manner, the slaves become ill-mannered; however, we should not become ill-mannered to enforce good conduct in our slaves."[1]

66. Backbiting

Allah, the Wise, has said:

وَلَا يَغْتَبْ بَعْضُكُمْ بَعْضًا

And do not backbite one another. (49:12)

The Holy Prophet said:

إِنَّ الْغِيبَةَ أَشَدُّ مِنَ الزِّنَا

Surely backbiting is worse than fornication.[2]

Short explanation

Backbiting, or speaking ill about a believer in his absence, is considered a major sin in Islam. One who indulges in this vice has transgressed two-fold: he has disobeyed Allah, and he has hurt the dignity, integrity, and feelings of his fellow brother in faith. Therefore, to make amends and attain forgiveness for his sin, he must seek forgiveness from Allah as well as from the one about whom he gossiped. Allah considers the dignity of a believer so sacred and lofty that destroying it through backbiting not only incurs punishment, but it also diminishes one's good deeds in the manner that fire burns wood.

Backbiting is often symptomatic of other spiritual illnesses including hatred, resentment, envy, malice, and rage. In the quest for self-purification it is important to refrain from backbiting as well as the destructive thoughts and emotions that motivate one to harm a believer's reputation. In redressing the negativity that induces a person to backbite, a person is able to remove the root cause of his sin.

---

[1] *Laṭāʾif al-Ṭawāʾif*, p. 94.

[2] *Jāmiʿ al-Saʿādāt*, vol. 2, p. 302.

1 – Unjust accusations

A man once passed by a group that was seated. Upon seeing the passer-by, a person from the group said: 'I harbour enmity towards him for the sake of Allah.'

The others retorted: 'By Allah! You have surely uttered an evil utterance! We will inform him of what you have said.' They then proceeded to do so.

The passer-by then approached the Holy Prophet and complained to him about what had been said against him. The Holy Prophet summoned the accused and asked him if the accusation was true. The man confirmed that it was. The Holy Prophet then asked: 'Why do you feel animosity towards him?'

He replied: 'I am his neighbour and am fully aware of his state. By Allah! I have never seen him offer any other prayer save the obligatory ones!'

Defending himself, the accused responded: 'O Prophet of Allah! Ask him if he has ever seen me delay my obligatory prayers or perform ablutions incorrectly or not perform my *rukū'* and *sujūd* correctly.'

When asked, the accusing neighbour replied that he had not, but he said: 'By Allah! With the exception of the month of Ramadan in which every person, whether pious or a sinner, fasts, I have never seen him fasting!'

The accused countered: 'O Prophet of Allah! Ask him if he has ever seen me not fasting in the month of Ramadan or disregarding any of the religious rulings associated with it.'

When the Holy Prophet enquired, the neighbour again replied in the negative before adding: 'By Allah! With the exception of the zakat that every person, pious or otherwise, pays, I have never seen him give any charity to a poor person!'

The accused responded: 'Ask him if he has ever seen me pay less than what was my duty or haggle with those who had come to collect the poor-rate from me.'

The reproachful neighbour was again forced to concede that the one he accused had fulfilled his obligations correctly.

The Holy Prophet then turned to the man who begrudged his neighbour and said: 'Depart from my presence for it is very likely that he is superior to you.'[1]

2 – The punishment for backbiting on the Day of Judgement

Shaykh Bahā'ī relates:

'It so happened that in a prominent gathering held in my absence I once became the topic of conversation. I later came to know that one who claimed to be my friend began backbiting about me and speaking ill of me; he seemed fully heedless of the verse in which Allah says: [Nor] backbite one another. Will any of you love to eat the flesh of his dead brother? You would hate it [49:12].

'When he [i.e. the one who had gossiped about me] came to know that I had become aware of his actions, he wrote me a lengthy letter in which he expressed his regret over the deed and sought forgiveness from me. In reply to his letter, I wrote: "May Allah reward you for the gift you have sent me! Your gift will cause the scale of my good deeds to become heavier on the Day of Judgement! It has been narrated that the Holy Prophet said: 'On the Day of Judgement, a person will be brought forth for the reckoning of his deeds; his good deeds will be placed in one pan of the balance while his evil deeds will be placed in the other, and it will be observed that the pan of evil deeds is heavier than that of his good deeds. At this juncture a sheet of paper will be placed upon his good deeds as a result of which the pan containing his good deeds will become heavier than the one containing his sins. Astonished, the person will ask: "O Lord! All the good deeds that I possessed had been placed in the pan so what is this sheet of paper? I never performed this good act." He will be informed: "This is in exchange for the evil words that were spoken about you which were not true.'" This tradition compels me to thank you for the gift that you have presented to me. Had you acted in this manner or even worse in front of

---

[1] *'Ilm-i Akhlāq-i Islāmī*, vol. 2, p. 399.

me, let me assure you that you would not have witnessed any response from me except forgiveness, pardon, friendship, and faithfulness. The years of life that remain are much too precious to waste in attempting to punish individuals for their deeds; rather, it ought to be spent in reflecting over that which has been lost and attempting to make amends for that which has passed.'"[1]

3 – The sin that impeded rainfall

The Banī Isrāʾīl were once afflicted with famine and drought. When Prophet Mūsā ﷺ offered prayers asking for rain on numerous occasions, Allah revealed to him: 'I have not answered your prayers because of a person from amongst you who constantly engages in backbiting and calumny.'

Prophet Mūsā ﷺ asked: 'O Lord! Who is the person?'

Allah revealed: 'O Mūsā! How can I backbite when I command you to refrain from backbiting? Tell all the people to seek forgiveness in order that I answer their prayers.'

When everyone had sought forgiveness, Allah showered them with His mercy in the form of abundant rainfall.[2]

In another tradition, it has been reported that a person had backbitten about Prophet Mūsā ﷺ who then requested Allah to reveal the person's identity to him. Allah replied: 'I consider telling tales to be abhorrent and reprehensible, and yet you desire that I should indulge in it?'

4 – A thousand lashings

Hārūn al-Rashīd once received some distinguished and valuable garments as gifts which he then gifted to his minister, ʿAlī ibn Yaqṭīn; amongst them was fur armour embroidered with gold. In grandeur and magnificence it resembled the garments worn by emperors.

ʿAlī ibn Yaqṭīn sent these garments to Imam al-Kāzim ﷺ along with numerous other valuables. The Imam, however, returned the armour and

---

[1] *Pand-i Tārīkh*, vol. 5, p. 160; *Kashkūl*, vol. 1, p. 196; *Kashkūl*, vol. 1, p. 196.

[2] *Jāmiʿ al-Saʿādāt*, vol. 2, p. 277.

wrote him a letter, advising: 'Keep it with you and do not take it out of your house; a time will come when you will be in need of it.'

A few days later, 'Alī ibn Yaqṭīn grew angry with one of his slaves and had him dismissed from service. This slave presented himself before Hārūn al-Rashīd, saying: "Alī ibn Yaqṭīn believes in the Imamate of Imam Mūsā ibn Ja'far and sends his *khums* to him every year. Even the armour that you gifted to him was sent to Mūsā ibn Ja'far on such and such day!'

Hārūn was enraged when he heard this and resolved to uncover the truth immediately. He ordered for 'Alī ibn Yaqṭīn to be summoned. When 'Alī ibn Yaqṭīn arrived, Hārūn bellowed: 'What have you done with the armour I gave you?'

'Alī ibn Yaqṭīn replied: 'It is in the house. I have wrapped it up in a piece of cloth and every morning and evening I open it to invoke the blessings it carries.'

Hārūn ordered: 'Bring it to me immediately.' 'Alī ibn Yaqṭīn directed one of his slaves to the location of the armour and asked him to bring it. The slave did as he was instructed and returned with the armour. When Hārūn observed that the armour he had given was perfumed and wrapped in a piece of cloth, his fury subsided and he said: 'Take this back to your house; henceforth, I will never pay heed to any words spoken against you.' He then showered 'Alī ibn Yaqṭīn with more gifts.

As for the slave, Hārūn ordered that he be subjected to 1000 lashes; upon suffering a few hundred lashes, he passed away.[1]

5 – The tale-telling slave

A person wished to purchase a slave and so set out for the slave market, whereat a slave was shown to him; he was told by its owner: 'This slave possesses no flaw except that he is a tale-bearer.' The person decided to purchase the slave and brought him to his house.

After a few days had passed, the slave approached his master's wife and said to her: 'Your husband does not love you anymore and intends to

---

[1] *Dāstān-hā Wa Pand-hā*, vol. 1, p. 52; *Kashkūl of Baḥrānī*, vol. 2, p. 132.

take another woman as his wife. If you desire, I will cast a magic charm on him to keep him besotted by you; however, to do so, I would need you to procure a few strands of your husband's hair for me.'

'How can I bring his hair for you?' the wife asked.

The slave replied: 'When your husband is asleep, cut some of his hair by means of a razor and bring it to me so that I can create a charm by which he will begin to love you!'

The slave then approached the husband and said to him: 'Your wife has found a lover for herself and desires to kill you, so beware.'

Hence, when night arrived, the husband pretended to be asleep; believing her husband to be asleep, his wife entered the room with a razor in hand. Assuming that his wife had come to kill him, the man lunged towards his wife and killed her. When the wife's relatives learned about what had happened, they murdered the husband. The husband's tribe then rose up in arms against the wife's tribe, leading to war, bloodshed, and long-standing enmity between the two tribes.[1]

67. Obscene Language

Allah, the Wise, has said:

$$وَلَا تَسُبُّوا الَّذِينَ يَدْعُونَ مِنْ دُونِ اللّٰهِ فَيَسُبُّوا اللّٰهَ عَدْوًا$$

Do not abuse those whom they invoke besides Allah, lest they should abuse Allah out of hostility. (6:108)

The Holy Prophet said:

$$إِنَّ اللّٰهَ لَا يُحِبُّ الْفُحْشَ وَالتَّفَحُّشَ$$

Surely Allah does not like obscene language and abusiveness.[2]

Short explanation

Obscene language is speech that is vulgar and foul. As speech and actions are manifestations of a person's inner state, coarse speech reflects foul

---

[1] *Shanīdanī-hā-yi Tārīkh*, p. 302; *al-Maḥajjah al-Bayḍāʾ*, vol. 1, p. 289.

[2] *Jāmiʿ al-Saʿādāt*, vol. 1, p. 314.

thoughts and a character lacking modesty, shame, and God-wariness. A true believer's speech is always refined and beautiful; he does not use his tongue to praise and worship Allah in seclusion and thereafter engage in lewd and crude conversation in the company of others. Conversely, indecent speech indicates a heart that has succumbed to hypocrisy, aligning itself to satanic temptations rather than the love and pleasure of Allah.

Speech mirrors a person's soul and so every effort should be made to ensure that one's thoughts, ideas, and attachments are also pure, constructive, and godly. Through self-discipline, sincere supplication, engaging in continual remembrance of Allah, and abstaining from vulgar pastimes and company, a believer can ennoble and uplift both his character and speech.[1]

1 – The Imam's reaction

'Amr ibn Nu'mān Ju'fī relates:

'Imam al-Ṣādiq ﷺ had a companion who accompanied him wherever he would go. The companion and his slave once joined the Imam in his journey to a place called Hadhaain. During the course of the journey, the Imam's companion suddenly realised that his slave was no longer by his side. The companion searched the nearby area three times but to no avail. The fourth attempt proved successful; as soon as the companion's eye fell upon his slave, he shouted angrily: "O son of an adulteress! Where have you been?"

'The companion's cry reached the Imam, who placed his hand on his forehead and said: "*Subḥān allāh*! You have ascribed an evil act to his mother! While I had always regarded you as a man of piety, I realise now that this is not the case."

'In an attempt to justify his statement, the companion responded: "May I be made your ransom! But his mother is a polytheist."

'The Imam rebuked him: "Do you not know that every community has its own marriage customs and they deserve to be respected? Withdraw

---

[1] *Iḥyā' al-Qulūb*, p. 65.

from my company."

'From that day on, I never saw him in the company of the Imam for as long as they were alive.'[1]

2 – Usāmah's reply

Usāmah ibn Zayd was the son of Zayd ibn Ḥārith, a slave freed by the Holy Prophet and adopted as his son. Like his father, Usāmah was much-loved by the Holy Prophet and a staunch and upright believer. The Holy Prophet once remarked: 'He [Usāmah] is an individual of whom I am particularly fond and he is one of the pious ones amongst you.' Just before his demise, the Holy Prophet entrusted the entire command of the Muslim military expedition against the Byzantine Empire to Usāmah, who was only seventeen years of age at the time.

It has been reported that once, Usāmah was engaged in prayers near the grave of the Holy Prophet. As he was praying, Marwān ibn Ḥakam, the governor of Medina, arrived to lead the funeral prayers for a man who had just passed away. Upon completion of the prayer, Marwān noticed Usāmah engaged in worship near the door of the house of the Holy Prophet. Offended that Usāmah had not participated in the funeral prayers that he had led, Marwān sneered: 'You want the people to see you engaged in prayers, don't you?' He then launched into a long tirade of insults and obscenities.

After completing his prayers, Usāmah approached Marwān and said: 'You have hurt me and used obscene and abusive language towards me. I have heard the Holy Prophet say: "Allah abhors a person who uses obscene and abusive language."'[2]

3 – Shayṭān accompanies one who uses foul language

The Holy Prophet and Abū Bakr were once seated together when a person

---

[1] The Arabic text of this is:

$$\text{أَمَا عَلِمْتَ أَنَّ لِكُلِّ قَوْمٍ نِكَاحًا}$$

[2] *Payghambar Wa Yārān*, vol. 1, p. 194.

approached Abū Bakr and began to mock and revile him. Abū Bakr responded by defending himself and slighting the offender in return. The Holy Prophet watched the exchange in silence. However, as soon as Abū Bakr's speech turned foul, the Holy Prophet stood up and moved away from the conversation, saying: 'O Abū Bakr! When you were being abused, an angel of Allah was responding in your defence; however, as soon as you began abusing him, the angel left you and his place was taken by Shayṭān; and I am not one who would

sit in a gathering wherein Shayṭān is present.'[1]

4 – Imam al-Ṣādiq's forbearance

A person once said to Imam al-Ṣādiq: 'Your such and such cousin was talking about you; all that he uttered was abusive and foul.'

The Imam requested his slave-girl to bring him water to perform *wuḍū*; he then performed *wuḍū* and began his prayers. When the Imam had concluded his two-unit prayer, he beseeched: 'O Lord! It was my right [which he transgressed] and I have forgiven him [for his insults and abuse]. Your kindness and mercy is far greater than mine, so forgive him and do not punish him for his conduct.'

A companion who observed the exchange, commented when reporting the incident: 'Upon witnessing the compassion [and forbearance] of the Imam, I was overcome with astonishment and amazement.'[2]

5 – Ibn Muqaffaʿ

Ibn Muqaffaʿ was an erudite scholar and a translator of several academic works from Persian into Arabic. Proud of his literary renown and academic proficiency, he began to look down on others. In his arrogance he even resorted to belittling and disparaging his companions in public gatherings.

Amongst those whom Ibn Muqaffaʿ humiliated was Sufyān ibn Muʿāwiyah, the governor of Basra during the caliphate of Manṣūr Dawānīqī.

---

[1] *Iblīs Nāmih*, vol. 1, p. 73; *Iḥyāʾ al-ʿUlūm*, vol. 3, p. 370.

[2] *Muntahā al-Aʿmāl*, vol. 2, p. 127; *Miskāht al-Anwār*.

Sufyān had a disproportionately large nose and whenever Ibn Muqaffaʿ would arrive before him, he would call out loudly: 'Salutations to both of you [i.e. Sufyān and his large nose].' At other times, Ibn Muqaffaʿ would attack Sufyān with obscenities and insults or mock him by demeaning his mother. One day, in a public gathering, Ibn Muqaffaʿ loudly addressed Sufyān, calling him 'O son of a lecherous woman!'

Angry at being the object of constant verbal abuse, Sufyān grew vengeful. He bided his time, waiting for an opportune moment to seek his revenge. Due to a sudden political turn of events, the moment soon arrived.

ʿAbd Allāh ibn ʿAlī initiated an uprising against his nephew, Manṣūr Dawānīqī. In response, Manṣūr dispatched Abū Muslim Khurāsānī to Basra to quell the rebellion. Abū Muslim emerged victorious in the battle that ensued and ʿAbd Allāh ibn ʿAlī fled the warfront, eventually finding refuge with his brothers, Sulaymān and ʿĪsā. They interceded on Ibn ʿAlī's behalf before Manṣūr and requested that he be pardoned. Successful in their intervention, Manṣūr's uncles returned to Basra and asked Ibn Muqaffaʿ to write an official letter of pardon for ʿAbd Allāh ibn ʿAlī.

Ibn Muqaffaʿ's conceit prompted him to write within the letter of pardon: 'In the event that Manṣūr Dawānīqī deceives his uncle ʿAbd Allāh ibn ʿAlī and troubles him, all his wealth will be considered as having become the property of the people, all his slaves will be considered free, and all Muslims will be considered free from their pledge of allegiance to him.' The letter was brought before Manṣūr to sign and seal. Upon reading its contents, Manṣūr was enraged and immediately ordered that Ibn Muqaffaʿ be killed.

Having received the perfect mandate for revenge, Sufyān instructed the guards to lock Ibn Muqaffaʿ in a room to await his punishment. Sufyān then turned to his helpless prisoner and asked derisively: 'Do you recall the abuses and obscene language that you had used for my mother and me?' He ordered a furnace to be lit and Ibn Muqaffaʿ, as per the command of Manṣūr Dawānīqī, was hurled into the flames and burned alive.[1]

---

[1] *Dunyā-yi Jawān*, p. 64; *Jawān*, vol. 2, p. 21.

68. Poverty

Allah, the Wise, has said:

الشَّيْطَانُ يَعِدُكُمُ الْفَقْرَ

Shayṭān frightens you of poverty. (2:268)

The Holy Prophet said:

تُحْفَةُ الْمُؤْمِنِ فِي الدُّنْيَا الْفَقْرُ

Poverty is a gift for a believer in the world.[1]

Short explanation

Wherever poverty is rife, so is suffering. Malnourishment, homelessness, disease, illiteracy, and high infant mortality are amongst the various ills associated with destitution. In situations where the poor are trapped in a persisting cycle of suffering and helplessness, they may turn to crime, drugs, and alcohol in a desperate bid to escape their misery. Others may fall into depression, despair, and even reject their belief in divine love and mercy.

Poverty is therefore an arduous test of patience, contentment, and faith in Allah. One who endures indigence without complaint, trusts in the wisdom of Allah's distribution, and relies on Him for strength and assistance, attains a lofty position in the eyes of Allah. In fact, the Holy Prophet states: 'The best of this ummah are the indigent ones and they shall enter heaven before everyone else. Poverty is my glory; heaven is desirous of the indigent ones and they are the kings of the inmates of heaven.'[2]

1 – The poor pious person

Saʿdī relates:

'I heard that a pious person was enduring the hardship of poverty [with patience]. He would repeatedly stitch his torn garment, piece by piece,

---

[1] *Jāmiʿ al-Saʿādāt*, vol. 2, p. 83.

[2] *Iḥyāʾ al-Qulūb*, p. 89.

all the while consoling himself, saying: "With dry bread and a patched woollen garment I shall content myself; my heavy burden I shall endure but not the burden of someone's obligation."

'A person once asked him: "Why do you sit here? Do you not know that there is an honourable and magnanimous gentleman in the city who has resolved to help the needy and relieve their misery? Go to him and inform him of your state, for if he realises your condition he will provide you with food and new clothes and end your hardship."

'The pious pauper replied: "Keep quiet! Repeatedly patching one's clothes and exhibiting patience is better than seeking clothes [and assistance] from a wealthy man. Indeed, entering heaven as a result of a neighbour's intercession is equivalent to the tortures of the fire of hell."'[1]

2 – The destitute Christian

An elderly blind man once sought monetary assistance from Imam 'Alī . Imam 'Alī   asked those around him: 'Who is this person and how is his state?'

They replied: 'O Commander of the Faithful, he is a Christian.'

Their tone of voice implied that the man was not worthy of receiving assistance from the Imam. Seeing their reluctance to assist him, the Imam exclaimed: 'What?! While he had strength to work, you extracted work from him, and now that he has turned frail, you do not attend to his needs! It appears that when he was strong, he used to work and serve.' The Imam then instructed that funds from the public treasury be used to provide for the Christian's needs.[2]

3 – The benefits of assisting the poor

'Abd Allāh ibn Mubārak once resolved to go to Mecca to perform the hajj. Shortly thereafter, as he was passing through a lane, he saw a woman bend down, pick up a putrid fowl carcass from the ground, and hide it under her

---

[1] *Ḥikāyat-hā-yi Gulistān*, p. 151.

[2] *Bā Mardūm Īn Gūnih Barkhūrd Kunīm*, p. 30; *Tahdhīb*, vol. 6, p. 292.

cloak. ʿAbd Allāh asked the woman in surprise: 'O lady! Why have you picked up this dead fowl?'

The woman replied: 'Need and adversity have compelled me to resort to such an act!'

When ʿAbd Allāh heard this he led the indigent woman to his house and gifted her the 500 dinars that he had set aside for his pilgrimage. Unable to afford the trip, ʿAbd Allāh did not perform hajj that year. When some pilgrims returned after having performed their pilgrimage, ʿAbd Allāh welcomed and congratulated them. As soon as the pilgrims saw ʿAbd Allāh, they said to him: 'We saw you performing the rites of hajj at ʿArafāt, Mina, and other places.'

Bewildered by this news, ʿAbd Allāh narrated the episode to the Imam and asked him for an explanation, whereupon the Imam clarified: 'Allah created an angel in your likeness to perform the pilgrimage of the House of Allah [in your place].'[1]

4 – Sayyid Jawād's neighbour

The jurist and author of the book *Miftāḥ al-Karāmah*, Sayyid Jawād Āmulī, narrates:

'One night, as I was having my dinner, someone knocked at the door. Opening the door, I saw it was the servant of Sayyid Baḥr al-ʿUlūm. He said to me: "The dinner of Sayyid Baḥr al-ʿUlūm is ready and he awaits you."

'I accompanied the servant to the house of Sayyid Baḥr al-ʿUlūm. As soon as I arrived, he said: "Is it because you do not fear Allah that you tend to be so negligent?"

'I humbly responded: "O teacher! What is the matter?"

'Sayyid Baḥr al-ʿUlūm replied: "Due to his poverty, one of your brethren in faith has only been able to afford dates to feed his family, and that too [he bought] on credit. Seven days have passed and the family has eaten nothing but dates. Today, [this poor man] approached a grocer to obtain food but the grocer flatly refused, causing him immense embarrassment.

---

[1] *Namūnah-i Maʿārif*, vol. 2, p. 413; *Laʾālī al-Akhbār*, p. 253.

Hence, he and his family have gone to sleep without having eaten any dinner. You have devoured a full meal while your neighbour is needy [and requires assistance]!"

'In my defence, I pleaded: "I possessed no information whatsoever regarding his condition!"

'Sayyid Baḥr al-ʿUlūm replied: "And had you been aware of his state and yet not helped him you would have been regarded as a Jew or even an infidel! It troubles me that you did not investigate the state of your brother in faith. My servant will now carry these containers of food [to your neighbour's house]; go with him and tell [your neighbour]: 'I would be very pleased if you would join me for dinner tonight.' Then place this bag of money [containing 120 rials] under his carpet and do not bring back the food containers."

'I proceeded to the [poor] person's house in the company of the servant and acted as per my teacher's instructions. My neighbour said to me: "No Arab can prepare this kind of meal. Tell me, to whom does this food belong?"

'Upon his insistence, I confessed: "It belongs to Sayyid Baḥr al-ʿUlūm."

'Astonished by my response, he confided: "No one except Allah has been aware of my state – not even my next-door neighbours, let alone those individuals who stay far from me!"'[1]

5 – Greed for wealth

During the reign of King Ḥusayn Kurt (732-771 CE), there lived a very poor beggar known as Mawlānā Arshadī. He was gifted with a beautiful voice and excellent oratory power by which he could captivate the hearts of his listeners. Hence, when King Ḥusayn wished to send a messenger to convey a message to King Shoja of Shiraz, people advised him to appoint Mawlānā Arshadī, insisting that 'the speech of Mawlānā Arshadī, the beggar, is excellent'. Persuaded by their good opinion, King Ḥusayn summoned Mawlānā Arshadī and said to him: 'I intend to send you upon an important

____

[1] *Pand-i Tārīkh*, vol. 1, p. 140; *Kalimah-i Ṭayyibah*, p. 111.

mission. The only flaw discrediting you is that you beg. However, I am willing to send you to Shiraz if you promise not to bring my name into disrepute by begging [in the city].' Having obtained Mawlānā's solemn pledge to refrain from begging, King Ḥusayn gave Mawlānā 20,000 dinars as payment for his mission to Shiraz. Upon Mawlānā Arshadī's arrival to Shiraz, he delivered King Ḥusayn's message to King Shoja. However, before Mawlānā could return to King Ḥusayn with the response received from King Shoja, King Shoja and members of his royal court requested Mawlānā to deliver a sermon in his famed eloquent style. Upon their insistence, Mawlānā Arshadī agreed to deliver a sermon in the mosque after the Friday prayers.

On Friday, the mosque was attended in large numbers. Upon completion of the prayers, Mawlānā ascended the pulpit and began his sermon. His eloquence soon captivated the attention of his listeners. Exploiting the opportunity to his personal advantage, Mawlānā Arshadī shrewdly added: 'I have been placed under oath not to speak of my poverty and beggary. However, from the moment I set foot in your city, I did not witness any charity extended by you! Is it the case that all of you have taken an oath not to give me any alms?'

Taken aback by Mawlānā's brazen accusation, the silent crowd erupted into laughter. They rushed to Mawlānā and offered him generous sums of money. Having successfully manipulated people's kindness to satisfy his greed, Mawlānā Arshadī returned to his native city with bulging pockets.[1]

69. Adjudication

Allah, the Wise, has said:

$$\text{وَاللّٰهُ يَقْضِي بِالْحَقِّ}$$

Allah judges with justice. (40:20)

---

[1] *Laṭāʾif al-Ṭawāʾif*, p. 371.

Imam al-Ṣādiq ﷺ said:

مَنْ حَكَمَ فِي دِرْهَمَيْنِ بِغَيْرِ مَا أَنْزَلَ اللّٰهُ عَزَّ وَجَلَّ فَهُوَ كَافِرٌ بِاللّٰهِ الْعَظِيمِ

One who passes a judgement with respect to [even] two dirhams in a manner other than what God has stipulated, is a disbeliever in God, the Great.[1]

Short explanation

Adjudication is amongst the most challenging professions in its test of honesty, discretion, and accurate judgement. Every judge may be inclined to rule in favour of friendship when a conflict between justice and attachment arises. However, Islam identifies justice as an absolute principle to which all interests of kinship, friendship, and alliance must defer. Unless a judge wisely counters the biases of personal inclination, self-interest, and limited factual information, he may pass an unfair verdict, thereby violating the rights of others. An arbiter who fulfils his role in strict accordance with the principles of justice, wisdom, and integrity, will be rewarded a lofty position in the afterlife.

1 – Imam ʿAlī ﷺ and the peculiar judge

Imam ʿAlī ﷺ was once delivering a sermon in the city of Kufa when a python suddenly slithered up the steps of the pulpit upon which the Imam was seated. Terrified that the python would attack the Imam, people moved to ward the reptile away but the Imam signalled for them to stay where they were. As they watched in silent bewilderment, the snake slid up the final step of the pulpit, its tongue almost touching Imam's ear, as he lowered his head towards the python. The python then hissed audibly in Imam ʿAlī's ﷺ ear, to which the Imam replied quietly. Once the strange conversation ended, the python glided down the pulpit and suddenly disappeared from sight. Imam ʿAlī ﷺ then continued and concluded his sermon.

As the Imam descended from the pulpit people crowded around him, questioning him about the incident. The Imam explained: 'What occurred

---

[1] *Safīnat al-Biḥār*, vol. 2, p. 436.

was not as you perceived it to be. He [the python] was a judge from amongst the jinn. Since the jinn were confused in connection with a judgement, he asked me for an explanation. I explained the judgement to him, whereupon he prayed for me and departed.'[1]

2 – The partiality of the judge and his punishment

Imam al-Bāqir ﷺ relates:

'Once, there lived a scholar from the tribe of Banī Isrā'īl who also adjudicated cases brought to him by members of his community. When he was on his deathbed, he instructed his wife: "Upon my death, perform the [required] ablutions, wrap me in a shroud, place me within the coffin, and cover my face."

'When the scholar died, his wife did as she had been instructed. However, desiring to see her husband's face one last time, she moved aside the covering from over his face to take another look. She was shaken by what she saw – a worm was gnawing and eating her husband's nose. That same night she witnessed her husband in her dreams and asked him about the worm. The judge replied: "Once, your brother asked me to adjudicate a dispute that had arisen between him and his companion. In my heart, I felt inclined to pass the judgement in his favour. The proceedings of the trial also indicated that the judgement should be passed in his favour. However, because my judgement was based on my personal inclinations rather than objective analysis, I suffered the punishment inflicted by the worm on my face."'[2]

3 – Divine judgement

Prophet Dāwūd ﷺ once prayed to Allah to make manifest for him one of the judgements He would issue on the Day of Judgement. Allah revealed to him: 'You have asked me to manifest something I have never manifested for anyone; it is not suitable for anyone except Me to observe judgement

---

[1] *Kitāb al-Irshād*, p. 183.

[2] *Dāstān-hā Wa Pand-hā*, vol. 1, p. 55; *Anwār al-Nuʿmāniyyah*, p. 15.

in this manner.'

When Prophet Dāwūd 🕮 repeated his request, Jibrīl descended and said: 'You have requested Allah for something that has never before been requested by the prophets; nonetheless Allah has answered your prayer. The ruling of the Hereafter with regards to the first case that is brought to you for judgement will be made manifest to you.'

The following morning, an elderly man accompanied by a young boy carrying a bunch of grapes entered the court of Prophet Dāwūd 🕮. The old man complained: 'O Prophet of Allah! This youth entered my garden, spoilt my trees, and ate my grapes without my permission.'

Turning to the youth, Prophet Dāwūd 🕮 asked: 'What would you like to say [in this regard]?' The youth admitted that the accusations against him were true.

At this moment, Allah revealed to Prophet Dāwūd 🕮: 'If you were to pass judgement according to the ruling of the Hereafter, the Banī Isrā'īl would never accept it. O Dāwūd! The garden belongs to the father of this youth. [Previously] the old man killed the youth's father and stole 40,000 dirhams buried in a corner of the garden belonging to the father. Therefore, hand a sword to the youth and instruct him to behead the old man as just retaliation for the murder of his father. Thereafter, grant the garden to him and ask him to dig the garden [in the area where the money was buried] and extract the property which belongs to him.'

Prophet Dāwūd 🕮 then executed the judgement as commanded by Allah, the Exalted.[1]

4 – The Jew and Imam ʿAlī 🕮 in the presence of the judge

Imam ʿAlī 🕮 was seated in the Mosque of Kufa when ʿAbd Allāh ibn Qufl, a Jew from the tribe of Tamīm, passed by him, carrying a coat of armour. When the Imam saw the coat of armour, he exclaimed: 'This [armour] belonged to Ṭalḥah ibn ʿAbd Allāh and came into my possession as my share of the booty of the battle in Basra. [To take the armour from me]

---

[1] *Ḥayāt al-Qulūb*, vol. 1, p. 333.

amounts to treachery.'

The Jew agreed to accompany the Imam to the court where the case would be presented before a judge. The judge, by the name of Shurayḥ,[1] had been appointed by the Imam. The Imam then put forth his claim before Shurayḥ, who responded: 'Present witnesses to testify and corroborate your claim.' When Imam ʿAlī ﷺ brought his son Ḥasan ﷺ as his witness, Shurayḥ said: 'The testimony of one person is not sufficient.'[2] According to another narration of the same incident, Shurayḥ refused to accept the testimony of a son in support of his father. The Imam then presented his slave Qambar as his witness, whereupon Shurayḥ responded: 'I shall not issue a verdict based upon the testimony of a slave.'

Disturbed by the judge's rulings, Imam ʿAlī ﷺ then turned to the Jew and said: 'Take the coat of armour and go your way for this judge has ruled falsely and incorrectly three times.'

Shurayḥ asked: 'What are the three rulings that have been false and incorrect?'

The Imam replied: 'Woe unto you! Firstly, there is no need for witnesses for issues pertaining to treachery and disloyalty [it is the responsibility of the supposed owner to present witnesses to prove how he became the owner of the possession in question]. Secondly, I presented Ḥasan as my witness but you refused to accept him, whereas the Holy Prophet passed judgements on the basis of one witness if the claimant took an oath [testifying to his own truthfulness]. Thirdly, Qambar presented himself as a witness but you stated that you would not pass a ruling on the basis of a slave's testimony; however, the correct ruling is that if a slave is upright, his testimony should be accepted. Woe unto you! The Imam of the Muslims is trustworthy – so how can his claim not be acceptable?'

At the end of the Imam's speech, the Jew exclaimed: '*Subḥān allāh*! The

---

[1] In the year 640 CE or 644 CE, at the age of forty, he was appointed as the judge of Kufa by the Second Caliph and continued to adjudicate for sixty years. He lived for 120 years.

[2] According to one narration, he refused to accept the testimony of a son in favour of his father; but accepted the testimony of Qambar.

caliph of the Muslims accompanies me before a judge, the judgement is passed against him, and he complies with the verdict! O Commander of the Faithful! Indeed you have spoken the truth. This coat of armour belongs to you; it fell down from your saddlebag and I acquired it by picking it up.' He then testified to the unity of Allah and the prophethood of the Holy Prophet and became a Muslim. The Imam then gifted him the coat of armour and awarded him 900 dirhams.[1]

5 – The crime of blinding a Bedouin

'Uthmān ibn 'Affān's servant once slapped a Bedouin; consequently, the slave became blind in one eye. When the Bedouin complained, 'Uthmān promised to pay him compensation for the injury. The Bedouin refused, stating: 'I seek retaliation.' 'Uthmān offered him double the promised amount in compensation but the Bedouin refused and insisted on blinding the slave in one eye in retaliation for the injury he had suffered.

'Uthmān informed Imam 'Alī ﷺ about the matter and asked him to pass judgement according to his discretion. The Imam requested the Bedouin to accept the compensation offered but he refused. The Imam offered to double the compensation; again, the Bedouin refused. When the Imam saw that the Bedouin would not relent, he summoned 'Uthmān's slave. The Imam then instructed that a mirror and some cotton-wool be brought before him. He moistened the cotton-wool and placed it over and around the slave's eye-lid in order to keep it open. Then, positioning the mirror under the sun such that the sunlight was reflected into the slave's open eyes, Imam 'Alī ﷺ instructed the slave: 'Look into the mirror.' The slave looked into the mirror until the sun's reflective glare removed his vision in one eye; in this manner the Imam exacted the retaliatory punishment for the slave's crime of blinding the Bedouin.[2]

---

[1] *Payghambar Wa Yārān*, vol. 3, p. 286; *Biḥār al-Anwār*, vol. 4, p. 302.

[2] *Qaḍāwat-hā-yi Amīr al-Mu'minīn* ﷺ, p. 103; *al-Wāfī*, vol. 2.

70. Loans

Allah, the Wise, has said:

$$\text{مَنْ ذَا الَّذِي يُقْرِضُ اللّٰهَ قَرْضًا حَسَنًا فَيُضَاعِفَهُ لَهُ أَضْعَافًا كَثِيرَةً}$$

Who is it that will lend Allah a good loan that He may multiply it for him severalfold? (2:245)

Imam al-Ṣādiq ﷽ said:

$$\text{مَكْتُوبٌ عَلَى بَابِ الْجَنَّةِ: الصَّدَقَةُ بِعَشَرَةٍ وَالْقَرْضُ بِثَمَانِيَةَ عَشَرَ}$$

It is written upon the door of heaven: The reward for [giving] charity will be ten-fold and that of [extending] loans will be eighteen-fold.[1]

Short explanation

Providing loans to those in need is a service that extricates the poor from a cycle of destitution and dependence on charity. Giving generous loans without exploiting the indebted by charging interest, is a lofty act of virtue in the eyes of Allah. Its reward is greater than that of giving charity, perhaps because unlike the short-term fix provided by charity, loan-giving offers the poor a dignified means to work their way out of desperation, dependence, and deprivation in the long- term. As compassion towards the needy is a key to divine mercy, loan- giving ensures divine increase and flow in a person's sustenance and wealth, whilst multiplying his rewards in the Hereafter.

1 – Abū Daḥdāḥ

Upon revelation of the verse: Who is it that will lend Allah a good loan that He may multiply it for him severalfold? (2:245) Abū Daḥdāḥ[2] asked: 'O Prophet of Allah! May I be made your ransom! How is it possible that

---

[1] *Jāmi' al-Sa'ādāt*, vol. 2, p 159.

[2] His name was Thābit and he possessed strong faith. During the Battle of Uḥud, when rumours spread that the Holy Prophet had been martyred and the Muslims began to flee the battlefield, Abū Daḥdāḥ shouted: 'If Muḥammad has been killed, the God of Muḥammad is still alive. Fight the enemies of Islam, for God is your helper.' *(Safīnat al-Biḥār)*.

whilst Allah is Independent and Needless, He seeks a loan from us?'

The Holy Prophet replied: 'It is [a means] by which He desires to enable you to enter heaven.'

Abū Daḥdāḥ further questioned: 'If I give Allah a loan, do you guarantee heaven for me?'

The Holy Prophet responded: 'Yes; Allah will recompense in heaven the one who provides Him a loan.'

Abū Daḥdāḥ then asked: 'Would my wife, Umm Daḥdāḥ, be with me in heaven?'

The Holy Prophet replied: 'Yes.'

Abū Daḥdāḥ persisted: 'Would my daughter also be with me in heaven?'

When the Holy Prophet again replied in the affirmative, Abū Daḥdāḥ requested: 'Place your hand upon my hand to confirm what you have just stated!' The Holy Prophet gave Abū Daḥdāḥ his hand, whereupon he said: 'I have nothing but two gardens and I lend both of them to Allah.'

The Holy Prophet advised him: 'Keep one for yourself and lend the other.'

Abū Daḥdāḥ responded: 'I take you, the Prophet of Allah, to be my witness that from my two gardens, I have given the better one to Allah.'

The Holy Prophet promised him: 'Allah has granted you heaven in exchange for it.'

When Abū Daḥdāḥ informed his wife of the incident, she said to him: 'May Allah make blessed that which you have purchased for yourself.'[1]

2 – Imam al-Sajjād ﷺ repays the debt of Ibn Usāmah

Imam al-Sajjād ﷺ once visited a sick companion by the name of Muḥammad ibn Usāmah. When the Imam saw that he was weeping, he asked in concern: 'How do you feel?'

Ibn Usāmah replied: 'I am in debt [and I am worried about it].'

The Imam enquired: 'How much is your debt?'

---

[1] *ʿUnwān al-Kalām*, p. 175.

'15,000 dinars,' replied Ibn Usāmah.

The Imam assured Ibn Usāmah that he would pay off his debt, and departed to fulfil his promise.[1]

3 – The reward of granting respite to a debtor

According to a hadith of Imam al-Ṣādiq 🕮: 'One who wishes Allah to shelter him on the day when there shall be no shelter except His shelter, should either grant respite to one who owes money to him or relinquish the debt that is owed to him.'

The Holy Prophet once asked while sheltering his face from the hot sun with his hands: 'Who desires to be sheltered from the intense heat of hell?'

All the companions who were present replied: 'We [do], O Prophet of Allah!'

The Holy Prophet repeated his question three times and each time, his companions repeated the same answer. He then said: 'One who grants respite [in the repayment of debt] to his debtor or relinquishes the money that is owned to him by an indigent person, will be protected from the intense heat of hell.'[2]

4 – The ignorant debtor

During *miʿrāj*, the Holy Prophet witnessed a person who was attempting to pick up a bundle of firewood. Each time he attempted to pick up the bundle of wood, the bundle would fall down and the amount of firewood would increase. The Holy Prophet asked Jibrīl: 'Who is this person?'

Jibrīl replied: 'This person was in debt and desired to repay it but could not do so and so he took another loan, adding to the burden of his debt.'[3]

---

[1] *Shanīdanī-hā-yi Tārīkh*, p. 146; *al-Maḥajjah al-Bayḍā'*, vol. 4, p. 234.

[2] *ʿIlm-i Akhlāq-i Islāmī*, vol. 2, p. 214.

[3] *Namūnah-i Maʿārif*, vol. 5, p. 253; *Laʾālī al-Akhbār*

5 – The deceased debtor

Mu'āwiyah ibn Wahab narrates:

'I once said to Imam al-Ṣādiq 🕮: "We have heard that when a person from amongst the Anṣār died while in a state of debt, the Holy Prophet refused to offer the prayers over him, saying: 'First clear his debts and then offer prayers over him.'"

'Imam al-Ṣādiq 🕮 said: "What you have heard is true and correct. The Holy Prophet acted in this manner to discourage people from taking their debts lightly." The Imam then continued: "The Holy Prophet, the Commander of the Faithful, Imam al-Ḥasan, and Imam al-Ḥusayn all died while in a state of debt and all their debts were then cleared. Imam al-Sajjād 🕮 sold the garden of Imam al-Ḥusayn for 300,000 dirhams and paid off his debts; Imam al-Ḥasan sold the Commander of the Faithful's property for 500,000 dirhams and cleared the debts of his father; for three years, during the season of hajj, the Commander of the Faithful would call out: 'Whoever has lent money to the Holy Prophet should come to me so that I can clear the loan.'"'[1]

71. Qur'an

Allah, the Wise, has said:

$$\text{إِنَّ هَـٰذَا الْقُرْآنَ يَهْدِي لِلَّتِي هِيَ أَقْوَمُ}$$

Indeed this Qur'an guides to what is most upright. (17:9)

The Holy Prophet said:

$$\text{مَا آمَنَ بِالْقُرْآنِ مَنِ اسْتَحَلَّ مَحَارِمَهُ}$$

One who regards as lawful that which the Qur'an considers to be unlawful, has not brought faith upon it.[2]

---

[1] *Safīnat al-Biḥār*, vol. 1, p. 477.

[2] *Safīnat al-Biḥār*, vol. 2, p. 415.

Short explanation

For the recitation of the Holy Qur'an to penetrate a person's heart and soul, three requirements must be fulfilled: his heart must be humble and submissive, his mind must be clear and focused, and his environment should be secluded and free from the distractions of work and worldly affairs. When a person surrenders his heart to Allah's will and pleasure, he protects himself from the guile of Shayṭān; when he purifies his mind from worldly preoccupations, it becomes receptive and malleable to the spiritual values of the Qur'an; and when he secludes himself from people and material diversions, Allah becomes his intimate, speaking to him through the wisdom and inspiration of His word.[1]

1 – Dependence upon the Creator

A person once persistently visited the house of 'Umar ibn al-Khaṭṭāb, seeking material assistance. Exasperated by his frequent visits, 'Umar said in irritation: 'Have you emigrated to the House of Allah or to the house of 'Umar? Go and recite the Qur'an and learn its teachings, for this will remove your need to come to me for assistance.'

The beggar departed and did not return for several months. Upon enquiry, 'Umar learned that he had isolated himself from society to devote his life to Allah's worship in seclusion. His curiosity aroused, 'Umar decided to locate the beggar's whereabouts and visit him.

Upon meeting him, 'Umar said: 'I longed to see you [and enquire about your well-being]. Tell me, what caused you to distance yourself from society?'

The man replied: 'I read the Qur'an and it made me independent of both 'Umar and his people.'

'Umar asked further: 'What was the verse that you recited that made you take this decision?'

The beggar replied: 'I was reading the Qur'an when I came across the following verse: And in the sky is your provision and what you are

____
[1] *Tadhkirah wa al-Ḥaqā'iq*, p.16.

promised [51:22]. Upon reflection, I chided myself: "My sustenance is in the heavens whereas I search for it on the earth; I am indeed an ungrateful person."'

Moved by the wisdom of the man's response, 'Umar admitted: 'Indeed you speak the truth!'[1]

2 – The Holy Prophet's relationship with the Holy Qur'an

The Holy Prophet's deep intimacy with the Holy Qur'an was reflected in his every action. Sa'd ibn Hishām states: 'I asked 'Ā'ishah, the wife of the Holy Prophet, about the Prophet's ethics and conduct. In reply, she asked: "Do you recite the Qur'an?" I answered: "Yes, I do."

'She remarked: "The conduct of the Holy Prophet was in complete accordance with the Qur'an."

'The Holy Prophet's deep love of the Holy Qur'an resonated in the poignancy of his recitation. When the Holy Prophet recited the Holy Qur'an his listeners were enthralled by the beauty and soulfulness of his tone. According to the Holy Prophet's servant, Anas ibn Malik: "While reciting the Qur'an the Holy Prophet would stretch the tone of his voice."

'When the Holy Prophet listened to Qur'anic recitation, he was often moved to tears. A scribe who wrote down the verses of the Qur'an as they were revealed, says: "The Holy Prophet said to me one day: 'Recite the Qur'an so that I may listen to it.' I recited Sūrat al-Nisā' until I reached verse 41: So how shall it be, when We bring from every nation a witness and We bring you as a witness to them? As soon as I recited this verse, I observed that the Holy Prophet's eyes were filled with tears. He then said to me: 'What you have recited is sufficient.'"'[2]

3 – Aḥmad ibn Ṭūlūn

When the king of Egypt, Aḥmad ibn Ṭūlūn, died, the ruling administration

---

[1] *Ḥikayāt-hā-e-Shanidanī*, vol. 2, p. 65; *Sharḥ Nahj al-Balāgha*, Ibn Abī'l al-Ḥadīd, vol. 19, p. 320.

[2] *Dastān-hā Az Zindagī-yi Payāmbar*, p. 63, as quoted from *al-Maḥajjah al-Bayḍā'*, vol. 4, p. 120, *Biḥār al-Anwār*, vol. 92, p. 326, and *Kuhl al-Baṣar*, p. 79.

hired a Qur'an reciter to recite the Holy Qur'an at his grave. It was discovered one day that the reciter had left his post and was nowhere to be seen. Upon searching, he was found and was asked: 'Why did you run away?'

He merely replied: 'I shall not recite the Qur'an anymore.' Although the reciter was offered double payment for his services, he refused, stating: 'Even if you multiply it several times over, I shall not recite the Qur'an.'

Upon the royal courtiers' repeated demands for an explanation, the reciter clarified: 'Some days ago, Aḥmad ibn Ṭūlūn objected to my recitation and said: "Why do you recite the Qur'an over my grave?" 'I said to him: "I have been asked to recite the Qur'an for you so that you receive its rewards."

'Ibn Ṭūlūn responded: "I do not receive any reward for your recitation. On the contrary, with every verse that you recite the intensity of the fire engulfing me is increased. I am told: 'Do you hear the verses of the Qur'an? Whilst in the world, why did you not act in accordance with the [teachings of the] Qur'an?'"'

The reciter then pleaded: 'Relieve me of the responsibility of reciting the Qur'an for this impious king.'[1]

4 – 500 copies of the Qur'an atop the spears

When Muʿāwiyah's forces began to lose in the Battle of Ṣiffīn, Muʿāwiyah consulted ʿAmr ibn ʿĀṣ to work out a strategy to avoid imminent defeat. ʿAmr ibn ʿĀṣ suggested: 'All who possess a copy of the Qur'an should raise it on a spear and invite the people of Iraq towards an arbitration based on the Qur'an.' Abū Ṭufayl, a companion of Imam ʿAlī 🖎, narrates:

'On the dawn of the Night of Clamour (Laylat al-Ḥarīr), we observed that there appeared what seemed to be flags in front of the soldiers of Damascus. As the darkness cleared, we realised that they had tied Qur'ans to their spears. The great Qur'an of the Mosque of Damascus was tied atop three spears with ten people holding it aloft. In each of the five sections

---

[1] *Riwāyat-hā Wa Ḥikāyat-hā*, p. 131; *Dāstān-hā-yi Parākandih*, vol. 2, p. 55.

of their army there were 100 copies of the Qur'an, creating a total of 500 copies placed on raised spears. The army shouted the following slogan: "By Allah! By Allah! For your religion, this book of Allah shall arbitrate between you and us!"

'When Imam ʿAlī ﷺ observed this, he sighed: "O Lord! You are aware that their aim and objective is not the Qur'an. Judge between us and them for You are the true Judge."

'This act on the part of the people of Damascus provoked a split in the ranks of the Imam's companions and there arose a disagreement amongst them. One group of simple-minded individuals said: "It is not permissible for us to fight them anymore for they have invited us to the book of Allah." Another group said: "This act of Muʿāwiyah is deception and we should not allow ourselves to be deceived."

'The consequence of this disagreement was that Muʿāwiyah was able to extricate himself from the battle and hence achieve what he sought to achieve.'[1]

5 – Napoleon

Napoleon Bonaparte once asked: 'Where is their [the Muslims'] main centre?' He was informed that Egypt was the stronghold of Islamic knowledge and culture. Accompanied by a translator, Napoleon travelled to Egypt and visited its main library. When the translator opened a copy of the Qur'an in the library, the following verse appeared before him:

Indeed this Qur'an guides to what is most upright, and gives the good news to the faithful. (17:9)

When the translator translated this verse for Napoleon, he stepped out of the library and passed the entire night in reflection and meditation.

The following morning, Napoleon visited the library again and the translator translated other verses of the Qur'an for him. On the third day, when the translator had translated a portion of the Qur'an for him, Napoleon asked him to provide further information about the Qur'an. The

---

[1] *Rāhnumā-yi Saʿādat*, vol. 2, p. 478; *Humā-yi Saʿādat*, p. 96.

translator explained: 'They [the Muslims] believe that God has revealed the Qur'an upon the final Prophet, Muḥammad; Muslims believe this book will serve as a code of guidance until the Day of Judgement.'

On hearing this, Napoleon remarked: 'What I have concluded from this book is that firstly, if the Muslims act upon the comprehensive and extensive teachings of this book, they shall never face humiliation and ignominy; secondly, so long as the Qur'an continues to play a role in their lives, the Muslims shall never submit before us westerners. They will never surrender while their attachment to the ideals of the Qur'an remains unbroken.'[1]

72. Destiny And Decree

Allah, the Wise, has said:

$$وَخَلَقَ كُلَّ شَيْءٍ فَقَدَّرَهُ تَقْدِيرًا$$

He created everything and determined it in a precise measure. (25:2)

Imam al-Ṣādiq ﷺ states:

$$فِي قَضَاءِ اللهِ عَزَّ وَجَلَّ كُلُّ خَيْرٍ لِلْمُؤْمِنِ$$

There is, in every decree of God, absolute goodness for a believer.[2]

Short explanation

The decree of Allah encompasses every aspect of a person's life. Life, death, sickness, health, poverty, and affluence are all determined according to Allah's general will, the intricacies and wisdom of which elude human understanding and knowledge. While a believer may not fully comprehend the reason and purpose behind the trials and difficulties that befall him, he knows that all that Allah decrees is ultimately for his benefit and well-being. Conviction in Allah's prevailing mercy, wisdom, and omnipotence removes anxiety with respect to the security of his livelihood, health, family, and worldly affairs. He views health and sickness, wealth and

---

[1] *Namunah-e'Ma'arif,* vol. 3, p. 146.

[2] *Biḥār al-Anwār,* vol. 71, p. 152.

poverty, and joy and sorrow as divine opportunities through which he can strengthen his relationship with his Lord and grow spiritually.

1 – Fetters upon the feet

A minister by the name of Muḥammad Mahlabī, relates:

'Before I became a minister, I once embarked on a journey by ship from Basra to Baghdad. One of the passengers aboard the ship was very jovial and full of good humour. In jest, his friends bound his feet with chains. When they later attempted to remove the chains, they realised with horror that they were unable to do so. When we reached Baghdad, we called for a blacksmith to remove the chains but he refused, saying: "I cannot do so without an order from the judge."

'The passengers then narrated the entire episode to a judge and requested him to instruct the blacksmith to cut the chains. A youth suddenly entered, and glaring angrily at the person in chains, asked: "Are you not such and such person, who killed my brother in Basra and escaped? I have been searching for you for some time." He then brought witnesses to testify against the accused before the judge.

'On the basis of the testimony of the witnesses, the judge found the chained passenger to be guilty and ordered that he be put to death for his crime. The passengers were astonished at the strange turn of events whereby their practical joke had resulted in the capture and conviction of a murderer.'[1]

2 – Fish from the sky

The destiny of a human being is governed by divine decree; Allah grants to His servants what He knows is good and beneficial for them. The late Shaykh Muḥammad Ḥusayn Mawlawī narrates:

'In the midst of World War II, I was compelled to enter Bahrain. I met several Bahraini residents who said to me: "Due to the severe war- time rationing of food supplies, we remained without food for an entire week;

---

[1] *Namunah-e'Ma'arif,* vol. 3, p. 146.

moreover, we had no harvest to fall back on. We gathered in the local mosque and *ḥusayniyyah* in large numbers and began to pray. We later observed that by the order of Allah, vapour rose from the sea. This vapour soon condensed into a cloud, bringing rain. The rain was accompanied by fish and both poured down upon us. The fish was of excellent quality and managed to sustain us for an entire week until we received the food supplies we needed!"[1]

3 – 'Izrā'īl, the companion of Prophet Sulaymān ☙

'Izrā'īl once entered the assembly of Prophet Sulaymān ☙ and persistently stared at one of his companions. 'Izrā'īl departed after a short time, and once he had left, the companion that had caught the angel's eye asked Prophet Sulaymān ☙: 'Who was he?'

"'Izrā'īl,' replied Prophet Sulaymān ☙.

The companion remarked: 'He kept looking at me as though he intended to seize my soul.' Prophet Sulaymān ☙ enquired: 'What would you like to do now?'

The companion requested: 'Order the wind to take me to India so that I may be far away from him.'

Prophet Sulaymān ☙ complied and the companion was transported by wind to India.

When Prophet Sulaymān ☙ met 'Izrā'īl sometime later, he asked the angel: 'Why were you staring at one of my companions?'

'Izrā'īl replied: 'I had been ordered by Allah to seize in a short while the soul of the person [I was looking at] in India! Seeing him standing before me left me greatly astonished. However, when I went to India at the appointed[2] hour, I found him present and I seized his soul.'[3]

---

[1] *Dāstān-hā-yi Shigift*, p. 313.

[2] This event is presented in the following poem in Persian:

چون به امر حق به هندوسنان شدم دیدمش آنجا و جانش بستدم

تو همه کار جهان را همچنین کن قیاس و چشم بگشا و ببین

[3] *Dāstān-hā-yi Mathnawī*, vol. 1, p. 41.

4 – The hoopoe

The extensive army of Prophet Sulaymān ﷺ once convened a regal gathering before him. All members, exhibiting utmost decorum and grace, stood before Prophet Sulaymān ﷺ. Each bird then informed him of the skill and knowledge that it possessed. When it was the hoopoe's turn, he said: 'The skill that I possess is that when I am flying at great heights I am able to perceive through my sharp and penetrative eyes whether the water which lies in the depths of the ground gushes out of mud or from stone. It would be appropriate to grant me a rank in your army so that I can provide you information about the presence of water when you embark upon a journey.'

Prophet Sulaymān ﷺ agreed and granted him the task of finding water. When the crow learned of the hoopoe's new appointment, he approached Prophet Sulaymān ﷺ and said: 'The hoopoe has not spoken the truth; if he is truly able to perceive the water within the earth, how is it that he is not able to perceive the snare covered only by a handful of earth which traps him and lands him in a cage?'

The hoopoe responded: 'O Prophet Sulaymān! Do not pay heed to the words of my enemy! If I lie, you may sever my head from my body. Whilst I am in flight I am able to perceive the snare; however, when [divine] destiny and decree are at work, a curtain clouds my intellect and rational mind.'[1]

5 – Faghfur, the Chinese emperor

Having successfully conquered many lands and created a vast empire, Alexander the Great then set his ambitious sights upon China. Leading a vast army, he marched to China and surrounded its borders.

The emperor of China, in the guise of a doorkeeper, arrived in the presence of Alexander and said to him: 'Faghfur, the Chinese emperor, has sent a message that I must convey to you in privacy.' Alexander ordered everyone to leave; the gathering dispersed, leaving Alexander alone with the doorkeeper. Revealing his identity, the Chinese emperor said: 'I am

---

[1] *Tadhkirat al-Ḥaqāʾiq*, p. 32.

Faghfur, the emperor of China.'

Caught by surprise, Alexander said: 'Where did you find the courage to carry out such a daring move?'

Faghfur replied: 'I consider you to be a virtuous and rational ruler. There has never been any enmity between us and never have I harboured any evil thoughts about you. If you kill me, not a single person shall die from my army. But I have come to you personally so that I can give you whatever you desire from me.'

Alexander said: 'I want you to give me the Chinese taxes you have received in the last three years.' Upon Faghfur's agreement, Alexander enquired: 'How will your situation be once you hand over to me the taxes I demand from you?'

Faghfur confessed: 'The empire will be so weak that we would be forced to surrender to any army that attacks.'

Alexander then asked: 'If I was content with receiving two years' taxes, how would your position be?'

Faghfur replied: 'My condition would be slightly better.'

'What if I were to take the taxes of only one year?' Alexander queried.

Faghfur replied: 'In that case my empire shall suffer no burden and I shall not be distressed in the least.'

Upon hearing Faghfur's response, Alexander conceded: 'I shall be content with taking only six months' payment in taxes!'

Faghfur was very pleased and invited Alexander to a banquet on the following day during which he promised to hand to Alexander the agreed payment.

As Alexander entered China for the banquet in his honour, he was taken aback by the massive Chinese army, armed to the teeth, facing him. Alexander's entire armed force found itself ensconced within the Chinese army surrounding it. Alexander felt threatened and regretted that he had not arrived better armed. Upon meeting Faghfur, Alexander asked him accusingly: 'Did you intend to play a trick on me by surrounding me with such a large army?'

Faghfur replied: 'I know that you have been granted a great empire by means of divine decree, and that you are backed by divine assistance; whoever opposes the prosperous ones is bound to taste defeat. This army bows in submission to your power and authority.'

Flattered by Faghfur's response, Alexander said: 'In appreciation of your deference, I return to you as a gift the taxes promised to me.'[1]

73. Contentment

Allah, the Wise, has said:

$$\text{وَأَطْعِمُوا الْقَانِعَ وَالْمُعْتَرَّ}$$

And feed the self-contained needy and the mendicant. (22:36)

The Holy Prophet said:

$$\text{كُنْ قَانِعًا تَكُنْ أَشْكَرَ النَّاسِ}$$

Be contented so that you may be the most thankful of all people.[2]

Short explanation

Undoubtedly, all the blessings a human being receives are in accordance with the will and decree of Allah. One who has conviction in the wisdom and justice of Allah's distribution knows that all hardship and ease are a measure of divine grace. He therefore bears difficulties with patience and turns only to Allah for the fulfilment of his needs.

Alluding to the spiritual strength and value of contentment, the Holy Prophet has said: 'Contentment is an empire that never collapses.' Satisfaction with Allah's decree elevates and ennobles the character of a human being. Therefore, one should always face deprivation with patience, and be content and pleased with the blessings that Allah has bestowed upon him.[3]

---

[1] *Khazīnat al-Jawāhir*, p. 676; *Zīnat al-Majālis.*

[2] *Jāmiʿ al-Saʿādāt*, vol. 2, p. 102.

[3] *Tadhkirat al-Ḥaqāʾiq*, p. 32.

1 – The conduct of Imam al-Ṣādiq ﷺ

Contentment is an admirable and noble attribute, loved by Allah. An example of the contentment of Imam al-Ṣādiq ﷺ in times of scarcity is provided by Muʿattab, a housekeeper in the house of the Imam, who narrates:

'Due to food shortages in the markets of Medina, the prices of commodities had shot up. The Imam asked me: "How much food do we have in the house?"

'"Enough to last us for several months," I replied. Upon hearing this, the Imam said: "Place all the food supplies for sale in the market."

'Astonished, I responded: "What kind of directive is this that you give?"

'The Imam repeated emphatically: "Take all the provisions of the house and sell them in the market."

'When I had acted as per the Imam's instructions and sold everything in the market, he said to me: "Your duty is to procure food supplies for my house on a day-to-day basis just as the average person does. Furthermore, the food for my family should be prepared by mixing fifty percent of barley and fifty percent of wheat."'[1]

2 – Salmān

Abū Wāʾil narrates:

'My friend and I visited Salmān's house. He said to us: "Had the Holy Prophet not prohibited exhibiting formalities towards guests, I would have taken the trouble of preparing some delicious food for you." He then proceeded to place some bread and salt before us.

'Seeing the food, my friend commented: "Had there been some vegetables in addition to this salt, it would have made a great meal!"

'Upon hearing this remark, Salmān pawned his pitcher, and with the money procured, purchased some vegetables. He then prepared the vegetables and laid them on the table alongside the rest of the meal. After the meal, my friend said: "All praise be to Allah who made us content with

---

[1] *Dāstān-hā Wa Pand-hā*, vol. 1, p. 31.

respect to what He gave us."[1]

'Upon hearing this, Salmān remarked: "Had you really been content, my pitcher would not have been pawned."'[2]

According to another narration of this incident, the host was Abū Dharr al-Ghifārī and the food desired was mint instead of vegetables.

3 – By means of contentment the soul becomes submissive

One of the signs of a content person is moderation and satisfying oneself with that which restrains the soul's carnal desires.

Aswad and 'Alqamah narrate:

'One day, when we approached Imam 'Alī ☸, we observed that before him lay a tray containing some date fibres upon which lay two loaves of barley bread, the chaff of barley flour being clearly visible upon the loaves. The Imam picked up the loaves and struck them on his knees until they broke, and then proceeded to eat them with some salt. Observing this, we said to Fiḍḍah, the slave-girl: "Why did you not remove the chaff from the flour for the Imam?"

'She replied: "Had 'Alī ☸ eaten the delicious bread, its sin would have fallen upon my shoulders."

'Hearing the conversation, Imam 'Alī ☸ smiled and said: "I instructed her not to remove the chaff."

'We asked: "But why, O 'Alī?"

'He replied: "In this way, my [carnal] soul is better subjugated, it becomes content, and the believers will continue to follow my example until I depart from this world."'[3]

4 – Your food or your ruler

Sa'dī, in his magnum opus Gulistān, has recorded twenty-four narratives

---

[1] The Arabic of this line:

الْحَمْدُ لِلّهِ الَّذِي قَنَّعَنَا بِـمَا رَزَقَنَا

[2] *Payghambar Wa Yārān*, vol. 3, p. 206.

[3] *Dāstān-hā Az Zindagī-yi 'Alī*, p. 119; *Anwār al-Nu'māniyyah*, p. 18.

pertaining to the virtue of contentment. The last of the narratives is the story of a devout worshipper, who upon eating the food of a king, abandons his piety and contentment and succumbs to greed and avarice.

Saʿdī relates this story as follows:

'A pious worshipper once took up dwelling in a cave, where he engrossed himself in worship far away from the people; he looked upon the kings and affluent ones in contempt and was uninterested in and indifferent to the glitter and dazzle of the world. One of the prosperous kings of the region sent the following message to the worshipper: "I hope that your esteemed and noble self would agree to be my guest and grace us by joining us for our meal." The worshipper was beguiled; accepting the invitation, he arrived for dinner and ate the food in accordance with customary practice.

'The following day, the king set out for the worshipper's cave in order to thank him in person. As soon as the worshipper's eyes fell upon the king, he stood up in respect, seated the king beside him, and began praising him. The king soon bid the worshipper goodbye and left. Some of the worshipper's friends objected to his behaviour, saying: "Why did you lower yourself so much before him, and, contrary to the conduct of distinguished and eminent worshippers, display such affection towards him?"

'The worshipper replied: "Have you not heard that if you consume someone's food it becomes incumbent upon you that you become servile towards him and repay his right?"'[1]

5 – The conduct of the content ones

Power, fame, and promotion are often exploited by people to derive maximum worldly advantages for themselves and their families. However, the example of Shaykh Anṣārī serves as a model of moderation and simplicity in the face of improving fortunes.

Shaykh Anṣārī began his studies in Najaf as a poor student from Dezful.

---

[1] *Ḥikāyat-hā-yi Gulistān*, p. 184.

Upon the death of the author of Jawāhir, he became the most prominent jurist of his time. In spite of his eminent position, Shaykh Anṣārī's house bore resemblance to that of the poorest of people. This was despite the fact that every year, more than 100,000 tumans in legal taxes would be handed over to him; yet, he would content himself with the most nominal of incomes, such that when he died, he possessed only seventeen tumans, the exact amount required to pay off his remaining debt. His survivors did not even have the means to establish mourning ceremonies for him; it was a wealthy person who established mourning ceremonies for Shaykh Anṣārī for six days and nights after his demise.

Shaykh Anṣārī's contentment with a life of austerity and simplicity is further reflected in the manner in which he conducted his daughter's wedding arrangements. Upon receiving an offer by his representative in Baghdad to arrange a dowry for his daughter who was to be wed to Shaykh Muḥammad Ḥasan Anṣārī, Shaykh Anṣārī refused. Instead, he chose to marry his daughter to his nephew upon payment of a very meagre dowry.[1]

74. The Day Of Judgement

Allah, the Wise, has said:

$$وَإِنَّمَا تُوَفَّوْنَ أُجُورَكُمْ يَوْمَ الْقِيَامَةِ$$

And you will indeed be paid your full rewards on the Day of Resurrection.

(3:185)

Imam ʿAlī ﷺ said:

$$إِنَّ الْخَلْقَ لَا مَقْصَرَ لَهُمْ عَنِ الْقِيَامَةِ$$

There is no escape for people from the Day of Judgement.[2]

Short explanation

The journey of the afterlife begins with death, followed by the intermediary stage of barzakh, and culminates in the resurrection of the Day of

---

[1] *Sīmā-yi Farzānigān*, p. 457.

[2] *Nahj al-Balāghah* of Fayḍ al-Islām, p. 488.

Judgement. On this day, the dead will be raised to receive the records of their deeds, await Allah's judgement, and enter their final abode of heaven or hell. Those who lived in deliberate rejection and denial of the truth will be dragged by angels towards a torturous chastisement, while those who strengthened their faith in hardship, purified their souls, and refrained from sin will be welcomed into heaven. On the Day of Judgement, every sin committed and virtue upheld will be made manifest, leaving no room for excuses, justification, or protest. All verdicts of punishment and reward will be clearly evidenced and decided by the Almighty according to His justice tempered by mercy.

1 – The plaintiff on the Day of Judgement

Five years after the proclamation of prophethood by the Messenger of Allah, the Muslims made their first migration to escape religious persecution by the Quraysh in Mecca. Ja'far Ṭayyār, the brother of Imam 'Alī ﷺ, together with eighty-two Muslims, migrated to Ethiopia. These migrants stayed in Ethiopia for approximately twelve years, returning to Medina shortly after the Muslim victory at Khaybar.

It has been reported that the Holy Prophet asked Ja'far upon his return: 'During your stay in Ethiopia, what strange incident did you witness?'

Ja'far replied: 'I witnessed a black Ethiopian woman walking whilst carrying a large basket on her head. A passer-by elbowed her, causing her to fall down, as a result of which the basket on her head fell to the ground as well. The woman turned to the person who had tripped her and said: "Woe unto you from the Judge of the Day of Judgement who shall grant justice to the oppressed from the oppressor."'

The Holy Prophet was also astonished by the startling insight of the woman.[1]

2 – The most sinful people on the Day of Judgement

'Abd Allāh ibn Ubayy Salūl (one of the most tenacious of the hypocrites

______

[1] *Ḥikāyat-hā-yi Shanīdanī*, vol. 2, p. 12; *I'lām al-Warā'*, p. 21.

and a staunch enemy of the Holy Prophet) once sought permission to meet the Holy Prophet. When the Holy Prophet realised who had arrived, he expressed his displeasure. However, he ordered that 'Abd Allāh be allowed to enter. As soon as 'Abd Allāh entered, the Holy Prophet seated him and spoke to him in a warm and friendly manner.

When 'Abd Allāh departed, 'Ā'ishah queried: 'O Prophet of Allah! You did not speak well of him before he entered, but once he entered you spoke to him in a very cordial manner.'

The Holy Prophet replied: 'O 'Ā'ishah! The most wretched of all people on the Day of Judgement will be one whom people respected in order to protect themselves from his evil actions.'[1]

Therefore, a person should ensure that he is respected due to his noble and righteous character, and not due to a sinister and menacing character that inspires fear.

3 – Fear of the Day of Judgement

Whenever the Holy Prophet left for battle, he would establish a bond of brotherhood between two of his companions; he did so between Sa'īd ibn 'Abd al-Raḥmān and Tha'labah Anṣārī before he left for the Battle of Tabūk.

Sa'īd accompanied the Holy Prophet in battle while Tha'labah stayed back and was responsible for looking after Sa'īd's family.

One day, when Tha'labah went to Sa'īd's house to arrange food provisions for his family, Shayṭān tempted him to look at Sa'īd's wife and he was soon overcome with lust. He approached her and placed his hand upon her, at which point she cried out: 'Is it appropriate that while your brother has gone for war you intend to violate the chastity of his wife?'

Her rebuke filled Tha'labah with such remorse that he set out into the wilderness, and upon reaching the base of a mountain he fell to the ground and remained there, weeping day and night to atone for his sin.

When the Holy Prophet and his companions returned from battle, all the inhabitants of the city except Tha'labah rushed to welcome their

---

[1] *Bā Mardūm In Gūnih Barkhūrd Kunīm*, p. 129; *Mustadrak al-Wasā'il*, vol. 2, p. 92.

brothers. Sa'īd went home and asked his wife about Tha'labah, whereupon she informed him of what had transpired. Sa'īd immediately left his house in search for Tha'labah; he eventually found Tha'labah seated near a stone, repeatedly slapping his head and wailing aloud: 'Woe on you for the shame and humiliation of the Day of Judgement!'

Sa'īd embraced Tha'labah, consoled him, and requested him to meet the Holy Prophet and seek forgiveness. Tha'labah agreed and requested Sa'īd: 'Tie my hands and place a rope around my neck similar to the manner in which slaves who have attempted to run away are tied.'

When Sa'īd and Tha'labah arrived before the Holy Prophet, he said to Tha'labah: 'You have indeed committed a grave offence. Go away from me, seek forgiveness from Allah, and await His orders.'

Upon revelation of the verse of forgiveness and repentance [3:135], the Holy Prophet sent Imam 'Alī ﷺ and Salmān to bring Tha'labah to him. They set out into the desert in search of Tha'labah, eventually finding him conversing with his Lord and seeking His forgiveness. Observing Tha'labah's penitent state, Imam 'Alī's ﷺ eyes filled with tears and he gave Tha'labah the good news that Allah had forgiven him.

It was nightfall by the time Imam 'Alī ﷺ, Salmān, and Tha'labah reached Medina. The Holy Prophet was reciting Sūrat al-Takāthur aloud in his prayers. As soon as Tha'labah heard the first verse,[1] he gave out a cry; hearing the second verse,[2] he shrieked loudly; and upon hearing the third verse,[3] he fell down unconscious. Upon concluding their prayers, the people around Tha'labah discovered that he had died.

The Holy Prophet and his companions wept profusely. The Holy Prophet then instructed that Tha'labah be provided the funeral rites of ablution, prayers, and burial. The Holy Prophet accompanied Tha'labah's funeral procession, walking on tip-toes for the entire journey. When people questioned his actions, the Holy Prophet replied: 'The angels who

---

[1] أَلْهَاكُمُ التَّكَاثُرُ

[2] حَتَّى زُرْتُمُ الْمَقَابِرَ

[3] كَلَّا سَوْفَ تَعْلَمُونَ

had come to participate in his prayers and join his funeral procession were so great in number that I had to walk upon my toes [for fear of treading on them]!'[1]

4 – Imam al-Ḥasan 🕮

When Imam al-Ḥasan's 🕮 companions observed that he was weeping on his deathbed, they asked: 'O son of the Prophet of Allah! In spite of your relationship with the Holy Prophet and the rank and status that the Holy Prophet has ascribed to you, why do you weep? You have performed hajj on foot twenty times; you have given away half your wealth in the way of Allah three times; and yet you weep?'

The Imam replied: 'I weep due to fear of the Day of Judgement and separation from my friends.'[2]

5 – Tawbah ibn Ṣummah

Tawbah ibn Ṣummah spent most of his days and nights examining and purifying his soul. He once counted the number of days he had lived, calculating the figure to be 21,500. Struck by the enormity of the number, he cried: 'Woe unto me! Will I be meeting the exalted Allah on the Day of Judgement having lived this many days? If I have committed even one sin per day, I will be carrying the burden of 21,500 sins; what then will be my state?'

Deeply troubled by his thoughts, Ibn Ṣummah fell down, unconscious. When people found him, they discovered that he had died; his fear of the Day of Judgement was so palpable and acute that his soul could not bear it.[3]

75. Working

Allah, the Wise, has said:

---

[1] *Khazīnat al-Jawāhir*, p. 315; *Rawḍat al-Anwār* of Sabzawārī.

[2] *Pand-i Tārīkh*, vol. 4, p. 208.

[3] *Sarmāyih-i Saʿādat*, p. 39.

$$\text{وَأَنْ لَيْسَ لِلْإِنْسَانِ إِلَّا مَا سَعَى}$$

And that nothing belongs to man except what he strives for. (53:39)

The Holy Prophet said:

$$\text{الْمُؤْمِنُ إِذَا لَمْ يَكُنْ لَهُ حِرْفَةٌ يَعِيشُ بِدِينِهِ}$$

If a believer does not have a profession, he shall earn his livelihood by exploiting his religion [which is highly reprehensible].[1]

Short explanation

Lawful food that nourishes both the body and the soul is the fruit of lawful and legal labour. The position of one who struggles to work and provide for himself and his family in an honest way, is comparable to that of a soldier striving in the way of Allah. Hence, earning money lawfully with integrity, honesty, diligence, and hard work, is considered an act of jihad. Lawful earnings ensure well-being and fortune both in this world and the Hereafter. Conversely, those who yield to laziness and lethargy are unable to fulfil their financial responsibilities and will be more likely to succumb to the temptations of illegal work to extract themselves from poverty and financial hardship. Hence, one who fails to earn a lawful living not only deprives himself of financial security and independence, but also the rewards and prosperity of the afterlife.

1 – The endowment letter

During his caliphate, Imam ʿAlī 🕮 once said: 'Throughout Iraq, my subjects are in ease and comfort; they drink sweet water and eat bread made of wheat.'

Imam ʿAlī 🕮 once freed Abū Nayzar, one of his slaves, on the condition that he would work for the Imam in his plantation for five years. The Imam later granted him the task of supervising his fields and springs, one of which came to be popularly known as the 'River of Abū Nayzar'.

Abū Nayzar relates:

'One day, the Imam came to inspect his field and, dismounting from his

---

[1] *Biḥār al-Anwār*, vol. 103, p. 9.

horse, enquired: "Do you have some food with you?"

'I replied: "Yes, although I fear it does not befit your rank; I have gourd with some fat oil." The Imam requested me to bring it to him. When I had brought the food, he washed his hands and proceeded to eat. The Imam then washed his hands again, drank some water, and requested me to bring him a pickaxe. He took the pickaxe from me, entered into a dry well, and dug energetically until he was overcome with exhaustion and fatigue. He came out of the well to rest, wiping the perspiration dripping from his holy forehead. Within a few moments, he again entered the well and began digging diligently.

'As he was digging, a fountain of water suddenly gushed out of the well like the neck of a camel. The Imam immediately emerged from inside the well and, still perspiring, repeatedly cried: "This is charity! This is charity! Bring me some ink and paper." I hurriedly brought ink and paper for the Imam who then wrote the following bequest: "This is an endowment from the servant of Allah, the Commander of the Faithful, given to the needy ones of Medina as charity – a charity that cannot be sold, gifted, or transferred so long as Allah is the owner of the heavens and the earth. Only Ḥasan and Ḥusayn may claim it if they fall in need of it, for then this well would become their property."'[1]

2 – 'Umar ibn Muslim

Imam al-Ṣādiq ﷺ once enquired about one of his companions by the name of 'Umar ibn Muslim, whereupon a person informed him: 'He has confined himself to acts of worship and has totally abandoned his trade.'

On hearing this, the Imam said: 'Woe unto him! Does he not know that the prayers of one who abandons his work and profession are not answered?' The Imam then continued: 'When the second and third verses of Sūrat al-Ṭalāq were revealed, stating: And whoever is wary of Allah, He shall make a way out for him, and provide for him from whence he does not reckon. And whoever puts his trust in Allah, He will suffice him

____
[1] *Islām Wa Kār Wa Kūshish*, p. 24.

[65:2-3], some of the companions of the Holy Prophet enclosed themselves in their houses, abandoned their work, and confined their daily routine to acts of worship, saying: "Allah is sufficient for us in providing sustenance."

'When the Holy Prophet was informed of their actions, he asked them: "Why have you adopted this attitude?"

'They replied: "According to the second and third verses of Sūrat al-Ṭalāq, Allah has taken upon Himself the responsibility to provide us our sustenance, and hence we have restricted our activities to acts of His worship."

'The Holy Prophet rebuked them, saying: "The prayers of one who abandons his work and busies himself in worship are not answered. It is incumbent upon you to work and earn your sustenance."'[1]

3 – Working is better than receiving charity

The Holy Prophet was once informed that a person from Medina was living in abject poverty. The Holy Prophet requested that the man be brought before him. Once the pauper arrived, the Holy Prophet said to him: 'Bring me whatever you possess in your house; do not regard anything as insignificant.'

The man went home and returned with a bowl and sackcloth. The Holy Prophet placed the items for auction and they were eventually purchased by a person at the price of two dirhams. Handing the money to the poor Muslim, the Holy Prophet advised: 'Use one dirham to buy some food for your family and use the other dirham to purchase an axe for yourself.'

The man did as instructed; he then returned to the Holy Prophet who said to him: 'Go into the desert and collect firewood; collect every piece of wood that you find and do not consider anything to be trivial and insignificant; thereafter, sell the wood you have collected.'

The man acted upon the instructions of the Holy Prophet. Within fifteen days, his financial state improved significantly. When the poor man returned to the Holy Prophet, the Holy Prophet told him: 'It is better that

---

[1] *Dāstān-hā Wa Pand-hā*, vol. 9, p. 73.

you work and earn a wage instead of receiving charity and rising on the Day of Judgement with the ugly sign of receiving charity manifested upon your face.'[1]

4 – Hard labour

Faḍl ibn Abī Qurrah relates:

'We once approached Imam al-Ṣādiq 🕮 and found him hard at work in his field. Observing this, we said to him: "May we be your ransom! Either permit us to do the work or let your servants do it."

'The Imam replied: "No; let me work. I desire that I meet Allah after having exerted myself and worked with my own hands in order to obtain lawful sustenance. Even 'Alī used to work hard to earn a lawful income."'[2]

5 – Ya'qūb ibn Layth Ṣaffār

The Ṣaffār dynasty enjoyed power over an extensive empire for fifty-six years. All seven dynastic rulers who assumed power were Shi'as, the first of them being Ya'qūb ibn Layth Ṣaffār (d. 878 CE).

Ya'qūb was initially a coppersmith by profession, earning him the title 'Ṣaffār'. He gradually recruited a powerful army and extended his power base by killing off his enemies. His military conquests were so successful that he eventually occupied Khorasan, Sistan, and several other cities.

Ya'qūb was a highly proficient administrator with extensive management skills. He was also a powerful military leader, commanding the obedience and unwavering loyalty of his troops. When Ya'qūb ordered his army to proceed for battle, the soldiers would immediately obey, saddling their mounts even as they were grazing. In fact, once, a soldier's horse was chewing some hay when Ya'qūb's battle call came; the soldier pulled the hay out of the horse's mouth to circumvent the slightest delay in carrying out Ya'qūb's command. He rebuked the horse sternly, saying: 'King Ya'qūb has prohibited the animals from eating their food.'

---

[1] *Ḥikāyat-hā-yi Shanīdanī*, vol. 3, p. 57; *Biḥār al-Anwār*, vol. 103, p. 10.

[2] *Shanīdanī-hā-yi Tārīkh*, p. 47; *al-Maḥajjah al-Bayḍā'*, vol. 3, p. 147.

Another loyal soldier was once found to be naked under his battle-dress. When questioned, he replied: 'I was engaged in performing the ablution of *janābah* when the king's announcer proclaimed: "Get ready for battle." Not wanting to delay myself in complying with the king's order, I did not wear my clothes and satisfied myself with wearing only the battle-dress!'[1]

76. Begging

Allah, the Wise, has said:

$$\text{وَأَمَّا السَّائِلَ فَلَا تَنْهَرْ}$$

And as for the beggar, do not chide him. (93:10)

The Holy Prophet said:

$$\text{لَوْلَا أَنَّ السَّائِلَ يَكْذِبُ مَا قُدِّسَ مَنْ رَدَّهُ}$$

If it were not for the telling of lies by the beggars, one who rebuffed them, would not be consecrated.[2]

Short explanation

To beg for provision from others out of greed rather than necessity is considered an act of disgrace in Islam. Those who have enough to meet their needs but still humiliate themselves by extending their hands to beg from others, will be raised on the Day of Judgement with faces devoid of flesh. A true believer's desires are few; he is satisfied with the provision he receives from Allah and does not lust for the wealth of others. If he desires to increase his sustenance he works hard to earn it, whilst also prostrating in prayer to beg from the one who owns the treasures of the heavens and the earth. He humbly seeks his needs from the divine and does not debase himself by relying on others for his sustenance. Believers are also charitable and compassionate, giving generously to the poor so that the poor are not forced by desperation to beg from others.

---

[1] *Tatimmat al-Muntahā*, p. 262.

[2] *Jāmi' al-Sa'adāt*, vol. 2, p. 98

1 – Imam al-Ṣādiq ﷺ and the beggar

Masma' ibn 'Abd al-Malik relates:

'We were in the company of Imam al-Ṣādiq ﷺ in Mina [during the hajj pilgrimage] and engaged in eating grapes that lay before us in a vessel, when a beggar approached us and asked the Imam for some help. The Imam requested that a bunch of grapes be given to him. When the grapes were offered to him, the beggar refused, saying: "I am not in need of this. I require dirhams." 'The Imam said: "May Allah increase your sustenance." The beggar departed but returned shortly after, saying: "Give me that bunch of grapes."

'The Imam responded: "May Allah increase your livelihood." However, he did not give the beggar any grapes.

'After a short while, another beggar arrived and asked the Imam for something to be given to him. The Imam picked up three grapes with his own hands and handed them to him. The beggar took the grapes and said: "Praise be to the God of the worlds, who provided me with these grapes." Upon hearing his response, the Imam asked him to wait a moment. Filling his two palms with grapes, the Imam handed them to the beggar. The beggar took the grapes and again praised Allah, whereupon the Imam turned to his slave and enquired: "How much money do you have with you?" 'The slave replied: "Twenty dirhams." The Imam took the money from the slave and gave it to the beggar.

'The beggar once again praised Allah, saying: "O Lord! Praise is for You, this money is from You, and You do not have any partner." The Imam then removed his garment and handed it to the beggar. The beggar took the garment and upon wearing it, said: "Praise be to Allah who has dressed and covered me." Addressing the Imam, he said: "O Abā 'Abdillāh! May Allah grant you a bounteous reward!" Thereafter, the beggar began to leave and this time the Imam did not request him to stay. We realised that had the beggar not prayed for the Imam and had continued only to praise Allah, the Imam would have continued to bestow him with gifts.'[1]

---

[1] *Bā Mardūm Īn Gūnih Barkhūrd Kunīm*, p. 123; *Biḥār al-Anwār*, vol. 47, p. 42.

2 – The poor have a share in the wealth of the rich

Abū Baṣīr relates:

'I once informed Imam al-Ṣādiq ﷺ: "One of your Shiʿas, a pious person by the name of ʿUmar, approached [another person called] ʿĪsā and sought help from him. However, ʿĪsā responded: 'I have some zakat in my possession but I shall not give it to you, for I have observed you purchasing meat and dates which indicates that you are not indigent.' ʿUmar responded: 'In a business transaction, my share of profit turned out to be one dirham; I spent a third of it to purchase some meat, another third for purchasing some dates, and I utilised the remaining third to fulfil other requirements of the house.'"

'Upon hearing the account, the Imam was visibly disturbed, and placing his hand upon his forehead in distress, said: "Allah has stipulated for the impoverished a share in the wealth of the affluent ones in a measure that would enable them to lead their lives in a good manner; had that measure not been sufficient, He would have stipulated an even greater share. Therefore, the poor should be given enough that they are able to provide for themselves with respect to food, clothing, marriage, charity, and hajj; strictness and stringency should not to be exhibited towards them, especially towards someone like ʿUmar, who is of the pious ones."'[1]

3 – The respectable pauper

Imam ʿAlī ﷺ once sent 900 kilogrammes of dates from his own farm situated in Yanbu (on the outskirts of Medina), to a poor person. Whilst the person was in need of financial help, he never permitted himself to seek assistance from the Imam or anyone else.

Observing the Imam's generosity, a companion said to the Imam: 'By Allah! That person never sought any help from you and you gave him this gift. It would have been quite sufficient had you given him just one kilogramme!'

---

[1] *Pand-i Tārīkh*, vol. 1, p. 142; *Sharḥ Man Lā Yaḥduruhu al-Faqīh*, Book of Zakat, p. 36.

The Imam responded: 'May Allah never increase the likes of you among the people! I show munificence whilst you exhibit stinginess? If I gave him what he expected after he asked me for it, I would not be doing him any favours. I would have compelled the face which prostrates on the ground before Allah and worships Him to plead before me. And one who acts in this way towards his Muslim brother, despite knowing that he is deserving of assistance, has not spoken the truth to Allah. When he prays for his Muslim brother, saying "O Allah! Forgive the male and female believers", he is effectively seeking heaven for his brother. How is it possible that at the same time, when it comes to giving him the temporal provisions of this world, he exhibits stinginess?! Hence, it is inappropriate for him to pray [for a believer's well-being] when he does not act in accordance with that prayer.'[1]

4 – The young beggar

A young man and his wife were once having a meal of roast chicken when a beggar came to the door and asked for help. The young man rose up angrily from his meal and harshly drove him away. Rebuffed, the beggar turned around and walked away.

It so happened that after a period of time, the young man lost all his wealth, became destitute, and divorced his wife. The divorced woman subsequently remarried. Her second husband was well-off and the couple lived comfortably.

They were once having a meal of roast chicken when suddenly a beggar came to the door and sought help. The man said to his wife: 'Arise and hand this chicken to the beggar.'

The lady picked up the food and approached the beggar; when her eyes fell upon the man, she recognised him to be her former husband. Handing him the chicken, she returned to the table, her eyes swimming with tears. When her husband saw her distraught face, he asked her why she was distressed. She replied: 'This beggar was my former husband.' She then

---

[1] *Islām Wa Mustamandān*, p. 251; *Furū' al-Kāfī*, p. 167.

narrated the incident of her former husband and the beggar who had been turned away.

Upon completing the narrative, her husband exclaimed: 'O wife! By Allah! I was that beggar!'[1]

77. Helping Others

Allah, the Wise, has said:

$$\text{فَوَجَدَا فِيهَا جِدَارًا يُرِيدُ أَنْ يَنْقَضَّ فَأَقَامَهُ}$$

There they found a wall which was about to collapse, so he erected it.
(18:77)

The Holy Prophet states:

$$\text{مَنْ قَضَى لِأَخِيهِ الْمُؤْمِنِ حَاجَةً فَكَأَنَّمَا عَبَدَ اللّٰهَ دَهْرَهُ}$$

One who fulfils the desire of his believing brother will be regarded as one who has worshipped God for his entire life.[2]

Short explanation

Allah has endowed human beings with the natural capacity to be compassionate, empathetic, and selfless, such that they are moved by the plight of others and seek to alleviate it. When they see someone in need and they are able to help, they desire to do so. However, altruism and generosity are often overpowered by selfishness and greed, restraining people from offering financial or personal help even when it is desperately required. Those who withhold assistance due to self-interest, stinginess, or conceit, incur Allah's wrath and punishment on the Day of Judgement. In contrast, those who strive hard to help others, fulfil their needs, and ease their difficulties, warrant Allah's pleasure and bountiful reward in the Hereafter.

Kindness and munificence are highly recommended in Islam, especially towards a fellow believer. According to a hadith by Imam al-Ṣādiq ﷺ:

---

[1] *Dunyā-yi Jawān*, p. 331; *Athar al-Ṣādiqīn*, vol. 8, p. 139.

[2] *Jāmiʿ al-Saʿādāt*, vol. 2, p. 230.

'Fulfilling the need of a believing brother is better than liberating 1000 slaves and giving 1000 horses in the path of Allah.'[1]

1 – 9000 years

Maymūn ibn Mahrān narrates:

'I was sitting beside Imam al-Ḥasan ☙ when a man came up to him and said: "O son of the Holy Prophet! I am indebted to a person but do not possess any money to repay the debt, and so he intends to send me to prison."

'The Imam responded: "Presently, I do not possess any money by which I can pay off your debt."

'The man pleaded: "Then do something whereby I am saved from imprisonment."

'Although the Imam was in a state of *i'tikāf* in the mosque, he put on his shoes and was about to leave the mosque when I said to him: "O son of the Prophet of Allah! Have you forgotten that you are in a state of spiritual retreat [and therefore are not permitted to leave the mosque]?"

'The Imam replied: "No, I have not forgotten. However, I have heard from my father that the Holy Prophet used to say: 'One who strives to fulfil a desire of his Muslim brother is like one who has spent 9000 years fasting during the days and worshipping during the nights.'"[2]

2 – Breaking the *ṭawāf*

Abān ibn Taghlib narrates:

'I was engaged in the *ṭawāf* of the Ka'bah in the company of Imam al-Ṣādiq ☙ when one of my friends asked me to come aside and listen to his request. Not wanting to leave the company of the Imam, I ignored his request. As we continued to perform the *ṭawāf* of the Ka'bah, the person signalled me to come towards him; this time, however, the Imam happened to see him and so asked me: "O Abān! Does he have some work with you?"

---

[1] *Iḥyā' al-Qulūb*, p. 121.

[2] *Riwāyat-hā Wa Ḥikāyat-hā*, p. 122; *Dāstān-hā-yi Parākandih*, vol. 2, p. 152.

I replied in the affirmative, whereupon the Imam enquired: "Who is he?"

'I said: "One of my friends."

'The Imam further asked: "Is he also a believer and a Shi'a?"

'I replied: "Yes."

'Upon hearing my reply, the Imam instructed: "Go to him and fulfil his desire."

'"Should I discontinue my *ṭawāf*?" I queried.

'He replied: "Yes."

'I asked: "Is it permissible to discontinue even the obligatory *ṭawāf* and leave it midway if it is for the purpose of fulfilling the needs of a believer?"

'The Imam replied: "Yes."

'Hence, I halted my *ṭawāf* and proceeded towards the man. After assisting the person, I returned to the Imam and requested him to inform me about the rights that a believer holds over another believer.'[1]

3 – Fulfilling the needs of others

Wāqidī relates:

'It once so happened that I was faced with abject poverty, and particularly as the month of Ramadan was approaching I was compelled to seek a loan from a friend who was a descendant of Imam 'Alī ﷺ. I wrote him a letter [requesting his assistance], and in response he sent me a sack containing 1000 dirhams. Soon after, I received a letter from another friend requesting me to assist him with a loan. I sent him the sack containing the thousand dirhams which I had accepted as a loan so that he would be relieved of his difficulty.

'It was not long before both my friend [who had helped me] as well as the one to whom I had sent the money, arrived at my home. The former enquired: "What did you do with the money that I sent to you?"

'I said: "I have used it for a good deed."

'On hearing this he laughed, and, placing a sack of money before me, said: "Having sent you the money, I had no more money left. With

____

[1] *Shanīdanī-hā-yi Tārīkh*, p. 69; *al-Maḥajjah al-Bayḍā'*, vol. 3, p. 356.

the month of Ramadan approaching, I decided to seek some money from this friend only to receive the sack with my own seal upon it which I had sent to you. As we are all in need and have gathered here, we can distribute the money amongst ourselves until Allah provides a way out of our predicament." We divided the money amongst ourselves and parted company. Unfortunately, all the money was exhausted within the first few days of the month of Ramadan.

'Some time thereafter, Yaḥyā ibn Khālid summoned me; when I arrived, he said: "I dreamt that you were faced with poverty. Inform me about the truth [of your situation]." When I informed him [of my recent troubles], he was taken aback and subsequently ordered 30,000 dirhams to be given to me and 10,000 dirhams to be given to each of my other two friends. The unexpected blessing that came our way was due to our efforts in fulfilling the needs of fellow believers.'[1]

4 – Extinguishing the lamp

Ḥārith narrates:

'I was engaged in conversation one night with Imam ʿAlī ﷺ. I said to him: "I am in need of something."

'The Imam said: "O Ḥārith! Do you regard me worthy of informing me of your need?"

'"Of course, O ʿAlī," I replied.

'Upon hearing my response, the Imam rose from his place and extinguished the lamp. He sat down beside me and said compassionately: "Do you know why I have extinguished the lamp? I have done this so that you can reveal all that is in your heart without any formality and so that I do not see the embarrassment upon your face. Now speak all that you desire for I have heard the Holy Prophet say: 'When the needs of a person are placed in the heart of another, they become a divine trust which must be concealed from others; the one who conceals them shall be given the rewards of worship. But if they are divulged, it befits all those who become

---

[1] *Namūnah-i Maʿārif*, vol. 2, p. 438; *Farajun Baʿd al-Shiddah*, p. 186.

aware of the person's needs to fulfil them.'"[1]

5 – Lettuce

A scholar from Najaf relates:

'I once saw the late Ayatollah Sayyid 'Alī Qāḍī[2] (d. 1946 CE) busy selecting some lettuce at a greengrocer's shop. However, contrary to usual custom, I observed him selecting the lettuce that had become withered and which possessed large and coarse leaves. He passed the selected lettuce to the owner of the shop who weighed it for him. Tucking the lettuce under his cloak, Ayatollah Qāḍī left the shop. I hastened after him and enquired: "Sir, why did you select the lettuce that was inferior and undesirable?"

'He replied: "This greengrocer is a poor person and I occasionally help him. However, I do not wish to give him something gratuitously, so that firstly his esteem and honour do not suffer, and secondly so that he does not, God forbid, habituate himself to taking things free of charge and thus become lax in his work. I am aware that no one will purchase this lettuce from him and he will have to throw it away when he closes his shop and so, in order to prevent him from incurring any losses, I purchased the lettuce from him. As for me, it does not make any difference to me whether I eat lettuce that is delicate and tender or that which is large and coarse!"'[3]

78. Malice

Allah, the Wise, has said:

$$\text{وَنَزَعْنَا مَا فِي صُدُورِهِمْ مِنْ غِلٍّ}$$

We will remove whatever rancour there is in their breasts. (7:43)

The Holy Prophet said:

---

[1] *Bā Mardūm Īn Gūnih Barkhūrd Kunīm*, p. 95; *al-Wāfī*, vol. 6, p. 59.

[2] He was the teacher of mysticism (*'irfān*) of 'Allāmah Ṭabāṭabā'ī, Ayatollah Bahjat, Ayatollah Sayyid 'Abd al-Karīm Kashmīrī, and numerous others, and the like of him has rarely been seen in the past sixty years.

[3] *Sīmā-yi Farzānigān*, p. 349; *Mihr-i Tābān*, p. 20.

الْمُؤْمِنُ لَيْسَ بِحَقُودٍ

A believer is never malicious.[1]

Short explanation

Nurtured by enmity, resentment, anger, and other negative emotions, malice is a spiritual disease that manifests itself as malevolence and spite towards another person. When a person harbours malice towards another, he is perpetually disturbed by a desire to hurt or destroy him. If unchecked, vindictiveness can overpower a person's intellect and moral reasoning, thus reducing his capacity to forgive, forbear, and refrain from revenge and harm.

A true believer is never malicious or vengeful; he either forgives the wrong perpetrated against him or entrusts the matter to Allah's justice and decree. Even in the heat of anger he is rational, quenching his rage before it hardens into rancour and drives him to abuse or injure another person.[2]

1 – Walīd's maliciousness

'Aqabah, the father of Walīd, the governor of Kufa during the caliphate of 'Uthmān, once spat upon the face of the Holy Prophet in Mecca. He had joined the ranks of the infidels in the Battle of Badr. When the infidels were defeated, 'Aqabah was taken captive and brought before the Holy Prophet, who ordered Imam 'Alī ﷺ to put him to death. Consequently, 'Aqabah's son, Walīd, always harboured malice towards Imam 'Alī ﷺ and often mocked and insulted him.

In spite of Walīd's mistreatment of his father, Imam al-Ḥasan ﷺ once visited Walīd when he fell ill. Seeing the Imam standing before him as he opened his eyes, Walīd said: 'I repent for all my past misdeeds and seek Allah's forgiveness for them, except the abuses which I hurled at your father for which I am not repentant.'

The Imam responded: 'My father killed your father and punished you [for consuming wine] and this is the reason for your animosity towards

---

[1] *Jāmi' al-Sa'ādāt*, vol. 1, p. 311.

[2] *Iḥyā' al-Qulūb*, p. 64.

him [and it is this malice that prompted you to abuse him].'[1]

2 – Ibn Sallār

During the sixth century, an officer in the Egyptian army by the name of Ibn Sallār rose to the rank of minister, wielding great power and authority over his subjects. He was courageous and intelligent whilst also self-centred and malicious. Hence, whilst he was a minister, Ibn Sallār not only served the people, but also committed numerous acts of oppression and vengeance.

Whilst Ibn Sallār was a soldier in the army, he was ordered to pay certain damages and compensation. He appealed to Abī al-Karam, the clerk of the treasury, for justice, but Abī al-Karam refused to consider his explanations and upheld the sentence, saying: 'Your words do not enter my ears.' Ibn Sallār was infuriated and deeply resented the judge who had rejected his plea of defence.

When he became the minister and an opportunity presented itself for revenge, Ibn Sallār had Abī al-Karam arrested, and ordered that a long nail be hammered into one of his ears such that it emerged from the other ear. As the nail was being hammered, Abī al-Karam repeatedly shrieked in pain. Each time he cried out, Ibn Sallār taunted him, saying: 'Now my words have entered your ears!'

Upon Abī al-Karam's death, Ibn Sallār ordered that Abī al-Karam's lifeless body be hung up on the gallows.[2]

3 – Rancour transforms into love

'Uthmān, the father of Shaybah, was killed in the Battle of Uḥud. Since the Holy Prophet had killed his father and eight other family members in battle, Shaybah held a deep grudge against him. He reports:

'There was none towards whom I harboured more animosity than Muḥammad, for he had killed eight members of my family, all of whom

---

[1] *Kayfar-i Kirdār*, vol. 1, p. 109.

[2] *Dāstān-hā Wa Pand-hā*, vol. 1, p. 163; *Lughat Namih-i Dihkhudā*, p. 320.

possessed the competence and ability to be leaders and commanders. I had always intended to kill him, but after the conquest of Mecca I lost hope of achieving my goal for I considered it impossible to achieve my objective when all the Arabs had flocked into his religion. However, when the people of Hawāzin united in their opposition towards him and declared their intention to fight him, my ambition was, to a certain extent, rekindled within my heart. However, the problem that lay before me was that he [Muḥammad] was surrounded by 10,000 soldiers! When the Muslim forces fled during their first encounter with the forces of Hawāzin, I said to myself: "This is the opportunity to achieve my objective and take revenge for the killings [of my family members]."

'I attacked the Holy Prophet from the right flank but found 'Abbās, his uncle, guarding him. Coming up from the left flank, I realised that Abū Sufyān ibn Ḥārith was protecting him and so I withdrew, thinking: "This person guarding Muḥammad is also a brave person." I then approached from behind and reached so close that my sword was about to reach him. Suddenly, a veil of fire appeared as a barrier between me and him, leaving my eyes dazzled by the intense light. Covering my face with my hands, I retreated, realising that he was under Allah's protection. The Holy Prophet became aware of my presence and said: "Shaybah, come near." When I had done so, he placed his hand upon my breast and said: "O Lord! Ward Shayṭān away from him." Then he looked at me and I found him to be dearer to me than my own self; all malice had been transformed into friendship and love. I then fought against the enemies [of the Holy Prophet] and was so devoted in assisting the Holy Prophet that even if my father had stood against me, I would have killed him. Once the battle was over, he [the Holy Prophet] said to me: "What Allah desired for you is better than what you desired for yourself."[1]

4 – The vindictive hypocrite

Rancour and malice are signs of hypocrisy. During the life of the Holy

---

[1] *Payghambar Wa Yārān*, vol. 3, p. 298; *Biḥār al-Anwār*, vol. 21, p. 156.

Prophet, the hypocrites harboured deep resentment and animosity towards the Holy Prophet and his progeny.

The Holy Prophet was once seated in the mosque in the company of a group of the Muhājirūn and Anṣār, when suddenly Imam ʿAlī 🖎 entered. The companions present rose up in respect and warmly welcomed him until he sat in his usual place near the Holy Prophet. As Imam ʿAlī 🖎 sat down, two individuals in the gathering began to whisper to each other. Seeing them whispering, the Holy Prophet grew angry. The Holy Prophet then said: 'By the one in whose power lies my soul! None shall enter paradise except he who loves me. And know that one who imagines that he loves me but regards this person [Imam ʿAlī 🖎] as an enemy, is a liar.' As the Holy Prophet spoke, ʿAlī's 🖎 hand was in the hand of the Holy Prophet. As soon as the Holy Prophet finished speaking, the following verse was revealed:

O you who have faith! When you talk secretly, do not hold secret talks [imbued] with sin and aggression and disobedience to the Apostle, but talk secretly in [a spirit of] piety and God-fearing, and be wary of Allah toward whom you will be mustered. (58:9)[1]

5 – Hind, the liver-eater

Ḥamzah, once known as the Chief of the Martyrs, was the uncle of the Holy Prophet. He killed nearly thirty people in the Battle of Uḥud before he was eventually martyred.

Hind, the wife of Abū Sufyān, was the most malicious and vengeful of all the women of Mecca. She promised Waḥshī, the slave of Jubayr ibn Muṭʿim, great wealth and riches as a reward if he killed Ḥamzah. Waḥshī accepted the challenging task and ambushed Ḥamzah from behind, piercing him with a dagger that killed him. He then split open Ḥamzah's stomach as per Hind's instructions and removed his liver. When the liver was brought before Hind, she chewed it, earning her the notorious title, 'liver-eater'.

In fulfilment of her promise, Hind gave all her ornaments to Waḥshī.

---

[1] *Ḥikāyat-hā-yi Shanīdanī*, vol. 4, p. 159; *Biḥār al-Anwār*, vol. 39, p. 270.

Overcome by malice as she approached the body of Ḥamzah, Hind cut off his ears, nose, and lips, and proceeded to make a crude necklace out of them so that she could take it to Mecca and display it to the womenfolk. The women of Mecca followed Hind's example and mutilated the bodies of other martyrs. Abū Sufyān also demonstrated a similar barbaric vindictiveness when he stood over the body of Ḥamzah, and he pierced his spear into a corner of Ḥamzah's mouth, and said derisively: 'O disowned one! Taste this!'[1]

79. Weeping

Allah, the Wise, has said:

$$فَلْيَضْحَكُوا قَلِيلًا وَلْيَبْكُوا كَثِيرًا$$

So let them laugh a little; much will they weep. (9:82)

Imam ʿAlī states:

$$بُكَاءُ الْعُيُونِ وَخَشْيَةُ الْقُلُوبِ مِنْ رَحْمَةِ اللّٰهِ تَعَالَى$$

The weeping of the eyes and the fear of the hearts is amongst the mercies of God, the Exalted.[2]

Short explanation

Weeping in humility, love, and fear of Allah reflects a soft heart that is the recipient of divine mercy and inspiration. A true believer cries out of love for the beloved, the grief of separation from Him, compassion for the oppressed and suffering, and other noble and lofty sentiments. A person may also weep for material losses or in pretence, as did the brothers of Prophet Yūsuf after throwing their younger brother in a dry well; these tears are superficial and are inspired by selfish interests.

It is only when a person undergoes a spiritual revolution, journeying from sin to repentance, apathy to compassion, and ignorance to illumination, that his ego crumbles, heart breaks, and divinely inspired

---

[1] *Muntahā al-Aʿmāl*, vol. 1, p. 61.

[2] *Tafsīr al-Muʿīn*, p. 122.

tears flow. Hence, the weeping that emerges from spiritual growth rather than unfulfilled desires is highly recommended and amply rewarded in Islam. It is so desirable that even if a person is unable to cry in fear of Allah or in solidarity with the sacrifice and principles of Imam al-Ḥusayn ☙, he is advised to appear sad and weepy so that He is included amongst those whose hearts are moved by love for Allah and His appointed guides.

1 – Prophet Nūḥ ☙

After the storm subsided, Prophet Nūḥ ☙ guided the ark that had carried him and his few followers across the rising water to dry land. Upon disembarking and settling down, the archangel Jibrīl approached Prophet Nūḥ ☙ and said: 'Previously, your profession was carpentry; now focus your attention upon developing your skills in a new field – pottery.' Hence, Prophet Nūḥ ☙ learned how to construct pots and utensils from clay.

Once, Prophet Nūḥ ☙ had created a vast array of pots, and Jibrīl said to him: 'Allah has commanded you to break the pots.' In obedience to divine orders, Prophet Nūḥ ☙ began to throw pots to the ground, letting them crumble and break. Often he threw them lightly to the ground, destroying them with some hesitation and reluctance.

After a few moments he stopped. Jibrīl asked Prophet Nūḥ ☙ why he had stopped destroying the pots when there were many left unbroken. He replied: 'My heart is unwilling to break them for I have spent a lot of effort in constructing them.'

Jibrīl said to him: 'O Nūḥ! Do any of these pots possess life? Do they have fathers, mothers, etc.? The earth and water are from Allah. Your only contribution was that you exerted yourself and constructed them and yet you are reluctant and unwilling to break them. So how did you permit yourself to curse the people and call for their destruction when they had been created by Allah and possessed life and had fathers and mothers?'

Intensely regretting his earlier sentiments, Prophet Nūḥ ☙ wept bitterly and profusely. Thereafter, while his name was 'Abd al-Ghaffār, Prophet Nūḥ ☙ came to be known as 'Nūḥ', meaning 'one who laments and cries intensely'.[1]

2 – Prophet Yaḥyā

Prophet Yaḥyā once came to Jerusalem and saw some clerics and priests wearing coarse garments and woollen caps. He requested his mother to arrange for him to wear a similar dress so that he too could engage himself in worship with them. When his mother gave him the outfit, he wore it and busied himself in worship.

One day, looking at himself in the mirror and observing that he had become very thin, he began to weep. Allah revealed to him: 'Do you weep because your body has become thin? By My honour and glory! If you were to possess the slightest awareness of the fire of hell, you would have worn a garment made of iron rather than one made of fabric.' In fear of Allah's punishment and wrath, Prophet Yaḥyā began to weep intensely.

Prophet Yaḥyā's father, Prophet Zakariyyā, once said to him: 'Dear son! Why do you weep so much? I had prayed for you to be born so that you may be the apple of my eye!'

Prophet Yaḥyā replied: 'But were you not the one who had said that between heaven and hell lies a pass that none shall be able to traverse except those who weep intensely out of fear of Allah?'

Prophet Yaḥyā used to weep so much that his mother gave him two pieces of felt to absorb the tears which flowed profusely from his eyes. When they would become drenched with his tears, he would squeeze the pieces of felt and his tears would flow out of them from between his fingers. Sometimes, Prophet Zakariyyā would look at his son, raise his head towards the heavens, and say: 'O Lord! This is my son and these are his tears and You are the Most Merciful of the merciful ones.'

When Prophet Yaḥyā would hear 'Sukran' – the name of a mountain in hell – he would rush out into the desert in distress, crying: 'Woe [unto me] due to my heedlessness [with respect to Allah]!'[2]

---

[1] *Jāmiʿ al-Nūrayn*, p. 122.

[2] *Risālah Liqāʾ Allāh*, p. 157; *al-Amālī* of Shaykh Ṣadūq.

3 – The intense weeping of Lady Zahrā'

The loss of the Holy Prophet, the sacrilege committed in connection with the usurped right of Imam 'Alī, and the abuses she suffered, made Lady Zahrā' weep bitterly. Inconvenienced by her weeping, the people of Medina complained to Lady Zahrā': 'We are troubled by your wailing and lamenting!' She was compelled to leave the city and travel to the graves of the martyrs of Uḥud to weep and mourn unheard by the people of Medina.

According to a reported tradition, the elders of Medina approached Imam 'Alī and complained: 'O Abū al-Ḥasan! Fāṭimah weeps during the day and night; none of us are able to sleep at night. During the day we are unable to rest due to our involvement in earning the livelihood, while at night we are unable to do so due to her weeping. Ask her to weep either during the day or during the night.'

The Imam conveyed this message to Lady Fāṭimah who replied: 'O Abū al-Ḥasan! I will not remain in this world for long and will shortly depart from the people. I will not be able to refrain from weeping until I am united with my father.'

Imam 'Alī constructed a room of bricks and date-palm leaves in the cemetery of Baqī', to which Lady Fāṭimah could withdraw to grieve and weep; it therefore came to be known as House of Sorrows (Bayt al-Aḥzān). Every morning, Lady Zahrā' would visit Baqī' with her children and weep incessantly amongst the graves; when night fell, Imam 'Alī would come to the cemetery and bring her and the children home with him.[1]

4 – Thirty-five years of weeping

Imam al-Ṣādiq states: 'The Fourth Imam wept for his father for almost forty years, the days of which he fasted and the nights of which he passed in worship. When it was time to open his fast, the Imam's slave would bring him food and water, and placing them before him, would say: "Eat it."

---

[1] *Muṣībat-i Buzurg*, p. 47; *Biḥār al-Anwār*, vol. 43, p. 155, 177.

'The Imam would respond: "My father was killed in a state of hunger and thirst," and then he would weep so intensely that his food would become moistened by his tears. And this continued for as long as he was alive.'

One of the friends of Imam al-Sajjād ﷺ reports:

'One day, the Imam journeyed into the desert and so I proceeded after him. When I found him, I saw him prostrating upon a rough stone, weeping and wailing; by my count, he recited a particular supplication 1000 times. He then raised his head [and I observed] that his face and beard were moistened with tears. I said to him: "O my master! End your sorrow and reduce your weeping!"

'He responded: "Woe unto you! Ya'qūb, the son of Isḥāq, was a prophet and the son of a prophet. He had twelve sons, and when one of them was lost he was so grieved that his hair turned white, his body became bent, and due to his intense weeping, his eyes lost their vision, and all this occurred despite the fact that his son was still alive. Yet I have seen my father, brother, and seventeen members of my family killed and lie martyred on the ground with my own eyes. Therefore, how can my sorrow end and how can my tears dry up?"'[1]

80. Sins

Allah, the Wise, has said:

$$\text{فَكُلًّا أَخَذْنَا بِذَنْبِهِ}$$

So We seized each [of them] for his sin. (29:40)

Imam al-Ṣādiq ﷺ states:

$$\text{أَمَا أَنَّهُ لَيْسَ مِنْ عِرْقٍ يُضْرَبُ وَلَا نَكْبَةٍ وَلَا صُدَاعٍ وَلَا مَرَضٍ إِلَّا بِذَنْبٍ}$$

No vein is cut, nor is there adversity, headache, or sickness, except as a result of one's sins.[2]

---

[1] *Namūnah-i Ma'ārif*, vol. 2, p. 589; *Anwār al-Nu'māniyyah*, vol. 2, p. 27.

[2] *Jāmi' al-Sa'ādāt*, vol. 3, p. 47.

Short explanation

Sinfulness incurs the wrath of Allah and is punishable both in this world and in the Hereafter. Sinful actions are often symptomatic of spiritual illnesses such as anger, hypocrisy, and arrogance, which drive a person to sin in the first place. In treating the virulence of rage, malice, greed and other diseases, the tendency to sin is mitigated and spiritual health can be restored.

Whilst all sins are not equally reprehensible, considering one's sins to be trivial and insignificant is in itself a major sin. One who is complacent about his minor sins does not realise that even the smallest sin is a grave transgression because it is an act of rebellion against his Creator. The journey towards redemption begins with acknowledging the ugliness of one's sin and thereafter repenting to Allah, seeking His forgiveness, and resolving never to commit the sin again. If a person has sinned against another person, the forgiveness of the one against whom he sinned must also be sought. Thereafter, he should be vigilant so that if the temptation to sin recurs, he does not succumb to it, but fights his desire, seeking Allah's assistance and guidance in his struggle.

1 – The banishment of the sinner

The tribe of Banī Isrāʾīl once prayed to Allah to save them from the sins of a licentious and corrupt man living amongst them. Allah revealed to Prophet Mūsā ﷺ to banish the youth from the city so that the inhabitants of the city would not be affected by the punishment ordained for him.

After Prophet Mūsā ﷺ banished the sinner from the city, the sinner proceeded to another city. Allah commanded that he should be removed from that city also. Thereafter, he sought refuge in a cave and fell ill. In his solitary and ill condition, the sinner repented, weeping and crying out: 'O Allah! Forgive me! Had my wife and children been here, they would have wept at my wretchedness and desolation. O Allah! You who have separated me from my father, mother, and wife, do not burn me in Your fire for my sins.'

In response to the sinner's supplication, Allah created angels in the form of his father, mother, wife, and children and sent them to him. The youth was delighted that his family would be near him in his final hours and died soon thereafter. Allah revealed to Prophet Mūsā ﷺ: 'Our friend has died in such and such place. Go and perform the necessary ablutions and bury him.' When Prophet Mūsā ﷺ reached the specified place, he saw that the deceased was the same sinner who had been banished from the cities; Prophet Mūsā ﷺ queried: 'O Lord! Is he not the same sinning youth whom You ordered me to expel from the city?'

Allah revealed: 'O Mūsā! I exhibited mercy towards him. Due to his weeping, lamentations, sickness, separation from his land and relatives, confession of his sins, and seeking forgiveness, I forgave him.'[1]

2 – Prophet 'Īsā ﷺ prays for rain

Prophet 'Īsā ﷺ and his companions came out of the city and went into the desert to pray for rain. Prophet 'Īsā ﷺ then said to his companions: 'Those of you who have committed sins should return to the city.' Obeying the instructions of the prophet, all the companions except one, returned to the city. Turning to the lone companion who remained behind, Prophet 'Īsā ﷺ asked: 'Have you not committed any sin?'

He replied: 'I don't remember having committed any sin except in one instance when, as I stood engaged in prayers, a woman passed in front of me. I looked at her and my eyes continued to follow her. But as soon as she left, I thrust my finger into my eye and pulling it out, threw it in the direction where the woman had gone.'

Prophet 'Īsā ﷺ said: 'Pray and I shall say *āmīn*.' The companion prayed and rain soon began to pour down.[2]

3 – The expiation of sins

One of the prophets of Banī Isrā'īl passed a person who had died under a

---

[1] *'Unwān al-Kalām*, p. 87; *Jāmi' al-Akhbār*.

[2] *Shanīdanī-hā-yi Tārīkh*, p. 22; *al-Maḥajjah al-Bayḍā'*, vol. 1, p. 299.

collapsed wall. Half his body lay protruding from under the wall and had been torn apart by wild beasts. He passed through this city and entered another. When he entered the second city, he saw that one of the elders of the city had died; shrouded with a brocaded cloth and perfumed with the fragrance of incense and amber, his lifeless body was placed in an expensive coffin and a large crowd had gathered to attend his funeral procession.

The prophet asked: 'O Lord! You are the Just and Wise and never approve of injustice. Why is it that a person who had never been tainted by polytheism died in that manner [that I witnessed in the previous city] while this person who never worshipped You died in this fashion?'

Allah revealed to him: 'It is just as you have stated; I am the Wise and never approve of injustice. That servant [in the previous city] had performed some sins and I desired that his death should serve to expiate his sins so that he could return to Me in a purified state. As for this person, he had performed some good deeds and I desired to reward him in this world so that he returned to Me requiring no recompense for his good deeds.'[1]

4 – Ḥumayd ibn Qaḥṭabah Ṭāʾī

ʿAbd Allāh ibn Bazzāz narrates:

'Ḥumayd and I were friends. One afternoon during the month of Ramadan, I visited his home. When Ḥumayd was informed that I had come to meet him he asked someone to welcome me inside.

'I greeted Ḥumayd as I entered and sat down, whereupon food was laid before me. He washed his hands and asked me to do likewise so that we could begin our meal. When he requested me to begin eating, I hesitated because I was fasting. I said: "O chief! It is the month of Ramadan and I am not sick [so as to be exempted from fasting]." Hearing this, Ḥumayd wept and then proceeded to eat his food. After he finished, I enquired: "Why did you weep while eating your food?"

'He explained: "One night, I was summoned by the Abbasid caliph,

---

[1] *Namūnah-i Maʿārif,* vol. 5, p. 299; *al-Kāfī,* vol. 2, p. 288.

Hārūn al-Rashīd. Upon arriving before the caliph, he raised his head and asked me: 'In what measure do you obey the caliph?' I replied: 'I obey him with my life and wealth.' He then lowered his head and permitted me to leave. No sooner had I returned to my house when the caliph's messenger summoned me to return to the caliph. I feared that the caliph had decided to kill me and so I began to supplicate to Allah. Upon arriving before the caliph, he raised his head and asked: 'How much is your obedience to your caliph?' I replied: 'With my life, wealth, wife, and children.' Hearing this, he smiled and granted me permission to return home. As soon as I arrived home, the caliph's messenger arrived to inform me that the caliph had summoned me once again. As I stood before the caliph, he again asked me: 'How much do you obey your king?' I replied: 'With my life, wealth, wife, children, and religion.' This time the caliph laughed and said: 'Take this sword and comply with what this slave orders you to do.'

"'The slave led me to a house with a locked door. He opened the door and I entered inside with him. Looking around, I noticed that there were three locked rooms and one well which lay in the middle of the courtyard. When the slave opened one of the rooms, I observed that it contained twenty descendants of varying ages of the Holy Prophet, fettered with chains. The slave instructed me to kill them. As instructed, I killed each of the descendants of the Holy Prophet, 'Alī ﷺ, and Fāṭimah ﷺ. Thereafter, the slave pushed all the dead bodies into the well. He then opened the door to the second room and brought out another twenty descendants of the Holy Prophet to the mouth of the well and I killed them also. Opening the door of the third room, the slave brought another group of twenty and I began to sever their heads from their bodies. I had severed the heads of nineteen individuals from this group when the last person, an old man with overgrown hair [due to his protracted stay in prison], said to me: 'O evil one! May you be cursed! What excuse will you have on the Day of Judgement when you shall stand before our grandfather, the Holy Prophet, after having killed sixty of his children?' Hearing this, a sudden tremor ran through my arms and body. The slave looked at me and ordered: 'Kill him.' I killed him and the slave hurled his body into the well. O 'Abd Allāh! After having killed sixty persons from the descendants of the Holy Prophet, how can prayers and fasts ever benefit me? I am certain that my abode is the fire of hell."[1]

81. Pleasure

Allah, the Wise, has said:

$$يُطَافُ عَلَيْهِمْ بِكَأْسٍ مِنْ مَعِينٍ ۝ بَيْضَاءَ لَذَّةٍ لِلشَّارِبِينَ$$

Served around with a cup from a clear fountain. Snow-white, delicious to the drinkers. (37:45-46)

Imam ʿAlī has said:

$$شَتَّانَ مَا بَيْنَ عَمَلَيْنِ عَمَلٍ تَذْهَبُ لَذَّتُهُ وَتَبْقَى تَبِعَتُهُ وَعَمَلٍ تَذْهَبُ مَؤُونَتُهُ وَيَبْقَى أَجْرُهُ$$

What a difference between two acts – an act [of sin], whose pleasure goes away while its detriment continues to remain, and an act [of goodness], whose hardship goes away while its rewards continue to remain.[2]

Short explanation

The human nature is inclined towards all kinds of pleasures. Pleasures are either those that have been lauded by the shariah, such as those derived out of worship, seeking knowledge, etc., or have been denounced by it, such as those derived by way of lust, consumption of unlawful food, etc. As such, an individual must strive to refrain from pleasures that have been forbidden by the shariah.

Just as bounties are of different kinds, the pleasures associated with them are also different; an academic derives pleasure with the acquisition of knowledge, while a child by the milk of the mother, and a businessman by the accumulation of his wealth. Consequently, the description by someone of the pleasures experienced by another would always be figurative.

Whilst engaging in pleasures that are forbidden may not even merit a

---

[1] *Kayfar-i Kirdār*, vol. 1, p. 302; *ʿUyūn Akhbār al-Riḍā*, vol. 1, p. 109.

[2] *Nahj al-Balāghah* of Fayḍ al-Islām, p. 1143.

discussion, however, care ought to be exercised that extravagance does not to come into play even with respect to pleasures that have been deemed lawful, because excessive involvement even in lawful pleasures could later lead to consequences and ramifications that could be detrimental in nature.

1 – The seven pleasures

One day, whilst in the presence of Imam 'Alī ⁅, Jābir ibn 'Abd Allāh Anṣārī heaved a deep sigh. Imam said to him: 'Is the deep breath and the long sigh of yours related to the affairs of this world?'

Jābir replied: 'Yes; I recalled the affairs of the life of this world and sighed because of this.'

Imam said: 'O Jābir! All pleasures, happiness, and enjoyment of this world are encompassed in seven things: things that are eaten, things that are drunk, things that are heard, things that are smelt, things that are means of travel, sex, and clothes. However, the most delicious thing that can be eaten is honey, which is the saliva of an insect – the honeybee. The most salubrious drink is water, which is abundantly found everywhere. The best of the things that can be listened to is music, which is sinful. The most pleasurable of things that can be smelt is the fragrance of musk, which is prepared from the dried blood of the umbilicus of an animal. The best of the sexual act is with one's wife, which is basically the interaction of two places of urination. The best of the means of travel is a horse, which, at times, can cause death. The best of clothes is one made of silk, which itself is acquired from the silkworm. A world, the best pleasures of which are of this kind, does not befit an intelligent person to heave a deep sigh for it.'

Jābir says: 'By Allah! After this preaching[1] love for this world never entered into my heart!'

2 – A beautiful description

During the time of the Holy Prophet there lived in Medina two men. They were immoral in behaviour and had scant regard for decent speech. They

____

[1] *Dāstān-hā Wa Pand-hā*, vol. 10, p. 153.

would engage in vulgar talks and make people laugh.

One day, whilst these two men were conversing with one of the Muslims, the Holy Prophet, who was at a few paces from them, overheard them say: 'When you attack the city of Taif and conquer it, keep a watch for the daughter of I'lān Thaqafī. Capture her and keep her for yourself, for she is a maiden who is tall and attractive, with large eyes, slim waist, and a cheerful demeanour. Whenever she sits she exhibits dignity, and when she speaks her words are attractive and captivating. Her cheeks are such and ...' endeavouring to incite the person by means of such a vivid description of the lady.

The Holy Prophet said to them: 'I don't suppose you to be men who are sexually inclined towards women; on the contrary, I think you are individuals that are foolish and have no sexual ability at all, as a result of which you only bring out the beauty of women in words [without actually experiencing the pleasures].'

The Holy Prophet subsequently exiled them from Medina, allowing them to come to Medina to procure food supplies and other living necessities only every Friday of each week.[1]

3 – The pleasure of *munājāh*

There once was a slave who had an understanding with his master that he would give one dirham to his master, daily, upon the condition that he be allowed to go wherever he desired during the night.

Once, when the master was praising his slave to some people, one of them said: 'This slave is probably digging up graves, stealing the shrouds, and selling them, and is thus able to give you the dirham.' This left the master distressed, and so, when the slave sought permission and left that night, he began to follow him. He observed that the slave had gone out of the city and entered a cemetery. There, he entered a wide grave, put on black clothes, placed a chain around his neck, rubbed his face on the earth, and began praying to his Lord, deriving pleasure from this conversation

---

[1] *Ḥikāyat-hā-yi Shanīdanī*, vol. 3, p. 89; *Biḥār al-Anwār*, vol. 22, p. 88.

with Him. Witnessing this, the master broke down in tears and sat near the grave till morning, while the slave, throughout the night, continued to remain engrossed in prayers and worship.

When morning dawned, the slave supplicated: 'O Lord! You are aware that my boss needs to be given one dirham while I do not have any. You are the one who helps the needy!' No sooner had the supplication ended when a light appeared in the air and a dirham came out of it and dropped into the hands of the slave.

Seeing this, the master moved forward, took the slave in his arms, and embraced him. Realising that his secret had become exposed, the slave was overcome with sadness and prayed: 'O Lord! Now that You have torn apart my veil of secrecy and exposed my secret, seize my soul.' No sooner had he completed his supplication when his soul departed the body. The master informed the people about the incident and they buried the slave in the same grave.[1]

4 – The pleasure of murder

Ḥajjāj ibn Yūsuf Thaqafī, who had been given the authority to rule by the Banī Umayyah and had committed numerous killings, used to say: 'One of the things that I derive great pleasure from is the murder of a human being, especially when, in my presence, his head is severed from his body and the blood gushes out from the veins in his neck and the person lies writhing in his own blood. The pleasure that I get out of this is better than the pleasure of marrying a beautiful virgin maiden.'[2]

He used to derive such great pleasure out of this that once, when three kilogrammes of flour was brought for him, he ordered: 'Prepare a dough out of this by mixing the blood of the sayyids with it and bake for me a bread, for I would like to open my fast with this bread.'[3]

---

[1] *ʿUnwān al-Kalām*, p. 30.

[2] *Jāmiʿ al-Nūrayn*, p. 331.

[3] *Pand-i Tārīkh*, vol. 3, p. 164.

82. Wealth

Allah, the Wise, has said:

$$لَتُبْلَوُنَّ فِي أَمْوَالِكُمْ وَأَنْفُسِكُمْ$$

You will surely be tested in your possessions and your souls. (3:186)

The Holy Prophet said:

$$حُبُّ الْمَالِ والشَّرَفِ يُنْبِتَانِ النِّفَاقَ فِي الْقَلْبِ$$

Love of wealth and status brings about the growth of hypocrisy in the heart.[1]

Short explanation

Whilst there are certain issues of this world that keep us attracted and engrossed for a short period of time such as food and sexual intercourse, there are others that tend to keep us occupied for most of our time, such as love and accumulation of wealth and riches.

Wealth, legitimately accumulated and correctly spent, can be a saviour for man, but if accumulated illegitimately and spent on fulfilling carnal desires, or if it leads him towards extravagance or parsimony, can destroy him. The mere possession of wealth is not the only indication of someone's love for it, for there are numerous people who, though not possessing it, are very desirous of it. They greedily eye the riches of others and intensely desire it for themselves. Both these groups have become engrossed with the material life of this world and overcome by hypocrisy and heedlessness towards Allah, such that the light of faith has left their hearts.[2]

1 – All this money from where?

'Amr ibn 'Āṣ,[3] the vizier of Mu'āwiyah, having realised his death was approaching, was seen to be weeping. His son, 'Abd Allāh, enquired: 'O father! Why do you weep? Are your tears out of fear of the severity of

---

[1] *Jāmi' al-Sa'ādāt*, vol. 2, p. 46.

[2] *Iḥyā' al-Qulūb*, p. 86.

[3] He died in Egypt in the year 43 AH at the age of seventy-seven.

death?'

'Death I fear not,' he replied. 'However, what is going to happen with me after death is what I am fearful of.'

'Abd Allāh said to him: 'But you have been a companion of the Holy Prophet ﷺ and have led a good life.'

'Amr explained: 'My son! I have been associated with three categories of people. At the outset I was a non-believer and was the staunchest of the enemies of the Holy Prophet ﷺ. If I had died then, undoubtedly, I would have gone to hell. Subsequently I pledged allegiance to the Holy Prophet ﷺ and used to hold him dear to me. Had I died then, my place would have been in paradise. After the Holy Prophet ﷺ I became absorbed in the affairs of the world and sultanate, and it is here that I do not know what my outcome is going to be.'

Since the time 'Amr ibn 'Āṣ became engrossed in the affairs of the world and the government machinery of Mu'āwiyah, he had managed to accumulate seventy cow-skins filled with money and gold. He ordered all his wealth to be brought before him and then asked: 'Who is it that would be willing to take all of this wealth along with all the evil consequences associated with it?'

His son replied: 'I cannot accept it as not knowing how much of this wealth belongs to which individuals, I would be unable to return the property to their rightful owners.'

Word of this reached Mu'āwiyah, who responded: 'I will accept this wealth with all its associated evils.' All this wealth was thus transferred from Egypt to Mu'āwiyah in Damascus.[1]

2 – The price of silence

Imam 'Alī ﷺ relates:

'One day, in the intense midday heat, the Third Caliph sent someone to summon me to his presence. So, wearing a head cover and covering my

---

[1] *Rāhnumā-yi Sa'ādat*, vol. 1, p. 22; *Nāsikh al-Tawārīkh*, volume on Imam al-Ḥasan ﷺ, p. 29.

face with a cloth, I presented myself before him only to see him stretched out on his bed with a stick in his hand and immense wealth in the form of two bags filled with gold and currency lying before him. As soon as he saw me, he said: "Take however much you wish from these two bags to your heart's content."

'I replied: "If this wealth belongs to you, which you have acquired by means of inheritance, gift, or other means of income, I might choose to either take it and thank you for it, or decline it. However, if it is from the public treasury with the rights of Muslims, orphans, and the poor associated with it, then, by Allah, neither can you gift this wealth to me nor can I accept it from you." ... Having wrapped my headscarf around my head, as I turned to return home, I said to him: "If I have done the enjoinment of good or forbidding evil to you then Allah shall be the judge between you and I."'[1]

3 – Correct utilisation of wealth

During the conquest of Iran at the hands of Muslims which took place during the time of the Second Caliph, one of the spoils of war that came into the hands of the Muslims was a large gold-brocaded carpet that was in excess of 350 metres in length. When this carpet was brought to Madain, it was cut into several pieces and subsequently distributed amongst the people.

Imam ʿAlī ﷺ used his share of this carpet to expand his farming and production work. He purchased a derelict plot of land that had a canal of water flowing through it and worked on it to bring it to life. He sowed 300,000 seeds of dates and irrigated the plants by means of the water from the canal, and in this manner he brought into existence a huge garden of date palms, which provided daily food for several people.

Subsequently, the Imam declared one part of the garden as an endowment for the benefit of those soldiers who fought in the way of Allah,

---

[1] *Bā Mardūm Īn Gūnih Raftār Kunīm*, p. 82; *Sharḥ Nahj al-Balāghah* of Ibn Abī al-Ḥadīd, vol. 9, p. 16.

and the other part as an endowment for the use of the general populace so that the annual harvest from this garden could be used for these two purposes.[1]

4 – Immense wealth

When Maʾmūn, the Abbasid caliph, was getting married to Purān, the daughter of Ḥasan ibn Sahl, the immense amount of money he spent on the wedding is beyond description. On the wedding night, pellets of musk were fired into the air, each pellet containing a piece of paper with the name of a garden, a slave-girl, a prize, or some other valuable item written on it. Whoever found a pellet would return it and receive whatever was inscribed on the paper within it.

Around 36,000 workers were involved in organising the wedding. A carpet was made from gold fibres for the bride to sit upon. Maʾmūn asked his wife Zubaydah: 'How much did Ḥasan ibn Sahl spend on the wedding?'

'Around thirty-seven million dinars,' she replied.

4000 mules over a period of four months carried firewood for the eve of the wedding, which got exhausted by the morning of the wedding! Subsequently, clothes made of linen were burnt under the cooking vessels to cook food.[2]

5 – Four dinars

One day, whilst ill, Abū Dharr, with the help of his walking stick, came to ʿUthmān. There, he observed 100,000 dirhams lying before ʿUthmān and a group of people seated around him in anticipation that ʿUthmān might perhaps distribute this money amongst them. Abū Dharr said: 'Whose wealth is this, from where has it come, and where is it to be used?'

ʿUthmān replied: 'This is 100,000 dirhams that have been brought to me from a certain region. We are anticipating another 100,000 to be added to this, before we decide what needs to be done with the money.'

---

[1] *Ḥikāyat-hā-yi Shanīdanī*, vol. 2, p. 75.

[2] *Pand-i Tārīkh*, vol. 3, p. 212; *Kashkūl* of Baḥrānī, vol. 2, p. 49.

Abū Dharr said: 'Which of these is more – 100,000 dirhams or four dinars?'

'Uthmān: 'Obviously, 100,000 dirhams.'

Abū Dharr: 'Bring to mind that night when the both of us were honoured to be in the presence of the Holy Prophet ﷺ. He was so disturbed and distressed that even his reply to our greeting was very uncharacteristic of him. The next day when we visited him, we found him to be smiling and happy whereupon we asked him: "May our parents become sacrificed for you! Why is it that last night you appeared immensely distressed, whereas today you look very happy?" He had said: "True! Last night four dinars from the public treasury of the Muslims remained with me as I was unable to distribute them. I was fearful that I might die while this amount remained with me; however, today I have distributed it and now am at ease."'[1]

83. Love

Allah, the Wise, has said:

$$\text{قُلْ إِنْ كُنْتُمْ تُحِبُّونَ اللهَ فَاتَّبِعُونِي يُحْبِبْكُمُ اللهُ وَيَغْفِرْ لَكُمْ ذُنُوبَكُمْ وَاللهُ غَفُورٌ رَحِيمٌ}$$

Say: 'If you love Allah, then follow me; Allah will love you and forgive you your sins, and Allah is All-forgiving, All-merciful.' (3:31)

Imam al-Ṣādiq ﷺ said:

$$\text{مَا الْتَقَى مُؤْمِنَانِ قَطُّ إِلَّا كَانَ أَفْضَلَهُمَا أَشَدُّهُمَا حُبًّا لِأَخِيهِ}$$

No two believers meet each other except that the most meritorious of the two is the one with more intense love for his [believing] brother.[2]

Short explanation

Love with Allah, the Holy Prophet, fellow believers, parents, etc., emanates from one's faith; the more the faith, the more the love.

---

[1] *Payghambar Wa Yārān*, vol. 1, p. 54; *A'yān al-Shī'ah*, p. 359.

[2] *Jāmi' al-Sa'ādāt*, vol. 3, p. 184.

On one hand, every person shall be resurrected with the thing that he loved in this world, and on the other, a love and friendship not based on Allah would remain distanced from the mercy of Allah.

When Allah loves someone He places his love within the hearts of angels, inhabitants of the skies, and the pure people so that they too begin to love him.[1]

Love is akin to a beautiful breeze that rejuvenates and makes vibrant everything that it touches, and to water, which brings about the growth of flora and foliage.[2]

1 – Allah's love for His creations

Once, as a person headed towards Medina from the desert, he observed a bird fly into its nest towards its young ones. The person approached the nest and picked up the young ones of the bird so as to carry them to Medina as a gift for the Holy Prophet.

Arriving in the presence of the Holy Prophet, who had a group of companions around him, the man placed the young ones of the bird before him. All of a sudden the people witnessed that the mother of the young birds, without exhibiting any fear, flew in amidst them and flung herself upon her young ones.

It was clear that the mother bird, out of love for her young ones, had followed the person to Medina. Her love towards her young ones was so great that she flung herself upon them without any fear of the people standing around.

Observing this, the Holy Prophet addressed those present around him: 'You have just observed the intense love that a mother has for her young ones. However, do know that the love and attachment that Allah has towards His creations is a thousand times more than what you have just witnessed.'[3]

------

[1] As per a hadith of the Holy Prophet.

[2] *Tadhkirat al-Ḥaqāʾiq*, p. 89.

[3] *Dāstān-hā Wa Pand-hā*, vol. 5, p. 12.

2 – Love for wood

Abū Ḥanīfah once went to Imam al-Ṣādiq ﷺ to acquire some knowledge and hear some traditions. The Imam had just come out of his house and was leaning on a wooden walking stick. Seeing this, Abū Ḥanīfah said: 'O son of the Holy Prophet ﷺ, you are not of an age that would require you to become dependent upon a walking stick.'

The Imam explained: 'You are right; however, this walking stick that you observe is the same one that was used by the Holy Prophet ﷺ and so I desired to derive some blessings from it.'

Hearing this, Abū Ḥanīfah rushed forward to kiss the stick, whereupon the Imam folded up his sleeves to expose his arm and said to him: 'By Allah! Despite knowing that the flesh of my hand is from the flesh of Holy Prophet ﷺ you do not kiss my hand, whereas you wish to kiss the walking stick of the Holy Prophet ﷺ knowing full well it is nothing but wood!'

3 – The oil seller

Imam al-Ṣādiq ﷺ narrates:

'There was once an individual who used to sell olive oil. He harboured such immense love for the Holy Prophet ﷺ that whenever he would want to go for some work, he would first go to see the Holy Prophet ﷺ and then go about his work. When in the presence of the Holy Prophet ﷺ, he would continue to gaze at him till such time that the Holy Prophet ﷺ turned and looked at him.

'One day he came to the Holy Prophet ﷺ to have a look at his face, and then left for his work. However, within a very short time he returned. The Holy Prophet ﷺ, saw him and beckoned him to sit down, and then asked: "What happened for you to do something today that you have never done before?"

'The man replied: "By the Lord that has sent you as a prophet! My heart is so filled with your love and remembrance that I just could not go about my work and have had to return to you." Hearing this, the Holy Prophet ﷺ prayed for him.

'It so happened that the Holy Prophet ﷺ did not happen to see him for a few days and so he asked the companions about him. They replied: "We too have not seen him for the past few days." The Holy Prophet ﷺ and the companions decided to visit him at his shop at the marketplace. When they reached the shop they noticed that there was no one in his shop. Upon making enquiries, the neighbours informed him: "O Prophet of Allah! That man has died. He was a very good, truthful, and trustworthy person, except for one bad trait in him."

'The Holy Prophet ﷺ asked: "And what was that?"

'They replied: "He had a roving eye for women and would not refrain himself from non-*mahram* ladies, at times even following them around."

'The Holy Prophet ﷺ said: "Allah shall forgive him! He had such immense love for me that even if he had committed a greater sin Allah would have forgiven him.""[1]

4 – The Jewish youth

Once, Salmān Fārsī requested the Commander of the Faithful to manifest for him one of the secrets of the unseen. The Commander of the Faithful directed him to go to the grave of a Jewish youth.

As instructed by the Commander of the Faithful, Salmān proceeded to the cemetery. There, he witnessed the *barzakh* of the youth, who had possessed the love of the Commander of the Faithful whilst alive in this world. Salmān saw the youth seated inside a palace which was in an extremely beautiful and attractive locale. Salmān asked him: 'What act of worship made you reach this position and status despite the fact that you died upon the Jewish faith?'

The youth replied: 'I was not a Muslim, but I used to love the Commander of the Faithful. It was this sincere love towards him that graced me with this status in *barzakh*.'[2]

---

[1] *Namūnah-i Maʿārif*, vol. 4, p. 135; *Rawḍat al-Kāfī*, p. 77.

[2] *Riyāḍ al-Muḥibbīn*, p. 133.

5 – A true friend

Muslim was a youth from the city of Madain, who, during the governorship of Ḥudhayfah ibn Yamān, had become friends with him.

Because of Ḥudhayfah, Muslim had become one of the most sincere followers of Commander of the Faithful. In the Battle of Jamal, the Commander of the Faithful, in order to complete his argument over the people of Basra and the army of ʿĀʾishah, held up the Holy Qurʾan and announced: 'Who is it that would take this Qurʾan to the opposition and invite them for an arbitration under the rules of the Holy Qurʾan?'

The young Muslim took the Holy Qurʾan from the Imam and proceeded towards the battlefield. As he set out, the Imam remarked: 'This young man is one whose heart Allah has filled with faith and guidance. I love him immensely due to the faith he possesses. However, he shall be killed and the army that will kill him shall never taste salvation.'

Muslim, holding up the Holy Qurʾan, invited the people of Basra and the army of ʿĀʾishah towards an arbitration governed by the rules of the Holy Qurʾan, but they responded by cutting his right hand. He transferred the Holy Qurʾan to his left hand, but they severed it. He then held the Qurʾan between his cut hands and his chest as blood began to flow over it. At this point, the soldiers rushed upon him and cut him into pieces.[1]

84. Death

Allah, the Wise, has said:

$$كُلُّ نَفْسٍ ذَائِقَةُ الْمَوْتِ$$

Every soul shall taste death. (3:185)

The Holy Prophet said:

$$كَفَى بِالْمَوْتِ وَاعِظًا$$

Death suffices as a preacher.

---

[1] *Shāgirdān-i Maktab-i Aʾimmah*, vol. 3, p. 361; *Tuḥfat al-Aḥbāb*, p. 360.

Short explanation

Remembrance of death kills the corrupt desires of the soul, severs the roots of heedlessness, extinguishes the fire of greed, and makes the world appear trivial in one's eyes.

Death is the last of the stages of this world and the first of the stages of the Hereafter. Bravo to the person who continuously improves his stages of this world and leaves it in the best stage, and whose entry into death is honourable.

The sincere servants of Allah covet death while the sinning ones loathe it. And while man considers death to be far away, it is, in fact, very near to him. Man tends to be fond of pleasures and does not like to be severed from the comforts of this world. Consequently, death, which means abandoning this world, is regarded by many as the most difficult of moments for them.[1]

1 – The old man of 150 years

Sa'dī says:

'Once, as I was engaged in debates and discussions with some scholars in the main mosque of Damascus, a young man entered the mosque and enquired: "Is there anyone from amongst you who speaks Persian?" Those present pointed towards me, whereupon the young man said: "An old man aged 150 years is on the verge of death. He speaks Persian and so we are unable to comprehend what he is saying. It appears that he might be intending to state his last will. If you could take the trouble of coming to him, you would have done him a favour and we could find out what his will is."

'I got up, and together with the young man proceeded to see the old man. Reaching there, I observed that he was saying: "I have been enjoying for a few moments the things I like, but alas, these moments have now been hindered. Alas! In this journey of my life it suffices to know that I have hardly enjoyed a few moments and consumed a few morsels when the order to depart has reached me."

---

[1] *Tadhkirat al-Ḥaqā'iq*, p. 83.

'Yes! Despite having lived for 150 years, he was ruefully stating: "I have hardly lived in this world". When I had translated his words into Arabic for the others they were left amazed over the fact that despite the longevity of his life, the old man was still harbouring regrets over his life coming to an end. I turned to the old man and said: "How do you feel?"

'He replied: "What can I say when I see my life about to separate from me?"

'I said to him: "Do not think about death; focus your attention upon recovery. Greek philosophers have stated: 'However good one's health may be, never believe in immortality; and however dangerous an illness may appear, it is never a definitive indication of death.' If you prefer, I can bring a doctor to treat you."

'Opening his eyes he gave out a laugh and said: "An intelligent doctor, when witnessing a patient in a critical state, clasps his hands in regret, for when the health of a person takes a turn for the worse, neither prayers nor treatment yield any benefit."'[1]

2 – Conversation at the time of death

When Bilāl, the muezzin of the Holy Prophet, was on the verge of dying, his wife who was beside him cried out: 'O woe that I am being subjected to such a trial!'

Hearing this, Bilāl said: 'Rather, this is an occasion of happiness and celebration, for what do you know how enjoyable death is?'

His wife wept: 'The moment of separation has arrived!'

Bilāl said: 'Rather, the time for communion has arrived.'

The wife cried: 'Tonight you shall go to the house of the desolate ones.'

Bilāl said: 'Rather, my soul shall return to its place of origin.'

The wife asked: 'After this where will I set my eyes upon you?'

Bilāl replied: 'In the company of the special servants of Allah.'

His wife said: 'With your passing away our house and family shall turn into ruins.'

---

[1] *Ḥikāyat-hā-yi Gulistān*, p. 229.

Bilāl explained: 'This body is similar to clouds; they gather together only to separate from each other a short while later.'[1]

3 – The Angel of Death

The Holy Prophet said:

'On the night of *mi'rāj*, as Allah journeyed me through the skies, I witnessed an angel holding in his hand a tablet made of light. He was so intently focused on the tablet that he neither looked to the left nor to the right, and, like a man drowned in sorrow, appeared totally immersed in his task. "Who is this angel?" I asked Jibrīl.

'"This is 'Izrā'īl, the Angel of Death, who is responsible for the seizing of the souls," he replied.

'I said to Jibrīl: "Take me to him so that I may speak to him." When Jibrīl took me to the angel, I said to him: "O angel! Do you seize the soul every person that has died or is about to die?"

'He replied: "Yes."

'"Do you present yourself before them?" I enquired further.

'He replied: "Yes, I do. Allah has placed the entire universe under my control like coins placed in the palm of a person who is able to twist and turn the coin as and how he pleases. There is no house upon the earth except that I visit it five times a day. When I hear them wailing and grieving over their deceased, I tell them: 'Do not weep for I shall keep coming to your house till I take away every single one of you from this world.'"[2]

4 – 'Allāmah Majlisī

Sayyid Ni'mat Allāh Jazā'irī, a close student of 'Allāmah Majlisī, relates:

'I had entered into an agreement with my teacher, 'Allāmah Majlisī, that whoever from amongst us dies earlier would appear in the dreams of the other to inform him of some of the events experienced by him. It so happened that my teacher passed away before me. A week later, when the

---

[1] *Dāstān-hā-yi Mathnawī*, vol. 2, p. 127.

[2] *'Ālam-i Barzakh*, p. 38; *Biḥār al-Anwār*, vol. 6, p. 141.

commemoration ceremonies had concluded, I remembered the agreement that I had with him and so I went to his grave. There, reciting the Qur'an and weeping, I fell into a sleep. In my dreams I saw my teacher appearing to come out from the grave dressed in beautiful clothes. I held his thumb and said to him: "In fulfilment of your promise, relate to me the events leading up to and after your death."

'He said: "When I fell ill and the illness had reached a level that I could no longer bear, I prayed: 'O Allah! I am unable to bear this anymore. By Your mercy, relieve me from this predicament.' I was still supplicating when I observed a dignified entity [an angel] arrive and sit next to me beside my legs, enquiring about my health. I informed him of my grievance whereupon that angel placed his hand upon my toes and asked: 'Do you feel better?' The pain in my toes had immediately subsided and so I replied in the affirmative at which, very gradually, he began moving his hand up my body towards my chest. As his hand moved over my body, the pain in those regions would subside, till his hand reached my chest, at which point my body fell to the ground. My soul, from a corner, was now witnessing my body. My relatives, friends, and neighbours arrived and began weeping and wailing over my body. My soul kept saying to them: 'Why do you weep? I am in a good state and not in any difficulty.' But not one person would hear me.

'"A short while later they took my body, performed the *ghusl*, covered it with a shroud, and placed it within the grave. At this point of time, suddenly, I heard a voice addressing me, saying: 'O My servant Muḥammad Bāqir! What have you prepared for this day?' I kept listing out my prayers, fasts, preaching, the books that I had authored, etc., but none of these was accepted. At this point I recalled one act – once, a believer was being beaten on the road because he was unable to repay his debts. I had intervened and paid his debts, and in the process I saved him from further beatings at the hands of the people. I presented this act, and Allah, because of this sincere act, accepted all the other acts of mine and granted me entry into paradise [of *barzakh*]."[1]

5 – Mālik Ashtar

When the Commander of the Faithful appointed Mālik Ashtar as the governor of Egypt, Muʿāwiyah was profoundly disturbed. He was worried that if Mālik Ashtar were to reach Egypt, things would become very difficult for the people of Shām, and so he ordered some people to poison and kill him while he was on his way to Egypt from Kufa. Muʿāwiyah had Mālik poisoned by means of a drink made from honey, and eventually Mālik departed from this world.

Muʿāwiyah, upon learning of the death of Mālik, remarked: "ʿAlī possessed two arms,[2] one of which was severed in the Battle of Ṣiffīn [i.e. ʿAmmār Yāsir], and the other, today [i.e. Mālik Ashtar].'

When the news of the martyrdom of Mālik reached Imam ʿAlī ☙, he said: '*Innā lillāhi wa innā ilayhi rājiʿūn*. The death of Mālik is one of the painful incidents of history.'

After Mālik's death, when a group of people came to visit the Imam, they observed him in a state of immense regret, rubbing one hand upon the other and saying: 'O Mālik! By Allah, your death has left dejected a large group, and delighted a large group [i.e. the people of Shām]. Those who desire to weep ought to weep over people such as Mālik. Can there ever be another Mālik?'[3]

85. The Oppressed

Allah, the Wise, has said:

$$\text{وَمَنْ قُتِلَ مَظْلُومًا فَقَدْ جَعَلْنَا لِوَلِيِّهِ سُلْطَانًا}$$

And whoever is killed wrongfully, We have certainly given his heir an

---

[1] *Muntakhab al-Tawārīkh*, p. 752.

[2] Or: Two individuals were the right hand of Imam ʿAlī ☙.

[3] *Shāgirdān-i Maktab-i Aʾimmah*, vol. 3, p. 196; *Sharḥ Nahj al-Balāghah* of Ibn Abī al-Ḥadīd, vol. 6, p. 76.

authority. (17:33)

Imam 'Alī ﷺ said:

يَوْمُ الْمَظْلُومِ عَلَى الظَّالِمِ أَشَدُّ مِنْ يَوْمِ الظَّالِمِ عَلَى الْمَظْلُومِ

The day when the oppressed has an upper hand over the oppressor will be more severe than when the oppressor had [the upper hand] over the oppressed.[1]

Short explanation

Those who defend the rights of the oppressed against the oppressors shall be the ones who will be in the company of the Holy Prophet in paradise.[2]

Since an oppressed person lacks wealth, strength, and power, assisting such a person is regarded as an act of justice. An hour of assisting an oppressed person is more virtuous than a month spent in fasting and observing the *i'tikāf* within the precincts of Masjid al-Ḥarām.

Allah, upon hearing the helpless wailing and the supplication for assistance of an oppressed person, hastens to assist him, as there is no wailing in the world that is more heart-rending than that of a person being oppressed.

1 – Khwarazm Shāh

After Khwarazm Shāh fought and lost against the Mongol army, he initially went to Iraq and then to Nishapur, where he began to busy himself in acts of fun and pleasure. During this period, there were certain people that were being oppressed for the past two years but had no one to turn to as there was no one willing to solve their problems. Desperate, these people collectively approached the minister in the sultan's court and pleaded: 'By Allah! Plan out a solution for us!'

The minister of Khwarazm Shāh replied: 'I am unable to help you with your problems now as the sultan has ordered me to supervise the beautification of a bevy of female singers.'

---

[1] *Nahj al-Balāghah* of Fayḍ al-Islām, p. 1193.

[2] *Tafsīr Mu'īn*, p. 271. This is a hadith from the Holy Prophet.

A few days later, news reached Khwarazm Shāh that Sunta Bahādur, with an army of 30,000 soldiers, was on his way to attack them. He fled to Iraq, but the Mongol army followed him. Khwarazm Shāh was forced to flee to Rey and from there to Mazandaran and finally Gorgan, where he hid his family and wealth in a fortress, and himself sought refuge on an island.

Sunta Bahādur laid siege to the fortress, eventually forcing those inside to surrender. He then ordered Khwarazm Shāh's sons to be killed, his womenfolk to be gifted to his generals, and his mother to be seated on a saddle-less horse and made to weep in front of the entire army. Khwarazm Shāh, upon hearing of this, was overcome with such intense grief that he died three days later.[1]

2 – O Allah! Are You asleep?

Once, Fir'awn issued a command for the construction of a towering palace. His generals started gathering all the men and women they could for this task, not sparing even pregnant women. Amongst the pregnant ladies was a young woman who was forced to carry heavy rock-slabs for the construction, since everyone was under the control of these barbaric supervisors. If she were to refrain from carrying the rocks, she would be killed by the lashing of the supervisors. Faced with this scenario, she continued carrying the heavy rocks.

One day, all of a sudden, she fell intensely ill and suffered a miscarriage. In that dire situation, from the depths of her grieving heart, whilst weeping, she beseeched: 'O Allah! Are You asleep? Do You not witness what these evil people are doing to us?'

Hardly had a few months passed since this incident when the same young woman, seated near the river Nile, suddenly saw the dead body of Fir'awn floating in the water before her eyes and heard a voice address her, saying: 'Do take note, O lady! We are not asleep; rather, We lie in ambush of those who oppress.'[2]

---

[1] *Pand-i Tārīkh*, vol. 3, p. 170; *Tārīkh Ṭabarī*, p. 50.

[2] *Ḥikāyat-hā-yi Shanīdanī*, vol. 3, p. 52.

3 – The grave of Imam al-Ḥusayn 🕮, the oppressed

Mutawakkil, the Abbasid caliph, ruled for fourteen years and was one of the vilest of all the Abbasid caliphs. His hatred towards the children of Abū Ṭālib was of such intensity that not only would it never allow him to stop harassing and oppressing them, but also exhorted him to denigrate the grave of Imam al-Ḥusayn 🕮. He converted the entire land of Karbala into an agricultural region and placed cows around the grave to plough and furrow the land.

When, upon the orders of Mutawakkil, a Jew by the name of Dizaj excavated the holy grave, he found the mat that had been brought by the tribe of Banī Asad when they had arrived to bury the Imam, completely intact with the holy body of the Imam lying on top of it. However, he wrote a letter to Mutawakkil, stating: 'I, as per your orders, excavated the grave but I did not see anything inside it.'

Nevertheless, Dizaj had brought along with him a few Jewish individuals whom he ordered to plough the land around the grave, flow water over it, and guard the area around it with strict instructions to arrest and punish anyone who came there with the intention of performing the *ziyārah* of Imam al-Ḥusayn 🕮.

Aḥmad ibn al-Juʿd al-Washā states:

'The reason for Mutawakkil's efforts to erase all signs of the holy grave was that prior to his becoming the caliph, there was a female singer who used to regularly send him a slave-girl who would sing for him and keep him entertained. One day, after having become the caliph and while in a state of inebriety, he sent a message to the female singer to send him the slave-girl so that he could be entertained. However, he was informed: "Both of them have gone on a journey." It was the month of Shaʿbān and they had gone to Karbala for *ziyārah*.'

Returning from her trip, she arranged for the slave-girl to go to Mutawakkil. When the slave-girl arrived before Mutawakkil, he questioned her: 'Where had you travelled?'

She replied: 'I had gone for pilgrimage along with my mistress.'

'You had gone for hajj in the month of Sha'bān?' asked Mutawakkil in astonishment.

'In fact, we had gone to visit the grave of Imam al-Ḥusayn 🕮,' she explained.

Hearing this he flew into a rage and ordered the mistress to be imprisoned, all her wealth to be confiscated, and the grave of Imam al-Ḥusayn 🕮 and every structure in Karbala to be destroyed.[1]

4 – O Allah! You are awake!

One night, one of the sultans of the Ghaznavid dynasty, unable to sleep, came out of his palace and began to roam in the streets. Having reached the door of a mosque, he saw a person in prostration, saying: 'O Lord! The sultan has shut the doors of help upon those who are being oppressed, but You are awake, so help me!'

The sultan came forward and asked: 'What is your problem?'

The person recognised the sultan and complained: 'One of your officials close to you comes to my house and sleeps with my wife, but I do not have the means to stop him.'

The sultan said to him: 'The next time this individual comes to your house, inform me.' He also instructed the guards of his palace: 'Whenever this person comes to meet me, do not stop him.'

The following night, as the officer of the sultan came to the house and slept with the wife, the oppressed person informed the sultan. The sultan came to the house, ordered the lanterns in the house to be extinguished, unsheathed his sword, and killed the immoral official. He then asked for the lanterns to be turned on and said: 'Bring me some food as I am hungry.'

The sultan, when asked for the reason for extinguishing the lanterns, replied: 'I was worried that the individual might be my son and if I saw him I might have been unable to kill him. I thank Allah that the person did not turn out to be my son. Since last night, out of distress at your state, I have been unable to eat any food. But now, having delivered you from the

---

[1] *Tatimmat al-Muntahā*, pp. 238-241.

oppression, I felt the desire to eat.'[1]

5 – The young Muḥammad and Ibrāhīm

Subsequent to the martyrdom of Imam al-Ḥusayn 🕮, the two young sons of Muslim ibn ʿAqīl were captured and sent to ʿUbayd Allāh ibn Ziyād, who threw them into prison and instructed the prison officer to be strict with them. After a year had passed, they revealed their identity to the old prison officer who, in the darkness of the night, freed them and allowed them to escape. They travelled some distance until they reached a village and sought shelter in a house. The lady of the house, upon realising their relationship to the Holy Prophet, took them in.

When ʿUbayd Allāh was informed of their escape from prison, he announced: 'Whoever brings me the head of one of them, I shall reward him with 1000 dirhams, and 2000 for both their heads.'

Coincidentally, the lady's son-in-law, Ḥārith, came to the house at midnight. He went to sleep, only to be woken by the heavy breathing of the two young boys. He went to the room where the boys were located, and, after identifying them, tied them up with a rope and waited for morning to dawn.

The following morning Ḥārith ordered his slave: 'Take these two boys to the banks of the river Euphrates and sever their heads.' However, the slave refused to carry out the order and so he himself brought the boys to the banks of the river to kill them.

Realising his intentions, they pleaded: 'Do not kill us for we belong to the family of the Holy Prophet; sell us in the market and make use of the money, or hand us over to ʿUbayd Allāh ibn Ziyād.' When he refused to relent, they pleaded: 'In that case at least allow us to offer our prayers.' He agreed.

When they had finished their prayers, he said to them: 'Allah has not placed mercy in my heart. I desire to get into the good books of ʿUbayd Allāh by killing you as he would then be pleased with me.'

---

[1] *Dāstān-hā Wa Pand-hā*, vol. 2, p. 160

He then severed the head of the elder brother, whereupon the younger brother smeared his face with his brother's blood and kept saying: 'I wish to meet the Holy Prophet in this state.' The man then proceeded to sever the head of the younger brother, and threw their bodies into the Euphrates and brought the two heads before 'Ubayd Allāh, with the intention of receiving the reward from him.[1]

86. The Guile Of Allah

Allah, the Wise, has said:

$$وَلَا يَحِيقُ الْمَكْرُ السَّيِّئُ إِلَّا بِأَهْلِهِ$$

And evil schemes beset only their authors. (35:43)

The Holy Prophet said:

$$لَيْسَ مِنَّا مَنْ مَاكَرَ مُسْلِمًا$$

One who deceives another Muslim is not from us.[2]

Short explanation

One of the vile traits is the trait of deception, which is employed by individuals that do not possess faith, in order to achieve their objectives.

Not utilising one's intelligence in the correct manner to achieve one's goals, and instead resorting to the use of surreptitious and clandestine means which involve hurting and deceiving others, is the conduct of deceitful individuals.

A deceitful individual will not present himself as an enemy; rather, by manifesting a façade of friendship and religiosity and other similar ways, he would seek to deceive individuals after having secured their trust.[3]

1 – Qur'an upon the spears

In the Battle of Ṣiffīn, as the forces of Muʿāwiyah were on the verge of

---

[1] *Muntahā al-Aʿmāl*, vol. 1, p. 317.

[2] *Jāmiʿ al-Saʿādāt*, vol. 1, p. 203.

[3] *Iḥyāʾ al-Qulūb*, p. 30.

being decimated and victory was within reach of Imam ʿAlī ﷺ, Muʿāwiyah said to ʿAmr ibn ʿĀṣ: 'We need to come up with some deception otherwise the forces of ʿAlī shall kill us all.'

ʿAmr ibn ʿĀṣ suggested: 'Let's raise copies of the Holy Qur'an upon the spears and announce that the Qur'an should serve as the arbitrator between us. If all of them accept, the battle will stop; and if only a segment of the forces of ʿAlī accept, a disagreement would erupt amongst his entire army.'

They implemented this tactic as a result of which the erstwhile fervour of battle that had existed within the forces of Imam ʿAlī ﷺ died down. Imam ʿAlī ﷺ called out to them: 'O servants of Allah! Remain steadfast upon the truth. I know these people very well; they are not the type who would adhere to the religion or the Qur'an. The only reason they have resorted to the Qur'an is because you have gained dominance over them in this battle.'

In response, the soldiers of Imam ʿAlī ﷺ argued: 'Now that they have resorted to the book of Allah, it is impossible for us to disregard their offer.' A group from amongst them said to him: 'They are inviting you towards the book of Allah, so accept their offer, otherwise we shall regard you as our enemy and do the same thing with you as we did with ʿUthmān ibn ʿAffān.'

They put such intense pressure upon the Imam that he was forced to order Mālik Ashtar to stop the battle; thus succeeded ʿAmr ibn ʿĀṣ in his deception.[1]

2 – The minister's answer

Countries that are super powers and colonial in nature are always on the lookout to destroy small nations, utilising various guiles and deceits under the veneer of friendship to achieve their objectives.

When Mīrzā Muḥammad Taqī Khān Amīr Kabīr was the chief minister of Nāṣir al-Dīn Qajar, one of the teachers of the Dār al-Funūn school

---

[1] *Jawāmiʿ al-Ḥikāyāt*, p. 99.

by the name of Nadhr Agha used to say: 'Whenever Amīr Kabīr would receive envoys of foreign countries, he would summon me to translate the discussions. During one of his meetings with the envoy of Russia, an interesting incident took place. The Russian minister made a certain inappropriate request regarding the boundaries that existed between Iran and Russia, which I translated for Amīr Kabīr. Amīr Kabīr said to me: "Ask him if he has ever eaten aubergine with yoghurt?"

'"No," replied the Russian minister in astonishment, when I translated the sentence for him.

'Hearing the reply, Amīr Kabīr said: "Tell the Russian minister that at home I have a wife by the name of Fāṭimah, who makes wonderful food of yoghurt and aubergine. Incidentally, she has cooked some today; I shall send some over for you so that you may see how wonderful it tastes!"

'The Russian minister said to me: "Say to him: 'Thank you, but what do you have to say about the issue of the boundaries?'"

'In response, Amīr Kabīr said to me to tell the Russian minister: "O the yoghurt and the aubergine! O my love Fāṭimah!" And in this manner Amīr Kabīr replied to the beguiling talks of the Russian minister, who, in a state of total disappointment, got up and left.'[1]

3 – Busr ibn Abī Arṭa'ah

In the Battle of Ṣiffīn, Busr ibn Abī Arṭa'ah found himself face to face in battle with the Commander of the Faithful. This was at a time when Imam had entered the battlefield to fight and had called out to Mu'āwiyah, saying: 'How many people do we allow to be killed, and for how long? Come forth so that you and I fight with each other so that the battle can conclude.'

Mu'āwiyah replied evasively: 'The number of people from Shām that you have killed in the battle suffices for me. I do not wish to come and fight you.'

At this point Busr contemplated fighting the Imam, thinking: 'If I

---

[1] *Ḥikāyat-hā-yi Shanīdanī*, vol. 2, p. 172; *Dastān-hā Az Zindagī-yi Amīr Kabīr*, p. 139.

am able to somehow kill 'Alī, I shall be looked upon with great honour amongst the Arabs.'

He consulted his slave, Lāḥiq, who said: 'Embark on this idea only if you are confident of yourself, for you do realise that 'Alī is a warrior who has no equal. Be aware that death flows from the spear and sword of 'Alī.'

'Is there anything else to life other than death? Man must die; either by a natural death or by being killed,' Busr said as he proceeded towards the battlefield. Entering it, he did not recite any boastful poetry but chose to remain silent so that the Imam would not recognise him.

The very first attack of the Imam felled Busr from atop his horse. At that point, bringing deception into play, he raised his legs and exposed his genitals. Seeing this, Imam immediately turned his face away, whereupon Busr got up and fled towards the safety of his camp leaving behind his battle helmet.

Mu'āwiyah burst out laughing as he witnessed the antics of Busr and said: 'A deception of this kind is perfectly fine since such an incident had also taken place with 'Amr ibn 'Āṣ.'

Hearing this, a young soldier from Kufa shouted out: 'Do you not feel embarrassed that 'Amr ibn 'Āṣ taught you this deception: that at a time of danger in a battle you expose your genitals?!'[1]

4 – The deception of Zarqā'

When Lady Āminah 🕮, the mother of the Holy Prophet, conceived him in her womb, the prophecies of the soothsayers began to go haywire.

Saṭīḥ, a prominent soothsayer from the tribe of Ghasān, wrote a letter to Zarqā' Yamāmah, another soothsayer, stating that every guile and deception would need to be employed if they were to put an end to the Holy Prophet.

The beautician of Lady Āminah 🕮, a lady by the name of Taknā, was known to Zarqā'. One day, Zarqā' happened to meet her and noticed that she look distressed, and therefore enquired: 'Why do you appear distressed?'

---

[1] *Dastān-hā-yi Zindagī-yi 'Alī* 🕮, p. 74; *Biḥār al-Anwār*, vol. 8, p. 479.

She complained of the birth of the child that had caused the idols to break and the soothsayers to become humiliated. Hearing this, Zarqā' showed Taknā a sac containing gold coins and told her that it could become hers if she helped Zarqā' execute a plan. The enticement worked and Taknā agreed. It was decided that the next time Taknā would go to beautify Lady Āminah ☸, in the course of her task she would stab her with a poisoned dagger, causing both the mother and the child to die.

On the appointed day, Taknā arrived and set about her task of beautifying Lady Āminah ☸. In the midst of her work, Taknā removed the poisoned dagger to stab Lady Āminah ☸ when a hand from the unseen hit Taknā, who fell to the ground. Seeing this, Lady Āminah ☸ screamed out and soon all the ladies of Banī Hāshim had gathered around them, seeking to know what had happened. When Lady Āminah ☸ described to them what had happened they turned to Taknā and asked: 'What made you embark on such an act?'

'I did this upon the orders of Zarqā',' she confessed.

Shortly after this incident Taknā died, while Zarqā' was forced to return to her place of origin, Yamāmah. And in this manner her deception failed to cause any harm to Lady Āminah ☸ or the child in her womb.[1]

5 – 'Amr ibn 'Āṣ

'Amr ibn 'Āṣ was a shrewd and politically motivated individual who has been attributed with perpetrating one of the greatest acts of deception in history.

Ja'far Ṭayyār, the brother of the Commander of the Faithful, left for Ethiopia together with a group of people upon the orders of the Holy Prophet. When 'Amr ibn 'Āṣ came to know of this he clandestinely left for Ethiopia to meet the Ethiopian king, Najjāshī. Upon meeting him he said: 'I have seen an individual leaving your presence who has been sent by an enemy of ours. Allow me to kill him so that I may exact my revenge on him as these people have greatly humiliated our elders.' Hearing this, Najjāshī

---

[1] *Khazīnat al-Jawāhir*, p. 48; *Biḥār al-Anwār*, vol. 6.

was greatly infuriated and, in anger, landed a blow upon the face of ʿAmr ibn ʿĀṣ!

During the caliphate of Abū Bakr, given the command of a huge army, he left for Syria. During the time of ʿUmar, for a brief period, he was given the authority to rule over Palestine, subsequently proceeding towards Egypt which he eventually conquered and over which he became the ruler.

He continued to rule over Egypt for four years after the death of ʿUmar until ʿUthmān dismissed him, causing their relationship to turn sour. He would not miss an opportunity to criticise ʿUthmān, such that once, when ʿUthmān was on the pulpit, ʿAmr ibn ʿĀṣ said to him: 'Things are really bad for you. Due to your deviation the entire *ummah* is getting deviated. Either act justly or abdicate your position.'

At times he would go to the Commander of the Faithful with the intention of instigating him to rise up against ʿUthmān, whilst at other times this cunning individual would go to Ṭalḥah and Zubayr, exhorting them to kill him. He even ended up divorcing his wife who happened to be the maternal cousin of ʿUthmān.

From the time ʿUthmān was killed, most of the deceptions and trickeries, such as raising the copies of the Qurʾan upon the spears in the Battle of Ṣiffīn, reciting the Friday prayer on a Wednesday, slaughtering a gourd in a manner similar to a sheep, etc., emanated from this cunning person.

And because of Muʿāwiyah, the foolish people of Syria acted on the deceptions of ʿAmr ibn ʿĀṣ with such absolute subservience and meekness that when they heard the Commander of the Faithful was killed in the *miḥrāb* of the mosque, due to the negative propaganda of ʿAmr ibn ʿĀṣ, they asked: 'But did ʿAlī even pray?'[1]

87. A Believer

Allah, the Wise, has said:

$$\text{وَاللهُ وَلِيُّ الْمُؤْمِنِينَ}$$

---

[1] *Payghambar Wa Yārān*, vol. 5, pp. 54-72.

And Allah is the guardian of the faithful. (3:68)

The Holy Prophet said:

$$\text{إِنَّ الْمُؤْمِنَ أَعَزُّ مِنَ الْجَبَلِ}$$

A believer is tougher than a mountain.[1]

Short explanation

A believer can be so tough and reach such a lofty spiritual status that he becomes more recognisable to the inhabitants of the skies than to those living on the earth, more elevated in rank than the Ka'bah, and one whom Allah loves more dearly than anyone else.

Amongst the numerous traits that a believer possesses, some are: he conceals his sorrows within his heart while his face always manifests happiness, he exhibits great forbearance, he is not lazy and constantly keeps himself engrossed in work, he is patient in times of calamities and thankful when in ease, he remains contented with the sustenance given to him by Allah, and people are never troubled by him. While his tongue remains protected from gaffes, his hands are embellished with generosity, and his eyes always desirous of the bounties of Allah.

1 – A complete believer

Once, the Commander of the Faithful happened to pass by some people who were seated in a group. He observed that they were wearing white and expensive clothing, laughing excessively, and ridiculing everyone that passed their way.

The Imam then passed by another group of people who had bodies that were lean and thin, their skins pale in colour, and who were humble in their speech.

The Imam, in a state of amazement, reached the Holy Prophet and related the states of the two groups of people he had encountered – both of whom claimed to be believers – and sought to know the traits of a believer. The Holy Prophet remained silent for some time and then explained: 'A

---

[1] *Jāmi' al-Sa'ādāt*, vol. 1, p. 260.

believer ought to possess certain traits; if he lacks even one of them, his faith is incomplete: he should pray in congregation, pay out the zakat at its appropriate time, assist the poor, express affection for the orphans, wear clean clothes, spend time in worship of Allah, be truthful, fulfil what he has promised, not be treacherous with respect to trusts placed with him, be a humble devotee in the night and a courageous lion during the day.'[1]

2 – A believer is never bitten twice

In the Battle of Badr, which took place in the second year after migration, an enemy soldier by the name of Abū ʿAzzah Jumaḥī, was captured by the Muslim forces. When he was taken to Medina and brought before the Holy Prophet, weeping and wailing he beseeched: 'I am a person with a family. Do me a favour by setting me free.'

The Holy Prophet freed him on the condition that he would never participate in a battle against the Muslims again. However, on returning to Mecca, he began to boast to the disbelievers: 'I managed to fool Muḥammad as a result of which he freed me.'

The following year he was once again in the army that fought against the Muslims in the Battle of Uḥud. Seeing him in the battlefield, the Holy Prophet prayed that he should not escape from the battlefield. As fate would have it, in this battle he again ended up becoming a captive of the Muslim forces. Standing before the Holy Prophet he once again pleaded: 'I am a person with a family. Do me a favour by setting me free.'

In reply, the Holy Prophet said to him: 'Should I set you free so that you return to Mecca and tell the people there that you have fooled Muḥammad? A believer is never bitten from the same hole twice.'[2]

3 – Indifference towards a complete believer

Muḥammad ibn Sinān related:

'I was with Imam al-Riḍā ﷺ when he said to me: "O Muḥammad!

---

[1] *Shanīdanī-hā-yi Tārīkh*, p. 254; *al-Maḥajjah al-Bayḍāʾ*, vol. 4, p. 362.

[2] *Ḥikāyat-hā-yi Shanīdanī*, vol. 2, p. 96; *Mustadrak al-Wasāʾil*, vol. 2, p. 267.

During the time of Banī Isrāʾīl there lived four believers. One day, one of them went to the house of another not knowing that the other three believers happened to be in the house. When he knocked on the door and the slave opened the door, he enquired: 'Where is your master?' 'He is not at home,' lied the slave. Hearing this, the believer went away. The master, despite knowing that the slave had lied, remained quiet and indifferent to what had happened and did not consider it necessary to rebuke his slave. The other believers also did not get upset over the actions of the slave and instead continued with their conversation.

'"The following day, as the three believers were on their way to a garden belonging to one of them, the fourth believer came up to them and said: 'I would like to join you.' He began to accompany them but they did not apologise to him over the incident that had taken place the previous day. They had travelled some distance when they observed that a cloud, having positioned itself over their heads, was casting a shadow over them. Suddenly, they heard a voice call out: 'O fire! I am Jibrīl, who has been sent by Allah. Encompass the three within your embrace!' No sooner was this said when a flame of fire emanated from the cloud and encircled the three believers, killing them on the spot. The fourth believer, however, remained unscathed, although he was frightened and stunned over what had happened.

'"Returning to the city, he proceeded to meet the prophet of the time, Yūshaʿ ibn Nūn (the successor of Prophet Mūsā ﷺ) and narrated the entire incident. Prophet Yūshaʿ said to him: 'Do you not know that Allah was displeased with them and thus manifested His anger upon them for their behaviour towards you?'

'"'But what did they do to me?' the believer asked. Prophet Yūshaʿ related the entire incident to him. Hearing this, the believer said: 'I have forgiven them for what they had done.'

'"Prophet Yūshaʿ explained: 'Your forgiveness could have been beneficial had it come prior to the descent of punishment. It may, perhaps, benefit them hereon.'"¹

4 – Calamity is warded off because of a believer

Zakariyyā ibn Ādam was a close companion of the Imams and possessed such a lofty position in their eyes that once, during a journey from Medina to Mecca, he accompanied Imam al-Riḍā 🕮 and was seated with him on the Imam's horse.

Imam al-Riḍā 🕮 had stationed him as his representative in the city of Qum and had instructed the people to get their answers on religious issues from him. His presence in the city was said to be the reason the punishment of Allah did not descend upon the inhabitants of Qum. This is known by the fact that once, when Zakariyyā said to Imam al-Riḍā 🕮: 'I wish to leave the city of Qum and sever my association with it, for amongst the people there are numerous ignorant and foolish individuals who do acts that are bound to make Allah angry,' Imam al-Riḍā 🕮 advised him: 'Refrain from doing this, since Allah, by means of your presence, wards off the calamities from the people of Qum just as He warded them off from the people of Baghdad due to the presence of my father, Imam al-Kāẓim 🕮 there.'

After the death of Zakariyyā, Imam al-Jawād 🕮, in a letter to Muḥammad ibn Isḥāq, wrote: 'May Allah shower His mercy upon Zakariyyā ibn Ādam for he possessed profound cognisance of Allah, was patient and forbearing, always desirous of divine rewards, and adherent to acts that pleased Allah and His Messenger.'²

5 – The believer from Khorasan

Imam al-Bāqir 🕮 once asked a man who had come to Medina from Khorasan: 'How was your father when you left?'

The man replied: 'He was very well.'

The Imam said to him: 'Your father has passed away. This happened at

---

¹ *Uṣūl al-Kāfī*, vol. 2.

² *Shāgirdān-i Maktab-i A'immah*, vol. 2, p. 208; *Rijāl Kashshī*, vol. 2.

the time when, during your journey, you had reached the region of Jorjān.' The Imam then enquired further: 'How was your brother when you left?'

'He was in good health,' the man replied.

Imam al-Bāqir ﷺ said: 'On such a date and such a time your brother was murdered by his neighbour by the name of Ṣāliḥ.'

The man from Khorasan began to weep and recited: 'Innā lillāhi wa innā ilayhi rāji'ūn,' whereupon the Imam said to him: 'Be patient and do not grieve. Their abode is paradise, which is a much better place for them than this temporal world.'

The man then asked: 'O son of the Holy Prophet! When I was leaving to come to you I had left behind a son who was sick and in great pain and distress. Why have you not asked me about him?'

The Imam replied: 'Your son has recovered and his uncle has got him married to his daughter. By the time you meet him, Allah shall have graced him with a son. His name shall be 'Alī and he shall be from our Shi'as. However, your son is not our Shi'a, rather he is our enemy!'

Immensely distressed, the man from Khorasan asked: 'Is there any solution for this?'

The Imam replied: 'His enmity towards us is inherent to his disposition and this is how it shall remain.'

The narrator of this tradition, Abū Baṣīr, says: 'As the person left, I asked the Imam: "Who is this person?"

'The Imam replied: "He is from Khorasan – a believer and our Shi'a."'[1]

88. Guests

Allah, the Wise, has said:

$$\text{هَلْ أَتَاكَ حَدِيثُ ضَيْفِ إِبْرَاهِيمَ الْمُكْرَمِينَ}$$

Did you receive the story of Ibrāhīm's honoured guests? (51:24)

---

[1] *Muntahā al-A'māl,* vol. 2, p. 104.

The Holy Prophet said:

إِنَّ الضَّيْفَ إِذَا جَاءَ فَنَزَلَ بِالْقَوْمِ جَاءَ بِرِزْقِهِ مَعَهُ مِنَ السَّمَاءِ

Indeed, whenever a guest arrives at someone's place, he carries with himself his own sustenance from the sky.[1]

Short explanation

Hospitality is a trait of Allah such that all His creations – believers, disbelievers, idol-worshippers, cow-worshippers, etc. – benefit from His banquet. Great prophets such as Ibrāhīm 🕮, Ya'qūb 🕮, Lūṭ 🕮, and the Holy Prophet, have benefitted immensely from this banquet.

A guest, in reality, is a gift from Allah, because while he brings his own sustenance along with him, his arrival causes the sins of the host to be forgiven and the calamities of the house to be warded off.

On the Day of Judgement, the faces of these individuals would be so luminous that people would reckon them to be prophets; but, it would be said to them: 'This is a believer who used to love his guests and honour them. The only destination for him is paradise.'[2]

1 – Feeding a guest

There lived in Kerman a king who was extremely generous and hospitable. It was an established norm with him that any stranger that would enter the city would be entertained as his guest for three days.

When 'Aḍud al-Dawlah Daylamī attacked Kerman, a battle ensued between them. Every morning, as the sun rose, the king would battle against the forces of 'Aḍud al-Dawlah killing numerous soldiers, but as night would fall he would arrange to have some food sent to them.

'Aḍud al-Dawlah sent someone to him to ask: 'What kind of behaviour is this that you exhibit? You fight and kill the soldiers during the day but then feed them during the night!'

The king replied: 'Fighting a battle is a manifestation of manhood,

---

[1] *Jāmi' al-Sa'ādāt*, vol. 2, p. 151.

[2] *'Ilm-i Akhlāq-i Islāmī*, vol. 2, p. 205.

whereas extending hospitality is a manifestation of magnanimity. The forces of 'Aḍud al-Dawlah may be my enemies but are strangers here and hence my guests; it is contrary to the etiquettes of magnanimity to keep a guest hungry.'

Hearing this, 'Aḍud al-Dawlah remarked: 'To battle someone possessing such humanity and magnanimity is surely a mistake,' and proceeded to make peace with the king.[1]

2 – The people of Prophet Lūṭ 🕮

The people of Prophet Lūṭ 🕮 lived in a city that lay on a caravan route that led to Syria and Egypt. As caravans would pass by their city and the travellers would stop by for some rest, the people of the city would extend their hospitality towards them. Eventually, after adhering to this norm for numerous years, they grew tired of it and resorted to becoming stingy. It was this stinginess that caused them to fall prey to the abhorrent act of sodomy. Whenever a caravan would stop by their city they would indulge in acts of sodomy with them with a view to refrain them from stopping by their city again, thus obviating the need to extend hospitality towards them. All the men of the city became involved in this act save Prophet Lūṭ 🕮, who was a man of generosity and magnanimity, extending hospitality towards every person who would come to him.

He would warn his people of the punishment of Allah and would seek to alert every person coming to him as a guest of the evils of his people. Whenever a guest would come to him, the people would object, saying: 'Have we not asked you to refrain from entertaining guests? Should you choose to continue, we shall cause evil to your guests so that you are left humiliated before them.' Consequently, Prophet Lūṭ 🕮 resorted to hosting the guests secretly, as he did not have any relatives in that city.

When Jibrīl and a few other angels came to his house in the form of humans, his wife lit up a fire on the roof of their house. The people, witnessing this, came to the house of Prophet Lūṭ 🕮 and said to him: 'Did

---

[1] *Jāmi' al-Ḥikāyāt*, p. 216.

we not tell you to not host guests in your house?'

When they desired to engage in sodomy with the guests, the punishment descended upon their city and they were annihilated.[1]

3 – Respecting a guest

'Ubayd Allāh ibn 'Abbās, the first cousin of the Holy Prophet, was a person who used to repeatedly send food to his neighbours. He would spread his tablecloth by the side of the road for people to consume his food to their heart's content.

During one of his travels with his slave, they came upon an Arab Bedouin tent and so he said to his slave: 'Let us be the guests of this Arab tonight.'

Since 'Ubayd Allāh was very handsome and well-spoken, the Bedouin exhibited great deference towards him. He said to his wife: 'A respectable person has come to us as a guest. Do we have something to extend our hospitality to him tonight?'

'We do not possess anything except one sheep which is a source of milk for our infant daughter,' replied the wife.

The man declared: 'There appears to be no other option except to slaughter it.' Saying this, he picked up the knife to slaughter the sheep.

Observing this, the wife said: 'You wish to kill your child?'

'While it may come to this, we have no choice except to show respect to a guest,' the man said. He then recited a couplet, which meant: 'O lady! Do not awaken this girl, for if she wakes up she would cry and the knife would fall out of my hand.'

Eventually, they slaughtered the sheep and arranged food for the guest. Little known to them, 'Ubayd Allāh had heard their entire conversation. In the morning, 'Ubayd Allāh asked his slave: 'How much money do we have with us?'

'We have 500 coins left with us at the moment,' the slave replied.

'Ubayd Allāh said to him: 'Give all the money to this Arab.'

____

[1] *Ḥayāt al-Qulūb*, vol. 1, p. 152.

Incredulous, the slave asked: 'For a sheep that costs five coins you are willing to give him 500 coins?'

'Ubayd Allāh explained: 'Not only did he sacrifice for us all that he possessed, he also gave us preference over his own daughter!'[1]

4 – An informal hospitality

Ḥārith Aʿwar, one of the special companions of the Commander of the Faithful, once approached the Imam and politely requested: 'O Commander of the Faithful! I would like you to honour us by having a meal in our house.'

The Imam agreed, saying: 'I shall accept your invitation upon the condition[2] that you shall not inconvenience yourself or indulge in any extravagant formalities for the purpose of hosting me.'

When the Imam went to Ḥārith's house, Ḥārith brought forth a piece of plain bread for the Imam. As the Imam began eating the bread, Ḥārith revealed some dirhams that he had concealed in his clothes and said: 'If you permit me I can buy something other than bread for you with this money that I possess.'

In response, the Imam said: 'This bread is something that was present in your house [and did not require you to be inconvenienced], however, arranging something else would be tantamount to a formality, which I did not wish you to engage in as a condition for accepting your invitation.'[3]

5 – On the table of Imam al-Ḥasan

Once, an Arab who possessed a very ugly appearance, while sitting at the table of Imam al-Ḥasan, greedily consumed all the food available. Imam al-Ḥasan, whose generosity was well-known to all, appeared very

---

[1] *Payghambar Wa Yārān*, vol. 5, pp. 54-72; *Asad al-Ghābbah*, vol. 3, p. 341.

[2] Actually it was upon three conditions: 'Firstly, you shall place before me only that which is present in the house. Secondly, you shall not procure anything for me from outside the house. Thirdly, you shall not put your family to inconvenience [because of me].' *Khiṣāl*, vol. 1, p. 188.

[3] *Bā Mardūm Īn Gūnih Barkhūrd Kunīm*, p. 204; *Furūʿ al-Kāfī*, vol. 3, p. 261.

happy to see the person eating to his heart's content and asked him: 'Are you single or married?'

'I have a family,' he replied.

The Imam further enquired: 'How many children do you have?'

He said: 'I have eight daughters, and while I am better looking than them all, they are more voracious eaters than I.'

The Imam smiled and, gifting him 10,000 dirhams, said: 'This is for you, your wife, and your eight daughters.'[1]

89. Intention

Allah, the Wise, has said:

$$قُلْ كُلٌّ يَعْمَلُ عَلَى شَاكِلَتِهِ$$

Say: 'Everyone acts according to his character.' (17:84)

Imam 'Alī ﷺ said:

$$عِنْدَ فَسَادِ النِّيَّةِ تَرْتَفِعُ الْبَرَكَةُ$$

When the intention becomes corrupt, blessings get taken away.[2]

Short explanation

One who possesses sincere intentions shall possess a pure heart. This is because a heart can only remain safe from satanic thoughts and whisperings if the intention, in all actions, is sincerely for Allah.

The Holy Prophet has stated: 'The intention of a believer is superior to his action.' A person's actions are associated with his intentions and thus every individual shall be rewarded or punished based on his intentions. Of course, intentions can be of various levels, based on situations and circumstances.

A person who possesses sincere intentions, despite the demands of his desires, subjugates them before the lofty Lord.[3]

---

[1] *Laṭāʾif al-Ṭawāʾif,* p. 139.

[2] *Ghurar al-Ḥikam,* h. 6228.

[3] *Tadhkirat al-Ḥaqāʾiq,* p. 5.

1 – The companion of Prophet Mūsā ﷺ

It has been reported in the traditions that there was a person from the Banī Isrā'īl who used to be in the company of Prophet Mūsā ﷺ most of the time, learning jurisprudence and the Torah from him and then explaining that to others.

It so happened that for a long period of time Prophet Mūsā ﷺ did not see him. One day, Jibrīl was with Prophet Mūsā ﷺ when suddenly a monkey passed by in front of them. Jibrīl asked him: 'Do you recognise this monkey?'

'No,' Prophet Mūsā ﷺ replied.

Jibrīl said: 'This is the same person who used to learn the Torah from you. This shall be the inner, real form of this individual in the Hereafter.'

'How did he come to acquire this form?' Prophet Mūsā ﷺ asked in astonishment.

Jibrīl said: 'This is because his aim and intention of learning the Torah from you was so that people would look upon him as a great religious scholar. Since his intention lacked sincerity and was not for Allah, he shall appear in the Hereafter in the form of a monkey.'[1]

2 – Knowing the intention

When Imam Mūsā al-Kāẓim ﷺ was in Baghdad, one of the Shi'as said to him: 'I was passing through a field in Baghdad when I saw a group of people gathered there. When I queried as to why they had gathered there, I was told: "There is a person here, a non-Muslim, who can inform people of their intentions." I went to the person and found that he was able to do so, just as the people had said.'

Hearing this, the Imam said: 'Come, let us go to him for I have some work with him.' When the Imam reached the field, he took the non-Muslim to one side and asked: 'How did you manage to learn this?'

'By opposing the dictates of my soul,' he replied.

The Imam asked further: 'Do you, in every act, oppose the dictates of

---

[1] *Riwāyat-hā Wa Ḥikāyat-hā*, p. 129; *Dāstān-hā-yi Parākandih*, vol. 4, p. 138.

your soul?' When he had replied in the affirmative, the Imam said to him: 'I am presenting Islam to you; see if your soul accepts it.'

The man said: 'No, it is not accepting it.'

The Imam now said decisively: 'In which case you ought to oppose this dictate of your soul and accept Islam.'

He accepted Islam and became one of the followers of the Imam. However, he was now unable to inform the people about the intentions in their minds. Coming to the Imam, he complained: 'When I was a disbeliever I was able to inform the people of their intentions. However, now that I have become a Muslim I am unable to do so, whereas I should now be able to inform them better about their intentions.'

The Imam explained: 'The reward that you were being given in this world due to your control over your soul, now that you have become a Muslim, is being collected to be given to you in the Hereafter.'[1]

3 – The king's intention

Once, Qubbad, the father of Anoushirwan, went hunting. Chasing an animal, he got separated from his soldiers and soon found himself alone. Thirsty, he looked around and observed a tent in the distance and so moved towards it. Reaching the tent, he called out: 'Would you appreciate a guest?' An old woman came forth, welcomed him, and then proceeded to lay out some food for him. After the meal, he rested for some time. When he woke up he realised it was almost dark and so decided to stay there for the night.

At nightfall, the cattle of the lady had returned from their grazing and so she asked her twelve year old daughter to milk the cows and take some milk for the guest.

The cows gave a lot of milk; when Qubbad observed this, a thought crossed his mind. These people were his subjects living in the wilderness; it would be good idea to pass a law that once a week such individuals should bring milk for the king; this way, the treasury would benefit from an increased revenue. He made up his mind that once back in his capital,

---

[1] *Khazīnat al-Jawāhir*, p. 388.

he would promulgate the new law.

The following morning the lady woke the daughter to milk the cows. The daughter got up, but as she started to milk them she realised that unlike before, the cows were not giving milk. She called out to her mother, saying: 'O mother! The king has planned something bad. Arise and say your prayers.'

The old lady started praying; when Qubbad witnessed this, he asked her the reason for her prayers. She related the incident of the cows not yielding any milk and then explained: 'When a king intends something bad, blessings and blessedness go away from the lands.'

Qubbad remarked: 'You speak the truth. I had made a bad intention, but I now turn away from it.'

Hearing this, the daughter went back to milk the cows who were now yielding milk as before.[1]

4 – Shaqīq Balkhī[2]

Shaqīq Balkhī narrates:

'In the year 149 AH I had gone for hajj. When I reached the region of Qādisiyyah I witnessed a large number of people with their assets and provisions making their way for hajj. As I was watching them, my eyes fell upon a good-looking youth who was wheat-like in complexion and appeared weak in body. With slippers on his feet and wearing a woollen apparel over his clothes, he sat isolated, away from the others. I said to myself: "This young man appears to belong to the Sufi sect who seek to be dependent upon the people so that they give them food to eat. By Allah! I shall go to him and rebuke him."

'As I drew up to him, he looked at me and said: "O Shaqīq! Abstain from most suspicion for surely suspicion in some cases is a sin."[3] Having

---

[1] *Jawāmiʿ al-Ḥikāyāt*, p. 70.

[2] He is the teacher of Ḥātim Aṣamm and was killed in the Battle of Kulān against the Turks in the year 194 AH.

[3] A reference to Qur'an, 49:12.

said these words, he went away.

'I wondered to myself: "This young man addressed me by my name and stated what I had intended. I must go and seek his forgiveness, for most surely he is a pious servant of Allah."

'Despite my best efforts, I failed to locate him. Time passed and I reached Wāqisah, the next place of halt. It was there that I saw him again, offering his prayers such that his body was shivering and tears flowed from his eyes. I waited till he had completed his prayers and then moved towards him. As he saw me, he said: "O Shaqīq! I have forgiven you," and then left. I said to myself: "Surely he is one of the close friends of Allah since, on two occasions, he had spoken about the thoughts that were in my mind."

'Once again, despite all my efforts, I failed to locate him till I reached the next place of halt, Zubālah. There, he was standing at the mouth of a well and was wanting to pull up some water when the bucket fell into the well. The young man raised his head towards the heavens and supplicated: "O Allah! You are the Satiated one and I am the one who is thirsty. And You are my resort when I need my sustenance."'

Shaqīq says: 'I observed that the water in the well began to gush forth and, ultimately, rose up to the mouth of the well. The young man stretched out his hand, lifted the bucket that was now filled with water and subsequently performed the *wuḍū'* to offer his prayers. He then proceeded towards a small hillock, picked up some pebbles and, dropping them into the bucket, he shook the bucket and then drank the liquid. I went up to him and extended my salutations to him, to which he responded. I then said to him: "Grace me with the bounty that Allah has graced you with!"

'He said: "O Shaqīq, the bounties, whether manifest or hidden, have always been with us. Ensure that you harbour a goodly opinion about Allah," and he then handed the bucket to me. As I drank the liquid I realised it was sugary and possessed such taste and fragrance the like of which I had never tasted before. For several days after this incident I did not experience the need or the urge to eat or drink anything.

'Following this incident, I did not see the young man till I reached

Mecca, where, in the middle of the night I saw him again. After *ṭawāf*, prayers and supplications I went closer to him, only to find that he was not alone but had slaves and friends around him. I turned to an individual, who was near the young man, and asked: "Who is this young man?"

'The person replied: "He is Mūsā ibn Jaʿfar 🕮!"'[1]

5 – Abū ʿĀmir and the construction of the mosque

Prior to the arrival of Islam there lived a famous monk by the name of Abū ʿĀmir, who would wear thick and coarse clothes and practice asceticism. He was held in very high esteem by the people until the Holy Prophet came to Medina, after which his popularity waned. Consequently, he rose up in opposition to the Holy Prophet and instigated the Battle of Khandaq. However, having faced defeat in these battles, he joined hands with a few of the hypocrites from Medina and planned to set up a base in Medina with the help of twelve individuals from the tribe of Banī Gham, such as Thaʿlabah ibn Ḥāṭib, Muʿattib ibn Qushayr, Nabtal ibn Ḥārith, and others.

With this objective in mind, he embarked on the construction of a mosque near the Mosque of Quba. When the construction was completed, a group of people approached the Holy Prophet and requested him to inaugurate this mosque just as he had done for the Mosque of Quba. Explaining to the Holy Prophet the reason for the construction of this new mosque, they said: 'Many people are unable to come to your mosque as the inclemency of the weather makes it very difficult for them.'

The Holy Prophet said: 'I am currently leaving for Tabūk. God-willing, I shall inaugurate it once I am back.'

When the Holy Prophet returned from the Battle of Tabūk, the group once again approached him to inaugurate the mosque. It was at this time that three verses of Sūrah Tawbah were revealed,[2] exposing their disbelief and the evil intention associated with the construction of that mosque. Based on the orders of Allah, the Holy Prophet sent two individuals to

---

[1] *Muntahā al-Aʿmāl,* vol. 2, p. 204.

[2] Verses 107-110.

break down the mosque. After the demolition they also set the remains on fire.[1]

90. Bounty

Allah, the Wise, has said:

$$\text{وَٱشْكُرُوا نِعْمَةَ اللّٰهِ إِنْ كُنْتُمْ إِيَّاهُ تَعْبُدُونَ}$$

And give thanks for Allah's blessing, if it is Him that you worship. (16:114)

Imam al-Ṣādiq said:

$$\text{كَانَ رَسُولُ اللّٰهِ (ص) إِذَا وَرَدَ عَلَيْهِ أَمْرٌ يَسُرُّهُ قَالَ الْحَمْدُ لِلّٰهِ عَلَى هَذِهِ النِّعْمَةِ}$$

Whenever the Holy Prophet would face a situation that would make him happy, he would say: 'I praise Allah for this bounty.'[2]

Short explanation

A true servant of Allah should always believe that all bounties have been given by Allah, and should be pleased with whatever has been granted to him by Him, and should not be desirous of procuring a bounty from anyone other than Him. When graced with a bounty from Allah, he should endeavour to always remain His thankful servant and not become disobedient towards Him.

The ability to thank Allah for a bounty is, in reality, a new bounty in itself and for which another thanksgiving becomes compulsory.

In view of all the innumerable favours and bounties from Allah, who is it that can thank Him appropriately and fully? However, care ought to be exercised to utilise every bounty in its correct manner and to refrain from excessiveness and extravagance in order that we continue to be the recipients of divine grace.

1 – The garden of Dharwān

In ancient times in a village near Yemen called Dharwān, there lived a

---

[1] *Payghambar Wa Yārān*, vol. 2, pp. 103; *Majmaʿ al-Bayān*, vol. 5, p. 70.

[2] *Jāmiʿ al-Saʿādāt*, vol. 3, p. 236.

pious and godly individual who owned a garden filled with fruit-laden trees. He would never hesitate to assist those who were underprivileged, to the extent that, in appreciation and thanks to Allah for His bounties, he would even distribute the entire harvest of crops and fruits from his garden amongst the poor, retaining for himself a measure just sufficient to fulfil his needs. His house was the focal point for the poor as most of the poor people would approach him to have their needs fulfilled.

Repeatedly, this godly man would gather his children and recommend to them to care for the poor and downtrodden, saying: 'All bounties are from Allah and so, to acquire His pleasure, do not forget to spend in His way.'

Whilst his children had heard these recommendations on numerous occasions, their wealth had made them haughty and arrogant.

Eventually, one day, this man passed away. The children forgot the recommendations of their father and decided that they would, henceforth, not distribute the harvest amongst the poor, but instead share it amongst themselves. As in the past, the poor people would come to the garden, but now the children would not give them any of the bounties they had received from their father.

Allah became wrathful upon these impudent children and a lightning struck their garden, burning everything to ashes. The following morning when they reached their garden, they saw everything had been burnt down![1]

2 – Excessiveness in utilising bounties

One day, Hārūn al-Rashīd – the fifth Abbasid caliph – announced his desire to consume meat of a special young camel – one that has entered its sixth month. However, that kind of meat was unavailable then.

Time passed. One day, Hārūn al-Rashīd once again experienced a desire to have that meat. The cook prepared a delicacy out of this meat and placed it along with other food items before the caliph. As Hārūn picked

---

[1] *Dāstān-hā-yi Mathnawī,* vol. 4, p. 15.

up a portion from this delicacy and placed it in his mouth, his vizier, Ja'far Barmakī, began to laugh. Hārūn asked him: 'Why do you laugh?'

Ja'far said: 'Do you know how much this morsel has cost us?'

'No; how much?' asked Hārūn.

Ja'far replied: '100,000 dirhams.'

'How is this possible?' asked Hārūn, incredulously.

Ja'far Barmakī said: 'On the first occasion when you had desired to eat this meat it was unavailable and so I had issued instructions that henceforth a young camel should be slaughtered daily and the delicacy prepared from it so that whenever you felt the desire to have this meat, it would be ready for you. Today you expressed a desire to have this meat; in preparation for this day, I have spent 400,000 dirhams on the purchases of this specific type of young camel. It was in light of this amount that I stated that the morsel that you had consumed was worth 100,000 dirhams!'[1]

3 – Thanks for a bounty

Abū Hāshim Ja'farī relates:

'There was a time when I was in a state of intense poverty and so I decided to visit Imam al-Hādī ﷺ. Having just sat down after having received permission to enter the house and seat myself, the Imam ﷺ said: "O Abū Hāshim! For which of the bounties of Allah that He has graced you with do you wish to thank Him? Do realise, expressing thanks for a bounty increases the bounty."'

Abū Hāshim says: 'I was stunned and was at a loss for words, whereupon the Imam ﷺ himself explained: "Allah has graced you with faith and helped you to obey Him; He graced you with contentment and in this way protected you from extravagance and excessiveness." The Imam ﷺ continued further: "O Abū Hāshim! I commenced my speech in this manner because I realised you had come to me with a complaint about being placed in such poverty. However, I have instructed my servant to

---

[1] *Ḥikāyat-hā-yi Shanīdanī*, vol. 3, p. 66; *al-Bidāyah Wa al-Nihāyah*, vol. 10, p. 216.

hand over to you 100 dinars, so take the money!'"[1]

4 – Detachment with respect to the bounties of this world

Once, Manṣūr Dawānīqī told ʿAmr: 'Give me a piece of advice.'

ʿAmr said: 'Would you like me to relate to you something from what I have witnessed or from what I have heard?'

'Tell me something that you have seen,' said Manṣūr, at which point ʿAmr said: 'When ʿUmar ibn ʿAbd al-ʿAzīz passed away, he was survived by eleven sons and had left behind seventeen dinars which were distributed amongst his sons. When Hishām ibn ʿAbd al-Malik died, he too was survived by eleven sons, however, each of them received one million dinars as inheritance from their father. After the passage of some time I happened to witness one of the sons of ʿUmar ibn ʿAbd al-ʿAzīz having reached such levels of wealth and richness that he had gifted 100 horses in the way of Allah, whereas I saw one of the sons of Hishām in a state of such abject poverty that he was seated by the side of the road, seeking charity from the passers-by.

'A person of intellect, if he were to ponder, would come to realise that one ought not to attach one's heart to this world or its bounties for they are prone to change.'[2]

5 – What is a true bounty?

A scribe of Imam al-Riḍā ﷺ by the name of Ibrāhīm ibn ʿAbbās, says:

'We were in the presence of Imam al-Riḍā ﷺ when one of the scholars asked: "Does the term 'bounty' in this verse: Then, that day, you will surely be questioned concerning the blessing [102:8], refer to 'cool water'?"

'The Imam ﷺ asked loudly: "What meaning do you make of it?" Each one from amongst those present stated a meaning; one said it could be 'cool water', while another stated it could be 'sleep', while yet another said it could mean 'tasty food delicacies'. Visibly upset, the Imam ﷺ said: "My

---

1 *Bā Mardūm In Gūnih Barkhūrd Kunīm*, p. 130; *al-Amālī* of Shaykh Ṣadūq, p. 412.

2 *Jawāmiʿ al-Ḥikāyāt*, p. 136.

father has narrated from his father Imam al-Ṣādiq ﷺ, who said: "Never will Allah question His creations nor will He ever manifest His obligations upon them by reminding them about things that He has graced them with. These are acts of people that are menial in that they place obligations on others for the food and drink they may have provided to them. How can acts considered inappropriate even for the creation of Allah be attributed to Allah? The term 'bounty' in the verse refers to the love and *wilāyah* of our family, about which Allah will question His creations after having questioned them about *tawḥīd* and prophethood. If a person has fulfilled his obligation with regards to the love and *wilāyah* of the Ahl al-Bayt, he would reach the bounties of paradise that are eternal and see no end."[1]

91. Prayers

Allah, the Wise, has said:

$$إِنَّ الصَّلَاةَ تَنْهَى عَنِ الْفَحْشَاءِ وَالْمُنْكَرِ$$

Indeed the prayer prevents indecencies and wrongs. (29:45)

The Holy Prophet said:

$$مَنْ صَلَّى رَكْعَتَيْنِ وَلَمْ يُحَدِّثْ فِيهِمَا نَفْسَهُ بِشَيْءٍ مِنْ أُمُورِ الدُّنْيَا غَفَرَ اللّٰهُ لَهُ ذُنُوبَهُ$$

One who offers a two-unit prayer in a manner that no thought of any affair of this world passes through his mind, all his sins would be forgiven by Allah.[2]

Short explanation

Know that Allah is not dependent of our services and nor is He in need of our worship. Rather, He has invited us towards His grace so that He may shower His mercy upon us, open the doors of forgiveness, and protect us from His punishment.

Allah, in ordaining acts of worship like prayers, has no intention except to manifest His generosity and power.

---

1 *Dāstān-hā Wa Pand-hā*, vol. 4, p. 103; *Yanābīʿ al-Mawaddah*, vol. 1, p. 111.

² *Tadhkirat al-Ḥaqāʾiq*, p. 15.

Thus, when the *takbīr* is recited and the prayer is commenced, everything between the heavens and the earth other than Allah ought to be considered as insignificant and trivial, and pushed into the oblivions of forgetfulness.[1]

1 – Prayer out of fear

A Bedouin Arab entered the Mosque of the Prophet at a time when the Commander of the Faithful was in the mosque. He started offering his prayers in haste and without diligence and adherence to any of the etiquettes of prayer such as recitations, and actions, etc. As he was about to leave the mosque after his prayers, the Commander of the Faithful summoned him and said: 'Offer your prayers again but slowly and with all its etiquettes, for the one offered by you was incorrect.'

Out of fear of the Commander of the Faithful the Arab once again offered his prayers, but this time with humility and with adherence to its etiquettes. When he had finished, the Commander of the Faithful asked: 'O Arab! Was this prayer not better than the first one?'

'By Allah! Yes, O Commander of the Faithful, because the first prayer I had offered was out of fear of Allah, while the second prayer I offered was out of fear of your shoes.'

Hearing this, the Commander of the Faithful burst out in laughter.[2]

2 – Arrow in the foot

An arrow had penetrated the foot of Imam 'Alī 🖂 and the intense pain was making it impossible for it to be extracted. Lady Fāṭimah Zahrā' 🖂 said to the companions: 'Try extracting the arrow from his leg whilst he is in his prayers, for while in prayers he is totally heedless of anything except Allah.'

They tried this and were successful in extracting the arrow from his

---

[1] Ibid.

[2] *Laṭā'if al-Ṭawā'if*, p. 139.

leg![1]

In another tradition it has been reported that in the Battle of Ṣiffīn an arrow penetrated his holy thigh. Try as they would, the companions were unable to remove it due to the pain being experienced by the Imam. They approached Imam al-Ḥasan 🕮 and informed him of the situation. The Imam advised them: 'Do not attempt to remove the arrow until such time that my father commences his prayers, for once in prayer he is so focused towards Allah that he becomes completely oblivious of everything else.'

While in a state of prayer and completely engrossed in Allah, the arrow was pulled out of his leg. The Imam realised this after the prayers and so asked: 'What happened?'

The people told him: 'While you were praying, we pulled the arrow out of your leg.'[2]

Dear readers, do not even for a moment, think: how can such a thing even be possible?[3] Have you not heard of the incident of Abū al-Dardā', who was on one night observing the Imam in a state of prayers and supplications near the wall of the tribe of Banī Najjār, and as he watched he saw Imam fall to the ground and was no longer able to hear the voice of the Imam. Worried, he approached stealthily, only to find the body of the Imam lying motionless on the ground like a log of dried wood. Rushing to Imam's house, he related the incident to Lady Zahrā' 🕮, who calmly explained to him: 'This is a state of unconsciousness that overcomes him out of fear of Allah. Go and sprinkle some water over his face and he shall regain consciousness.'[4]

Abū al-Dardā' rushed back and sprinkled some water, and subsequently the Imam regained his consciousness.

---

[1] *Shanīdanī-hā-yi Tārīkh*, p. 13; *al-Maḥajjah al-Bayḍā'*, vol. 1, p. 397.

[2] *Dāstān-hā Wa Pand-hā*, vol. 4, p. 147; *Anwār al-Nuʿmāniyyah*, p. 342.

[3] Note that the ladies of Egypt were so overcome by the handsomeness of Prophet Yūsuf 🕮 that they ended up cutting their fingers instead of the lemons. See Qur'an, 12:31.

[4] *Laʾālī al-Akhbār*, vol. 4, p. 36.

3 – Congregational prayers

One of the companions of the Holy Prophet once happened to remain awake for a whole night engaged in acts of worship till the time of *fajr* prayers. Due to fatigue and sleepiness, he did not go to the mosque for the congregational prayers, preferring instead to offer his prayer at home.

When the Holy Prophet did not see him in congregation, he went to his house after the prayers and asked his wife: 'Why did your husband not come for the congregational *fajr* prayer?'

The wife replied: 'He had spent the entire night in a state of worship and hence was overcome with sleepiness.'

Hearing this, the Holy Prophet commented: 'The rewards that would have been given to him for the congregational *fajr* prayer would have been far superior to the rewards of all the prayers recited by him in the night.'

As this conversation ensued, the companion, hearing the voice of the Holy Prophet, came out to meet him. Seeing him, the Holy Prophet said: 'A person who offers the *fajr* prayer in congregation is like one who has passed his entire night bowing and prostrating. Do you not know that the earth complains to Allah about the individual who, before sunrise, is still sleeping?'[1]

4 – Cheated

Once, a Bedouin Arab entered a mosque and observed an old man offering his prayers with immense humility and submissiveness. Evidently impressed, he said to him: 'How beautifully you offer your prayers!'

The old man said: 'I am also fasting, as the rewards of a person offering his prayers while fasting is twice that of a person who is not fasting.'

The Bedouin said to him: 'Do me a favour and take care of my camel; I need to go to for some work but shall return shortly.' No sooner had the Bedouin handed over his camel to the old man and left, when the old man stole the camel.

Returning and seeing neither his camel nor the old man, the Bedouin

____

[1] *Safīnat al-Biḥār,* vol. 1, p. 177.

embarked upon an extensive search. When he drew a blank, he recited this couplet: 'Amazed me his prayer, and attracted me to him, his fast; but of what use, as my camel he stole despite his prayer and fast.'[1]

5 – Friday prayers

Famine and drought had overwhelmed the city of Medina, as a result of which hunger and poverty had wreaked misery on the people of the city. With circumstances being such, if a caravan containing food and other provisions of life were to enter the city, it was obvious that people would create a near-stampede in their endeavour to procure food items for themselves. It was a norm that when a merchandise-laden caravan would enter the city, the people, excited and beating the drums, would rush to welcome it with even the womenfolk emerging from their houses and joining them in such celebrations.

It was Friday and the Muslims had gathered for offering Friday prayers led by the Holy Prophet. It was when he was engaged in delivering the sermon for the Friday prayers that some people brought the news that a merchandise-laden caravan had entered Medina. (Diḥyah Kalbī was a trader, who had arrived from Syria bringing along with him wheat, barley, flour, etc. for sale. People began beating the drums to inform the others of the arrival of this caravan.)

Hearing the drumbeats, the Muslims in the mosque, thinking that if they remained in the mosque for the Friday prayers they would lose out on the merchandise that had arrived from Syria, rushed out to procure the provisions for themselves. Only eight people remained in the mosque with the Holy Prophet. Addressing them, he said: 'I swear by the Lord in whose control lies my soul! Had you also left and had the mosque become empty, fire [as the wrath of Allah] would have descended upon this land and engulfed the people.'

According to another tradition, the Holy Prophet said to them: 'Had you not remained in the mosque, stones would have rained down from the

---

[1] *La'ālī al-Akhbār*, vol. 4, p. 62.

sky.'

It was at this time that the eleventh verse of Sūrat al-Jumuʿah was revealed:

When they sight a deal or a diversion they scatter off towards it and leave you standing! Say: 'What is with Allah is better than diversion and dealing, and Allah is the best of providers.' (62:11)[1]

92. Cursing

Allah, the Wise, has said:

أُولَٰئِكَ يَلْعَنُهُمُ اللهُ وَيَلْعَنُهُمُ اللَّاعِنُونَ

They shall be cursed by Allah and cursed by the cursers. (2:159)

The Holy Prophet said:

لَيْسَ الْمُؤْمِنُ بِالطَّعَّانِ وَلَا اللَّعَّانِ

A believer does not taunt nor does he curse.[2]

Short explanation

If a curse has been uttered by the Holy Prophet or an Imam, then it must be realised that the person who has been cursed fully deserved it. However, if an ordinary person who has been a victim of an injustice or false accusation or has been deprived of a legal right wishes to invoke the curse [of Allah], despite the fact that it may be permissible for him to do this, nonetheless a better option would be to adopt the path of forgiveness and to pray to Allah to guide the perpetrator to the right path.

However, if the person for whom the curse of Allah was invoked was not deserving of this, the curse would return back to the person invoking the curse! For example, if a person were to ram into a stone and injure his foot and subsequently embark on cursing the stone despite the stone not being at fault, the effects of this curse would return to this person.

---

[1] *Dāstān-hā Wa Pand-hā*, vol. 9, p. 37; *Tafsīr Nūr al-Thaqalayn*, vol. 5, p. 329.

[2] *Jāmiʿ al-Saʿādāt*, vol. 1, p. 314.

1 – Instead of cursing, he supplicated

Ibrāhīm Atrush relates:

'I was seated with Maʿrifat Karkhī and some others on the bank of the river Tigris when we observed a group of youths seated in a small boat, and engaged in playing music, singing, and consuming alcohol. Some from amongst us requested Maʿrifat Karkhī to curse them. He stretched his hands and said: "O Lord! As You have made them joyful in this world, make them joyful in the Hereafter too."

'The friends turned to Maʿrifat and objected: "Why did you supplicate for them when we had asked you to curse them?"

'He replied: "If Allah wills them to be joyful in the Hereafter, He would inspire them to seek forgiveness and mend their ways."'[1]

2 – ʿUbayd Allāh ibn Ziyād

For almost six years after the martyrdom of Imam al-Ḥusayn 🖏, the families of the martyrs of Karbala were always in a state of grief and anguish, such that the ladies of Banī Hāshim would neither apply kohl to their eyes nor dye their hair. Six years after Karbala, ʿUbayd Allāh ibn Ziyād, the right-hand man of Yazīd, was eventually killed at the hands of Ibrāhīm, the son of Mālik Ashtar, on the day of ʿĀshūrāʾ of the year 67 AH, at the age of thirty-nine.

When Mukhtār sent the head of ʿUbayd Allāh to Imam al-Sajjād 🖏, the Imam was having his meal. He immediately fell into prostration; when he had raised his head, he said: 'When we were made to enter the court of Ibn Ziyād, he was engrossed in having his meal. The head of my esteemed father lay before him as he ate his food. I had prayed to Allah that I should not die before seeing ʿUbayd Allāh's head at a time when I am having my meal. May Allah reward Mukhtār for the revenge that he has taken on behalf of us.'

The Imam then instructed those present to also offer thanks to Allah.[2]

---

[1] *Shanīdanī-hā-yi Tārīkh*, p. 393; *al-Maḥajjah al-Bayḍāʾ*, vol. 7, p. 268.

[2] *Tatimmat al-Muntahā*, p. 62.

3 – Ḥurmalah

Minhāl ibn ʿAmr relates:

'Once, with the intention of going for hajj, I set off from Kufa. On this trip, I met Imam al-Sajjād 📿, who asked me: "What news do you have of Ḥurmalah [the murderer of the six-month old ʿAlī Aṣghar]?"

'"He lives in Kufa," I replied.

'The Imam 📿 raised his hands and cursed him, praying to Allah to punish him by making him taste the punishment of iron and fire.'

Minhāl continues:

'I subsequently returned to Kufa. One day it so happened that I went to meet Mukhtār. As I came before him he called for his horse, climbed upon it, and asked me to climb up along with him. We rode till we had reached the periphery of Kufa, when he stopped as if waiting for someone. All of a sudden, I saw Ḥurmalah being brought before him as a captive. Seeing him, Mukhtār praised Allah and ordered Ḥurmalah's hands and legs to be cut and then for him to be thrown into the fire. As I saw this, I uttered: "*Subḥān allāh.*"

'Hearing this, Mukhtār asked me: "Why did you recite this?"

'I narrated the incident of Imam al-Sajjād's 📿 curse for Ḥurmalah, and how the curse had come to pass that day. Mukhtār got down from his horse and began offering a protracted two-unit prayer after which he went into a long prostration of thanks to Allah.

'On our way back, as we neared our houses, I invited Mukhtār to join me for a meal. Mukhtār said to me: "O Minhāl! Having informed me about the curse of Imam al-Sajjād 📿 which came to fruition at my hands, you now want me to have some food! Rather, today is a day when I should be observing a fast as a way of expressing thanks to Allah."'[1]

4 – Sent as a prophet of mercy

For a period of twenty-three years, the Holy Prophet had to bear immense troubles in his endeavour to guide the people. Physically and

---

[1] *Muntahā al-Aʿmāl*, vol. 1, p. 451.

psychologically, a lot of tribulations and calamites were inflicted upon him to the extent that in the Battle of Uḥud his face was left injured and his teeth were broken.

Some of his companions urged him to curse the enemies, to which the Holy Prophet replied: 'I have not been sent as a prophet to curse the people; rather, I have been sent as a mercy to the people, and to invite them towards Allah.' He then prayed: 'O Allah! Guide my people for they know not what they do.'[1]

93. Soul

Allah, the Wise, has said:

$$لِتُجْزَى كُلُّ نَفْسٍ بِمَا تَسْعَى$$

So that every soul may be rewarded for what it strives for. (20:15)

Imam al-Ṣādiq ﷺ has said:

$$طُوبَى لِعَبْدٍ جَاهَدَ نَفْسَه وهَوَاهُ$$

Bravo to the servant [of Allah] who strives against his soul and his base desires.[2]

Short explanation

Man is made up of two things: body and soul; the body being the mount, while the soul the rider.

If righteous, the soul will not incite towards evil acts; but if not so, it will exhort towards evil and ungodly acts.

In order to have the reins of the soul firmly under control so as to not fall prey to satanic deceptions, it is essential to subject it to scrutiny and surveillance and to hold it accountable for its actions. Great care ought to be exercised with respect to one's thoughts and intentions, for the soul is akin to a python which, if left neglected even momentarily, can lead a

---

[1] *Safīnat al-Biḥār*, vol. 1, p. 412.

[2] *Safīnat al-Biḥār*, vol. 2, p. 603.

person to the fire of hell, and ultimately, to annihilation.[1]

1 – The python of the soul

It has been reported in history that there once lived a snake-catcher. He would go to the mountains to catch snakes and bring them to Baghdad in order to conduct shows before the people, and in this way earn some money for himself.

Once, in winter, after a great effort, he managed to locate a large python in the mountains. Since it was cold, the python was listless and motionless and it took him a lot of work to be able bring it to the city of Baghdad, located near the river Tigris. Reaching there, he called out to the people to come and have a look at the reptile he had captured. Hundreds of people gathered to catch a glimpse of the captured python.

The weather had gradually turned warm, as a result of which the python had begun to regain its strength and mobility. As the snake-charmer brought it out of its sac, it suddenly lunged at him, attacking him and killing him in full view of the people that had gathered. Terrified, they fled from the scene of the incident.

O my brother! Do not remain heedless, for your soul is like this python;[2] if it acquires enough strength it would destroy your life. Do not think that you would be able to gain control over it by means of gentleness; the only way to be dominant over it is by way of suppressing and opposing its whims and caprices![3]

2 – Lemon juice of Shiraz

The deceased Shaykh ʿAbd al-Ḥusayn Khwānsārī has narrated:

'In Karbala there lived a perfumer who was very renowned and famous. Once, he happened to fall ill and the illness prolonged for a long time. In

---

[1] We have penned some explanations about the soul in the book *Tadhkirat al-Nufūs*.

[2] Rumi says: Your soul is a python, when has it ever died? It only lies dormant, for an opportunity it awaits.

[3] *Dāstān-hā-yi Mathnawī*, vol. 2, p. 73.

his quest to get cured, he was forced to sell the entire stock of his shop as well as many of the items of his house, but it was to no avail as all the doctors pleaded their inability to cure him.

'One day, I decided to pay him a visit. Reaching him, I saw that he was in a very bad state of health. The perfumer, in my presence, turned to his son and said: "Go to the market, sell some other items of the house, and get some money so that I may be comforted either by getting cured, or by means of death."

'I said to him: "What kind of talk is this?"

'He took a deep sigh and then said to me: "I had managed to acquire a lot of wealth and the reason for this was that once, Karbala was plagued by an epidemic. Doctors believed the only cure for this disease was a certain lemon juice of Shiraz. As a result, lemon juice was in short supply. My soul instigated me, saying: 'If you adulterate the pure lemon juice with something else and sell this concoction as pure lemon juice, you shall become very wealthy.' I did this and soon I had monopolised the lemon juice in Karbala to such an extent that in the entirety of Karbala it could only be found in my shop. I had acquired such immense riches that amongst the traders I came to be popularly known as 'The Father of Millions'. Not long afterwards, I found myself afflicted with this disease. I was forced to sell all that I had towards the treatment of this disease, but to no avail. All that remained were these few possessions which I have just told my son to sell so that I may be freed from this disease, either by means of a cure or by means of death."'[1]

3 – The best and the worst

Initially, Luqmān, who was a contemporary of Prophet Dāwūd ﷺ, was a slave of one of the kings of Banī Isrā'īl. One day, the king ordered him to slaughter a sheep and bring before him the best part of the animal. Luqmān slaughtered a sheep and brought its heart and tongue before the king.

A few days later the king ordered him to slaughter another sheep, but

---

[1] *Muntakhab al-Tawārīkh*, p. 813.

on this occasion asked him to bring the worst part of the animal. Luqmān slaughtered a sheep and once again presented its heart and tongue to the king. Surprised, the king remarked: 'The two actions of yours appear to be contradictory.'

Luqmān explained: 'If the tongue and the heart were to act in tandem, they become the best parts of a body, but if they were to act in opposition to each other, they become the worst parts of a body.'

This impressed the king so much that he set Luqmān free.[1]

4 – Abū Khaythamah

Mālik ibn Qays, popularly known as Abū Khaythamah, was a companion of the Holy Prophet. He had participated in many battles but, along with a few others, had refrained from participating in the Battle of Tabūk. On a very hot summer afternoon, ten days after the Holy Prophet had left for the battle, Abū Khaythamah, who had gone out, returned home and seated himself in his garden under a gazebo that he had set up for his two wives. They had, while awaiting his return, readied for him a pitcher of cool water, some delicious food, and sprinkled the walls of the gazebo with water so as to keep the interior cool.

As Abū Khaythamah looked at the cool water, the delicious food, and his beautiful wives living in ease, he began to think of the Holy Prophet, and, overcome by a feeling of guilt, he said to himself: 'It is surely not right that while the Holy Prophet ﷺ is facing the heat and hardships, I place myself here in ease and comfort. The hypocrites may harbour scepticism towards the religion, but my soul is firm in belief.' Packing his luggage, he took off on his camel towards the Battle of Tabūk.

On the way, he met and became friends with 'Umayr ibn Wahab. As they neared the camp of the Holy Prophet, Abū Khaythamah said to 'Umayr: 'As I had desisted from accompanying the Holy Prophet ﷺ, allow me to go to him alone and seek forgiveness from him.'

A person informed the Holy Prophet: 'Someone is approaching us.'

---

[1] *Ṭarā'iq al-Ḥaqā'iq*, vol. 1, p. 336.

The Holy Prophet prayed: 'I pray to Allah it be Abū Khaythamah.'

Abū Khaythamah reached the camp, dismounted from his camel, and arrived in the presence of the Holy Prophet. Seeing him, the Holy Prophet said: 'I was expecting this from you.'

When Abū Khaythamah related to him the incident of his soul experiencing guilt at not having accompanied him, the Holy Prophet prayed to Allah for him.[1]

5 – The capable soul

Not everyone possesses the ability to be the recipient of divine grace and be elevated to lofty ranks. Abū Ḥamzah Thumālī was one such individual who possessed this ability, and thus found himself receiving special attention from four infallible Imams to the extent that Imam al-Ṣādiq ﷺ has been reported as saying to him: 'Whenever I see you, I experience a sense of peace and tranquillity within myself.'

He had come to possess such a pure soul that he would spend most of his time in the Mosque of Kufa, engaged in acts of worship. He relates:

'One day, as I was seated in front of the seventh pillar of the Mosque of Kufa, I saw a person wearing a turban enter the mosque. I had never seen anybody as good-looking, as fragrant, and as well-dressed as this person. He took off his Arabic slippers and stood next to the seventh pillar to offer his prayers. The manner in which he recited the *takbīrat al-iḥrām* made such an impact upon me that my body broke out in goose bumps and I became totally captivated by his pure and enchanting accent. Having offered a four-unit prayer, he left the mosque.

'I began to follow him until he reached the periphery of Kufa, where I observed that a slave had readied a camel for him. I moved towards the slave and enquired: "Who is this gentleman?"

'The slave replied: "Do you not recognise him? He is ʿAlī ibn Ḥusayn, Zayn al-ʿĀbidīn."'

As soon as he heard this, Abū Ḥamzah fell at the holy feet of the Imam

---

[1] *Payghambar Wa Yārān*, vol. 5, p. 210; *Sīrah Ibn Hishām*, vol. 4, p. 163.

and began kissing them. The Imam held him by the arms and raised him up, saying: 'Don't do this, for it is inappropriate to prostrate before anyone other than Allah.'

Thenceforth, Abū Ḥamzah became one of the special companions of Imam al-Sajjād ﷺ and went on to become the companion of Imam al-Bāqir ﷺ, Imam al-Ṣādiq ﷺ, and Imam al-Kāẓim ﷺ, and benefitted greatly from them.

Imam al-Riḍā ﷺ has been reported to have stated: 'Abū Ḥamzah was the Luqmān of his time, for he has served four Imams from our family.'[1]

94. *Wilāyah*

Allah, the Wise, has said:

$$\text{لَا يَتَّخِذِ الْمُؤْمِنُونَ الْكَافِرِينَ أَوْلِيَاءَ}$$

The faithful should not take the faithless for allies. (3:28)

Imam al-Ṣādiq ﷺ has said:

$$\text{وِلَايَةُ عَلِيٍّ (ع) مَكْتُوبَةٌ فِي صُحُفِ جَمِيعِ الْأَنْبِيَاءِ}$$

The *wilāyah* of ʿAlī has been prescribed in the scriptures of all the prophets.[2]

Short explanation

From the beginning of creation, Allah had conferred the position of caliph upon His chosen servants so that His creations are not bereft of a leader and a guide.

In the current time, the *wilāyah* belongs to Imam al-Mahdī ﷺ, who is the manifestation of the traits and attributes of Allah.

Any person who stands in opposition to the dictates of the *walī* of Allah shall become the object of the wrath of Allah. The fundamental criterion, with regards to *wilāyah*, is complete obedience to and love towards the *walī* of Allah, and the best recommendations in this regard are those, as

---

[1] *Shāgirdān-i Maktab-i Aʾimmah*, vol. 3, p. 196.

[2] *Safīnat al-Biḥār*, vol. 2, p. 619.

witnessed by history, of the Holy Prophet with respect to the Commander of the Faithful.

In our times, when the grace of Imam al-Mahdī ﷺ encompasses us all, it behoves us to not become heedless towards him, and to constantly seek his assistance and succour.

1 – The black slave

A black slave, accused of stealing, was once brought in the presence of the Commander of the Faithful. The Imam asked him: 'Have you committed the theft?'

'Yes, O 'Alī,' he replied.

The Imam said to him: 'I shall ask you one more time. If you confess again, I shall have to cut your fingers.' When asked again about the theft, the servant once again confessed to it, whereupon the fingers of his right hand were severed.

The slave, holding the severed fingers in his other hand and with blood oozing out, went away. On the way he came across 'Abd Allāh ibn al-Kawwā',[1] who questioned him: 'O slave, who has severed your fingers?'

The slave replied emphatically: 'The king of *wilāyah*, the Commander of the Faithful, the leader of the pious ones, the successor of the Final Prophet, and he who is my master and master of all the people is the one who has severed my fingers!'

Taken aback at hearing such lavish praises of Imam 'Alī ﷺ, Ibn al-Kawwā' asked, incredulously: 'He has severed your fingers and yet you laud and praise him?'

The slave replied: 'How can I not praise him when his love is enmeshed in my flesh and blood? He has rightfully severed my fingers.'

Ibn al-Kawwā' came before the Commander of the Faithful and related to him all that had transpired with the slave, whereupon the Imam said: 'We have such friends that even if we were to cut them into pieces, their

---

[1] He was a hypocrite who belonged to the Kharijite group. He used to question Imam 'Alī ﷺ a lot about various things.

love for us would only increase; and we have such enemies that even if we were to pour honey down their throat, it would only cause their enmity towards us to increase.' Then, turning to Imam al-Ḥasan ☙, the Imam said: 'Go and bring that slave to me.'

When the slave was brought before him, the Imam asked: 'O slave, how is it that even though I have cut your fingers you still continue to praise me?'

The slave replied: 'Who am I to praise you? It is Allah who praises you.'

The Imam placed the severed fingers at the locations from where they had been severed from the hand, covered it with his cloak, and recited a prayer (some have said the Imam recited Sūrat al-Ḥamd), and lo and behold the fingers had joined the hand as if they had never been severed in the first place![1]

2 – The spouse of the poet ʿAbdī

The poet ʿAbdī[2] relates:

'Once, my wife said to me: "It has been a long since we last visited Imam al-Ṣādiq ☙. It would be a good idea to go for hajj and then also visit the Imam."

'I said to her: "Allah is my witness that I do not have the means to shoulder the expenses of the trip."

'She said: "I have some clothes, gold, and jewellery. Sell them so that we can undertake this journey."

'Acting upon her advice, I sold her items and subsequently we embarked on the journey. It so happened that as we were nearing Medina, my wife fell ill; her condition continued to deteriorate rapidly to such an extent that she looked certain to die. As we entered Medina, I placed her in the house and rushed to meet the Imam ☙. When I saw the Imam, I observed that he was wearing a red apparel. I extended my salutations to him to which he

---

[1] *Tuḥfat al-Majālis*, p. 133.

[2] Abū Sufyān ibn Muṣʿab ʿAbdī was a poet from Kufa (d. 120 ah). About him, Imam al-Ṣādiq ☙ has been reported to have said: 'O Shiʿas! Teach your children the poems of ʿAbdī, for he is steadfast on the religion of Allah.'

replied, and then enquired after my wife. I informed him of the state that she was in and said to him: "I have come to you out of utter helplessness at the condition of my wife."

'The Imam lowered his head for a while and then, raising it, said: "Do not worry, for she shall recover. I have prayed to Allah to grant her recovery from her illness. As you return to your wife, you shall observe your slave-girl giving her some sugar to eat."'

'Abdī says:

'I hurried back to my wife, only to witness the situation exactly as the Imam had indicated to me. I asked her: "How do you feel?" She replied: "Allah has cured me and, subsequent to my recovery, I developed an urge to have some sugar."

'I said to her: "As I left you to go to the Imam I had given up hope. The Imam asked me about your health, and I explained the situation to him. He said you would recover and, when I return to you, I would see that you would be having some sugar."

'My wife said to me: "When you left me, I was on the verge of death. Suddenly I witnessed a person wearing red clothes come to me and ask: 'How are you?' I replied: 'I am about to die. The Angel of Death is about to seize my soul.' At that moment the person turned to the Angel of Death and said: 'O Angel of Death! Are you not ordained to obey us and listen to our commands?' 'Yes,' responded the Angel of Death. The man then said: 'I am ordering you to delay her death by twenty years.' The Angel of Death said: 'I shall obey your orders.' That man then left along with the Angel of Death, and I regained consciousness."'[1]

3 – Mu'āwiyah's maternal cousin

Muḥammad ibn Abū Ḥudhayfah was the maternal cousin of Mu'āwiyah. When his father was killed, he was raised under the care of 'Uthmān; however, he was one of the staunchest followers of the Commander of the Faithful.

---

[1] *Pand-i Tārīkh*, vol. 5, p. 89; *Biḥār al-Anwār*, vol. 11, p. 137 (Old Edition).

In battle, the forces of Mu'āwiyah killed Muḥammad ibn Abū Bakr – the governor of Egypt, and Muḥammad ibn Abū Ḥudhayfah sustained injuries. Taken captive by 'Amr ibn 'Āṣ, he was sent to Syria where Mu'āwiyah put him into prison.

One day, Mu'āwiyah said to his coterie of friends and advisors: 'Why don't we bring this thick-headed relative of mine here and reprimand him? Perhaps that may get him to abandon 'Alī and begin speaking bad about him.' Those around him agreed with this suggestion.

When Muḥammad was taken out of the prison and brought before him, Mu'āwiyah said: 'Is it not time yet that you mend your errant ways and forsake that lying individual, 'Alī? Do you not know that 'Alī was involved in the murder of 'Uthmān and that we intend to avenge the murder?'

Muḥammad replied: 'Mu'āwiyah, is it not that I am the closest to you amongst all and know you better than any other individual?'

'Yes,' said Mu'āwiyah, at which Muḥammad said: 'By Allah other than whom there is no god, no one has killed 'Uthmān other than you and your people. O Mu'āwiyah! You have been the same whether it be in the Age of Ignorance or in Islam, as acceptance of Islam has not brought about any change in you. Do not rebuke me for my friendship with 'Alī ◌ because all the pious and righteous people – those who fast during the days and pass their nights in worship – are with 'Alī, whereas those that are around you happen to be either the children of hypocrites or the children of those disbelievers who had been freed after the conquest of Mecca. By Allah! Till I am alive I shall always treat 'Alī as a friend and you as an enemy for the sake of Allah and for the pleasure of the Holy Prophet ◌!'

Hearing this, Mu'āwiyah said: 'It seems you continue to be deviated,' and ordered him to be thrown back into prison.

Muḥammad remained in prison for some time and then managed to escape. Mu'āwiyah sent a force under the command of 'Ubayd Allāh ibn 'Amr to search and apprehend him. They eventually found him hiding in a cave and subsequently killed him.[1]

---

[1] *Payghambar Wa Yārān*, vol. 5, p. 241; *Qāmūs al-Rijāl*, vol. 7, p. 500.

4 – Benefiting from *wilāyah*

One day, as Imam ʿAlī 🖼 came out of his house, he saw a group of people. He asked them: 'Who are you?'

'Your Shiʿas,' they replied.

The Imam said to them: 'I do not see on your faces the signs of a Shiʿa of mine.'

Embarrassed, one from amongst them asked: 'What are the signs of your Shiʿas?'

The Imam remained silent, whereupon a pious person by the name of Hammām ibn ʿUbādah,[1] placed the Imam under oath and insisted that he inform them of the signs. At this point, the Imam delivered the Sermon of the Pious.

However, this has been differently related in *Nahj al-Balāghah*, according to which, Hammām queried the Imam about the traits of the pious,[2] saying: 'Describe to me the pious so vividly that it is as if I am seeing them with my eyes.' The Imam hesitated for a few moments and then said to him: 'O Hammām! Fear Allah and do good acts, for surely Allah is with those who fear Him and who do good deeds.' Not satisfied with this response, Hammām requested him to elucidate further, at which the Imam began to enumerate the qualities of the pious.

In the course of his sermon, when the Imam reached this sentence: 'The pious isolate themselves from the people, but not out of arrogance; and they mingle with the people, but not out of deceit and shrewdness,' Hammām suddenly gave out a shriek and fell down dead.

Seeing this, the Imam remarked: 'By Allah! This is what I was fearing for him. This is how an appropriate admonition affects an appropriate individual.'[3]

---

[1] Ibn Abī al-Ḥadīd and the author of *Tuḥaf al-ʿUqūl* are of the opinion that his father's name was Shurayḥ and not ʿUbādah.

[2] *Nahj al-Balāghah* of Fayḍ al-Islām, Sermon 184.

[3] *Awṣāf-i Pārsāyān*, pp. 27-35.

5 – Witnessing the king of *wilāyah*

Hārūn al-Rashīd, the Abbasid caliph, had a son by the name of Qāsim who had detached himself completely from the world, and was habituated to repeatedly visit the cemetery, spending his time there, weeping immensely. One day, as Hārūn was seated in a meeting, Qāsim entered. Seeing him, Jaʿfar Barmakī, the minister of Hārūn, burst out laughing. Hārūn asked him: 'Why do you laugh?'

He replied: 'This boy just does not resemble you; he sits with the poor and spends his time in the cemetery.'

'Perhaps he is behaving in this fashion because I have yet to make him the ruler of a region,' Hārūn mused. Then, turning to his son, Hārūn began to advise him: 'I would like to make you the ruler of Egypt. And if you wish to simultaneously carry on your acts of worship, I can even avail you an able minister who can assist you in your work.'

Qāsim, however, declined the offer.

Despite this, Hārūn wrote down the decree handing over the rule of Egypt to him. People kept coming up to Qāsim, congratulating him on this new position. However, the night prior to the day when he was to leave for Egypt, Qāsim fled from his house. Hārūn was able to follow his son's trail till the banks of the river, after which the trail was lost. Qāsim had actually boarded a boat and left for Basra.

ʿAbd Allāh Baṣrī relates:

'A wall of my house had become dilapidated and so I went out to look for a mason to set it aright. I came across a young man seated and reciting the Qur'an, with a shovel and a bucket lying beside him. I approached him and enquired if he would work, to which he asked me: "How much would you pay?"

'"One dirham," I said, and he accepted. From morning till sunset he worked in a measure equivalent to two persons, but when I sought to pay him more, he declined.

'The following day I went out in search of that young man but failed to find him. Upon making enquiries, I was told: "That young man only works on Saturdays, remaining engrossed in worship for the remainder of the week!"

'The following Saturday I went to look for him again. He came, worked for me, I gave him his wages, after which he left. The Saturday of the following week I went to locate him but couldn't find him. I was informed: "For the past two to three days he has been sick and not keeping well."

'I managed to find out that he lived in a house that was desolate and in ruins. Going up to him, I said: "I am ʿAbd Allāh Baṣrī."

'"I have recognised you," he replied.

'I asked him: "Who are you?"

'He replied: "Qāsim, son of Hārūn, the Abbasid caliph." Hearing this, a shiver ran through my body. He continued: "I am about to die; when I am dead give my shovel and bucket to the person who digs my grave, and my Qurʾan to someone who will recite it on my behalf. Also, take this ring of mine to Baghdad on a Tuesday as my father holds open sessions with the people on this day. Hand this ring over to him and convey this message to him: 'Place this ring along with your other riches, and answer Allah on the Day of Judgement yourself.'"'

ʿAbd Allāh Baṣrī says: 'I saw Qāsim making an effort to move but he could not. He tried for a second time but failed once again. Turning to me, he said: "ʿAbd Allāh, help me to stand, for my master, the Commander of the Faithful ﷺ, has come to pay me a visit." No sooner had I made him stand when his soul departed from his body.'[1]

95. Whisperings

Allah, the Wise, has said:

$$\text{مِنْ شَرِّ الْوَسْوَاسِ الْخَنَّاسِ ۞ الَّذِي يُوَسْوِسُ فِي صُدُورِ النَّاسِ}$$

From the evil of the sneaky tempter, who puts temptations into the breasts of humans. (114:4-5)

---

[1] *Jāmiʿ al-Nūrayn*, p. 317.

سَأَلْتُ أَبَا عَبْدِ اللهِ عَلَيْهِ السَّلَامُ عَنِ الْوَسْوَسَةِ وَإِنْ كَثُرَتْ، فَقَالَ: لَا شَيْءَ فِيهَا، تَقُولُ:
لَا إِلٰهَ إِلَّا اللّٰهُ

[The narrator says:] 'I asked Imam al-Ṣādiq ﷺ what should be done for excessive evil whisperings?' He said: 'No problem; recite *lā ilāha ill-allāh*.'[1]

Short explanation

Shayṭān cannot assert domination over man except when man turns away from the remembrance of Allah, considers trivial the commands of Allah, and engages in acts that have been forbidden by Allah.

Whisperings, if they penetrate the heart, can drag an individual towards confusion and deviation. Therefore, man should never consider himself secure from the guiles of Shayṭān, and ought to always be watchful of himself so as to not fall prey to such whisperings, and must never become heedless of Allah for He is the best helper to ward away satanic whisperings.[2]

1 – Devotion

A person once approached the Holy Prophet and said: 'O Prophet of Allah! It appears that I have turned into a hypocrite.'

The Holy Prophet said to him: 'By Allah, you have not become a hypocrite, for had you turned into one, you would have never come to me to inform me about it. What is it that has caused you to fall into doubt and scepticism? I have a feeling that Shayṭān has been whispering into your mind the question: "Who has created you?" And when you replied: "Allah has created me," Shayṭān whispered to you again: "Then who has created Allah?"'

No sooner had the person heard this from the Holy Prophet when he uttered: 'By the Lord that sent you as a prophet, the reality is exactly as you have stated.'

The Holy Prophet explained: 'When Shayṭān fails to acquire influence

---

[1] *Uṣūl al-Kāfī*, vol. 2, p. 310.

[2] *Tadhkirat al-Ḥaqā'iq*, p. 40.

over you by means of your actions and deeds, he resorts to acquiring influence over your thoughts so that he may then deviate and misguide you. Whenever you happen to experience this, recall the remembrance of the oneness of Allah [*lā ilāha ill-allāh*] so that the satanic whisperings get distanced from you.'[1]

2 – Not providing an opportunity to the whisperings of Shayṭān

An upright and pious trader was once conversing with a group of friends in the courtyard of the shrine of Imam al-Ḥusayn 🌼, when a person came up to them and informed them: 'Such and such trader has just passed away.'

As soon as this trader heard the news, he announced to his companions: 'Gentlemen, bear witness that I owe him such and such amount of money.'

Surprised at his sudden announcement, one of them asked: 'What has prompted you to state this at this point of time?'

The trader replied: 'I had borrowed a certain sum of money from this deceased trader. However, there is no written record of this; no one knows of this loan except the deceased himself. I became fearful that Shayṭān might attempt to deceive me by whispering to me that since no one knows of this loan, there is no need to hand over the money to his heirs. As such, I have stated this openly before you all so as to negate any opportunity that Shayṭān might seek to take advantage of in his endeavour to deceive me, and thus nip his evil machinations in the bud.'[2]

3 – Shayṭān in three states

The reason why the hajj pilgrims pick up stones from three places in Mina to strike the pillars representing Shayṭān is[3] that when Prophet Ibrāhīm 🌼 dreamt of Allah telling him to sacrifice Prophet Ismāʿīl 🌼, initially, without explaining anything to his son, he said to him: 'Take a knife and

---

[1] *Uṣūl al-Kāfī*, vol. 2, h. 5.

[2] *Ḥikāyat-hā-yi Shanīdanī*, vol. 3, p. 65.

[3] This reason has been reported by Shaykh Ṣadūq from Imam al-Ṣādiq 🌼.

some rope so that we go to a ravine and collect some firewood.'

Shayṭān came before Prophet Ibrāhīm ﷺ in the form of an old man, and asked: 'What are you intending to do?'

'I intend to obey the orders of Allah,' replied Prophet Ibrāhīm ﷺ.

Hearing this, Shayṭān said to him: 'It was Shayṭān and not Allah who came into your dreams and ordered this.' Prophet Ibrāhīm ﷺ realised this was Shayṭān and shooed him away.

His whispering failed to have any effect on Prophet Ibrāhīm ﷺ, so Shayṭān came to Prophet Ismāʿīl ﷺ and disclosed to him that his father intended to kill him. Hearing this, Prophet Ismāʿīl ﷺ queried: 'But why?'

'Because he imagines it to be the order of Allah,' Shayṭān explained.

Hearing this, Prophet Ismāʿīl ﷺ declared: 'If it is indeed the order of Allah, I shall submit to it.'

With the intention of continuing his whisperings, Shayṭān approached Hājar, the mother of Prophet Ismāʿīl ﷺ, and narrated the episode to her. Hājar said: 'Knowing the love that Ibrāhīm has for Ismāʿīl, I am sure he would not kill him.'

Shayṭān persisted: 'But he thinks it is the order of Allah.'

'If this is so, then we shall submit to His orders,' said Hājar, emphatically.

Shayṭān went away having failed to turn away Prophet Ibrāhīm ﷺ by means of his whisperings from obeying the divine order. It was on three occasions that Prophet Ibrāhīm ﷺ picked up stones to repel Shayṭān, and so Allah declared it to become a custom that would be enacted by the pilgrims of hajj every year the hajj is performed.[1]

4 – Whisperings in *wuḍū*

One of the Muslims happened to be plagued by whisperings with respect to the performance of *wuḍū*. While performing his *wuḍū*, he would wash his hands and face numerous times and yet remain unconvinced that it was done correctly, and thus embark on redoing his *wuḍū* repeatedly.

'Abd Allāh ibn Sinān says:

---

[1] *Tārīkh-i Anbiyā*, vol. 1, p. 69.

'I approached Imam al-Ṣādiq 🙼 and, informing him of the state of that individual, said to him: "Despite the fact that he is a person of great intelligence, he has become overwhelmed by whisperings when it comes to performing his *wuḍū*."

'Imam remarked: "What kind of intelligence does he possess and what kind of an intelligent person is he that he follows Shayṭān?"

'Astonished, I asked: "How is it that he is following Shayṭān?"

'Imam elucidated: "Ask him what the cause is of this whispering that he is entangled with, and he himself would acknowledge: 'This is the handiwork of Shayṭān.'"'[1]

96. Neighbours

Allah, the Wise, has said:

$$\text{وَالْجَارِ ذِي الْقُرْبَى وَالْجَارِ الْجُنُبِ}$$

[And be good to] the near neighbour and the distant neighbour. (4:36)

The Holy Prophet said:

$$\text{وَأَحْسِنْ مُجَاوَرَةَ مَنْ جَاوَرَكَ تَكُنْ مُؤْمِنًا}$$

Be a good neighbour to your neighbours so that you may be [regarded as] a believer.[2]

Short explanation

The discussion on the rights of neighbours is one of the areas of discussion under the topic of rights. According to a tradition of the Holy Prophet, if the neighbour is a non-believer he possesses one right, and if he is a believer then two, and if a relative then three.

As such, someone not honouring the rights of a neighbour (including neighbours that are non-believers) and acting in a manner that is hurtful to him, would seem to have a shortcoming in his faith.

According to a tradition: 'The reverence that must be exhibited by a

---

[1] *Iblīs Nāmih*, vol. 1, p. 96; *Biḥār al-Anwār*, vol. 21, p. 336.

[2] *Jāmiʿ al-Saʿādāt*, vol. 2, p. 267.

neighbour towards another neighbour is similar to the reverence that must be exhibited to a mother.'

Therefore, kindness needs to be exercised towards a neighbour for it results in an increase in lifespan and brings about happiness in society.

It is necessary, if a neighbour is known to be hungry and needy, to feed him and provide him his wants; and if ignored, then one should fear the consequences.[1]

1 – Selling a house with its neighbour

Muḥammad ibn Jahm put up his house for sale at an exorbitant price. When some interested individuals had gathered, they asked him: 'At what price do you wish to sell your house?'

He said: 'In addition to the house, how much will you pay to purchase the rights to be the neighbour of Saʿīd ibn ʿĀṣ?'

Surprised, they asked: 'But who sells or purchases the rights of being a neighbour?'

Muḥammad replied: 'Why not? Especially when you have as a neighbour a person who gives you things when you seek from him and gifts you things even when you do not seek from him; a person, who does good to you even when you do evil to him!'

When Saʿīd ibn ʿĀṣ came to know of this he was overjoyed and sent 100,000 dirhams to Muḥammad along with a message: 'Do not sell your house.'[2]

2 – A non-believer and a believer

ʿAlī ibn Yaqṭīn relates:

'Once, Imam al-Kāẓim ﷺ said to me: "In the community of Banī Isrāʾīl there lived a believer who had a neighbour who, despite being a non-believer, was always kind and helpful to the believer. When the non-believer died, Allah ordained for him, in the hell of *barzakh*, a house from

---

[1] *Iḥyāʾ al-Qulūb*, p. 132.

[2] *Namūnah-i Maʿārif*, vol. 3, p. 336; *Thamarāt al-Awrāq*, vol. 2, p. 36.

a special soil that protected him from the fire of the hell of *barzakh* and provided him his sustenance. The non-believer was informed: 'Due to the goodness that you exhibited towards your neighbour, Allah has graced you with this so that you may not suffer the burning of the fire here.'"[1]

3 – Disciplining the neighbour

A person once approached the Holy Prophet and complained about the inconveniences his neighbour was causing him. The Holy Prophet advised: 'On Friday morning strew the furniture of your house on the road such that the people who are going for the Friday prayers witness this. Whenever someone asks you the reason for this act, tell them you have done this because of the problems your neighbour is causing you.'

As per the advice of the Holy Prophet, the person began placing the contents of his house on the road in front of his house. When the neighbour realised what was happening, he rushed to the person and, pleading him to take them back into the house, promised: 'Upon the oath of Allah, I shall never inconvenience you again.'[2]

4 – Forty houses

'Amr ibn 'Ikramah relates:

'One day, I approached Imam al-Ṣādiq ☙ and complained: "My neighbour troubles me immensely."

'Imam said to me: "You behave in a goodly manner with him."

'"May Allah never shower His mercy upon him," I murmured. The Imam heard this and, visibly upset, turned away from me. I did not wish to go away while the Imam remained upset with me, so I tried to explain: "But he continually inconveniences me in various ways."

'The Imam asked: "Do you think that if you manifest your enmity and behave with him in the same manner as he does with you, you would be able to extract your revenge?"

---

[1] *La'ālī al-Akhbār*, vol. 3, p. 6.

[2] *Safīnat al-Biḥār*, vol. 1, p. 192.

"'I should think so," I said.

'The Imam then explained: "Your neighbour happens to be an individual who gets overcome with jealousy if he sees someone having been graced with a bounty from Allah; an individual, if he has a family, would be harsh upon them, and if he does not have a family, would be harsh upon and troublesome towards his subordinates. Do know that once, a person from the Anṣār came to the Holy Prophet ﷺ and said: 'I have purchased a house in such and such locality, however, the nearest neighbour to me is a person from whom I can never expect an act of goodness and can never feel safe from his evils.' When the Holy Prophet ﷺ heard this, he instructed 'Alī, Salmān, Abū Dharr, and Miqdād to go to the mosque and announce loudly for all to hear: 'He who troubles his neighbour does not possess faith.' The Holy Prophet ﷺ then pointed to forty houses in all four directions, indicating these were to be considered as neighbours."'[1]

5 – Genghis Khan's law

The Mongol king, Genghis Khan, ordained several laws which the people were obliged to follow. One of these was that if an animal had to be killed, it should only be by means of strangulation. Killing an animal by means of a knife was prohibited and anyone caught doing this would be killed by having his head severed.

A Muslim lived in a house that was next door to a person belonging to the Mongol tribe and who was not on good terms with him. One day, this neighbour observed that the Muslim had purchased a sheep and so thought to himself: 'Surely he is going to slaughter this by means of a knife.' He brought a couple of his friends as witnesses and climbed to the roof of the house to keep a watch on the activities of his Muslim neighbour.

In his house, the Muslim slaughtered the sheep. As soon as they witnessed this, the Mongol and his two friends barged into the Muslim's house. They caught him and, together with the slaughtered animal, took him before Genghis Khan.

____

[1] _Uṣūl al-Kāfī_, vol. 2, chapter on The Rights of Neighbourhood, h. 1.

Genghis Khan, after hearing the entire story, turned to the men and asked: 'Did this Muslim do this in the street or in his house?'

'In his house,' they replied.

'Where did you see this?' he queried further.

They replied: 'We saw him doing it from the top of the roof of my house.'

Genghis Khan said: 'Our law was not violated in the streets or in public. It is God that knows things that are hidden, and He conceals the hidden actions of people.' Saying this, he turned to his executioners and ordered: 'Sever their heads from their bodies so that henceforth nobody dares to peep into the house of his neighbour.'[1]

97. Guidance

Allah, the Wise, has said:

$$وَيَزِيدُ اللّٰهُ الَّذِينَ ٱهْتَدَوْا هُدًى$$

Allah enhances in guidance those who are [rightly] guided. (19:76)

The Holy Prophet said to Imam ʿAlī:

$$(يَا عَلِيُّ) لَأَنْ يَهْدِيَ اللّٰهُ عَلَى يَدَيْكَ رَجُلًا خَيْرٌ لَكَ مِمَّا طَلَعَتْ عَلَيْهِ الشَّمْسُ$$

[O ʿAlī!] If Allah were to guide a person due to your efforts, this would be better for you than everything under the sun.[2]

Short explanation

When Allah created this world and placed the children of Ādam in it, it was only natural for Him to send illustrious guides for the purpose of guiding His creations. He revealed heavenly books so that His creations may tread the straight path and thus be protected from misguidance and deviation.

While some types of guidance are direct, like the guidance from the

---

[1] *Khazīnat al-Jawāhir*, p. 642.

[2] *Safīnat al-Biḥār*, vol. 2, p. 700.

prophets and the sincere friends of Allah, most of the instances of guidance take place through lofty personalities, parents, good books, and events.

It needs to be understood that neither is every speaker a guide, nor does every person possess the ability to tread the right path. Regardless, suffice to know that while the paths to success are numerous, individuals desirous of treading those paths are few and far between.[1]

1 – A liar is guided aright

Once, Khawwāt ibn Jubayr was seated and engaged in talks with some ladies belonging to the tribe of Banī Ka'b. Coincidentally, the Holy Prophet happened to pass by and, seeing him there, said: 'Why are you seated with the ladies?'

'I possess a camel that has become unruly and constantly attempts to run away. I have come here so that these ladies can spin for me a rope by means of which I can tie my camel.'

The Holy Prophet left without saying anything more. Having completed his work, the Holy Prophet was on his way back when he observed that Khawwāt was still seated with the ladies. He remarked: 'Hopefully that camel is not running away now!'

Khawwāt said: 'I was embarrassed and did not say anything, but from then on I would make a conscientious effort to avoid the Holy Prophet ﷺ for I felt ashamed at the prospect of facing him [as I realised that he knew I had been making up an excuse only to be with the ladies]. One day, as I was offering my prayers, I observed the Holy Prophet ﷺ approach me and seat himself by my side. I began to prolong my prayers, at which he said: "Do not prolong your prayers for I am waiting for you." When I had finished my prayers, he said to me: "Hopefully that unruly camel has not been running away from you anymore?" Feeling ashamed, I got up and went away.

'The next time I saw him he was seated on his donkey and crossing the

---

[1] Those interested can read the book *'Ilm-i Akhlāq-i Islāmī*, which is in three volumes and has been translated by Dr Sayyid Jalāl al-Dīn Mujtabawī.

street. No sooner had he reached me, he said to me: "I hope that camel is not running away now."

'I said to him: "By Allah! Since the day I have become a Muslim that camel has not run away [and I had spoken an untruth to you]."

'Having heard the truth, the Holy Prophet ﷺ prayed: "*Allāhu akbar, allāhu akbar.* O Allah! Do guide Khawwāt."'

From that day onwards, Khawwāt became one of the true and rightly guided Muslims.[1]

2 – Defeating the person who deviates

A person once brought a gift for Imam al-Ḥasan ﷺ. The Imam said to him: 'In response to your gift, which of the two options would you like to choose: either I give you twenty times the value of your gift [20,000 dirhams], or pass on to you a knowledge that would enable you to acquire dominancy over such and such a man who harbours animosity towards us, and in this manner prevent the weak-minded individuals of your village from being deviated by this person's talks. However, if you were to choose correctly, I shall grant you both gifts.'

The man enquired: 'Would the rewards of defeating that person [in a debate] and saving the weak-minded individuals from becoming deviated be the same as acquiring the 20,000 dirhams?'

The Imam said: 'The rewards would be better than everything that exists in this world.'

Hearing this, the man asserted: 'In which case I choose to gain the chapter of knowledge.'

'Well chosen,' commended the Imam, and then proceeded to impart to him the concerned chapter of knowledge and, in addition, gave him the 20,000 dirhams. The person left the presence of the Imam and proceeded towards his village. There, he set about to debate that individual and was successful in defeating him. This news reached the Imam.

Sometime later, he was graced with an opportunity to meet the Imam

---

[1] *Shanīdanī-hā-yi Tārīkh*, p. 188; *al-Maḥajjah al-Bayḍā'*, vol. 5, p. 235.

again. The Imam said to him: 'None has profited in the measure that you have profited. You have procured the friendship of Allah and that of the Holy Prophet ﷺ, the Ahl al-Bayt ﷺ, the angels, and your believing brothers. And, for every believer and non-believer in this world, you have acquired rewards that are a thousand times better than all that is in this world. Bravo to you!'[1]

3 – Sayyid[2] Ḥimyarī[3]

Sayyid Ismāʿīl Ḥimyarī, also called Abū Hāshim, was born in Oman, grew up in Basra, and died in Baghdad (in the year 176 or 179 AH). However, his parents belonged to the Kharijite group in Basra and were habituated to cursing Imam ʿAlī ﷺ, daily.

Although still a child then, he used to be very disturbed at the actions of his parents. In order to avoid hearing the words of his parents against Imam ʿAlī ﷺ, he would, at times, either sleep in the mosque and thus remain hungry, or he would go home to have his food and leave immediately.

Once, in his youth, when he sent poems to his parents with the intention of guiding them towards the love of Imam ʿAlī ﷺ, they were so incensed that they decided to kill him. However, a person by the name of ʿAqabah ibn Muslim arranged for him an accommodation and helped organise his life.

In the course of his life he happened to develop an inclination for the Kīsāniyyah sect, who believed in the Imamate of Muḥammad ibn Ḥanafiyyah – the son of the Commander of the Faithful. They claimed that he was alive in the Raḍawī mountains, protected by lions and leopards, and procuring his sustenance by means of two springs – one of water and the other of honey – till such day that he shall reappear and fill the earth with justice and equality.

---

[1] *Dāstān-hā Wa Pand-hā*, vol. 4, p. 91; *Iḥtijāj Ṭabarsī*, p. 6.

[2] 'Sayyid' was the name given to him by his mother and is not because he was from the lineage of the Holy Prophet.

[3] Ḥimyarī is either the name of a tribe in Yemen or a village in Syria.

'Abd Allāh ibn Najjāshī would try to guide Sayyid Ḥimyarī of the fallaciousness of this belief but to no avail, until one day he went to meet Imam al-Ṣādiq 🕮 and said: 'Due to my love for the family of the Holy Prophet 🕮 I have distanced myself from the attachments of this world and the enemies of this holy family, but word has reached me that you have been saying I am deviated and not on the right path.'

Imam al-Ṣādiq 🕮 said: 'The Holy Prophet 🕮, Imam 'Alī 🕮, Imam al-Ḥasan 🕮, and Imam al-Ḥusayn 🕮, despite being superior to Muḥammad ibn Ḥanafiyyah, passed away from this world; how then can he not have died?'

'Do you have proof of his death?' asked Sayyid Ḥimyarī.

Imam al-Ṣādiq 🕮 took hold of Sayyid's hand, brought him before a grave in the cemetery of Baqī', placed his hand on a grave, and recited a supplication. Suddenly, Sayyid Ḥimyarī saw an old man with white hair coming out of the grave and say to him: 'Do you recognise me? I am Muḥammad ibn Ḥanafiyyah. Do know that the Imam after Imam al-Ḥusayn 🕮 was his son, 'Alī ibn Ḥusayn 🕮. The Imam after him was Muḥammad al-Bāqir 🕮, and after him, the Imam is this person here.'

Sayyid Ḥimyarī entered the fold of Shi'ism having been guided by means of a mystical intuition. Subsequently, he wrote a poem, which meant:

I became an adherent of a faith different to what I was previously professing

For it was Ja'far ibn Muḥammad, the leader of all men, who guided me to it.[1]

4 – Ruby

Shaykh 'Alī Rashtī, a student of Shaykh Murtaḍā Anṣārī and a scholar of the region of Laristan, narrates:

'With the intention of returning home to Najaf after having performed the *ziyārah* of Imam al-Ḥusayn 🕮, I was on a small boat on the river

---

[1] *Shāgirdān-i Maktab-i A'immah*, vol. 1, p. 182; *A'yān al-Shī'ah*, vol. 3, p. 409.

Tigris traversing a stretch between Karbala and Tuwairij. The others on the boat were all residents of Hillah and were mainly engrossed in fun and enjoyment, except for one individual. While signs of sobriety and dignity were manifest from his face, I noticed that the others were continually mocking and ridiculing this person's religious affiliations.

'The boat reached an area where the water was shallow and so we disembarked. As we walked along the bank of the river, I asked this person to tell me something about himself. He said: "My name is Yāqūt and I sell oil in Hillah. My father is a Sunni while my mother is a Shi'a. I had travelled with a group of people from Hillah to far off regions to purchase oil. On the way back I fell asleep and the others went away without me. When I woke up, I was overcome with fright as the place was totally deserted with no one in sight. To relieve myself from this predicament, I sought the assistance of the lofty personalities of the Sunni faith, but to no avail. I then remembered my mother telling me: 'Whenever you are in a quandary, invoke our living Imam – Abā Ṣāliḥ – and he shall come to assist you.' No sooner had I prayed to him to assist me, when I saw a person wearing a green turban appear before me. He showed me the way I needed to take and advised me to adopt the religion of my mother. He then said to me: 'You will shortly reach a village that is full of Shi'as.' I asked him: 'Will you not come with me?' He replied: 'There are thousands of people calling out for help and I have to go to help them.'"

'Yāqūt said: "I had traversed only a short distance when I reached the village. However, the group of people from Hillah, who had abandoned me, only managed to reach the village the following day! I have now become a Shi'a as per the instructions of the Imam."'[1]

5 – 'Umayr ibn Wahab

'Umayr ibn Wahab was a warrior belonging to the tribe of Quraysh and one of those who had ignited the flames of the Battle of Badr. He managed to save himself in the battle, but his son was taken captive by the Muslim

---

[1] *Muntahā al-A'māl*, vol. 2, p. 437.

forces.

One day, as he was conversing with his cousin Ṣafwān ibn Umayyah near the Kaʿbah, the conversation reached a point where he said: 'Had I not been in debt and had my family not been suffering from poverty, I would have gone to Medina and killed Muḥammad with a sword, for I have heard he does not have a guard around him.'

Ṣafwān, hearing this, agreed to pay off his debts and take care of his family if ʿUmayr would go to Medina with the excuse of procuring the release of his captive son, and in the process kill the Holy Prophet.

Entering Medina, ʿUmayr got down from his mount in front of the Mosque of the Prophet and began to seek out the Holy Prophet. It so happened that ʿUmar noticed him and shouted out: 'Take hold of this dog.'

A group of people gathered and caught ʿUmayr, and ʿUmar took away his sword and brought him before the Holy Prophet. However, as soon as the Holy Prophet's eyes fell upon ʿUmayr, he said to ʿUmar: 'Release him.' Then, the Holy Prophet turned to ʿUmayr and asked him the reason for coming to Medina.

He replied: 'I have come to seek the release of my son, Wahab.'

The Holy Prophet countered: 'The reality is that you have covenanted with Ṣafwān near the Kaʿbah that you would come here with your sword and kill me, and in exchange Ṣafwān would pay off all your debts and take care of your family. However, Allah shall protect me, and you will not be successful in killing me.'

As the Holy Prophet exposed his secret, ʿUmayr recited the *shahādatayn*, became a Muslim, and then said to him: 'Until this moment I have always been sceptical about you receiving the revelation and having connection with the world of the unseen; but now that you have uncovered my secret I have brought faith upon Allah and His Messenger, and am thankful to Allah that He has guided me in this fashion.'[1]

---

[1] *Payghambar Wa Yārān*, vol. 5, p. 73; *Asad al-Ghābbah*, vol. 4, p. 149.

98. Associates

Allah, the Wise, has said:

إِذَا قِيلَ لَكُمْ تَفَسَّحُوا فِي الْمَجَالِسِ فَافْسَحُوا يَفْسَحِ اللّهُ لَكُمْ

When you are told: 'Make room,' in sittings, then do make room; Allah will make room for you. (58:11)

The Holy Prophet said:

لَا يَنْبَغِي لِلْمُؤْمِنِ أَنْ يَجْلِسَ مَجْلِسًا يُعْصَى اللّهُ فِيهِ وَلَا يَقْدِرُ عَلَى تَغْيِيرِهِ

It is inappropriate for a believer to be seated in a gathering where the disobedience of Allah is taking place and he is unable to stop it.[1]

Short explanation

A natural consequence of having relationships with relatives, believers, and people of other faiths is associating with them in gatherings and assemblies. Whenever a believer attends a gathering he should strive to sit facing the qibla, and ensure that he maintains confidentiality of the talks that have taken place in these gatherings and not disclose them to others.

He should associate with individuals that remind him of Allah, intermingle with those that are poor, and strive to participate in gatherings of knowledge so that he can benefit from the knowledge and blessings associated with such assemblies.

Simultaneously, he should refrain from associating with those that are immoral, ignorant, and excessively money-minded. And most importantly, one should select an associate that does not assert a negative and detrimental influence upon him.

1 – An untested associate

Sa'dī says:

'One year, I was travelling between Balkh and Herat. The journey was very dangerous as murderous dacoits lurked in the region and were known to ambush travellers and caravans. A young man, who was strong, heavily

---

[1] *Uṣūl al-Kāfī*, vol. 2, p. 374.

built, armed with a shield, and possessing great expertise in the art of archery, had accompanied me as my guide and bodyguard. However, while he possessed strength of ten men, his one flaw was that his upbringing had taken place in immense ease and comfort and with a great deal of pampering. Never having travelled before, he had not seen or experienced the world, nor had he ever experienced any fight or battle!

'While we were on our way, two dacoits suddenly emerged from behind a rock, one carrying a stick and the other a sledgehammer, and stood menacingly before us. I turned to the young man and exhorted him, saying: "Do not hesitate. This is the time to showcase your strength." However, I saw the bow and arrows fall from his hands in fear and his entire body was trembling with fright.

'Things reached a point where we had no option except to give in without resistance. We handed over all our belongings to the dacoits and managed to escape with our lives!'[1]

2 – The effects of an associate

Once, the French emperor, Napoleon Bonaparte, happened to visit a madhouse. As he entered, he noticed a man chained to a wall. Overcome with pity, he asked the supervisor of the madhouse: 'Why have you chained this insane person to the wall?'

'Because he utters things that are nonsensical,' he replied.

Napoleon asked: 'What does he say?'

The head replied: 'He says he is Napoleon Bonaparte.'

Napoleon smiled and said: 'It's OK for an insane person to imagine himself to be Napoleon.'

The head of the madhouse said forcefully: 'There is no way that I shall tolerate such talks from him because, in reality, I am Napoleon Bonaparte.'

Hearing this, Napoleon was so overcome with laughter that he could hardly control himself. He realised that the supervisor of the madhouse, due to effects of his constant interaction with insane people, had started

---

[1] *Ḥikāyat-hā-yi Gulistān*, p. 255.

speaking like them.[1]

3 – Birds of a feather flock together

There once lived in Mecca a lady who possessed a comical disposition and would keep people amused and entertained. Contemporaneous to her, there also lived in Medina a woman with a similar trait. One day, the lady from Mecca travelled to Medina and stayed over at the house of the lady from Medina. On one of the days of her stay in Medina, she visited ʿĀʾishah, who asked her: 'Where have you put up in Medina?'

'At the house of such and such lady,' she replied.

Hearing this, ʿĀʾishah replied: 'Allah and His Messenger have spoken the truth, for I have heard the Holy Prophet ﷺ say: "The souls of humans remain in groups that are similar to one another."'[2]

4 – Firʿawn and Hāmān

One day, Firʿawn had summoned Hāmān with the intention of discussing with him the way forward with regards to the warnings given by Prophet Mūsā ﷺ about the arrival of the punishments of Allah. When the evil-minded Hāmān heard what Firʿawn had to say, he gave out a shriek, began to weep, and, beating his face and head, said to him: 'O Great King! Why are you even pondering about this issue? Why have you been overcome by this deplorable state that has the potential to lead you to your doom? You are the king of the east and the west, and the world lies under your subjugation. Immeasurable wealth pours into your coffers in the form of taxes, as the kings of the world stand humbled before you. All worship you as their lord and stand in humility before your majesty and might. It would be better for you to burn in a thousand fires than to abdicate your god-ship and become a follower of someone like Mūsā. Were you to accept the truthfulness of Mūsā and follow him, your slaves shall become masters over you and your enemies would start planning your downfall.'

---

[1] *Ḥikāyat-hā-yi Shanīdanī*, vol. 3, p. 55.

[2] *Shanīdanī-hā-yi Tārīkh*, p. 64; *al-Maḥajjah al-Bayḍāʾ*, vol. 3, p. 294.

Fir'awn, due to his association and consultation with Hāmān, came to regard himself as the lord of the people, disregarded the warnings of Prophet Mūsā ◈, and eventually got entangled in Allah's punishment.[1]

5 – Punishment for associating with a sinner

Ja'farī relates:

'Imam Mūsā ibn Ja'far ◈ said to me: "Why is it that I see you associating with 'Abd al-Raḥmān ibn Ya'qūb?"

'"Because he is my uncle," I replied, humbly.

'The Imam said: "He speaks incorrect things about Allah. He attributes a body to Allah whereas Allah cannot be attributed such. Either continue to associate with him, in which case you will have to cease your association with us, or continue to remain with us and abandon him!"

'I tried to clarify: "But his ideas are not detrimental to me as I do not adhere to them."

'The Imam explained: "Do you not fear that the punishment which could descend upon him could also encompass you within its folds? Do you not know about the individual who was from amongst the companions of Prophet Mūsā and whose father was from amongst the followers of Fir'awn? At the time when the forces of Fir'awn were closing in on the people of Mūsā in the sea, this companion of Mūsā separated from the group of Mūsā and went to his father, who was in the army of Fir'awn, to advise him to leave Fir'awn and join Mūsā. When the waters joined and the people of Fir'awn were drowned, these two individuals were also amongst those that got drowned. When Mūsā was informed of this, he said: 'He is in the mercy of Allah. However, when the punishment of Allah arrives, the person who is near the sinner is also caught up in the punishment.'"[2]

---

[1] *Dāstān-hā-yi Mathnawī*, vol. 3, p. 84.

[2] *Uṣūl al-Kāfī*, vol. 2, Chapter on Associating with Sinners.

99. Orphans

Allah, the Wise, has said:

$$\text{فَأَمَّا الْيَتِيمَ فَلَا تَقْهَرْ}$$

So, as for the orphan, do not oppress him. (93:9)

The Holy Prophet said:

$$\text{مَنْ كَفَلَ يَتِيمًا وَكَفَلَ نَفَقَتَهُ، كُنْتُ أَنَا وَهُوَ فِي الْجَنَّةِ}$$

One who supports an orphan and provides for his expenses, he and I shall be together in paradise.[1]

Short explanation

A child that is deprived of a father and mother is in an exigent need for love and affection from other creations of Allah.

Caressing them, feeding them, making them happy by giving them clothes, and gifting them things are some of the numerous things that the believers can do with respect to orphans.

In paradise there is a special place exclusively reserved for those who have made orphans of the believers happy. However, in hell, certain individuals would have fire emanating from their rectums – a punishment primarily for those who had usurped and misappropriated the properties of orphans.[2]

1 – The orphan-carer of Basra

Once, a person died in the suburbs of Basra and since he was regarded as a corrupt individual, there was no one willing to perform his funeral rites. His wife managed to pay a few people to carry the dead body of her deceased husband to the cemetery so that he could be buried, even if it be without prayers being performed upon him. However, it so happened that a pious person who lived there and was well-known for his piety and truthfulness, arrived and performed prayers over the deceased, subsequent

---

[1] *Safīnat al-Biḥār*, vol. 2, p. 731.

[2] *Tafsīr al-Muʿīn*, p. 12.

to which the body was buried.

When the news of this reached the people, they came in droves to him seeking to know why he had performed prayers for such a sinning individual. He explained: 'In my dreams I was told: "Go to such and such place for a deceased shall arrive there accompanied by his wife. Perform the prayers upon him." I then asked the wife: "What acts was your husband doing that made Allah exhibit such mercy upon him?" She replied: "He used to consume alcohol. This was one evil behaviour of his."

'I persisted: "But what were his good acts?" She said: "Whenever he would come to his senses from his intoxication, he would begin to weep and say: 'O Allah! Which corner of hell would you place me in?' As morning would dawn, he would change his clothes, perform *ghusl* and then *wuḍū'*, and then offer his morning prayers. The second good act was that he would ensure to always have at least two or three orphans in his house, whom he would care for. The love and kindness that he would shower upon an orphan would be more than what he would towards his own children."'[1]

2 – Isfandiyār

When Rustam ibn Zāl fought against Isfandiyār, despite the valour that he possessed, he still found himself defeated by Isfandiyār. In the course of the fight, Rustam launched several attacks on Isfandiyār, but on each occasion he would be forced to retreat, having received fresh injuries. Isfandiyār was strong and heavily built as a result of which the attacks of Rustam failed to make much impact upon him.

Eventually, Rustam decided to turn to his father for advice. The father said to him: 'Construct an arrow with two heads and target the eyes of Isfandiyār so that he gets blinded.' Rustam did as his father had advised him and, having blinded Isfandiyār, eventually managed to become victorious over him.

The reason why Isfandiyār met such an end has been stated as follows: once, when young, Isfandiyār had used a branch of a tree to beat the head

---

[1] *Pand-i Tārīkh*, vol. 1, p. 155; *Shajarah-i Ṭūbā*, vol. 2, p. 278.

and face of an orphan, causing him to lose his sight and become blind. Subsequently, the orphan took the branch and planted it into the ground. Years later, in the fight between Rustam and Isfandiyār, it so came to pass that Rustam picked up that very branch that had been planted by the orphan and used it to make the arrow, which eventually ended up blinding Isfandiyār![1]

3 –Affection towards an orphan

A young child once approached the Holy Prophet and said: 'O Prophet of Allah! My father has died and I am left with my mother and sister. Please help us!'

The Holy Prophet said to Bilāl: 'Go into the house and bring to me whatever food you are able to find.' Bilāl entered the house and, after searching, located twenty-one pieces of dates which he brought before the Holy Prophet. The Holy Prophet said to the child: 'Seven pieces are for yourself, and seven each for your mother and sister.'

While this conversation was going on, a companion of the Holy Prophet by the name of Mu'ādh, placed his hand on the head of the child, caressed his hair, and said: 'May Allah grace you so that you may become like your father.'

Witnessing this, the Holy Prophet said to Mu'ādh: 'I have observed your affection for this orphan. Do know that whoever caresses the head of an orphan out of affection, for every strand of hair that passes under the hand Allah shall grant him numerous goodness, erase from him numerous sins, and elevate him numerous ranks.'[2]

4 – Recommendation about uncles and aunts

Imam al-Riḍā ﷺ, in a letter written to his son Imam al-Jawād ﷺ, advises: 'Whenever you intend to leave your house to go out, carry some money with you. Whenever someone seeks some money from you, help him by

---

[1] *Muntakhab al-Tawārīkh*, p. 815.

[2] *Dāstān-hā Wa Pand-hā*, vol. 4, p. 160; *Majma' al-Bayān*, vol. 1, p. 506.

giving him some. If your uncles seek financial assistance from you, be kind to them and ensure you do not give them less than fifty dinars. As for your aunts, do not give them less than twenty-five dinars. I desire that by means of these acts of generosity Allah further elevates your rank. Keep giving charity and do not fear poverty.'[1]

5 – The orphans of a martyr

Ja'far Ṭayyār, the brother of the Commander of the Faithful, was martyred in the Battle of Mu'tah in the year 8 AH. 'Abd Allāh, the son of Ja'far Ṭayyār, relates:

'When the Holy Prophet ﷺ came to our house to break the news of my father's death to my mother [Asmā' bint 'Umays], I can never forget the love and affection with which he caressed my brother's head and mine, as tears flowed from his eyes. Weeping so profusely that his holy beard became wet, he prayed: "O Allah! Ja'far has proceeded towards the best of the rewards. Support his family in the best way that You support families."

'The Holy Prophet ﷺ stood up, took hold of my hand, and continued to cuddle me and shower his affection upon me till he entered the mosque. In the mosque, as he climbed onto the pulpit, with signs of immense sadness writ large upon his face, he made me sit on a step just below the one he sat on. Later, as he proceeded towards his house, he took me with him. Reaching the house he asked for some special delicacies to be prepared and then sent someone to summon my brother. Later, my brother and I ate the delicious food prepared for us. After a while, he instructed Salmā, his slave-girl, to grind some barley and then proceed to make a dish out of this flour by mixing it with some olive oil and pepper. Once again, my brother and I were given this to eat.

'For three continuous days while my mother was in grief, we stayed at the house of the Holy Prophet ﷺ. In this period, whenever he would go to the houses of his wives he would take us along with him. It was after three

---

[1] *Namūnah-i Ma'ārif*, vol. 2, p. 407; *Uṣūl al-Kāfī*, vol. 4, p. 44.

days that we returned to our house.'[1]

100. Certitude

Allah, the Wise, has said:

$$\text{وَٱعْبُدْ رَبَّكَ حَتَّى يَأْتِيَكَ الْيَقِينُ}$$

And worship your Lord until certainty comes to you. (15:99)

The Holy Prophet said:

$$\text{مِنْ أَقَلِّ مَا أُوتِيتُمْ الْيَقِينُ وَعَزِيمَةُ الصَّبْرِ}$$

The least that you have been graced with is certitude and patience.[2]

Short explanation

The prophets of Allah, amongst themselves, possessed different ranks, and these ranks were directly proportional to the level of certitude they possessed. When the Holy Prophet was told: 'Prophet 'Īsā could walk on water,' he replied: 'Had he possessed a higher level of certitude, he would have been able to walk on air!'

The believers also vary in rank based on the measure of certitude they possess. A person whose certitude is strong, would realise that all power belongs to Allah and thus, strive greatly to obey His dictates. For such a person, wealth or poverty, fame or anonymity, praise or criticism appear to be the same, as he knows that everything is from Allah.

But those whose certitude is feeble, would always be on the lookout for worldly causes to help them out. They are inclined to attaching great significance to the opinions of the people, constantly remaining engrossed in worldly acts and engaged in gatherings of wealth and riches.[3]

1 – Remedy for obesity

Once, there lived a king who used to rule justly and with fairness. It so

---

[1] *Payghambar Wa Yārān*, vol. 2, p. 178; *A'yān al-Shī'ah*, vol. 16, p. 24.

[2] *Jāmi' al-Sa'ādāt*, vol. 1, p. 119.

[3] *Tadhkirat al-Ḥaqā'iq*, p. 87.

happened that with the passage of time he became overcome by obesity; his body had become so immensely bloated that he was unable to even move. His ministers sought the assistance of various doctors to treat him but it was to no avail.

A wise man who lived during the time approached the ministers and said to them: 'I have a cure for the king's problem.' Overjoyed, they took him before the king. The wise man looked at the king and then, having checked his pulse, announced: 'The king shall die within the next forty days. If he manages to survive the forty days, I shall then prescribe something for him.'

Hearing these words, a shiver ran through the king's body. With the fear and anxiety of his impending death constantly plaguing him, he began losing weight daily and started becoming weaker and thinner. This continued until, after forty days, his body had come down to its normal size.

After forty days, when the wise man was brought before the king for prescribing the medicine, he confessed: 'There never was any prescription in mind.'

The king understood what the wise man had done and rewarded him handsomely.[1]

2 – Muḥammad ibn Bashīr

On the eve of 'Āshūrā', Lady Zaynab 🕊 said to Imam al-Ḥusayn 🕊: 'O my brother! Hope your companions shall not desert you tomorrow and leave you alone.'

Imam al-Ḥusayn 🕊 replied: 'By Allah! I have tested them. They are as intensely desirous of martyrdom as a child is of the breast of the mother.'

On the eve of 'Āshūrā', when Imam al-Ḥusayn 🕊 addressed the companions and gave them permission to leave should they so desire, each of them stood up and declared their unflinching support for the Imam. He then showed them their places in paradise as a result of which their

---

[1] *Sarmāyih-i Saʿādat*, p. 24.

certitude became so strong and firm that the following morning – the day of 'Āshūrā' – they did not mind the pain of the injuries caused to them by the swords and spears of their enemies.

On the eve of 'Āshūrā', Muḥammad ibn Bashīr was informed that his son had been taken captive at the border of the region of Rey. Upon hearing the news, he remarked: 'I shall take compensation of his life and mine from Allah, the Creator of the universe. I do not wish to remain alive after he has been taken captive.'

When Imam al-Ḥusayn ﷺ heard these words, he said to him: 'I have freed you from the allegiance that you have pledged to me. Go and try to free your son from captivity.'

Muḥammad ibn Bashīr said to the Imam: 'May the animals of this wilderness tear me apart and eat me alive should I abandon you and leave your company.'

The Imam said to him: 'In which case take these apparels and hand them over to your other son so that he may try to secure the release of his brother,' and proceeded to gift him five apparels, collectively valued at 1000 dinars.

Muḥammad ibn Bashīr was amongst those who were martyred in the first wave of attack on the day of 'Āshūrā'.[1]

3 – Ferdowsi

Due to the great cruelty of the governor of Tus, Abū al-Qāsim Ferdowsi left his city and proceeded to Ghaznayn to lodge a complaint with Sultan Maḥmūd Ghaznawī. This, however, yielded no result.

Incidentally, it so happened that while in an assembly of the renowned poet Unṣurī, Ferdowsi recited a poem which was immensely appreciated and received wide acclaim. As a result of this, he was taken to the court of Sultan Maḥmūd Ghaznawī, who ordered him to recite the history of Iran in the form of a poem.

When Ferdowsi completed reciting the poem called *Shahnameh*, the

---

[1] *Muntahā al-A'māl*, vol. 1, p. 340.

sultan was very impressed and consulted with his ministers about the most appropriate reward to be given to him. While the ministers debated amongst themselves about the amount to be given to Ferdowsi, some individuals highlighted the fact that he was a Shi'a, and thus should not be given a large amount of money. Hearing this, the sultan ordered him to be paid a dirham for each line of his poem; as his poem consisted of 60,000 lines, he was given 60,000 dirhams.

Ferdowsi was greatly upset that they had reduced his prize because he was a Shi'a, and so, with the strength of the great certitude that he possessed, he added the following lines to the *Shahnameh*:

O Sultan Maḥmūd, the conqueror of countries ... if me you do not fear, at least have some fear of Allah

The fearlessness that I possess is due to the luminosity of my heart ... which has the stamp of the Ahl al-Bayt and the *walī* (of Allah)

Wherever I tread, this is how I am, and this is how I shall be ... I, the one, who praises the Prophet and Ḥaydar

I shall remain always the slave of these two ... even if my body is cut into pieces.

It is said that after Ferdowsi died, Shaykh Abū al-Qāsim Gurgānī refused to offer prayers over his body because of the poems he had recited in praise of the various sultans and magians. However, that very night he saw Ferdowsi in his dreams and observed that he had been graced with a lofty position in paradise. Seeing this, Shaykh Gurgānī asked him: 'How did you manage to acquire this position, whereas you had spent your entire life praising the people of this world?'

Ferdowsi replied: 'Because of this poem ... Allah forgave me my sins.'[1]

4 – Request for a greater certitude

Once, Ma'mūn – the Abbasid caliph – asked Imam al-Riḍā ﷺ about the commentary of the words of Prophet Ibrāhīm ﷺ, when he said: 'My Lord! Show me how You revive the dead.' (2:260)

---

[1] *Muntakhab al-Tawārīkh*, p. 703.

Allah asked him: 'And do you not believe?' Ibrāhīm said: 'Yes, but that my heart may be at ease.'

Allah then said: 'Take four birds, kill them, mix up their flesh, and spread out their pieces of flesh on the mountains. Then summon them towards you in order that they hasten to you.'

Prophet Ibrāhīm killed a vulture, a waterfowl, a peacock, and a cockerel, made mincemeat of their flesh, mixed the flesh of all the four birds, and placed a portion of this mixture on top of ten mountains that were close by. However, he held the beaks of the four birds between his fingers, placed some grains and water near him, and then began calling out the names of each of the birds. Upon the orders of Allah, the pieces of flesh of each of the birds gathered together, joined with the head, flew towards Ibrāhīm, joined with the beak, and began to eat the grains and drink the water!

Yes, Ibrāhīm – the *ulū al-'azm* prophet – requested this so as to increase his certitude, and Allah made him witness it in a manifest manner.[1]

5 – Ḥārithah ibn Nu'man

He was from the Anṣār and belonged to the tribe of Khazraj, and possessed a degree of certainty that remain untainted for the entire duration of his life.[2] He had participated in the majority of the battles of the Holy Prophet such as the Battles of Badr, Uḥud, and Khandaq. In the Battle of Ḥunayn, he remained steadfast alongside the Holy Prophet and did not abandon him and flee. After the Holy Prophet had passed away, he continued to participate in the battles alongside Imam 'Alī 🖄.

When the Commander of the Faithful was to get married to Lady Zahrā' 🖄, the Holy Prophet said to him: 'Procure a house for yourself and take your wife to your house.'

Imam 'Alī 🖄 said: 'O Prophet of Allah! The only person I can think of with respect to this issue is Ḥārithah ibn Nu'man.'

The Holy Prophet said: 'By Allah! I feel ashamed before Ḥārithah as we

---

[1] *Ḥayāt al-Qulūb*, vol. 1, p. 180.

[2] He had witnessed angel Jibrīl twice in his lifetime.

have used up all of his houses.'

When these words of the Holy Prophet reached the ears of Ḥārithah, he rushed to him and said: 'O Prophet of Allah! My wealth and I are at the disposal of Allah and His Prophet. By Allah! Nothing is dearer to me than what you take from me, and what you take from me is dearer to me than what you leave behind for me!'

The Holy Prophet prayed for him and instructed that Lady Fāṭimah be taken to his house.

Nearing the end of his life, Ḥārithah had lost his sight and had become blind. He had tied a rope from his place of rest in his room to the door of his house and would place a bowl of dates beside him. Whenever someone would come seeking alms, he would pick up some dates, reach the door with the help of the rope, and hand over the dates to the person. When his family members would tell him: 'Why do you trouble yourself so much? We can do this for you,' he would reply: 'I have heard the Holy Prophet say: "Giving something to a poor person by one's own hands protects a person from a bad death."'[1]

---

[1] *Payghambar Wa Yārān*, vol. 2, p. 204.